D0915541

AMERICAN COVENANT

AMERICAN COVENANT

———————★———————

A HISTORY OF CIVIL RELIGION FROM THE PURITANS TO THE PRESENT

———————★———————

PHILIP GORSKI

PRINCETON UNIVERSITY PRESS
Princeton & Oxford

Published by Princeton University Press,
41 William Street, Princeton, New Jersey 08540

In the United Kingdom: Princeton University Press,
6 Oxford Street, Woodstock, Oxfordshire OX20 1TR

press.princeton.edu

Jacket image © EastVillage Images/Shutterstock

ISBN 978-0-691-14767-3

Library of Congress Cataloging-in-Publication Data

Names: Gorski, Philip S., author.
Title: American covenant : a history of civil religion from the Puritans
    to the present / Philip S. Gorski.
Description: Princeton : Princeton University Press, [2017] | Includes bibliographical
    references and index.
Identifiers: LCCN 2016013496 | ISBN 9780691147673 (hardcover : acid-free paper)
Subjects: LCSH: Civil religion—United States—History. | United States
    —Religion—History.
Classification: LCC BL2525 .G667 2017 | DDC 306.60973—dc23 LC record available at
    https://lccn.loc.gov/2016013496

British Library Cataloging-in-Publication Data is available

This book has been composed in Miller

Printed on acid-free paper. ∞

Printed in the United States of America

10 9 8 7 6 5 4 3 2 1

CONTENTS

Three Trips to Philadelphia

I STARTED WRITING this book in early 2008. It was an exciting time in American politics. The Democratic presidential primaries were in full swing. ABC News had recently broadcast the Jeremiah Wright videos. And Barack Obama had just responded to the ensuing furor with a widely praised speech on race in America.

There was much discussion of the speech's contents, but it was the framing that especially caught my attention. It was a bit unusual for a speech on the history of race relations in the United States. The speech was delivered at the National Constitution Center in Philadelphia. The opening was taken from the preamble to the Constitution: "We the People . . . in Order to form a more perfect Union." The narrative drew from the Hebrew Bible. There was talk of founding covenants (the Declaration and the Constitution), of original sins (African slavery), of a people's backsliding and marching (Jim Crow and civil rights), of a Promised Land that was always just over the horizon.

I immediately recognized this blend of civic and religious motifs. The late Robert Bellah had famously described it as "the American civil religion" and, more generally, as America's "founding myth." I knew this because Bellah had been one of my mentors in graduate school. But I also knew that Bellah had later pronounced the American civil religion "an empty and broken shell." Had his epitaph been premature? Was the civil religious tradition still alive?

I sat pondering these questions onboard a train from New Haven to Philadelphia in March of 2008. The fact that Obama himself had just spoken in the latter a few days before made the questions feel more urgent. I started typing in New Jersey. I had a rough draft by the time I stepped off the train in Philadelphia, and a finished essay when I arrived back in New Haven the next day. I then posted the piece to *The Immanent Frame*, a blog on "religion, secularism and the public sphere."

A few days later, I received an email from Fred Appel, the religion editor at Princeton University Press. He had read the essay and wondered whether I might be planning a book. I told him I was—just not on that particular topic! I was a historical sociologist and early modern Europeanist by training. True, I did have a special interest in religion and politics—and I had been reading up on American religious history. Still, I had never contemplated writing a book on American political culture.

But I was tempted. The subject touched on many of my deepest concerns. Like most Americans, I was deeply distressed by the partisan vitriol that had flooded Washington, DC, and gradually seeped into every corner of our public life. Raised in a Christian family but now ensconced in the secular academy, I knew decent and reasonable people of faith and no faith, and I was dismayed by the way in which a small minority of culture warriors had managed to dominate the political dialogue for so long. At the same time, I was cautiously optimistic that Barack Obama might be able to fulfill George Bush's broken promise to be a "uniter, not a divider." Perhaps this young presidential hopeful could finally move the country beyond the fratricidal quarrels of the Baby Boom generation. And perhaps I could make a small contribution to that process by placing Obama's message within a deeper context. It wouldn't take long, I thought. I decided to submit a book proposal to Princeton. And so began a second and more figurative "trip to Philadelphia," a journey through the intellectual and cultural history of the United States. It would prove a much harder climb than I imagined.

I already had a map to guide me: Bellah's 1976 book, *The Broken Covenant.* In some ways I found it to be accurate and helpful. Bellah had argued that the American civil religion wove together two strands of thought: "civic republicanism" and "covenantal religion." This still seemed right. Bellah had then traced the history of the American civil religion through a series of formative crises in American history: Puritanism, the American Revolution, the Civil War, and so on. This too seemed like a good approach. I decided that my book would also be organized narratively and chronologically.

But I quickly concluded that Bellah's map needed some updating. For one thing, the American civil religion needed to be more clearly roped off from two close rivals. Bellah had not drawn a sharp enough line between the American civil religion and what I call *American religious nationalism*—the sort of apocalyptic and nativistic hyperpatriotism that has driven so many of America's witch hunts and imperial misadventures over the centuries. I also concluded that my account had to give more attention to what I call *radical secularism*—the sort of secular progressivism that seeks to dispense with any notion of tradition and bar all religious expression from the public square. I came to see the American civil religion as a *via media* between these two extremes.

My updated map also led to a revised storyline. Bellah had defined the civil religion as a "founding myth." His account was ultimately a jeremiad about cultural decline. This didn't seem quite right to me. I saw the civil religion as evolving, rather than declining. I wanted to show that the civil religion was a dynamic and living tradition; like a great river, it had deepened and widened over time. And it had not yet run dry. I also wanted to show that religious nationalism and radical secularism were not viable paths for the American project; they were both too shallow and too narrow to accommodate a people as metaphysical and diverse as the Americans.

As the manuscript grew, Obama was demoted from the leading man to a supporting actor, becoming just one voice in a large cast of civil theologians. That cast would eventually grow to include not only universally known figures such as Abraham Lincoln and Martin Luther King Jr. but also less familiar thinkers like Jonathan Mayhew and John Courtney Murray.

My list of republican prophets was long, but I worried that it was not exhaustive. Eventually, I realized it did not need to be. After all, I was not trying to write a comprehensive intellectual history of the civil religious tradition. I was attempting something far more modest: to show that the civil religious tradition had grown in a coherent way and been nurtured by a diverse citizenry. White Protestant men may have given the original formulation, but other thinkers—white and black, Jewish, Catholic, and agnostic—had helped to revise and reformulate it. My cast, the prophets of this tradition, needed to demonstrate these shifts, but I did not need to document their every nuance.

But why delve so deeply into the past? There are four reasons. First, some parts of this past are still usable. Civic republicanism provides a powerful language for thinking about issues like individual freedom and social inequality—a much more powerful language than that of contemporary conservatism or liberalism. Meanwhile, prophetic religion provides us with the original script for the American experiment—the Exodus story—and also with the primordial vision of a just society.

Second, some common interpretations of our shared past are badly in need of correction. Secular liberals who claim that the United States was built on Enlightenment foundations are just as mistaken as religious nationalists who believe that the American founders were "orthodox Christians." Revolutionary worldviews were actually a rich mixture of Jewish, Christian, liberal, and republican ideas and values.

Third, the past provides an important starting point for thinking about the future—perhaps the only starting point we all still share. We may disagree about the exact meaning of "liberty" or "equality" or "the pursuit of happiness," but we must all agree that these values and ideas have constituted us as a culture and a people.

Fourth, and finally, the past is still not really past. The history of our modern-day culture wars is deep, far deeper than many people understand. And if we do not reckon with that fact, we are doomed to reenact the struggles of the past yet again.

But why seek out the *via media*? Why not just fight it out: "Radical secularism versus religious nationalism: may the best (wo)man win!"? There are a myriad of reasons: Because we have been fighting for nearly four decades. Because we have fought to a standstill. Because American political institutions necessitate compromise. And, last but not least, because we have urgent business to attend to. Anyone who thinks America is still number one at anything other than military spending needs to wake up and pay more attention. At this point, the American federal government seems utterly incapable of addressing major challenges like income inequality and family breakdown; indeed, it barely manages to fulfill the most basic tasks of a night-watchman state, like fixing roads and bridges. Elections alone will not bridge this impasse—that much must be clear to all of us by now. The American political class simply cannot be counted on to make the necessary changes by itself. Some politicians and pundits are sincere and well meaning enough, but too many of them have too much to gain from our continued polarization—whether those gains come in the form of super PAC funding or advertising buys or consulting fees or Nielsen ratings. Real political change will have to be initiated by ordinary citizens working from within civil society rather than by the political professionals who currently dominate electoral politics.

But is this change worth the struggle? Perhaps we should all just shrug our collective shoulders and go on our separate ways, off to our own well-fortified little castles in the Lands of Whatever and Nevermind. That is what libertarians on both the left and the right now propose, and with increasing resonance. Their disgust with American politics is perfectly understandable. But their solutions are unworkable. The road to Libertaria does not lead to the Island of Prosperity; it actually leads to the chaos of Somalia.

Or perhaps we should find yet another foreign enemy who can temporarily distract us from our internal feuding? Maybe "radical Islam"? Then we can all take up our weapons, lock arms, and rebuild Fortress America, the greatest military power the world has ever known. That is what the neo-cons and their religious-nationalist accomplices recommend, and with puzzling resonance. Isn't it clear by now that the world's problems can't be solved through American arms?

Or perhaps what we really need is an internal enemy? "Illegal immigrants," for example: If we could just deport 11 million people, couldn't we "make America great again"? That is what the neo-nativists tell us. What they don't tell us is that this would mean betraying our founding ideals and turning the United States into a police state. Is that their definition of "greatness"?

As much as most Americans pretend to hate politics and government, the truth is that the kind of society they aspire to still requires both—and politics requires compromise, and compromise involves talk. So the goal of this book is to help us recover and rearticulate an older and better way of talking about the American project, one that can help us to reframe, rethink, and—who knows—maybe even solve a few of our current problems.

ACKNOWLEDGMENTS

I WOULD LIKE to thank Jonathan Van Antwerpen and Ruth Braunstein for inviting me to submit the original blog post on "Barack Obama and Civil Religion" to *The Immanent Frame* back in 2008, and Fred Appel of PUP for encouraging me to turn it into a book—and for being so patient with me as I did so. Over the years, I have had the privilege of presenting this work before audiences at the University of California, Berkeley, Boston College (Boisi Center), Boston University, the University of Chicago, the School for Advanced Studies in the Social Sciences (EHESS) in Paris, Harvard University (twice), New York University, the University of Virginia, and Yale University (three times). I am indebted to all of the faculty and students who attended those presentations and provided helpful feedback and to those who invited me and provided comments, especially Julia Adams, Nancy Ammerman, Orit Avishai, Joe Davis, Noah Feldman, Roger Friedland, Andreas Glaeser, Julian Go, Ron Hassner, Rita Hermon-Belot, James Hunter, Jill Lepore, Eric Nelson, Jeff Manza, Melissa Matthes, Orlando Patterson, Steve Pincus, Sadia Saeed, and Alan Wolfe. I owe a special thanks to those who read some or all of the manuscript at one stage or another: Jeffrey Alexander, Akeel Bilgrami, Hella Heydorn, Samuel Loncar, Margarita Mooney, Frederick Schneider, Samuel Stabler, Jeff Stout, and Bean Weston. My thinking about religion and politics was shaped by the MacMillan Initiative on Religion, Politics and Society at Yale. I would like to thank my co-conspirators in that endeavor—Bryan Garsten, Sigrun Kahl, and Vivek Sharma—for many stimulating conversations over the years, and also Ian Shapiro, the director of the MacMillan Center, for his generous support of the initiative. Finally, I owe a special debt to my wife, Hella, and our three sons, Jacob, Eric, and Mark, for sharing the pleasures of this project and enduring its sorrows.

INTRODUCTION

Prophetic Republicanism as Vital Center

Turning and turning in the widening gyre
The falcon cannot hear the falconer;
Things fall apart; the centre cannot hold;
Mere anarchy is loosed upon the world . . .
The best lack all conviction, while the worst
Are full of passionate intensity. . . .

And what rough beast, its hour come round at last,
Slouches towards Bethlehem to be born?

—W. B. YEATS, "THE SECOND COMING"

WRITING SHORTLY AFTER the close of World War II, Harvard historian Arthur Schlesinger Jr. spoke of the urgent need to fortify the "vital center" of the American polity against "centrifugal forces" that were threatening to tear it apart. By the "vital center," he meant an alliance between "the non-Fascist Right" and "the non-Communist Left" that was based on a shared belief in liberal democracy.[1] The "centrifugal forces" he spoke of emanated from rapid social change and radical ideologies.

The only way that the vital center could be held together, he argued, was if the Left and the Right both faced up to their own moral and political failures. The chief failure of the Left was a sentimental belief in human goodness and historical progress that led it to underestimate the human capacity for evil. The chief failure of the Right was a callous indifference to the dislocations and injustices produced by industrial capitalism and a self-serving faith that the market would sort them out.

Today, America's vital center is threatened by a new set of centrifugal forces: by economic changes that are steadily widening the gap between the haves and the have-nots; by partisan politics that are drawing a new Mason Dixon line between "red states" and "blue states"; by the Great Recession, which lasted longer than the Great Depression; by a series of small wars that have left the nation anxious and depleted; and by a

1

never-ending culture war now well into its fourth decade. These changes are pulling at the seams of the social fabric.

The vital center is also threatened by radical ideologies. Some are old, such as the revival of "states' rights" arguments hailing from the antebellum South. Others are newer, such as the antistatist "techno-libertarianism" that has taken hold among some on the Left. These ideologies are tearing the American tapestry apart.

The result of these changes is political dysfunction. Congress engages in unprecedented obstructionism. The executive branch responds with unprecedented unilateralism. Roads and bridges crumble. Cabinet posts go unfilled. Budgets get stuck in committee. Each side doubles down in the hope of scoring a knockout blow against the other. This endless gridlock and bare-knuckled partisanship is eroding the nation's power and standing in the world.

What is needed now is not another political speech about "American greatness." What is needed is a new vital center, a coalition of nonchauvinists and nonlibertarians on the Left and the Right, a coalition of ordinary citizens premised on a common vision of the American project that is grounded in America's civil religious tradition.

The vital center is not a mushy middle that splits the difference between Left and Right. It is a living tradition that cuts across these divisions. Some will argue that it is "neoconservative." Others will denounce it as "crypto-socialist." But they will be wrong: it is neither. It is something much older and also more radical.

The vital center does not purport to be a "third way" that "transcends" Left and Right. It is a political vocabulary that enables dialogue and debate between Left and Right. The point of reclaiming the vital center is not to end debate but to restart it. There is plenty of posturing in our public life right now but very little genuine engagement. There is lots of shouting but not much actual discussion.

Much of the shouting is coming from two directions. The first is American religious nationalism, a toxic blend of apocalyptic religion and imperial zeal that envisions the United States as a righteous nation charged with a divine commission to rid the world of evil and usher in the Second Coming. The other is American radical secularism, an equally noxious blend of cultural elitism and militant atheism that envisions the United States as part of an Enlightenment project threatened by the ignorant rubes who still cling to traditional religion.

Religious nationalism is not worthy of our allegiance. There are reasonable forms of nationalism, but religious nationalism is not one of them. At its core, religious nationalism is just national self-worship. It is political idolatry dressed up as religious orthodoxy. Any sincere believer should reject it, remembering that the line between good and evil does not run between people or nations; it runs through them.

Radical secularism is not worthy of our allegiance either. There are reasonable forms of secularism, too, but radical secularism is not one of them. At its core, radical secularism is little more than a misguided effort at cultural censorship, political illiberalism dressed up as liberal politics. Any serious liberal should reject it on the ground that liberal citizenship should not require that religious citizens shed their deepest beliefs before entering the public square. What liberal citizenship really requires is liberality—a spirit of ecumenism, generosity, and civic friendship.

How have religious nationalism and radical secularism come to exert so much influence over our public life? This situation has arisen in part because both sides have been supported by vocal and well-organized minorities, and in part because each tradition strongly confirms the other's prejudices. Christian nationalists conform to the stereotypes of the radical secularists, who equate religion with violence and intolerance. Radical secularists conform to the stereotypes of the Christian nationalists, who equate secularism with moral relativism and cultural condescension. Meanwhile, the chorus of shouting drowns out the quieter voices of the vital center.

That center consists of the many Americans—believers and nonbelievers, Republicans and Democrats—who support a moderate form of secularism and a liberal form of nationalism. They are concerned that church and state not become too entangled in one another's affairs, but they do not believe you can take religion entirely out of politics, or vice versa. They know that the American project has a moral and spiritual core. They also value American culture and institutions enough to cherish and defend them but without succumbing to the conceit that America is always and everywhere a "force for good in the world." They are the natural constituency of the vital center. This book is addressed to them. It is an effort to give voice to the historical tradition that undergirds their deepest convictions, in a time when the best are denounced for lacking all conviction.

This is mostly a book about important thinkers and their ideas, rather than about power and institutions. I am well aware that thinkers and their ideas are always influenced by power and institutions—I am a sociologist, after all!—but I also know that thinkers and their ideas are rarely sufficient to change power and institutions. For that, organizations and movements are generally required. But as a historical and cultural sociologist, I am equally convinced that thinkers and their ideas are always necessary to change power and institutions. They help us to express our highest ideals and to see how we fall short of them.

The thinkers and ideas I deal with in this book are not free-floating. They are all embedded in various traditions, and it is these traditions that I am most concerned with here. By a "tradition," I mean a culture that is self-conscious of its past. To be part of a tradition is to know certain stories, read certain books, admire certain people, and care about certain things. It is to knowingly enter into an ongoing conversation, a conversation that precedes one's birth and continues on after one's death.

Commitment to a tradition is not just a matter of opinion. It is not "subjective," like a preference about soda is. Traditions have been forged and tested through historical experience and collective debate. Some traditions stand the test of time; others don't.

Traditions have to be evaluated not only in relationship to historical experience but also vis-à-vis rival traditions: other accounts of how the world is and should be. Evaluating traditions fairly is difficult. In this book, I have used three criteria: internal consistency, historical accuracy, and sociological plausibility. I have asked whether each tradition remains true to its own highest values, gives a defensible interpretation of the nation's history, and yields a practicable vision of the American project.

I believe that the civil religious tradition passes these three tests, and that its two rivals fail them. Religious nationalism fails because it is idolatrous and thus irreligious, because America was not founded as a "Christian nation," and because many modern-day Americans are not believing Christians but are good citizens nonetheless. Radical secularism fails because restricting religious expression violates liberal principles, because the United States was not founded on a "total separation" of religion and politics, and because most Americans are still religious. Consequently, neither religious nationalism nor radical secularism provides a morally defensible, historically plausible, or sociologically practicable basis for the American project.

The civil religious tradition passes these tests because it is neither idolatrous nor illiberal, because it recognizes both the sacred and the secular sources of the American creed, because it provides a political vision that can be embraced by believers and nonbelievers alike, and because it is capacious enough to incorporate new generations of Americans.

I expect that some readers may be puzzled by my emphasis on the dynamism of tradition. "Isn't a tradition fixed?" they might ask. I agree that any tradition must have some foundations, and that the shape of those foundations influences the shape of what can be built on them. But any building must be renovated and expanded now and again if it is to withstand the tests of time and accommodate new occupants.

Let me put this less metaphorically. The foundations of a tradition are laid by certain people and composed of certain texts. To that degree, they are indeed fixed. But the meaning of those lives and texts is always and ever subject to debate. Even the names of the founders and the texts in a canon may be called into question. New founders and texts may be discovered and incorporated. That is the source of the tradition's dynamism.

For some, "dynamism" is just another word for corruption. I am not of this view. I believe that the full meaning of a tradition is only gradually disclosed over time as its implications are worked out in various contexts. For example, I think it is fair to say that the American founders did not fully understand the meaning of equality, even if they wrote that concept into the founding documents.

Nor is this to say that change is always for the good. Traditions really can be corrupted. Corruption occurs when the core values of a tradition are distorted to justify a particular status quo, as when equality is claimed to apply only to white, property-holding men. But sometimes change deepens or widens a tradition, making it more profound or inclusive. In this way, freedom of conscience was eventually understood to imply the free exercise of religious faith, and not only for Protestants. This sort of change is not corrupting. Indeed, a tradition that is no longer able to grow in this way may in fact be dying.

While some readers may find my definition of tradition peculiar, others may find it alarming. "Isn't tradition opposed to modernity, rationality, and progress?" they might ask. Not at all! Modernity and tradition are closely connected. It is precisely the rapid pace of social change in modern societies that has generated a stronger awareness of tradition in the first place and, for many, a deepened yearning for the bonds of tradition, as evidenced by the many traditions great and small that we moderns are continually inventing for ourselves.

Nor do I think that rationality is inherently opposed to tradition. I doubt that rationality in any deep sense is possible outside of a tradition, if by "tradition" we mean a certain language for talking about the world, and if by "rationality" we mean reasoning about ends as well as means. The various discourses of modernity—natural science, secular philosophy, abstract art, and so on—are all "traditions" in this sense. They tell us what we should strive for—be it truth or reason or beauty—and not just how to get there. It is therefore important to distinguish tradition in the sense I describe here from traditionalism in the sense of an instinctive resistance to change.

Finally, I do not believe that tradition is inherently opposed to progress. Tradition often serves as an inspiration for change, and sometimes even as a source of radicalism. Civic republicanism is a very old tradition, for example; its roots go back at least to ancient Athens. Nevertheless, it provided one inspiration for the American Revolution, which was a very radical experiment indeed. Prophetic religion is an even older tradition; its roots go back to ancient Israel. But it provided one inspiration for the civil rights movement, another very radical movement. Again, we must be careful not to confuse tradition and traditionalism.

"Fine," readers may respond. "But I am still an antitraditionalist. I prefer to think everything through on my own." I doubt this is really possible. By the time we are able to think on our own, we have already been socialized into any number of traditions: cultural, political, local, religious, and so on. We can be reflective about and even critical of these traditions. And we should be. That is what people really mean when they talk about thinking things through "on their own." My point is that there is a historical and social element to all of our thinking. We think in languages that have been handed down and taught to us.

What does it mean to be immersed in a tradition? A tradition is like a powerful river that cuts through a deep canyon. We can approach it in various ways. We can swim against the current, or we can just let it carry us along. We can also lie on our backs and gaze upward, wondering what lies above. All these are things we can do.

What we assuredly cannot do is climb up out of the canyon and gaze down at the river from some God's-eye perspective. For finite, cultural animals such as us, there is no "view from nowhere." It is because of this that independent, critical thinking is not necessarily opposed to tradition. In fact, I would argue that it is really possible only for those who have mastered a tradition.

To think critically within a tradition is to paddle to shore and walk upstream or downstream, reflecting on how the river and the canyon have shaped one another. To act critically within a tradition is to try to bend the river by altering the banks, or vice versa. This book does the former in order to enable the latter. It presses conservatives to embrace a more dynamic understanding of tradition, and it pushes progressives to take tradition more seriously. And it does both with an eye to action.

One of the scholarly traditions that I am working out of here is "critical hermeneutics." My method is "hermeneutic" in that it involves textual interpretation, but mine is not a sophisticated hermeneutics based on literary theory. Rather, it is a poor man's hermeneutics that simply tries to put texts into contexts—biographical, historical, and social.

I am interested in the standpoint of the author, the sources of his or her thinking, and how that thinking was related to the problems of the day. I am especially interested in thinkers who deepened or widened their traditions: deepened by going back to earlier texts within the tradition or widened by drawing in new sources.

My approach is critical insofar as it involves the *evaluation* of texts. I regard some interpretations as better than others, based on the three criteria enumerated previously. For example, I think Frederick Douglass's and Abraham Lincoln's interpretations of the nation's founding documents are much better than John C. Calhoun's (see chapter 4). And I think Reinhold Niebuhr's interpretation of Nazism is infinitely superior to H. L. Mencken's (see chapter 5).

My approach is also critical in several other senses, though. I criticize some thinkers for a one-sided reading of the civil religious tradition. In this way, I criticize Hannah Arendt for ignoring the prophetic side of the tradition (see chapter 6), and I criticize Barack Obama for underplaying its republican side. I criticize other thinkers for corrupting the civil religious tradition (see chapter 7). In this vein, I criticize Jerry Falwell for exempting the Christian churches from his prophetic critiques, and I criticize Ronald Reagan for absolving the American people of their collective sins (again, see chapter 7).

Another brief note on method is also necessary here: the central concepts of this book—"civil religion," "religious nationalism," and "radical secularism"—are all "ideal types" in the two senses delineated by the great German sociologist Max Weber. First, they are "ideal types" in the sense of a series of "unified analytical constructs" that are "formed by the one-sided accentuation of certain points of view" so as to sharpen their contrasts with each other.[2] An ideal type construct in this sense is a set of interrelated concepts that are more logically consistent within themselves and more sharply bounded off from one another than are the real phenomena to which they refer. In short, ideal types are useful exaggerations. By turning shades of gray into black and white, they make it easier for us to see real contrasts.

These concepts are also "ideal types" in a second sense: they articulate contrasting sets of ethical and political ideals and clarify what is at stake when we choose between them. So one function of ideal types is to draw out the underlying assumptions of civil religion, religious nationalism, and radical secularism so that we can subject them to logical, historical, and ethical evaluation. Another is to more precisely locate the boundaries between them so that we know when we are crossing over from one side to the other—when, for instance, a laudable sort of civic patriotism is devolving into a dangerous form of political idolatry, or when a reasonable concern with individual freedom is shading off into a malignant type of radical individualism.

I set out to write a book that is scholarly but accessible. That is easier said than done, and whether I have succeeded, only the reader can judge. Still, it may be helpful if I briefly explain how I have approached the task.

On the one hand, I have tried to read as broadly and deeply as possible—broadly in the general literature about each historical period I consider, and deeply in the writings of each individual thinker I examine. I have not delved into personal papers or archival sources but have relied exclusively on published materials and secondary literature. Consequently, whatever claim to originality this book may have resides exclusively in the overarching framework it develops—particularly its central thesis concerning America's three competing political theologies.

At the same time, I have tried to write as plainly and directly as possible. This is not how professors are taught to write, and I have learned that it is not easy. As far as possible, I have tried to keep the academic jargon to a minimum and to confine scholarly debates to the endnotes or, where this is not possible, to define my terms in ordinary language and paint the academic debates in very broad strokes.

Specialist readers who care about the scholarly debates can always turn to the notes, where they will easily discover my intellectual influences. Among other things, they will find that my interpretation of civic republicanism is shaped by the Cambridge School, that my understanding of the prophetic is similar to Walter Brueggemann's, that my understanding of hermeneutics takes its cues from Paul Ricoeur, and that my theory of tradition is inspired by Alasdair MacIntyre and Jeff Stout. Nonspecialist readers who do not care about such things can simply read on.

I have also structured the introductory and concluding sections of the book in a somewhat unusual way. The present introduction is addressed to a wide audience, and it may be all the introduction that many readers will want. In contrast, the next chapter is a bit more scholarly. It, too, is written for a general audience, but readers with a low tolerance for conceptual discussion may wish to skip it. The conclusion is likewise in two parts. Its first part, chapter 8, is, like chapter 1, a little more scholarly in tone. It contrasts civil religion with other political philosophies and political theologies, and argues that some of them are reasonable and others not. Readers who are not especially interested in political philosophy or political theology may want to skip directly to the conclusion proper, which sketches a vision of the righteous republic and considers how such an end might be achieved. I suspect that many academic readers will find chapters 1 and 8 much more interesting than the introduction and conclusion, while some political philosophers and theologians may find them to be the only interesting parts of the book.

Now, for a more detailed road map of what follows. In chapter 1, I define my key concepts in greater detail and situate my argument within current debates. I explain at more length what I mean by terms like "civic republicanism," "prophetic religion," "civil religion," "religious nationalism," "radical secularism," and "tradition," and I spell out how my definitions are similar to, or different from, those advanced by other scholars. Again, readers who are satisfied with the briefer explication of these terms I have already given may simply skip directly to chapter 2, though they may wish to circle back after reading a few of the historical chapters.

Chapter 2 is devoted to what I regard as America's first founding: the establishment of Puritan New England. There, I argue that covenantal religion provided the basic blueprint for Puritan society; that the Puritan polity was proto-republican; that American religious nationalism first arose out of the Puritans' wars with the Native Americans; and, finally, that Puritan society gave rise to proto-secularist views, but not radical secularist ones.

Chapter 3 focuses on what I regard as America's second founding: the American Revolution. There, I side with scholars who argue that the American revolutionaries were more influenced by civic republicanism than by "Lockean liberalism"; that the American founders generally saw Christianity and republicanism as complementary, rather than opposed; that the most influential model of republican government for most Americans was neither Rome nor Athens but Jerusalem; that apocalyptic religious nationalism was conspicuous mainly by its absence in this period; and that scholars who believe that radical secularism was the main inspiration for the American Constitution are seriously mistaken.

Chapter 4 turns to what may be seen as America's first refounding: the Civil War. It argues that Abraham Lincoln's understanding of the American Constitution was initially quite similar to that of John C. Calhoun, the most articulate defender of Southern slavery and "states' rights," but that Lincoln's thinking gradually converged around a new interpretation of the Constitution whose leading advocate was the abolitionist orator Frederick Douglass, himself an emancipated slave. For Calhoun, the articles of the Constitution overrode the preamble, and the Constitution overrode the Declaration, while Douglass's reading proceeded in the opposite direction: the preamble of the Declaration, with its promise of equality, overrode the articles of the Constitution, with their tacit recognition of chattel slavery.

Chapter 4 also details important developments within the rival traditions. It discusses the emergence of a new rhetoric of "blood sacrifice" and "blood atonement," first as a justification for the Civil War and later to legitimate American imperialism, and how this durably transformed American religious nationalism. It also discusses the new radical secularist movement that appeared during Reconstruction and the central role that nativist anti-Catholicism played in its emergence.

In chapter 5, I fast-forward to a second period of social upheaval, the first half of the twentieth century. This chapter focuses on four Progressive Era intellectuals—John Dewey, Jane Addams, Reinhold Niebuhr, and W.E.B. Du Bois—and their respective responses to America's increasing secularity, diversity, and power, as well as its continuing struggles over race. It also details the emergence of popular apocalypticism within American Christianity and discusses its influence on American religious nationalism via the example of Pentecostal evangelist Aimee Semple McPherson. Finally, it shows why modern-day radical secularists might want to think twice before lionizing H. L. Mencken.

In chapter 6, I turn my attention to the decades after World War II, the period of the "liberal consensus," the civil rights movement, and the final collapse of the WASP ascendancy in American society. I show how Hannah Arendt challenged an increasingly technocratic style of liberal governance by returning to the Athenian roots of Western democracy, how Martin Luther King's civic poetry wove several new strands into prophetic republicanism, and how John Courtney Murray incorporated Catholicism into the American story and resynthesized the prophetic and republican strands of the civil religious tradition via the theory of natural law.

In chapter 7, I trace the interaction between the civil religious tradition and partisan politics from the Reagan era up through the present day. In brief, I argue that liberal Democrats like Michael Dukakis and Walter Mondale jettisoned the civil religious tradition, while conservative Republicans like Ronald Reagan and George W. Bush corrupted it. I also argue that Barack Obama's 2008 presidential campaign can be seen as an attempt to revive that tradition, albeit a one-sided and anemic one that ignored its republican strand and then succumbed to the fundamental contradiction between power and prophecy.

In chapter 8, I explain in greater detail why I regard the civil religious tradition as superior to its two main rivals and compare this tradition to several other closely related standpoints, including "liberal nationalism" and "constitutional patriotism." Again, the general reader may find this discussion a bit too specialized.

Finally, in the conclusion, I offer some thoughts on how a revival of the prophetic republican tradition might be brought about and how it would reframe political debate and public policy in the contemporary United States.

In closing, let me offer a few caveats for both the scholarly and nonscholarly reader. The scholarly reader may wonder about my method. For example, cultural and historical sociologists may wonder why I have not spent more time trying to explain the series of social crises that frame each chapter of the book or placing the resulting conflicts in their social context. Intellectual historians may be unhappy that I have focused most of my attention on a few relatively well-known figures instead of trying to paint a more complete and bottom-up picture of the political debates within each period. Political philosophers might wish that I had parsed certain texts more finely or worked out some of my arguments in greater detail. Political scientists, finally, may wonder how the intellectual developments I discuss here may have interacted with electoral politics or public policy.

I have two answers to these concerns. The first is that I am addressing my readers as citizens first and scholars second. The second is that even a scholarly book's method must be appropriate to its purposes. The purposes of this book are to recuperate a certain tradition within American political culture, to demonstrate that it has been a living and evolving tradition, and to identify certain exemplary figures within that tradition from whom we might still draw some measure of inspiration today. While the book's methods may not be adequate to the current standards within any of the various disciplines on which they draw, I believe that they are adequate to their own purposes.

I'd also like to issue a further caveat for nonacademic readers who may wonder why a book about the present crisis gives so much attention to past events. Let me briefly reiterate the reasons:

1. To deepen our perspective on the present. Our current debates are often extensions of earlier debates that reach back to the founding generations and beyond. Consequently, revisiting past debates may help us to resolve present ones, or at least to understand them better.
2. To provide hope for the future. Viewed through the lens of a single lifetime, our politics may seem hopelessly static. When viewed in cross-generational perspective, however, the slow and halting progress becomes more visible. History can be an antidote for cynicism.
3. To challenge misleading narratives. Our positions on politics are often wrapped up with our understanding of the past. If this understanding is distorted or one-sided—and it often is—then our politics will be too. Better history may lead to better politics.
4. To provide a sturdier and more capacious frame for thinking about the American project. Nonacademics—which is to say, most people—do not usually reason in terms of abstract principles or values; they work through moral problems in terms of stories. Historical narratives help us to think about what should come next.

CHAPTER 1

The Civil Religious
Tradition and Its Rivals

MY ARGUMENT ABOUT civil religion is part of a long tradition in political philosophy and social theory. It is most immediately rooted in the
twenty-year-long debate about "civil religion in America" that was un-
leashed a half century ago by sociologist Robert N. Bellah's 1967 essay
of the same name, but its history is far deeper. Bellah may have injected
the notion of civil religion into modern sociology, but he did not invent
the concept. That honor goes to the political philosopher Jean-Jacques
Rousseau, who proposed the establishment of a civil religion to secure
his "social contract." Looking back further still, although Rousseau may
have introduced the idea of civil religion into political theory, the problem itself was already very old: how to coordinate the spiritual and secular kingdoms, or, in Jesus's words, how to render unto Caesar what is
Caesar's, and unto God what is his. The modern debate about civil religion is part of a debate about political theology that is as old as mono-
theism itself.

That it is an old debate does not mean that it is a dead debate—and
there are many reasons for revisiting it now. Over the last three decades,
there has been a massive resurgence of "public religion," not only in the
United States but also around the world.[1] Meanwhile, there has been a
rapid growth of the "religiously unaffiliated," initially in Western Europe
but increasingly in North America too. Simultaneously, there has been an
unprecedented movement of people and ideas around the globe. American religion and culture have been carried to every corner of the planet,
and not-yet-American religions and cultures have been imported into
every corner of the nation. The result is a new level of cultural pluralism
that goes well beyond denominational diversity within American Christianity. The old debate on civil religion provides one starting point for
thinking about how we can sustain democratic solidarity in this changing
context. It provides an alternative to a reactionary traditionalism that
seeks to restore cultural homogeneity and also to a radical individualism
that seeks to dissolve all political bonds. It is perhaps the best starting
point that we have for thinking about the future of America.

"BUT WHY 'CIVIL RELIGION'?!"

One question I was asked repeatedly as I presented this argument before various audiences—a question that some readers may now be asking themselves—was "Why 'civil religion'?" Secular audiences were often uncomfortable with the mention of "religion," while religious audiences sometimes bristled at its conjunction with "civil." Why not choose a more innocuous-sounding term, they asked? Perhaps something less irritating, like "public philosophy" or "political culture" or "civic creed"?[2]

I take these concerns seriously—but I decided to stick with "civil religion." Why? Partly because I wanted to signal continuity with the Bellah thesis, not out of filial piety, but because I think Bellah's interpretation is mostly right.[3] Another reason is that I found all of the alternatives to be unsatisfactory in one way or another. I was unhappy with "public philosophy" because the civil religious tradition long had—and, for some, still has—a genuinely religious meaning.[4] I did not like the singular "political culture" either because it suggests one unified culture, as opposed to multiple and competing traditions; nor did I like the plural "political cultures," which I found too static and unhistorical. "Civic creed" is perhaps the closest substitute I discovered, but it did not quite suit my purposes either—not because it leaves out the ritual aspects so important to civil religion, such as ceremonies, commemorations, parades, and so on, but because it lacks a narrative dimension. My account focuses more on stories. The civil religion is a narrative that tells us where we came from and where we are headed, not just what our commitments are. It embeds our values and commitments within particular stories of civic greatness—and collective failure.

Still, there is no denying that many regard "civil religion" as an irritating concept. But is that such a bad thing—especially if we understand "irritating" in the root sense of "disorienting"? Disorientation can lead to reflection, and perhaps it would be a good thing for the more secular minded to reflect on how their values are ultimately grounded in a certain "transcendent" understanding of reality, that is, a reality that transcends their physical self and its narrow interests.[5] As the late David Foster Wallace once put it, "In the day-to-day trenches of adult life . . . [t]here is no such thing as not worshipping. Everybody worships. The only choice we get is what to worship." Some may worship money and material things, others beauty and sexual allure, and still others "some sort of god or spiritual-type thing."[6] But we all worship something. In this sense, our lives always have a "spiritual" dimension, even if it remains implicit. And if we realize that, then perhaps the secular minded will not be so quick to dismiss the spiritual commitments of their co-citizens.

A related hope is that the civil religion concept may help the more religiously minded to see that their values necessarily have a civic dimension, and that their highest values can really be protected and exercised only in a certain kind of civic community. If one places a high value on freedom of religion, for example—and most people of faith in this country do—then one must also respect freedom *from* religion as one possible result of the freedom of conscience. Not everyone will choose to worship "some sort of god or spiritual-type thing." If the religiously minded are honest about their own doubts, perhaps they will not be so quick to judge the secular minded.

Nevertheless, even if one grudgingly admits the usefulness of the civil religion concept, one might still ask: In what sense is the civil religion actually "religious"?

The answer to that question depends a lot on the questioner. For the secularist, civil religion may be religious only in a historical or literary sense: historical insofar as contemporary progressivism owes a deep debt to the Hebrew prophets; literary insofar as the civil religion still supplies the lyric poetry of our public life. One need not be a Bible believer to draw inspiration from the life or oratory of a great civil theologian like Abraham Lincoln or Martin Luther King Jr., or to be compelled by their telling of the American story.

For the religionist, the civil religious tradition may also be religious in an ethical and even theological sense. If we really are all God's children, as King was fond of saying, then we are also equal in the most fundamental sense possible. If we really are commanded to care for "the least of these," as Matthew's Gospel urges, then the pursuit of social justice has the force of a divine command. And if we believe with our founding grandfathers John Locke and Roger Williams that genuine faith must be freely chosen, then religious freedom has a theological warrant.[7] More than that, if we believe, with some early modern thinkers, that the republic is the form of government that God prefers for his peoples (1 Samuel 8), then we must accept that religious freedom involves public expression.[8] Civil and religious liberties, on this view, are inextricably bound together.

Others have asked, "What's *civil* about civil religion?" The civil religionist sees the civic community as a positive good, even an end in itself, rather than as an instrumental good, a mere means to some other end. For that reason, he or she will try to engage other citizens with civility, that is, with forbearance and respect. And he or she will also strive to build civic friendships with ideological opponents, and not just political alliances with those who are like-minded.

However, civil religion should not be confused with mere civility in the sense of "politeness." The civil religionist is also concerned with the core values of the republic, and these may sometimes trump civic friendship. So the civil religionist will also be prepared to engage in civil disobedience when this is necessary. But the civil religionist will reject ideological absolutism and political violence in the understanding that civic life requires that we balance competing values and forge difficult compromises.

So not "public philosophy" or "political culture" or "civic creed" in the end, but "civil religion.

WHAT IS CIVIL RELIGION?

Bellah initially defined civil religion as the "religious dimension" of the "political realm." Importantly, he understood civil religion as distinct from, but not necessarily opposed to, organized religion.[9] In a later work, Bellah offered a more general definition: civil religion, he said, is the "founding myth" of a political community. This myth generates a "religious dimension, found . . . in the life of every people, through which it interprets its historical experience in the light of transcendent reality."[10]

Bellah's understanding of civil religion should not be equated with Rousseau's. It is different in a number of ways. First, it is voluntary rather than compulsory. No one is morally or legally obligated to affirm it. Second, it is more scriptural than ritual. It provides a conceptual framework for thinking about the American project rather than a liturgical one for celebrating it.[11] Third, it is not a replacement for organized religion. It "exists alongside of and rather clearly differentiated from the churches"—and the synagogues, mosques, and temples, one might add.[12] For all these reasons, Bellah's vision of civil religion is compatible with American traditions of religious freedom, individual rights, and cultural diversity in ways that Rousseau's was not, and it is immune from the legitimate criticisms sometimes directed against other versions of the civil religion idea.

Bellah's definition of civil religion does have one major weakness, though: it does not draw a clear enough line between civil religion and religious nationalism. After all, modern-day American exceptionalism can also be understood as a "religious orientation" or a "founding myth." It is partly for this reason that Bellah was sometimes (wrongfully) accused of promoting "national self-worship," and that modern-day Christian nationalism is sometimes (misleadingly) characterized as a civil religion.[13] This is why it is crucial to distinguish the two at the outset.

Civil religion also needs to be clearly distinguished from radical secularism. Civil religion recognizes the importance of an institutional separation between church and state. What it rejects—and what radical secularists embrace—is a total separation between religion and politics. Radical secularists insist that public life can and should be a "neutral" realm. What they really mean by this is that the public square must be made religion-free. This is neither possible nor fair. It is not possible because religious convictions have political implications. It is not fair because it requires that religious citizens translate their arguments into the secularists' language, but not the other way around. And it is probably not even desirable because so many of our deepest convictions are embedded in religious language—even if we ourselves happen to be secularists. Imagine Lincoln's or King's or Obama's speeches shorn of all religious references. Civic poetry would be transformed into political doggerel.

We can distinguish civil religion from its two rivals in terms of both form and substance. We can do so on the basis of form by comparing how each envisions the proper relationship between the religious and political realms (see fig. 1). The religious nationalist wishes to fuse religion and politics, to make citizenship in the one the mark of citizenship in the other, to purge all those who lack the mark, and to expand the borders of the kingdom as much as possible, by violent means if necessary. The radical secularist wishes to fortify the border; to build a wall that is so high and so well guarded that no traffic, no money, no people, no ideas even, can pass through it; and to punish anyone who dares cross from one side to the other. The civil religionist believes that each kingdom has its proper border, but that there is also a place where those borders crisscross with one another, creating a liminal zone where the ends of religion and the ends of politics overlap, and that preserving this space is of vital importance to both kingdoms. Religious nationalists advocate total fusion; radical secularists advocate total separation; civil religionists accept partial overlap.

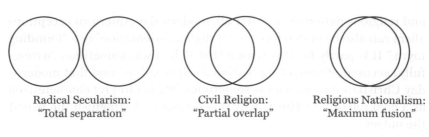

Radical Secularism: Civil Religion: Religious Nationalism:
"Total separation"   "Partial overlap"   "Maximum fusion"

FIGURE 1

We can also distinguish the three traditions in terms of substance. They all draw on two main sources: the Bible, both Hebrew and Christian, and Western political philosophy, both ancient and modern. But they draw on them in different ways. Western theology and philosophy both give rise to various streams that diverge from and converge with one another like a delta at the intersection of two rivers. The American civil religion is fed by biblical as well as philosophical sources, specifically prophetic religion and civic republicanism. Religious nationalism draws only on biblical sources, particularly biblical tales of conquest and apocalypse. Radical secularism draws only on philosophical sources, specifically libertarian liberalism and total separationism (see fig. 2).

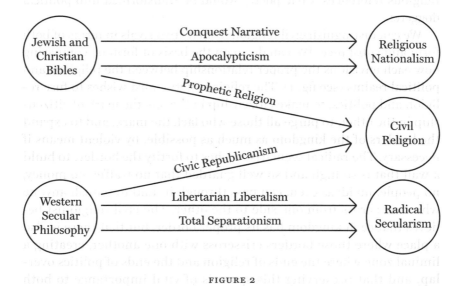

FIGURE 2

The relationship among religious nationalism, radical secularism, and civil religion is a bit like the relationship between two powerful clans.

Religious nationalists and radical secularists want to keep their bloodlines pure. They want nothing to do with each other. Civil religionists do not think this is possible. They see the lineages as intermixed and even intermarried.

For many Americans, the term "prophetic religion" conjures up visions of the Apocalypse and the Rapture such as one finds in the book of Daniel and the Revelation of John.[14] This, however, is not what I mean by "prophetic religion" but instead is related to a stream of thought generally known as "apocalypticism."[15] In American religious nationalism, apocalypticism flows together with a certain reading of the Hebrew Bible, which I will refer to as the "conquest narrative." This narrative highlights the martial exploits of the ancient Israelites described in Joshua, Judges, and Kings. *The basic formula for religious nationalism in American history has been apocalyptic politics plus the conquest narrative.*

The conquest narrative can be contrasted with another reading of the Hebrew Bible that draws mainly on "Latter Prophets" such as Amos, Isaiah, and Jeremiah. It is to this reading that I refer in using the term "prophetic religion."[16] It stresses the covenants formed between God and his people in the Pentateuch and then deepened and reaffirmed in the books of the prophets. *The basic formula for civil religion in American history has been prophetic religion plus civic republicanism, or, more succinctly, prophetic republicanism.*

It is now time to dive a little more deeply into these various streams of thought, to map out their divergences and convergences in a little more detail.

RELIGIOUS NATIONALISM
AND THE CONQUEST NARRATIVE

The Jewish and Christian Bibles are often read as a series of sacred agreements or "covenants" between God and his people.[17] Biblical scholars usually distinguish the covenants made by Noah, Abraham, and Moses. The terms of these covenants gradually evolved over time. In the first, or Noahide, covenant, established after the Great Flood, Noah and his descendants agree not to eat blood or kill one another.[18] In return God gives them "every moving thing that lives" as food and promises that they shall "be fruitful and multiply." The sign of the rainbow seals the first covenant. In the second, or Abrahamic, covenant, established after the destruction of the Tower of Babel, Abraham promises obedience to God, and God promises him land and progeny.[19] The rite of circumcision seals this covenant.[20] In the third, or Mosaic, covenant, established following the Exodus from

Egypt, the Israelites promise obedience to God's laws, and God promises to make them a "light unto the world"—and threatens to punish them should they backslide. The Ten Commandments seal this covenant.

Up to the point of the making of the Mosaic covenant, prophetic religion and the conquest narrative have been flowing along in the same streambed. With the arrival of the prophets, they begin to diverge, especially over the question of blood sacrifice. In the early covenants, blood sacrifice remains central: Noah makes a burnt offering to God, Abraham constructs an altar to God, and Moses includes sacrifice in the Law.[21] In the prophetic books, however, we find scoffing denunciations of blood sacrifice.[22] In the first chapter of Isaiah, we encounter these words: "'What to me is the multitude of your sacrifices?' says the LORD; 'I have had enough of burnt offerings of rams and the fat of well-fed beasts; I do not delight in the blood of bulls, or of lambs, or of goats. . . . Bring no more vain offerings.'"[23] If burnt offerings are made in "vain," then what exactly does God desire from his people? The prophet Micah provides part of the answer: "With what shall I come before the LORD, and bow myself before God on high? Shall I come before him with burnt offerings . . . ? . . . What does the LORD require of you but to do justice, and to love kindness, and to walk humbly with your God?"[24] The book of Amos adds the following: "Even though you offer me your burnt offerings and grain offerings, I will not accept them. . . . But let justice roll down like waters, and righteousness like an ever-flowing stream."[25]

The God of the prophets is not interested in blood sacrifice; he demands individual righteousness and social justice. But justice how, and to whom? Here is Jeremiah's rebuke to the king of Judah and the House of David: "Woe to him who builds his house by unrighteousness, and his upper rooms by injustice, who makes his neighbor serve him for nothing and does not give him his wages, who says, 'I will build myself a great house with spacious upper rooms,' who cuts out windows for it, paneling it with cedar and painting it with vermilion. Do you think you are a king because you compete in cedar?"[26] For the Latter Prophets, the covenant is recentered around individual righteousness and social justice, particularly toward the weak and the oppressed, rather than around blood sacrifice. And with the destruction of the Second Temple and the emergence of rabbinic Judaism, the old blood rituals are indefinitely suspended.

Of course, the metaphor of blood sacrifice does reappear in the "new covenant" pronounced by Jesus. During the Last Supper, on the eve of his crucifixion, Jesus holds up a chalice and says: "This is my blood of the covenant, which is poured out for many for the forgiveness of sins."[27] Later, Paul echoes Jesus's words: "Without the shedding of blood, there is no remission of sins."[28] But Jesus's sacrifice is to be the final sacrifice, the blood that puts an end to all bloodletting.

So why does talk of blood sacrifice remain a part of Western political theology? Because the conquest narrative helps legitimate political violence, particularly violent forms of nation building. Blood helps define the nation. Shared blood ("race") tells us who is and is not a member of the nation. Aren't the true Israelites the blood descendants of Abraham, Isaac, and Jacob?[29] Aren't they forbidden from intermarrying with other peoples?

Blood also defines Israel's most fundamental obligation to God: blood offerings.[30] The *locus classicus* is Leviticus 1–7, which discusses the rites of animal sacrifice.[31] Blood is to be sprinkled, daubed, or thrown as a means of atonement.[32] In this way, blood also brings blessings to the nation.

What's more, God himself seems to approve of war. In the historic books of the "Former Prophets," Yahweh often appears as a warrior god who leads his people into battle and intervenes on their behalf in exchange for blood offerings. The books of the Former Prophets are rife with stories of bloody conquest, altar building, and animal sacrifice. In the conquest narrative, war itself becomes a kind of sacrament.

Blood is also part of the act of bringing down vengeance on the unrighteous. This is where the conquest narrative flows together with apocalypticism. The crucial text is John's Revelation, which depicts violent retribution on a cosmic scale. Following the formula of blood for blood, the avenging angels of the Lord use blood to obscure the moon and poison the waters.[33] In the Pentateuch, blood is a symbol of life. In Revelation, blood becomes a symbol of death.[34]

So blood sacrifice marks the point of divergence between prophetic religion and the conquest narrative and also the point of convergence between the conquest narrative and apocalyptic religion. It is what makes religious nationalism nationalistic: religion, people, land, and polity are all cemented together with dried blood in the form of blood sacrificed to God, blood flowing in veins, blood spilled in battle, blood showering down from heaven. Modern-day American exceptionalists may be too squeamish to speak of blood in this way. They may prefer watered-down talk about "ultimate sacrifice." But their hands still drip with blood.

APOCALYPSE SOON?

In the most virulent strains of American religious nationalism, the conquest narrative flows together with an apocalyptic form of prophecy belief.[35] The apocalyptic storyline is familiar. The world enters into a period of rapid moral decline. Natural disasters occur with increasing frequency and severity. These are all "signs of the times"—the "end times." A climactic confrontation ensues between the forces of good and evil. Horrific warfare decimates the world's population and massive conflagrations consume the earth's surface. Finally, "like a thief in the night," Christ swoops down from the sky, accompanied by the hosts of heaven, to defeat the forces of evil and bind the power of Satan. Thus begins Christ's thousand-year reign over the earth, a period of peace and harmony during which the "lion lays down with the lamb."

The apocalyptic worldview is based on a certain way of reading biblical texts, namely: (1) predictively, as an encoded message about future events that can be decoded by modern-day prophets[36]; (2) literally, such that the mythical creatures of the texts are understood as material realities; (3) "premillennially," with the Second Coming of Christ understood to precede the earthly "millennium" of God's thousand-year reign on earth; and (4) vindictively, with the punishment of the godless occurring in the most gruesome and violent form imaginable.

This is not the only way the texts can be read; nor is it even the way they have been read traditionally. The early church read them allegorically, rather than predictively. The great battles depicted in the apocalyptic texts stood for great battles within the human heart. The premillennial interpretation is likewise a modern invention that did not become widespread in American Christianity until the early to mid-twentieth century. Before then, the general view was "postmillennial." Christ would not return until the church had already transformed the world. Literalist interpretation of Christian scripture is also not traditional but arose during the "fundamentalist/modernist" controversies of the early twentieth century. Before that time, scripture was read in multiple registers (e.g., the typological, the allegorical, the symbolic). Nor was revenge a central motif of traditional Christianity: the Roman church had emphasized redemption with its doctrine of purgatory. In short, the apocalyptic worldview is not an integral part of "traditional Christianity." Rather, it is characteristic of a certain kind of American Protestantism that arose during the early twentieth century.

What makes apocalyptic religious nationalism so dangerous? First, it leads to hubris. It seduces its followers into claiming to know things that no human being can possibly know. Second, it leads to demonization of others. Our enemies become physical embodiments of evil. Third, it leads to fatalism, suggesting that wars and other calamities are beyond human control. Finally, and most fatefully, it suggests that the ultimate solution to all problems is a violent one involving the annihilation of one's enemies.

It is not hard to understand the appeal of apocalypticism: it makes us feel in the know, in the right, and in on the action. We are drawn to it for the same reasons that we are drawn to adventure and fantasy novels such as the *Harry Potter* or *Lord of the Rings* series. It gives us the sense that we understand what is "really" going on, that the moral of the story is in black and white, and that we are the lead actors in the final showdown between good and evil. But apocalypticism dissolves the line between fiction and reality. And when it crosses over into politics and gains the force of arms, it can unleash forces that truly *are* demonic.

Fortunately, religious nationalism is not the only tradition in our public life.

CIVIC REPUBLICANISM VERSUS CLASSICAL LIBERALISM

Every morning, American schoolchildren rise from their desks, place their hands over their hearts, and "pledge allegiance to the flag, of the United States of America, and to the republic, for which it stands." In referring to the United States as a "republic," they are alluding—mostly unknowingly, no doubt—to a long tradition in the political and intellectual history of the West, a tradition that had a profound influence on the American founders.[37] This tradition links the city republics of the ancient world with the city-states of medieval Europe and the liberal democracies of the modern world. And it links ancient philosophers like Aristotle and Cicero with American thinkers like James Madison and John Adams.

Of course, it's not just today's schoolchildren who are unaware of the republican roots of the American project. If asked to characterize the political system of the United States, most of their parents would probably say that it is a "democracy" or, perhaps, a "liberal democracy." Few Americans would even think to identify the United States as a "republic," and those who would might not fully understand the term. As important as it was to the founders and as vital as it remained during the nineteenth century, the language of civic republicanism has been slowly supplanted by the vocabulary of liberal democracy.

Here, a brief clarification is in order: classical liberalism in the philosophical sense is not the same thing as modern liberalism in the partisan sense of "liberal Democrats." Nor is classical liberalism opposed to contemporary conservatism in the partisan sense of "conservative Republicans." Ironically, most liberal Democrats are not "classical liberals," and few conservative Republicans are "civic republicans." Rather, the former incline toward modern social liberalism, and the latter toward classical economic liberalism.

So, just how does republicanism differ from liberalism?

First, republicanism and liberalism have different understandings of human nature. On the republican view, human beings are inherently social. They naturally seek out the company and approval of other human beings, and not just for instrumental reasons of economic exchange. The republic is a natural result of this social disposition. As Cicero put it, "The original cause of [the republic] is not so much weakness as a kind of social instinct natural to man. For the human kind is not solitary . . . but it is so constituted that, even if it possessed the greatest plenty of material comforts, [it would nevertheless be impelled by its nature to live in social groups].[38] Furthermore, republicans generally agree that human beings are inherently political in the sense that they tend to form self-governing communities. As Aristotle famously put it, "Man is by nature a political animal. . . . Nature . . . has endowed man alone among the animals with the power of speech"—and this power can only be fully exercised in a self-governing community.[39] For all these reasons, republicans see self-government as a positive good rather than a necessary evil.

Contrast this with classical liberalism's assumptions about human nature and government. Many versions of liberalism assume that human beings are inherently unsocial and/or that they come together solely for the purpose of economic exchange.[40] Indeed, in the pessimistic liberalism of Thomas Hobbes's *Leviathan*, human beings are downright rapacious. The "state of nature" is a "war of all against all," and the only reason why human beings enter into a "social contract" with their ruler is to ensure their own physical security. (Nowadays, many American conservatives would not entrust even this task to government. They prefer to arm themselves.) On the liberal view, human beings band together for mutual advantage or self-protection rather than innate sociability or self-realization. Other things being equal, they would be just as well off all by themselves.

Republicanism and liberalism are also premised on different views of human freedom. On my reading, republican freedom is complex, having at least three meanings.[41] First, and most fundamentally, republican freedom means not being a slave in the literal or figurative sense, which is to say, not being subject to the arbitrary will of other persons. Slavery of either kind leads to personal servility and undermines the foundations of political independence. It is therefore incompatible with genuine citizenship. In a free society, the arbitrary rule of men gives way to the impersonal rule of law. Second, republican freedom means not being a slave to one's passions. Specifically, it means reshaping one's passions so that one naturally desires what is good and just and dislikes what is base and selfish.[42] Third, republican freedom means being an active citizen. For all these reasons, the republican understands freedom and government as complementary rather than opposed—so long as the government is a republican one.

What about liberal freedom? It, too, has various senses—but all of them are simple, rather than complex. On the classically liberal view, freedom means not being interfered with and, more precisely, not being subject to physical restrictions on one's movement.[43] Locke gives the example of a person locked in a room.[44] So long as that person has no desire to exit the room, he says, he or she is free. This is a very narrow conception of freedom: by this reasoning, a slave is free so long as he or she does not desire his or her freedom. On a more utilitarian view, being free means pursuing one's desires, whatever they may happen to be. In David Hume's formula, reason should be the slave of the passions; the passions provide the ends, and reason the means. But if reason cannot distinguish between good and bad ends, then it is not clear how one differentiates between, say, a passion for opera and a passion for heroin. On Hume's definition, the clever heroin addict is just as free as the clever opera buff. Such an example may seem contrived, but it has vexed some brilliant minds.[45] The liberal account of freedom reaches its logical conclusion in the libertarian views of Ayn Rand, for whom freedom is not being hampered by external limitations imposed by laws and the state. The possibility that the operation of markets or the power of firms might limit or undermine a person's freedom is not even seriously entertained, because freedom is understood exclusively in terms of private choices. Note that all three views assume that freedom and government are in inverse relation to each other.

Republicans and liberals often have very different views of virtue as well. Republican virtue is not Victorian virtue: it has little to do with sexual propriety or sensual restraint. Rather, virtue connotes ethical and practical skill, a knowledge of what is worthwhile and how to attain it.[46] For the ancients, civic virtue conjoined a devotion to civic life with training in oratory, persuasion, and other public skills.[47] For the Renaissance humanists, civic virtue acquired a further connotation inspired by Christianity: self-sacrifice for the common good.[48] Civic republicans generally believe that free institutions are inherently fragile and cannot survive very long without a virtuous citizenry to support them.

Virtue alone is not sufficient, however; a properly balanced constitution is also crucial. The mention of "balance" may evoke the "checks and balances" that one learns about in civics class.[49] In the republican tradition, however, "balance" has a sociological meaning as well. It presumes a balance between the different groups within society as well as between the various branches of government.[50] The underlying idea is that laws and institutions are rarely enough to prevent abuses of power; only a balance of power among different social groups can achieve that aim. Why? Because a powerful group will always find a way to subvert laws and institutions for its own gain, unless its power is checked by that of other groups. From a republican perspective, laws and institutions are important, but they are never sufficient to check "corruption."

But just what is "corruption"? Since the Progressive Era, the term has come to mean self-dealing and quid pro quos—bribery, nepotism, influence peddling, and so on. It suggests individual moral failings—the proverbial "bad apples." The republican, however, understands corruption in sociological terms, as the result of a political imbalance; corruption infects the whole tree, not just one apple. How so? Simply put, if one group can exercise power without being checked by another, it will elevate its corporate interests above the common good.[51] And when one segment of the population begins to pursue its interests at the expense of everyone else's, people become more concerned with their private interests than with the common good. No one wants to be a "sucker." They'd prefer to be a "free rider."

On the republican view, then, civic virtue and constitutional balance jointly counteract political corruption. On the liberal view, by contrast, institutional design is everything, and civic virtue and sociological balance are nothing. Indeed, according to Immanuel Kant, virtue is unnecessary because even "a people comprised of devils" can govern themselves through representative institutions. Once the proper laws are put in place, self-interest will automatically produce the common good.[52] The possibility that powerful individuals or groups not counterbalanced by other powerful groups might rewrite the laws to serve their personal or collective interests does not appear to have occurred to Kant, perhaps because he lived under an absolutist monarchy and had no personal experience with representative government. We can hardly afford to be so naïve today. On another view, originally put forth by the British essayist Bernard Mandeville, virtue is unnecessary because free markets magically transform private vices into public goods.[53] This is of course true if by "public goods" one means consumer goods, and if one cares about their production but not their distribution. We can no longer afford such a limited view. We know that extreme inequality is associated with a host of social pathologies, to which even the richest are not immune.

Republicans and liberals also have very different notions of historical time. For republicans, history is circular. In classical republicanism, the circle took the form of a cycle of regimes. Polybius's theory of "anacyclosis" distinguished six simple types of political regime: three good types and three corresponding corrupt types. The three good types were monarchy (rule by one), aristocracy (rule by the few), and democracy (rule by the many). The corresponding corrupt types were tyranny, oligarchy, and ochlocracy, respectively. Polities moved through a series of stages involving corruption and metamorphosis: monarchy degenerated into tyranny, aristocracy into oligarchy, and democracy into ochlocracy. The corrupt form of one regime gave way to the pure form of the next—tyranny to aristocracy, oligarchy to democracy, and ochlocracy to monarchy. Such, said Polybius, is the "cycle of political revolution, the law of nature according to which constitutions change, are transformed, and finally revert to their original form."[54] This cycle, however, could be halted, or at least slowed, by means of a "mixed constitution" that combined elements of monarchy, aristocracy, and democracy.[55] The political architecture of the United States was much influenced by the ideal of the mixed constitution (see chapter 3). Alas, this constitutional architecture has not proven sufficient to protect the American republic from the corruptions of oligarchy.

Following a certain school of thought in contemporary political philosophy, I have been emphasizing the differences between republicanism and liberalism.[56] But as various critics have rightly pointed out, one should not overdraw the contrast, and for at least two reasons. The first is that liberalism may be seen as an effort to adapt republican ideals to modern polities.[57] The United States and France are not Athens and Sparta, after all. They are far larger and much more complex. Their citizens cannot all assemble in a single public square. Nor can they be neatly divided into just two or three groups. Liberal thought provides insights about how republican principles might be realized under modern conditions. The second reason not to exaggerate the contrast is that there is actually a great deal of overlap between republican and liberal thought and ideals.[58] Consider Locke, Montesquieu, and Madison, all of whom had an enormous influence on American political discourse and institutions. To Locke, we owe the idea of "natural rights"; to Montesquieu, "checks and balances"; and to Madison, our "federalist" institutions. Yet none of these men can be neatly categorized as "republican" or "liberal"; they were, all three, both. Still, as I will argue in chapter 3, civic republicanism exerted a greater influence on the American founders than did modern liberalism.

WHAT IS RADICAL SECULARISM?

There is plenty of space between the conceptual poles of republicanism and liberalism. Thus, there are some types of modern liberalism
that are quite close to civic republicanism, and others that are much
further away. Those that are closer to republicanism embrace some of
the goals of social democracy. Those that are further away embrace one
or more variants of radical individualism. Similarly, there is also plenty
of space between secular humanism and total separationism, as well
as some types of secular humanism that are quite close to prophetic
religion, and others that are very far away. The types that are close have
a strong commitment to social justice. The types that are far away are
much more concerned with individual rights. This means that there are
some kinds of secular humanism that are really just secular versions
of civil religion and others that are radically opposed to civil religion. I
refer to the latter as "radical secularism." So, radical secularism does not
encompass all forms of secular humanism, just those that are at odds
with the civil religion.

What do I mean by "radical individualism"? If you've ever read
Hobbes's *Leviathan* or Locke's *Second Treatise*, you'll already know.
Radical individualism begins with presocial and often antisocial individuals who encounter each other in a state of nature and contract
with one other for the sake of safety and property. They see the protection of individual rights as the highest or even sole purpose of the
political order.

Radical individualism has deep roots in American culture. Alexis de
Tocqueville detected it as early as the mid-nineteenth century; indeed,
he invented the term "individualism" to describe what he observed. The
intellectual roots of radical individualism are much deeper, though. They
go all the way back to the ancient atomists of Greece and Rome and, in
particular, to the philosophies of Epicurus and Lucretius, who thought
the good life was the private life, and that public life was to be avoided.
(Of course, nowadays, Americans are more likely to pick up radical individualism in a microeconomics course or an Ayn Rand novel than to
encounter it in a philosophy class.) It is important to distinguish radical
individualism of this sort from broader conceptions of individualism.
Civic republicans are also very concerned with individual freedom, but
they are not radical individualists.

The idea of total separationism also circulates widely in our public
discourse. It can be found in high-minded works of legal philosophy as

well as in everyday discussions of American politics. Such a concept is not the same as American-style secularism. Secularism defends religious freedom, including the freedom to choose irreligion, and rejects religious establishments, with "establishment" meaning any special recognition of a particular church or any special privileging of religion over irreligion. Radical secularism goes much further. It attacks religious faith from the vantage point of scientific reason, claiming that the one cannot be reconciled with the other, and demands that religion be ejected from public life, which should be a realm of pure reason.

The American version of radical individualism draws on at least three different strands of secular philosophy. The first is social atomism, the modern-day descendant of ancient atomism. Social atomism is the scientific variant of radical individualism, the view that "individuals" are literally the elementary particles of social life and that, strictly speaking, "there is no such thing as society," as Margaret Thatcher once put it—just individuals.[59] Like society, culture, institutions, and traditions are just so many chimeras.[60] The social scientific version of social atomism is "methodological individualism." This is the view that all of social life results solely from interactions between self-interested individuals. By contrast, civic republicanism assumes that human beings are social creatures, that they are shaped by the society they are born into, and that their personal wellbeing is tied to the collective wellbeing of their society.

The second source of radical individualism is libertine liberalism. Libertine liberalism is the political philosophy of radical individualism. Libertine liberals define freedom as the absence of restraint and the pursuit of our desires, whatever they may happen to be.[61] This is a very superficial understanding of freedom. The problem is not only that people sometimes desire things that undermine their wellbeing, as in the addiction example given earlier, but also that they often have many different desires that conflict with one another. As any parent knows, learning to restrain our desires is a first step toward ordering them. And without this internal order, there is emotional chaos. Furthermore, in focusing on desire, libertine liberalism overlooks capability. Many of the things that are most worthy of our desire require the development of our physical, moral, aesthetic, and intellectual capacities. Desiring to run a marathon or play the piano or repair a car is not the same as having the capacity to do so. A free society is one that provides its citizens with the resources and opportunities to develop distinctly human capacities such as these. Finally, libertine liberalism is self-undermining. One of the central insights of the republican tradition is that if citizens do not use some of their freedom to sustain free institutions, they are apt to lose all of it. The preservation of individual liberty always requires some degree of civic virtue.

The third source of radical individualism in the United States is commonsense utilitarianism. Commonsense utilitarianism is the ethical system that underpins radical individualism. It defines a "good life" as one in which the sum total of pleasant experiences exceeds the sum total of painful experiences, and a "good society" as one in which the aggregate of individual utilities (pleasures minus pains) is positive rather than negative.[62] Typically, republicanism is accompanied by some form of "virtue ethics," in which a "good life" has a certain overall shape that is considered admirable by one's peers, as well as by a robust understanding of the "common good" as goods that are produced and enjoyed in common (e.g., a musical performance or a worship service). Indeed, "common good" and "common wealth" are both connotations of the Latin term *res publica*. In commonsense utilitarianism, by contrast, there are no common goods or common wealths, only individual utilities and private property.

Radical secularism combines one or more forms of radical individualism with the doctrine of total separationism. Total separationism seeks a total "privatization" of religion in the secret hope of its eventual extinction.[63] It sees religion as inherently and inevitably divisive and oppressive and therefore at odds with democratic ideals of equality and freedom. With Christopher Hitchens, it believes that "religion poisons everything." The American version of total separationism often appeals to the American Constitution, claiming that the founders were enlightened deists or closet atheists who authored a "Godless Constitution" that erected an impermeable wall between religion and politics. As we will see in chapter 3, they seriously overstate their case.

While some forms of liberalism and humanism can be part of a new vital center, radical secularism in the sense defined here cannot. While radical secularism may provide a strong bulwark against an overreaching state or church, it does not provide a tenable foundation for a diverse republic. Indeed, it tends to undermine the republic by leaving it exposed to the twin tyrannies of oligarchies and markets, the real tyrannies that currently threaten the American project.

A THEORY OF TRADITION

A tradition is like a river with many tributaries.[64] But what about the water itself? What is it made of? When it comes to tradition, the "water" comprises four basic elements: canon, archive, pantheon, and narrative.[65] By "canon," I mean a set of texts that are widely known and read, and that can serve as focal points for civic discussion and public debate. For example, one of the key "books" in the "Old Testament" of the civil religious tradition—discussed at some length in chapters 2 and 7—is John Winthrop's "City on a Hill" speech, the ur-text of a certain genre of civil religious writing that conceives of America as a "New Israel" (in the words of Timothy Dwight) and of Americans as an "almost chosen people" (in the words of Abraham Lincoln). The genre's "gospels" are, of course, the Declaration of Independence and the U.S. Constitution, particularly the preambles and the Bill of Rights. Under the Common Core standards recently introduced into most of the nation's public schools, all American children must read and understand these texts. Rounding out America's "New Testament" are the speeches and writings of the "founding fathers," particularly the *Federalist Papers* and various writings and speeches by the first three presidents. These are texts to which America's civil theologians and their rivals have returned again and again for inspiration and evidence.

By "pantheon," I mean the founders, heroes, saints, and martyrs of American civic life. At the apex of this pantheon, one presently finds King, Lincoln, and Washington, and in that order. Immediately below them one finds the rest of the "founding fathers," along with a few others who risked or gave their lives in the name of civic inclusion and democratic government, such as Rosa Parks or John F. Kennedy. In what follows, I will press for the canonization of a wider set of figures, some of them less well known to the broader American public, including Benjamin Rush, Frederick Douglass, Jane Addams, and Hannah Arendt. Why do I include a pantheon in my conception of tradition? Because abstract principles do not always provide an adequate guideline for human conduct. One needs moral exemplars as well, individuals who embodied these principles in their lives and can therefore serve as models of civic excellence in the present day.

By "narrative," I mean an interpretation of the past that generates a vision of the future. For example, many versions of the civic narrative are loosely modeled on the Exodus story in the Hebrew Bible. Thus, the Puritans crossed a great sea in search of a Promised Land. Once there, on their "errand into the wilderness," some fondly recalled the "fleshpots"—of England, not Egypt. For them, the narrative taught perseverance. The revolutionary generation focused on another moment in the Exodus story. In Washington, they saw their Moses; in the Declaration, their covenant; in the Constitution, their commandments. By the time of the Civil War, African Americans were telling a very different version of this story, in which they were the chosen people and white Americans were cast in the role of the Egyptians. And during the Progressive Era, the great Protestant theologian Reinhold Niebuhr focused on the jeremiads of the prophets, excoriating the American people for their unwarranted pride and their tragic tendency to confuse the material blessings of a bounteous continent with the just deserts of personal righteousness.

Lest we imagine that we have somehow risen above such rhetoric, that we are too cynical to be moved by stories any longer, consider the opening paragraphs of Barack Obama's 2008 "race speech." I quote at length:

> "We the people, in order to form a more perfect union . . ."—221 years ago, in a hall that still stands across the street, a group of men gathered and, with these simple words, launched America's improbable experiment in democracy. Farmers and scholars, statesmen and patriots who had traveled across an ocean to escape tyranny and persecution finally made real their declaration of independence at a Philadelphia convention that lasted through the spring of 1787.
>
> The document they produced was eventually signed but ultimately unfinished. It was stained by this nation's original sin of slavery, a question that divided the colonies and brought the convention to a stalemate until the founders chose to allow the slave trade to continue for at least 20 more years, and to leave any final resolution to future generations.
>
> Of course, the answer to the slavery question was already embedded within our Constitution—a Constitution that had at its very core the ideal of equal citizenship under the law; a Constitution that promised its people liberty and justice and a union that could be and should be perfected over time.

In this speech, Obama masterfully wove together the Exodus narrative and the American founding, yielding a seamless story that points toward the uncompleted and ultimately uncompletable project of a truly United States.

Finally, by "archive," I mean the vast inventory of texts, personages, and stories that are not presently part of the civil religious tradition but that might one day be incorporated into it. The civil theologians of America's past have spent many hours in this archive. Abraham Lincoln combed through debates surrounding the Constitution as he worked out his positions on union and abolition. Niebuhr worked through the writings of Cotton Mather as he thought about the legacy of Puritanism for modern America. And Barack Obama turned to the writings of Frederick Douglass and W.E.B. Du Bois in his quest to understand the place of the black man in American history and society. This book, too, is an example of "archival research" in this sense, though not in the historian's understanding of the term. No doubt, recent generations of immigrants will do research of their own as they begin to more fully write themselves into the American story, just as past generations have already done.

Of course, the other traditions have their own canons, pantheons, narratives, and archives. The secularist canon might include Thomas Paine's urgings to "begin the world anew" or H. L. Mencken's acid-tongued diatribes against the original Protestant fundamentalists. Its pantheon might place Thomas Jefferson above George Washington and Lionel Trilling above Reinhold Niebuhr. Its basic narrative is a story of individual emancipation from authority and the shift of authority from religion to science.

As for the nationalist canon, it would include the writings of the anti-Federalists and of John C. Calhoun, their nineteenth-century heir. Accordingly, it might rank anti-Federalists like Patrick Henry and George Mason above proto-liberals like Jefferson and Paine, and nowadays it would put Ronald Reagan on the highest pedestal of all, well above the likes of Martin Luther King. The religious nationalist narrative is best understood as an Americanized version of the "golden age" myth. It emphasizes the great deeds of the past, particularly the economic vitality and military strength of the United States, not to mention its sexual purity and religious piety. Its core trope is moral decline, which supposedly results from religious decline.

AN AMERICAN TRADITION

There is something very American about the civil religious tradition. A brief comparison with France can help us to see why. The French Revolution was also powerfully influenced by civic republicanism. In France, however, republicanism and religion were soon seen as fundamentally opposed.[66] Why this perception took hold there is an interesting question, but not one I can pursue here. In any event, the "de-Christianization" campaign of 1793 marked a fundamental turning point. Church properties were confiscated, altars stripped, monasteries dissolved, priests banished, and a "Cult of Reason" established in their place. Thus began the vaunted conflict between *"les deux Frances,"* republican and Catholic, that would help define French politics for more than a century and that still echoes in present-day debates. Many (though not all) modern-day French republicans believe that religions must be removed from public life. This is one reason they have been so vexed by Islam: it is not so easily privatized.[67] While there is no shortage of anti-Muslim sentiment in the United States, there is also no equivalent to the "headscarf affair" either. For most Americans, the Muslim headscarf is just another form of "personal" religious expression.

The American revolutionaries did not see republicanism and religion as inherently opposed; on the contrary, most saw them as deeply complementary (see chapter 3). This view is indicated by Jefferson's phrase "Nature's God" and by the copious citations to the Old Testament in Paine's *Common Sense*. Personally, Jefferson may not have seen much difference between Nature and God, and Paine would certainly have placed his bets on Nature.[68] Still, both invoked God, even if only for the sake of political compromise or audience appeal. And they were among the least orthodox of the American revolutionaries. There were also a great many orthodox Christians among the founders, men such as Jonathan Mayhew or Benjamin Rush, who saw the struggle for religious and political liberties as fully of a piece. For them, there was no conflict between traditional Christianity and civic republicanism. Indeed, many of them believed that the Israelites, rather than the Greeks, had established the first republic, and that republicanism thus had a theological as well as a philosophical warrant. Indeed, one might argue—and I *will* argue—that the dominant vision of civic republicanism during the American Revolution was Hebraic, or prophetic, republicanism. Such a form of republicanism truly is uniquely American.

CONCLUSION

Up until now, I have presented the three rival traditions as if they were dusty portraits hanging side by side on a wall. On the right-hand side we find *Religious Nationalism*, a red-hued canvas in heavy oils, filled with the blood and fire of war and Apocalypse, and replete with battle scenes in which the forces of good and evil square off on land, on sea, and in the air. It is a fantasy scene, filled with supernatural creatures—and vain hopes that justice and peace can be achieved through violence and bloodshed. On the left-hand side hangs *Radical Secularism*, a blue-toned watercolor in cheerful pastels that portrays a congeries of disconnected individuals pursuing their own private interests and pleasures without any especial regard for one another. It is a utopian tableau, which paints over human evil and vulnerability. Finally, in the middle, we have *Civil Religion*, a panoramic portrait of a diverse people marching together through time toward a Promised Land across landscapes both light and dark. It is hopeful without being fantastical, and progressive without being naïvely optimistic.

I have presented the three traditions in this static way in order to highlight certain key differences between them. For one, each is made of different materials. Religious nationalism uses a blend of the war stories of the Hebrew Bible and the divine vengeance of Christian apocalypticism, all against a red background of blood rhetoric. Radical secularism uses the solvent of total separationism to remove religion from the mix and thins down democratic solidarity with a healthy dose of libertarian self-worship. Civil religion uses the cement of the common good to bind together the prophetic voice of the jeremiad with traditional themes of civic republicanism.

The materials are different, but they are also related. The conquest narrative and prophetic religion are both taken from the Hebrew Bible. Add in a little blood rhetoric, and civil religion can quickly devolve into religious nationalism. The two traditions hang closer together than one might imagine. Religious nationalism is the dark side of civil religion. Similarly, both republicanism and liberalism emphasize human freedom. But if liberalism's simple "no restraints" version of freedom is substituted for republicanism's more complex understanding, then the civil religion begins to break down into radical individualism. Radical secularism is the libertarian version of civil religion. This is why it is important to highlight the differences between them.

Still, this static juxtaposition of the three traditions hides as much as it reveals. For one, it implies that the three traditions emerged simultaneously. They did not. Civil religion is the oldest of the three, having arrived with the Puritans (see chapter 2). Religious nationalism is only a little bit younger. It was born out of the Puritans' wars with the native peoples. Radical secularism can plausibly claim a revolutionary birthday (see chapter 3). Nevertheless, it cannot plausibly claim to be America's founding tradition; at best, it was a marginal movement. Full-blown radical secularism did not really appear on the scene until the late nineteenth century (see chapter 4).

These static portraits also suggest that the three traditions have not changed. But they have. Over time, apocalyptic rhetoric has become more central to American religious nationalism, while blood rhetoric has become more muted. There is more talk of cosmic showdowns between good and evil, while the language of blood sacrifice has slowly given way to the squeamish euphemism of "ultimate sacrifice." The rhetoric of radical secularism has also undergone a subtle shift. Early on, radical individualism was justified using arguments drawn from social Darwinism and laissez-faire economics—and in conservative libertarian circles, it still is. But among left-leaning secularists, the emphasis nowadays is on the romantic, whether in the high-minded sense of self-expression or in the carnal sense of sexual freedom (though the distance between the two has lately narrowed almost to a point of convergence in our sexually expressive culture). Justifications for total separationism have shifted even more radically. They first arose out of the nativist backlash against Catholic immigration. Today, they are couched in a gentler language of liberal "neutrality." Nor has the civil religious tradition been static either. Its prophetic strand has remained strong, but it has come to be flavored with less salt and more sugar. There is less talk of sin and more talk of justice. Meanwhile, the republican strand has grown weaker as liberal ideas have gained strength. This weakening of civic republicanism is perhaps the single greatest danger to the civil religious tradition today.

One of the biggest challenges facing the United States—and other countries around the world—is the task of reconciling a robust system of popular governance with increasing levels of cultural diversity. The radical secularist wager rests on the belief that this is just a temporary problem: soon enough, everyone will be an unbeliever. I wager that they are wrong. The metaphysical future of the American people is one of diversity, not disbelief. Religious nationalists also wager that this challenge is temporary: soon enough, the unbelievers will be defeated and punished. I wager that they, too, are wrong. If the world ends soon, it will be by human hands, whether through nuclear disaster or climatic catastrophe. In the meantime, we are stuck in history—together. The civil religion provides a framework for connecting past and future, and for conjoining sacred and secular. It is an antidote to the twinned hubristic stances of radical secularism and religious nationalism.

CHAPTER 2

The Hebraic Moment

THE NEW ENGLAND PURITANS

IN PRINCIPLE, a nation can only be founded once. But in practice, most nations have had multiple founders, some mythical, some historical, and most somewhere in between. Israel had Abraham, Moses, and David. Athens had Athena, Solon, and Cleisthenes. England had Albion, the Trojans, and King Arthur. The United States is no exception to the rule. It was founded at least twice, once by the New England Puritans, and then again by the American revolutionaries, both real enough, but somewhat mythologized as well.

I say "at least," because the Massachusetts Bay Colony was not the first permanent settlement in the future United States—that honor goes to St. Augustine in Spanish Florida. Nor was it even the first English colony— that honor goes to Jamestown, Virginia. And yet, it is the establishment of the Massachusetts Bay Colony that marks the founding moment in our collective memory (the Pilgrims), that is memorialized in our civic holidays (Thanksgiving), and that has been most studied by American historians (Puritan New England). Consequently, it is the Puritans who play the role of first founders in the civil religious tradition, and it is with the Puritans that I begin.

Is that the only reason to begin with them? Some might think so. The Puritans have had a foul odor about them ever since the early twentieth century, when H. L. Mencken caricatured them as straitlaced killjoys. More recently, James Sleeper has offered a more appreciative (though critical) remembrance. He reminds us that the Puritans left "everything they'd known and loved . . . to cross an ocean, under conditions we can barely imagine now, to a 'howling wilderness.'" In doing so, "they turned their backs on the golden thrones of popes and kings and countenanced neither aristocracy nor destitution." Throughout this journey, they "held convictions by which they could be"—and often were—"called to account" by their religious and political leaders. In an age as comfort obsessed, celebrity enthralled, and morally flaccid as our own, Sleeper concludes, there is still something to be gained from an encounter with America's first "Very Serious Persons."[1] They remind us of the higher purposes to which the American experiment was originally dedicated: not material consumption, but Christian charity; not imperial domination, but collective self-determination. We may find it hard to love or even like the Puritans. But we can still learn from them, and perhaps even admire them just a little.

COVENANT AND CONQUEST

However we retell it today, the Puritans understood their story as that of a new Israel established in a new England. Drawing on the books of the Pentateuch and the Former Prophets, which provided a rich trove of plot lines, they saw numerous parallels between themselves and the ancient Israelites: liberation from slavery, the delivery across the water, the sealing of the covenant, the wanderings in the wilderness, the conquest of Canaan, the lost tribes of Israel. The Puritan clergy cast themselves as the Latter Prophets, charged with calling the people back to the covenant when they strayed too far from their founding values. Puritan political leaders viewed themselves as latter-day versions of the Biblical "judges."

What did it mean to be a "New Israel"? It meant arduous flight from "Egyptian slavery." It meant wandering through a "howling wilderness." It meant being surrounded and pursued by great empires (British and French) and hostile tribes (the native peoples). But above all, it meant being "chosen"—although not for special blessings so much as for special judgment. The Puritans believed that they had entered into a covenant with God. They had pledged themselves to uphold God's laws. If they succeeded, he would protect them. But if they failed, he would punish them. And they *would* fail, and they *would* be punished; that much was certain. The ancient Israelites had, and so would they. But they, too, would return to the covenant to plod on toward the Promised Land. Of that, their prophets and preachers, their Jeremiahs and Aarons, would make sure.

The centrality of the covenant to Puritan theology and of the jeremiad to Puritan rhetoric are well-worn themes in Puritan scholarship.[2] But there were actually two quite different versions of the Puritan storyline: one that emphasized covenant and one that emphasized conquest (for the scriptural and historical background of these ideas, see chapter 1). The covenant story is told in a prophetic voice, couched in the terms of the jeremiad, denouncing the sins of the people and calling them back to the Law. This voice reminds the nation of its foundational commitments and warns of divine punishments if those commitments are breached.

This covenant narrative can be distinguished from the conquest narrative, which is governed by the metaphor of blood. It is declaimed in a warrior's voice that summons the nation to purify its ranks, gird up its loins, cross the Jordan, and conquer the Promised Land. This voice reminds the people of their blood ties and providential mission, and promises divine aid in that mission's realization. The covenant narrative is one root of America's civil religion—the prophetic one—while the conquest story is one root of its religious nationalism.

I use the term "root" because neither tradition is fully developed at this stage. The republican thread of the civil religion is still so thin that it can hardly be disentangled from the prophetic thread—if, indeed, it is really even distinct. In the seventeenth century, the "godly republics" of New England were still more godly than republican in their ambitions.[3] As for religious nationalism, it, too, is only half grown, being still more millennial than apocalyptic at this stage.[4] When the early Puritans cited Daniel or Revelation, they did so more out of hope than from despair. It was not until the end of the Puritan era that premillennial apocalypticism—the other thread of American exceptionalism—made its first, brief appearance.

BIBLICAL "TYPOLOGY" AND PURITAN THEOLOGY

By almost any reckoning, the composition of the Pentateuch and the departure of the *Mayflower* from England are separated by at least two millennia. For contemporary readers, jumping from one to the other at a single bound may seem too long a leap. For a Puritan reader, however, it would not have. The Puritans—and their Anglican contemporaries—were inclined to read history the same way that they read the Bible, namely, "typologically."[5] In a typological reading of the scriptures, the figures and events of the Old Testament are seen as prefiguring those of the New: Isaac, the son who was not sacrificed by his father, prefigures Jesus, the son who was; Noah's flood is the seagoing version of John's apocalypse, and so on. The Puritans—and the English in general—often read events in the same way and gave themselves the starring role: as the Pentateuch described the Old Israel, so would the English become the New Israel.

To us, this may seem a bold conceit. But to the Puritans themselves, the parallels probably seemed self-evident and only grew more so over time.[6] Consider: the ancient Israelites had been enslaved by Pharaoh, who refused them permission to worship their God. Weren't the English

Puritans also being enslaved by King Charles I, who refused to let them worship *their* God? Under Moses's leadership, of course, the Israelites fled Egypt and marched across the Red Sea. Weren't John Winthrop's Puritan followers doing the same thing when they boarded the *Arbella* and pushed out into the Atlantic? Was their deliverance across the stormy seas any less miraculous? Moses's followers soon found themselves in the wilderness, where they longed for the "fleshpots" of Egypt, were tempted by the altars of Baal, and eventually did battle against the Canaanites for their "inheritance." In the same way, Winthrop's followers were also plunged into "an howling wilderness" where they were deprived of the comforts of home, exposed to the strange gods of the natives, and eventually compelled to do battle with them to secure *their* "inheritance."

For context's sake, it is worth noting that the Puritans were hardly the first to cast themselves in the starring role of the New Israel.[7] In England, the Hebraic analogy goes back to at least the eighth century, and in France to the early Middle Ages.[8] Nor were the Puritans the first to reintroduce the concept either. That groundwork had already been laid in the early sixteenth century by John Foxe's *Book of Martyrs*, a best-seller in the Reformation era that made the case for England's status as an "elect nation."[9] Nor were the Puritans the last to make the analogy. The Afrikaaners and Scots-Irish adopted it, as did African Americans during the civil rights movement.[10] So the Hebraic analogy was not exceptionally American; on the contrary, it has been a seedbed, not only of most Western forms of nationalism, but also of revolutionary politics as well.[11]

JOHN WINTHROP: THE COVENANT OF CHARITY

Let us begin our examination of the Puritan worldview where most such discussions begin: with John Winthrop's sermon "Christian Charity, A Model Hereof." According to the traditional account, the sermon was composed and delivered onboard the *Arbella*. Recent research suggests that it was actually written before Winthrop's departure and circulated within the Puritan community in written form.[12] Be that as it may, the basic gist of Winthrop's speech would have been familiar to those who set sail with him, as would its two governing metaphors: "covenant" and "body." Both were meaning-laden terms that figured prominently in Christian theology and also in English legal and political thinking.[13] In Winthrop's day, contracts and treaties were often referred to as "covenants," while the term "body" was frequently used to refer to what are nowadays called "corporations" or "associations." As a lawyer admitted to the Inns of Court, Winthrop would have been aware of these connotations.[14] Both registers, the theological and the legal, can be clearly heard in what is probably the speech's most famous passage, worth quoting at length:

> Thus stands the cause between God and us, we are entered into a covenant with him for this work, we have taken out a commission, the Lord hath given us leave to draw our own articles[,] we have professed to enterprise these actions upon these and these ends, we have hereupon besought him of favor and blessing: Now if the Lord shall please to hear us, and bring us in peace to the place we desire, then hath he ratified this covenant and sealed our commission, [and] will expect a strict performance of the articles contained in it, but if we shall neglect the observation of these articles which are the ends we have propounded, and dissembling with our God, shall fail to embrace this present world and prosecute our carnal intentions, seeking great things for ourselves and our posterity, the Lord will surely break out in wrath against us [and] be revenged of such a perjured people and make us know the price of the breach of such a covenant.[15]

In Winthrop's view, those who joined the voyage and those who financed it, those who left England and those who stayed behind, were entering into both a sacred covenant and a legal contract with one another. Should their voyage succeed, he argued, this would be a sign that God had accepted their proposal and that he would enforce its terms. Should the Puritans live up to the bargain, great things could be expected; should they violate it, however, they would earn God's particular wrath.

What exactly were the terms of this covenant? Nothing less than charity itself, as Winthrop immediately went on to explain. Again, I quote at length:

> We must be knit together in this work as one man, we must entertain each other in brotherly affection, we must be willing to abridge ourselves of our superfluities, for the supply of others' necessities, we must uphold a familiar commerce together in all meekness, gentleness, patience and liberality, we must delight in each other, make one another's conditions our own, rejoice together, mourn together, labor, and suffer together, always having before our eyes our commission and community in the work, our community as members of the same body.[16]

Certainly, the terms of this covenant were not the limited ones of a legal contract, as we would understand such an instrument today; nor did they envision a "market society" driven by material self-interest. The obligations were open-ended and individual interests subordinated to the common good.[17] But the rewards were potentially unlimited, and the success of the project of the greatest importance. For if the Puritans succeeded, concluded Winthrop, then they would "be as a city upon a hill [and] the eyes of all people [would be] upon" them.[18]

This initial covenant was just the first of many. Like their Hebraic forebears, the New England Puritans reread, revised, and renewed their founding covenant at regular intervals.[19] To these serial covenants, however, they affixed numerous subsidiary covenants as well. There were, first of all, the "church covenants" that became the hallmark of the Congregationalist way.[20] The Puritans insisted that a "true church" could only be established by means of a sacred covenant between a group of "visible saints,"[21] that is, men who had demonstrated to one another a satisfactory knowledge of "true doctrine" and persuasive evidence of "saving grace," normally in the form of a public recounting of their own experience of conversion.[22]

The early covenants were spare and simple. The 1629 covenant of the Salem Church read as follows: "We Covenant with the Lord and one with an other; and doe bynd our selves in the presence of God, to walke together in all his waies, according as he is pleased to reveale himself unto us in his Blessed word of truth."[23] The renewed covenant of 1636 spelled out the duties of the saints in greater detail: "To beare and forbeare, give and forgive"; not "to shew oure owne gifts or parts in speaking or scrupling"; to live in concord with other settlers and with the native peoples; to obey "those that are over us, in Church or Commonweale"; and to work diligently "in our particular callings, shunning ydleness."[24]

The Puritans' reputation for moral rigor was not undeserved. Most church covenants also included a pledge of "holy watch," that is, the duty of mutual surveillance and admonition for the purpose of keeping church members on the straight and narrow.[25] While church attendance was mandatory in all of the colonies (except Rhode Island), church membership was far from automatic. Only the most upright were deemed worthy of that honor; in Thomas Hooker's words, "visible Saints are the only true and meet matter, whereof a visible Church should be gathered."[26] Initially, evidence of good behavior and knowledge of Calvinist doctrine were sufficient qualifications for membership.[27] Soon, however, most churches began to demand that prospective members show signs of having received saving grace as well. In practice, this meant a narration of one's conversion—which the Puritans understood as a lengthy process rather than a single event—and evidence of that experience in one's conduct.[28]

The covenanting model was extended to the civil polity as well.[29] In Winthrop's words, "No common weale can be founded but by free consent."[30] Winthrop was true to his principles. In the fall of 1630, just months after his arrival, he summoned a meeting of the colonists to discuss the "due form of government." The original charter for the Bay Colony envisioned a for-profit commercial venture, not a Puritan experiment in political theology. Only stockholders were to have political rights. Under the new constitution that Winthrop put forward, these rights were extended considerably—not to all members of the community, to be sure, but to all white male church members. Soon, outlying towns were authorized to send deputies to the General Court as well. In this way, a joint-stock company was effectively transformed into a civil polity.

Most early New England towns began in more or less the same way as the original Bay Colony, that is, with the drafting and signing of a "civil covenant."[31] The most famous of these documents is the Mayflower Compact, whose key passage is as follows:

> Having undertaken, for the Glory of God and advancement of the Christian Faith and Honour of our King and Country, a Voyage to plant the First Colony in the Northern Parts of Virginia, do by these presents solemnly and mutually in the presence of God and one of another, Covenant and Combine ourselves together into a Civil Body Politic, for our better ordering and preservation and furtherance of the ends aforesaid; and by virtue hereof to enact, constitute and frame such just and equal Laws, Ordinances, Acts, Constitutions and Offices, from time to time, as shall be thought most meet and convenient for the general good of the Colony, unto which we promise all due submission and obedience.

Some civil covenants invoked the Hebraic analogy much more explicitly. The civil covenant of Dedham, Massachusetts, for example, claims that the lands of the settlement were given "by God to *some of his people in this wilderness*."[32] While Dedham's covenant invokes an Old Testament God, the covenant of the settlement of Woburn pledges itself to "the full fruition of such libertys and prvileges of humanity civility and Christianity cals for as due to every man."[33]

Just as there is more to religion than scripture and theology, so there was more to these covenants than paper and words. The chief part of that "more" was ritual. We are better informed about the rituals surrounding church covenants than about those surrounding their civil counterparts.[34] Nathaniel Morton, a settler of the Plymouth Colony, described the founding of the Plymouth Church as follows:[35] Having assembled the requisite number of founding members and electing a pastor and a "teacher," the teacher drafted a "Confession of Faith and Covenant." Copies of this document were made for each of the founding members, thirty in all. The formal signing of the church covenant was planned for August 6, 1629, which was declared a day of fasting and prayer. On this day, each of the two ministers preached a sermon, and then the covenant was read aloud to the founding members, who "did solemnly profess their Consent thereunto." The ceremony concluded with a laying-on of hands. In contrast, we know much less about the signing ceremonies for civil covenants. Most of the early civil covenants were signed by all or most members of the new community,[36] and there is some evidence that suggests a ritual assemblage of some sort. But here is the crucial point: the Puritans did not envision their polities as mere aggregations of individuals pursuing their private welfare, but as sacred corporations dedicated to higher principles.

NEITHER THEOCRATS NOR SECULARISTS

The Puritan social order consisted of two different kinds of polity: ecclesiastical and civil. What exactly was the relationship between them? Was it theocratic? Or was it secular? In truth, the best answer is "neither." Of course, the Puritans themselves did sometimes characterize their polity as a "theocracy." But Puritan New England still did not satisfy the modern dictionary definition of "theocracy" as a polity in which God's "laws are taken as the statute-book of the kingdom, these laws being usually administered by a priestly order as his ministers and agents; hence (loosely) a system of government by a sacerdotal order, claiming a divine commission."[37] The Puritan statute book was hardly coextensive with the Bible. Many Old Testament laws did not find their way into the laws of the Commonwealth of Massachusetts, whereas many elements of the English common law did.[38] Similarly, when it came to the enforcement of the laws, religious and civil authority were not one and the same. It is true that the "ruling elders" were charged with maintaining "godly discipline." But their instruments were strictly churchly ones: admonition, penance, and, in extreme cases, excommunication. They had no power to impose civil penalties of any kind and thus did not enforce civil law. Nor were they members of the "priestly order," but simply lay officials elected from the ranks of church members. Further, none of the colonies allowed ministers to serve as magistrates, or magistrates as ministers. And many New England towns also prohibited church officers (e.g., ruling elders) from occupying civil office, and vice versa.[39] Nonmembers were not freed from attending church, however; church attendance was generally mandatory for all under the civil law, even if this rule was not necessarily enforced with great rigor. It is also worth noting that the records of local congregations and magistrates were always kept separately, in contrast to the practice of the state churches of Protestant Europe. But perhaps the most telling evidence that the Puritans generally viewed the religious and political orders as distinct is that church and civil covenants themselves were separate. The Puritans feared an amalgamation of the two, such as that which prevailed in England at the time.

Nonetheless, the New England "church-states" were not exactly "secular" states in the modern sense either. The civil covenants almost always contained explicitly theistic language. In theory, citizenship rights in the original Bay Colony were closely tied to church membership; technically, nonmembers, the so-called "inhabitants," could not vote or hold office there, even if these rules were not always strictly observed.[40] The same pattern obtained in most other early New England colonies, with the notable exception (as always) of Rhode Island. Also, while ministers were excluded from political office, this did not mean that they were excluded from political life. They were officially charged with delivering public sermons on Election Days, for example. It was also expected that the ministers would be consulted about the drafting and interpretation of laws to ensure that the civil and divine laws were not in conflict with one another. What is more, their salaries came from the public purse, and people who were not members of the church paid some of the moneys into that purse. There was also a considerable degree of informal cooperation between ruling elders and civil magistrates, particularly when their jurisdiction overlapped. Should a habitual drunkard or wife-beater be fined or forced to do penance—or both? Such questions were answered on a case-by-case basis. So although the line between church and state was more sharply drawn in New England than in Old Europe, that line was not impermeable either.

The practice of church–state relations in the Bay Colony corresponded quite well with the Congregationalist theory that had begun to take shape in sixteenth-century England. Nowhere was this theory of church–state relations more fully worked out than in the writings of John Cotton, perhaps the most prominent minister of the founding generation and without doubt the ablest and best-known defender of the Congregational system that became known as the "New England Way." The fundamental premise of the Congregational vision according to Cotton was that "God hath fitted and appointed two sorts of Administrations, *Ecclesiastical and Civil*," each with its own means—"Laws," "Officers," and "Power, whereby to reduce men to Order"—as well as its own ends.[41] The chief end of the civil polity, he argued, was "the publick and common Good, whether Natural, as in the preservation of Life and Safety; or Moral, as Justice and honesty in Humane Societies; or Civil, as Peace, Liberty of Commerce; or Spiritual as to protect the Church in Spiritual, though outward, Order and Administrations in peace & purity."[42] Of what did the "Spiritual, though outward" governance of the church consist? The Cambridge Platform of 1648 provides the following answer: "Idolatry, Blasphemy, Heresy, venting corrupt & pernicious opinions, that destroy the foundation, open contempt of the word preached, prophanation of the Lords day, disturbing the peaceable administration & exercise of the worship & holy things of God, & the like, are to be restrained, & punished by civil authority. If any church one or more shall grow schismaticall . . . the Magistrate is to put forth his coercive power."[43] Just as the civil authorities had a role to play in the "outward" governance of spiritual life, so, too, did the ecclesiastical authorities have a role to play in the "inner" governance of civil life. Specifically, it was the job of the churches to raise up "able judges" and "good rulers."[44]

But while Cotton clearly thought that the ecclesiastical and civil orders overlapped, he did not wish to see them confounded either, as he thought they had been in old England. When civil rulers seize "the horns of the church," he warned, "it makes the church a monster."[45] The experience of religious oppression in England always served as a check on the authoritarian impulses of the governing authorities in the Bay Colony. Similarly, Cotton was also concerned that an overly close relationship between church and state could harm the state. Because rulers are apt to abuse their power, he reasoned, no "mortal man" should be granted absolute power. Keeping civil and ecclesiastical governance separate would act as a check on tyranny. The relation between church and state, Cotton concluded, must therefore be strictly "civil": church members should participate in civil governance not *qua* church members but *qua* citizens, and vice versa. Cotton saw civil and ecclesiastical government as distinct but interrelated enterprises. As he put it, "God's institutions (such as the government of church and of commonwealth be) may be close and compact, and coordinate one to another, and yet not confounded." In this vision—and New England practice—the ends, laws, and offices of church and state were not to be "confounded."

Cotton's political theology may thus be seen as the first articulation of civil religion in American history. It envisioned the proper relationship between the religious and political orders not in terms of "total separation," as in radical secularism, nor in terms of complete fusion, as in religious nationalism, but as a dynamic state of overlap and tension.

Borrowing a phrase from Michael Winship, I call this first version of civil religion "godly republicanism."[46] It was "godly" in at least two senses. First, it was more theocentric than Christocentric: the God of the covenant was the God of the Pentateuch, and it was with this God that the Puritans had their "controversy." Second, the republic it envisioned was a republic of the "godly," a republic of and by the "saints." In what sense was it "republican," though? It was once thought that English republicanism had its beginnings in the English Civil War. However, recent research has shown that its roots can be traced back well into the Elizabethan era, that is, the era when the Puritan leaders first came of age.[47] And, indeed, a careful reading of Puritan tracts uncovers many of the typical tropes of republican thought: the argument for popular sovereignty and mixed government, a suspicion of absolute power and support for the establishment of constitutional checks, a concern with the corrupting influence of wealth and luxury, and an emphasis on the need for "virtue" in the citizenry.[48]

The institutional design of the Puritan polities also had republican features. In this regard, they were more like the city-states of Renaissance Italy than the present-day United States. The Puritan polities were organized into concentric circles marking off different degrees of political belonging and influence. The outermost circle consisted of the so-called "inhabitants," whom the charter guaranteed the "liberties and immunities of free and naturall subiects . . . as yf they . . . were borne within the realme of England."[49] What "inhabitants" lacked was the vote, a power that distinguished them from the next circle, the "freemen" or "citizens." To be a freeman, one had to be a church member—and a man. The distinction between "freeman" and "assistants," meanwhile, mirrored those between "small" and "large" councils in many of the Italian city republics. The governorship was a sort of elected monarch not dissimilar to the Venetian doge. Like Venice, then, the Bay Colony had a "mixed constitution" that combined democratic, aristocratic, and monarchical elements in perfect accord with republican theory.

Another reason for selecting the term "godly republic" is that the ideas that underlay the Puritan polity were derived from the nascent republican movement in England. Winthrop himself described the Bay Colony as a "popular state" where the power of the people was "unlimited in its own nature," a view that was seconded by some of the colony's ministers as well.[50] So the Bay Colony was "republican" both in conception and in organization.[51]

To us, of course, church–state relations in Puritan New England still look much too close. That church attendance was compulsory, that citizenship was limited to (male) church members, that nonmembers were required to pay church taxes—such arrangements grate on contemporary sensibilities. And so they did on historical ones. Cotton's vision had plenty of Puritan critics: libertines, such as Thomas Morton; proto-liberals, such as Roger Williams; and would-be sectarians like Anne Hutchinson. They would all press for a greater degree of separation between church and state, albeit one that fell far short of radical secularism. Later, during and after the conflicts with the indigenous Americans, zealous defenders of New England would push hard in the other direction, with political and military leaders like Samuel Nowell and religious and intellectual leaders like Cotton Mather using the rhetoric of blood and Apocalypse to articulate a religious nationalist version of the New England project. New England had its culture wars, too.

SCENE I: CONTESTING THE COVENANT: THOMAS MORTON

The first series of challenges to the nascent orthodoxy of godly republicanism coincided with the founding decades of the Puritan experiment. The opening scene was set during the early years of the Plymouth Colony and involved one Thomas Morton, who arrived on the colony's shores in 1624 with his business partner, a certain Captain Wollaston, and some thirty indentured servants. Morton was a trained lawyer and merchant adventurer who hailed from Devonshire, a stronghold of conservative Anglicanism and traditional culture despised by the Puritans as a "dark corner of the land." The two partners fell out shortly after their arrival when Morton discovered that Wollaston had sold a number of the indentured servants into slavery in Virginia. Wollaston departed southward, leaving Morton in charge of their thriving trade with the native peoples. But Morton soon ran afoul of the Plymouth Puritans as well. They accused him of selling alcohol and firearms to the natives (a charge he denied) and—what was worse, at least to Puritan eyes—of erecting a maypole and engaging in "Bacchanalians" with the natives, including sexual liaisons with native women. There is no reason to doubt the latter charges; they accord well with Morton's own published account of his life and times in what he called the "New English Canaan." According to William Bradford, the Puritans feared Morton and his consorts for another reason as well: "All the scum of the country or any discontents would flock to him from all places, if this nest was not broken." And break it they did, capturing, trying, and expelling Morton from the colony.

While Bradford painted Morton as a "dissolute" and "lecherous" "libertine," Morton characterized the Puritans as "precise separatists" who "trouble[ed] their braines more than reason would require about things that are indifferent" and as vile land-grabbers who practiced treachery toward the natives. Conversely, he portrayed himself as a defender of Anglicanism and an emissary to the Native Americans.[52] While Bradford portrayed Morton as a threat to the social order, Morton returned the favor. For Morton, however, the order in question was not the providential order of the New Israel, but the hierarchical order of Old England, which he perceived as being threatened by the social climbing, land grabbing, and self-promotion that were enabled by the sociological *tabula rasa* of the New World. Morton charged the Puritans with "degrading" the "gentry," his own class of origin and the natural rulers of the countryside. He found the Puritans too democratic and egalitarian.

While Morton himself was outmanned, the balance of forces would slowly shift in his favor as the English reasserted control over their colonies following the Restoration and the new gentry of the Southern colonies began to emulate the English aristocracy. For them, the New World was not to be a city on a hill but an outpost of empire, a land full of natural bounty and pliable laborers ready for exploitation. Morton would have a long line of successors in the centuries to come: plantation owners, railroad magnates, oil barons, and hedge funders—adventure capitalists all, whose vision of the American Dream boiled down to unfettered acquisition of material possessions, which they mistook for true freedom. Like Morton, they would often find clever ways to cloak their ambitions with the trappings of religion. They would recast Jesus as a business leader, the Puritans as zealous capitalists, and the free market as an instrument of divine Providence, dispensing to all their just deserts. Of course, these interpretations are gross distortions of the Puritan vision, not to mention of Christian theology. But the impulse to turn the austere city on a hill into a "shining" city on a hill is a very old one.

SCENE II: EXPANDING THE CIVIL COVENANT: ROGER WILLIAMS

The next scene took place just over a decade later in the newly established Bay Colony. It stars Roger Williams. Williams had been won over to the Puritan cause in early adolescence. With the sponsorship of Sir Edward Coke, the famous English jurist, he attended Cambridge and then secured a chaplaincy with a prominent family. In 1630, he embarked for Massachusetts with his wife and family. By this time, he had developed outspokenly "Separatist" views.[53] For him, it was not enough to join a Separatist church; one had also to publicly renounce the Church of England and refrain from any participation in its services. The refusal of even his fellow Separatists to separate themselves from the establishment to this degree provoked conflict and eventually led to his expulsion from Massachusetts and his emigration to Rhode Island, where he founded the colony of Providence. The logic of Separatism, and the principle of purity that underlay it, also led Williams to become one of the first American "Seekers"—a term whose origins lie in this era—and to reject not only the legitimacy of the existing churches but the very possibility of a true church of any kind in the present age and therefore (following Congregationalist ecclesiology) of an ordained ministry.

It might be imagined that Williams's uber-Puritan quest for complete purity would have led him to favor state-sponsored religious persecution of heretics and dissenters. But this was not the case, because the kind of purity that Williams sought was not the purity of a visible community of saints, much less a purity of blood, but a purity wholly invisible and spiritual. Williams came to believe that maintaining this purity required that the religious community retain its autonomy vis-à-vis the state. Indeed, in Williams's view, it was Constantine's takeover of the primitive church that had corrupted the institution in the first place; only upon Christ's return, he believed, would the true church be fully restored. Force was of no use. In a series of vituperative exchanges with John Cotton, he famously denounced the "bloudy tenent" of religious persecution as a form of "soule rape" that was at odds with the peaceful ministry of Jesus Christ and more likely to provoke conflict than to preserve order. At the same time, he elaborated an argument in favor of the freedom of conscience, not only for other Christians, but for all peoples.

But Williams was no world-fleeing sectarian either. Indeed, he served as the governor of the Providence Colony for a time. Perhaps because of his own practical successes in Rhode Island, he was quite optimistic about the possibilities for civil engagement across religio-cultural boundaries and the potential benefits of civil government. Moreover, Williams was optimistic *because* of his faith, rather than in spite of it. Like Calvin—and Calvin's scholastic predecessors—Williams believed that moral law and natural reason were part of the common inheritance of all human beings.[54] And because all humans shared certain basic moral principles and rational capacities, it was possible for them to achieve and even expand a basic agreement about the elements of the common good—a view that would gain more and more adherents within the Puritan camp by century's end.[55] Williams therefore disputed one of the central claims of godly republicanism: that only the godly were fit to rule. In Williams's view there was no necessary connection between godliness and leadership; non-Christians could make good leaders, and good Christians poor ones. However, Williams did not adopt the Machiavellian position that politics and morality are at odds with one another. On the contrary, he felt that the state should teach virtue and enforce the (natural) moral law. He did not want a confessional state. But neither did he want an amoral state.

Scholarly analysts sometimes portray Williams as the founding father of radical secularism.[56] It is not difficult to see why. After all, Williams did advocate a higher degree of separation between the religious and political realms than orthodox Puritans did. And he did not believe that first-class citizenship should be limited to godly Puritans or that the civil magistrate should enforce religious uniformity. What is more, he defended the rights of individual conscience against the demands of the dominant orthodoxy.

But Williams's legacy can also be read in another way, namely, as an effort to redefine the relationship between the religious and political orders rather than to sunder it altogether. This effort at redefinition revolved around two key terms: "civility" and the "common good." By "civility," Williams meant those moral virtues that facilitate peaceful coexistence in a pluralistic world, such as courtesy, respect, and toleration toward others. By the "common good," Williams meant those ends shared by all members of a society. Williams believed that the practice of civility enabled discovery of the common good through public deliberation. He also believed that the virtue of civility had to be cultivated not just by religious communities, but by the political community as well. Nor did he understand the good as purely private or subjective.

Williams's vision diverged from that of radical secularism on at least two crucial points: he believed that the substance and practice of politics involved morality and not just interests, and he thought that political as well as religious institutions should enforce basic morality and inculcate public virtue in their members. On these points, Williams's position was more akin to civic republicanism than to classical liberalism, not to speak of contemporary libertarianism.

Williams did not seek to abolish the civil covenant so much as to expand it beyond the ranks of the godly. He wished to transform godly republicanism into civil republicanism. On these and other scores, his vision anticipated the revolutionary settlement.

SCENE III: AN AMBIGUOUS LEGACY: ANNE HUTCHINSON

We now come to the third and final scene in this opening act: the antinomian or free grace controversy. This episode starred Anne Hutchinson, with John Cotton playing a supporting role. Hutchinson was born into a well-to-do family of the gentry. Her minister father was a man of Puritan conviction, and she was well educated and intellectually gifted. After marrying a prosperous merchant, William Hutchinson, she moved to Lincolnshire, where she came under the sway of a gifted young Puritan minister—none other than John Cotton. When Cotton fled to America, she and her family followed. Soon after her arrival in Boston, she began to hold private meetings in her home at which she parsed sermons and Bible verses, first with a small circle of women, and then with an ever-expanding group that included some of the most influential men in the colony, such as then-governor Henry Vane.[57] Gradually Hutchinson elaborated a heterodox theory of salvation. According to the Puritan divines, whatever certainty of saving grace that one attained was gained through the process of sanctification, that is, through the increasing godliness of one's conduct. But that certainty could never be absolute.[58] In Hutchinson's view, this emphasis on conduct smacked of a "covenant of works." In her heterodox theory, certainty of salvation came through inward experience of the Holy Spirit. As her following grew, Hutchinson took to denouncing members of the clergy who did not share her views. Despite her status and connections, Hutchinson and many of her supporters were eventually called before the General Court and banished from the Bay Colony. Many of them fled to Rhode Island.

The Hutchinson controversy is one of the most fascinating episodes in the history of New England, combining as it does the politics of gender, religion, and class. But what significance does it have for our particular story? On the one hand, it can be read as an attempt to expand the bounds of the religious covenant by challenging the patriarchal structure of its leadership. Hutchinson was a feminist *avant la lettre*. On the other hand, it can be understood as an attempt to shrink the bounds of the religious covenant by locating it in the individual heart. In this way, she anticipated the "heart religion" of American evangelicals stretching from Jonathan Edwards to Billy Graham. Finally, it can be understood as a revolt against the high theology of the seminary-trained clergy. In this regard, Hutchinson foreshadowed the egalitarian anti-intellectualism of low-church Protestantism—and its political cousin, the populist movement. Hutchinson's legacy is a complex and ambiguous one.

Morton, Williams, and Hutchinson each challenged the godly republicanism of the Puritan establishment from a different angle: Morton from the perspective of a traditionalistic folk religion emphasizing carnivalesque rituals and traditional hierarchies; Williams from the perspective of a hyperseparatist Calvinism that sought a radically purified religious community even as it acknowledged a universal moral law and the possibility of an expanded civic covenant; and Hutchinson on the basis of a mystical doctrine of saving grace that did away with the covenant of works and the need for a rational theology, thereby challenging the intellectual foundations of the New England Way.

While Morton, Williams, and Hutchinson were quickly expelled from the Bay Colony, many of their fellow travelers—and, with them, their ideas—were eventually incorporated into the Puritan fold. In 1638, Winthrop officially chartered the Ancient and Honorable Artillery Company of Boston. Modeled after the civic militias that had been established in many European cities during the Renaissance, the company gathered together a number of well-to-do citizens for the purpose of local self-defense.[59] In this way, Puritan society made room for the honor-based culture of English aristocrats like Morton but within a republican frame. [60] Hutchinson's vindication came next. During the 1660s, heated controversy over the "Halfway Covenant," concerning the admission of church members' children into local congregations, generated a series of schisms and migrations within the churches of Massachusetts and Connecticut. Some congregations resisted the loosened standards of church membership, which conferred automatic "half" membership on congregants' children. John Davenport's flock in New Haven was one of them. Other congregations pushed for their complete relaxation. For example, infant baptism entitled one to full membership in Boston's Old South Church. In this way, a certain measure of internal pluralism was introduced into the Puritan community. Williams's vindication came last. Following the Glorious Revolution of 1688–1689, which put the English throne back into reliably Protestant hands, the leaders of Puritan New England increasingly came to see themselves as part of a broader "Protestant Interest" that was centered in London and arrayed against France and the forces of Catholicism.[61] In this vision, the bounds of the polity were defined by civility rather than orthodoxy. In all these ways, the godly republicanism of Cotton and Winthrop proved surprisingly flexible—flexible enough, in the event, to accommodate an increasingly plural and cosmopolitan society. Godly republicanism was rapidly evolving into civil republicanism.

PURITAN EXCEPTIONALISM: NOWELL AND THE MATHERS

But there were limits to the pluralism and cosmopolitanism of this new New England—sharp limits. These limits were marked—in blood—by the initial emergence of an American version of religious nationalism. American exceptionalism has always had two main elements: the conquest narrative and premillennial apocalypticism. Neither was particularly salient during the first generation of the Puritan experiment, but by the end of the Puritan era both had taken hold within the community. They initially crystallized during the three decades stretching from the restoration of the English monarchy (1660) to the onset of the French and Indian Wars (1689), a period when the Puritan project seemed threatened from within and without.

With the collapse of Cromwell's Protectorate (1659) and the restoration of the Stuart dynasty (1660), the dream of a Puritan England collapsed, as did the vision of New England as a kind of Puritan avant-garde. As New England's eyes turned inward, a debate over communal boundaries ensued that came to be known as the "Halfway Covenant" controversy. Under the Congregational system, church membership was limited to "visible saints." But what of their children, particularly those who had been baptized into the church but had not given testimony of conversion? Were they no longer church members? For that matter, what about their children's children, especially the children of nonmembers? After all, only church members could have their children baptized. Were the grandchildren of the first generation to be cast out of the church altogether? The Puritan colonies had been quite successful at biological reproduction— the population had grown rapidly. But they had been less successful at cultural reproduction—at producing a new generation of "saints."

Such was the background of the Halfway Covenant controversy.[62] First advanced by Solomon Stoddard, the most influential minister in the Connecticut River Valley, the doctrine of the Halfway Covenant gave the children and grandchildren of church members the right to participate in church sacraments (baptism, communion, and marriage). Until they showed evidence of saving grace in their own lives, however, they were denied a vote in church affairs. They were half-members of the church, in much the same way that "inhabitants" were half-citizens within the polity. In this way, Stoddard effectively moved the Connecticut churches in the direction of a more traditional parish model in which individuals were essentially "born into" the church.

The Halfway Covenant solved a pastoral problem, but it created a theological one. Why should one assume that the children of the saints were among the saved? The most influential answer was given by Increase Mather, who proclaimed that "the vein of election doth run through the loins of godly parents for the most part" and "that for many generations successively." This was an extraordinary—and extraordinarily consequential—claim. It made blood descent rather than divine law the basis of the covenant, and it opened the door to a racialized understanding of the Puritan project.

Initially, some Puritan leaders tried to have it both ways.[63] Hadn't God loved Abraham for his righteousness *and* included his progeny in the covenant? But renewed war with the Native Americans soon pushed many Puritans through the door that Increase Mather had opened, and the path that they encountered on its other side was marked by a trail of blood. This conflict, known as King Philip's War (1675–1676), was bloody indeed.[64] In fact, relative to population, it was the bloodiest war in American history, claiming the lives of one in fifteen military-age men and leading to the destruction of around half of all English settlements. It also led to the death, removal, and enslavement of thousands of natives and the dissolution of several tribes. How was all this killing, savagery, and destruction—much of it by the colonists—to be reconciled with the Puritan project of a "city on a hill"?

Some writers began to answer in terms of the conquest narrative of blood sacrifice, blood belonging, and sacred lands. Take Samuel Nowell. A Harvard graduate and first-generation New Englander, Nowell wore many hats during his career, serving in turn as a preacher, soldier, and magistrate. He united these roles in his famous "artillery election sermon," *Abraham in Arms*, which he preached publicly before the election of many local artillery captains and subsequently published.[65] The principal argument of this sermon concerned the relationship between religion and soldiering. Where some descried a conflict, he saw none, for, he proclaimed, echoing a common refrain of such sermons, "the Lord is a Man of War."[66] Military service, he continued, is part of the "general calling" of all Christian men, and, indeed, the "holyest, the best, and wisest of men" have always taken it up. Toward the end of the sermon, he turned to the recent conflict, placing it in an apocalyptic frame as the opening chapter in the struggle against "Gog and Magog" foretold in the Revelation of John. The Native Americans he ranged on the side of Satan, warning that they could never "joyn or mix with us to make one Body" and reminding his listeners that God had forbidden the Israelites to intermarry with the Canaanites.[67] New England, he concluded, was the "heritage" of the Puritans, their Holy Land, and God would help them to conquer and defend it. There was nothing new about the individual elements of Nowell's narrative. The valorization of soldiering, the demonization of native populations, New England *qua* New Canaan—we have encountered all of these themes already. What was new about Nowell's rhetoric and that of others from this period was the fusion of these elements within the overarching framework of the conquest narrative.

Nowell's rhetoric also contained an apocalyptic element, though it was only weakly developed. Later writers would distill it further, yielding a high-octane version of premillennial apocalypticism. In this venture Increase Mather's son Cotton was the lead alchemist. To be sure, Cotton Mather was not the first Puritan to immerse himself in the apocalyptic texts. However, he was the first American Puritan to systematically combine the four elements of premillennial apocalypticism as defined in chapter 1, namely, predictive, literalist, premillennial, and violent readings of the apocalyptic texts.

Other Puritans had not gone this far.[68] Anne Hutchinson favored an allegorical reading of the texts. For her, the struggles between good and evil depicted in the book of Revelation were to be understood as struggles within the human heart. John Cotton had embraced a predictive reading, but one that was naturalistic, peaceful, and postmillennial. He believed that the reestablishment of true churches in New England would be followed by the preaching of the Gospel to the "heathen" peoples, which would in turn usher in an earthly millennium, to be followed by Christ's Second Coming. Other first-generation Puritan divines, such as John Eliot, even incorporated the native peoples into the eschatological drama by casting them as one of the "lost tribes" of Israel.[69] And since the conversion of the Jews was to precede the Second Coming of

Christ, these thinkers reasoned, a peaceful mission to the Native Americans had to be part of the millennial program. Ultimately, in a sort of multiculturalism *avant la lettre* Eliot even foresaw the civic incorporation of "praying Indians" into New England's church polities. Overall, the eschatology of the early Puritans was more millennial than apocalyptic. It envisioned the imminent arrival of the Kingdom of God, not the fiery return of Jesus Christ. And, in fact, this optimistic form of "civil millennialism" would reemerge during the Second Great Awakening and remain the dominant eschatology right through the American Revolution.[70]

However, in the decades around 1700, civil millennialism was temporarily displaced by premillennial apocalypticism. With the renewal of hostilities between New England and the native peoples and their mutual entanglement in England's and France's struggle to control North America, those who shared Eliot's views were quickly placed on the defensive, and those who shared Nowell's outlook suddenly found themselves in the ascendancy.[71] Once again, the Mathers played a leading role in this struggle. In his two histories of the conflict, both published shortly after the conclusion of the war, Increase Mather combined a covenantal and an apocalyptic frame. He argued that God was using the Indians to punish, test, and discipline his new chosen people, just as he had done with his first chosen people when *they* violated the covenant. But he then raised the temperature by styling the Native Americans as "tools of Satan" and embedding the conflict with King Philip into a cosmological struggle between good and evil.[72]

However, it was his son, Cotton Mather, who first developed a full-blown version of premillennial apocalypticism.[73] Cotton spent long hours poring over the works of European expositors of the apocalyptic texts. Schooled in typological interpretation of the Old Testament, he was already inclined toward a predictive reading of Revelation. Convinced that the Bay Colony was undergoing a precipitous moral decline, and vexed by his local enemies, he longed for Christ to return in glory and settle his accounts. "At no time in his vision of the end did he ever describe Christ's Second Coming as occurring in harmony and peace," Cotton Mather insisted. "Christ would descend upon the earth in smoke and fire with His angels. And the fire would rain down on degenerate men everywhere, and the heavens would be set on fire to torment the devils there."[74]

Even so, it would be premature to speak of a fully formed version of American religious nationalism at this point. Increase Mather's racialized vision of the Puritan community was not tightly linked to Cotton Mather's apocalyptic vision of the end times in either their respective writings or anywhere else. And the Mathers's star was sinking in any event. More openhearted and optimistic versions of Protestantism now came into the ascendancy and would remain there until the Civil War era. The twin seeds of American exceptionalism had surely been planted, but they would not reach full flower for two centuries.

CONCLUSION: THE HEBRAIC MOMENT

In his influential writings on civic republicanism, the intellectual historian J.G.A. Pocock speaks of a "Machiavellian moment" in North Atlantic political culture, a moment in time defined by the inner logic of Machiavellian republicanism. Perhaps one might also speak of a Hebraic moment in American political theology. This was, first of all, a time when the national storyline was modeled on the Hebrew scriptures. I say "national" because the vision of America as a "Promised Land" and of its inhabitants as a "chosen people" was soon extended from New England to the nation as a whole and persisted well into the nineteenth century and beyond.[75] It was, second, a moment of theological debate, in which different understandings of the Hebrew and Christian scriptures and their relationship to one another were at issue. Was the national covenant based on blood lineage or moral law? Were the apocalyptic texts to be understood allegorically or historically, naturally or supernaturally? The Puritans did not resolve these debates. Nor have we. Thus, the Hebraic moment was also, and still remains, a "moment" in the physicist's sense of a balancing point. Throughout its history, America has teetered back and forth between civil religion and religious nationalism, sometimes leaning more in one direction or the other, but without losing its balance altogether. So far.

How should we understand the Puritan story today? The Mathers and their followers understood it in terms of "declension," the ineluctable decline of Puritan society following the golden age of Winthrop's generation. This declensionist narrative eventually received a scholarly imprimatur from Perry Miller, the great twentieth-century historian of New England Puritanism, which then influenced Bellah's writings on civil religion a few decades later—too much so, I think. For the declensionist account tacitly presumes an intellectual consensus that never existed. Stephen Foster has therefore proposed that we think of Puritanism as a "long argument" that spanned the entire seventeenth century, an argument that included the various figures cited earlier and many more as well.[76] America had more than one founding myth.

Not everyone who lived in seventeenth-century America was part of this argument, of course. Some were never allowed to join—Catholics, for instance. A few were ejected—to Rhode Island usually. And many more were too busy to join in—such as the Jamestown planters, perhaps. But the argument was not a narrow one either, especially in the context of the times. It included many people of a "middling sort" who would have had little, if any, voice in their ancestral homelands.[77] At moments, the argument even included Puritan women and Native Americans. Far as they may have been from contemporary ideals of democratic life, the Puritan polities of New England were still remarkably egalitarian and participatory. Given the choice between the Bay Colony, that "city on a hill" built on a "Protestant work ethic," and Jamestown, that tobacco plantation built on indentured servitude and chattel slavery, should we not cast our votes for the Puritans?

What sustained the "long argument" was not an intellectual consensus so much as a shared vocabulary. The focal concept was the covenant. The Puritans debated its meaning, but they agreed on its significance: it was the central node that held together a cluster of interrelated ideas— chosenness, godliness, and civility, to name but a few. The result was a web of meaning strong enough to hold the Bay Colony together during its formative years and elastic enough to encompass the nation as a whole during later years.

What remains of the long argument are certain elements of the American tradition. Winthrop's *Arbella* sermon is now part of the national canon and is often cited even today. Roger Williams now stands above Winthrop in the national pantheon as the first defender of "religious liberty,"[78] alongside Anne Hutchinson, the "first American feminist." John Eliot, the "first American multiculturalist" is a more recent discovery in America's civil religious archive. Perhaps that archive holds further treasures as well.

Still, the greatest legacy of the Puritan founding is surely the Exodus narrative itself. This story of oppression, flight, and freedom has long had, and still has, an enduring resonance for an immigrant nation like the United States.

CHAPTER 3

Hebraic Republicanism

THE AMERICAN REVOLUTION

> The Americans combine the notions of liberty
> and of Christianity so intimately in their minds
> that it is impossible to make them conceive of
> the one without the other.
>
> —ALEXIS DE TOCQUEVILLE

IN RECENT DECADES, the history of the American Revolution has become a battleground in the "culture wars." Some Christian conservatives argue that the United States was originally founded as a "Christian nation" and that our political system rests upon "biblical principles."[1] They contend that the founding fathers were "orthodox Christians" and that the U.S. Constitution was "divinely inspired."[2]

Meanwhile, some radical secularists claim that the United States was actually founded as a "secular democracy" and that our political system is premised on "Enlightenment principles."[3] They insist that the founding fathers were "religious skeptics"—possibly even closet atheists—and that the U.S. Constitution drew its main inspiration from secular sources.

So who is right: the religious nationalists or the radical secularists? In my view—and that of most American historians these days, I think—the correct answer is "neither."[4] Religious nationalists tend to overestimate the religious orthodoxy of the revolutionary generation and underestimate the influence of liberal ideas on them. Radical secularists do the reverse. Meanwhile, both make the revolutionary generation more homogeneous than it really was. Neither understands the influence of civic republicanism on the founders.

The revolutionary coalition was remarkably broad. Theologically, it ran from Baptists to deists.[5] Philosophically, it ran from Cicero to Locke.[6] Still, its outlook was not incoherent. Its vital center—its civil religion— was what I will call "Hebraic republicanism."[7] Like godly republicanism, Hebraic republicanism was a complex synthesis of biblical and classical ideas. For the leaders of the revolution, who had been steeped in the

Greek and Roman classics, the republican element usually predominated.[8] But for their followers, who were far more familiar with the Old and New Testaments, the Hebraic element was likely stronger.[9] However, neither saw any contradiction between Christianity and republicanism.[10]

Hebraic republicanism differed from classical republicanism in two important respects. It incorporated a Lockean notion of natural rights[11] and a Protestant sort of moral egalitarianism.[12] Of course, rights and equality were not granted to natives, women, or slaves.[13] But hereditary aristocracy and absolute monarchy were firmly rejected. This was already pretty revolutionary in and of itself.

There were other sources of revolutionary ideology as well. There was a dark apocalypticism that envisioned the American Revolution as part of a cosmic showdown between Christ and Antichrist.[14] And there was a more optimistic "civil millennialism" that imagined the revolution as an attempt to "begin the world anew."[15] The optimistic vision was more influential. Religious nationalism was at this time still but a small stream within the revolutionary torrent.

There were also small pockets of proto-liberal and proto-secular thought.[16] I use the term "proto" here because the word "liberal" did not yet have its modern meaning and the word "secular" was not even in circulation. I say "small" because those who espoused strongly liberal and secular ideas were still a tiny minority. Radical secularism would not reach full maturity for almost another century.

REVOLUTIONARY POLITICS:
LIBERAL AND/OR REPUBLICAN?

There has been much debate about the intellectual origins of the American Revolution over the last fifty years. [17] During the mid-twentieth century, most scholars thought that the United States was built on liberal principles derived from the political philosophy of John Locke and, in particular, his *Second Treatise of Government.*[18] During the mid-1960s, several scholars challenged this view, arguing that the ideology of the American Revolution was based entirely on civic republicanism.[19] In the mid-1980s, a new generation of American historians countered that Lockean liberalism was actually more important to the American founders than the republican revisionists had allowed. Today, the general view is that revolutionary ideology contained republican as well as liberal elements.[20] (Later work would definitively show that republican ideas did remain influential until well into the nineteenth century.[21]) Today, the debate focuses on the relative weight of republican and liberal ideas. *My thesis in this chapter is that revolutionary ideology was about three-quarters republican and one-quarter liberal.*

One reason why the debate has not been settled is that the participants have not usually been clear enough about what they mean by "republicanism" and "liberalism." In chapter 1, I contrasted republican and liberal ideas about human nature, freedom, virtue, balance, and corruption. I noted that republicans view human beings as inherently sociable and see the polity as a result of this innate sociability. By contrast, liberals believe human beings are inherently selfish and see the state as an artificial construction. I argued that republicans have a complex idea of freedom that involves: (1) freedom from arbitrary authority through rule of law, (2) mastery of one's passions and a sense of justice, and (3) active participation in political affairs. By contrast, liberals have a simple idea of freedom that consists of not being interfered with in the pursuit of one's desires. I showed that republicans believe that civic virtue is crucial to the proper functioning of a free government, while liberals believe that good institutions are sufficient. Republicans therefore believe strongly in civic education, while liberals think it is unnecessary and coercive. As regards constitutional balance, liberals believe that institutional checks and balances are enough, while republicans insist that sociological balance between different social groups is also necessary. Too, liberals and republicans have very different definitions of corruption. Liberals understand it transactionally, that is, as a *quid pro quo* between corrupt individuals. Republicans understand it culturally, specifically, as a pervasive tendency to put self-interest ahead of the common good. In this context, I would like to add one further contrast: classical republicans believe that human beings are naturally unequal, whereas classical liberals believe they are naturally equal. These contrasts are summarized in table 1 (for a more detailed discussion, please see chapter 1).

With these distinctions in mind, it is easy to show that the founders were strongly influenced by civic republicanism, albeit to varying degrees. At one end of the spectrum, we find someone like John Adams, whose views were classically republican. In his "Dissertation on Canon and Feudal Law" (1765), he urged his readers to "read the histories of ancient ages" and "contemplate the great examples of Greece and Rome."[22] He would do so himself two decades later in his "Defense of the Constitutions of the United States" (1786), a primer on republican governments from antiquity through the present. Adams's views of human nature were also strongly influenced by classical thought. "Men, in their primitive conditions," he argued, "were undoubtedly gregarious; and they continue to be social, not only in every

TABLE 1.1. CIVIC REPUBLICANISM VS.
CLASSICAL LIBERALISM

	Civic Republicanism	Classical Liberalism
1. Human Nature	Inherently sociable	Inherently selfish
2. Human Freedom	Complex: self-mastery, rule of law, active citizenship	Simple: noninterference
3. Free Institutions	Require civic virtue as well as proper design	Require proper design only
4. Constitutional Balance	Institutional and sociological	Institutional only
5. Corruption	Cultural: putting self-interest before the common good	Transactional: *quid pro quo*
6. Human Equality	Natural inequality	Natural equality

stage of civilization, but in every possible situation in which they can be placed."[23] To say that human beings are sociable, however, is not to say that they are virtuous. Still, virtue is the greatest thing to which human beings can aspire, for "the happiness of man, as well as his dignity, consists in virtue."[24] To attain virtue, Adams believed, it is necessary to control the passions. However, the capacity for virtue is not equally distributed: human beings are naturally unequal, and attempts to make them equal are doomed to failure.[25] He believed that American society would be—indeed, already was being—divided up into distinct social orders. One means of preserving popular liberty was to establish a republican constitution that would hold the "three different orders of men *in equilibrio*."[26] Another was to promote civic education, for "liberty cannot be preserved without a general knowledge among the people." Consequently, "no expense" should be spared in providing for "the liberal education of youth, especially for the lower class of people."[27] Only in this way could a republic instill the modicum of civic virtue that is necessary for its own preservation. In sum, John Adams was the classical republican of the revolutionary generation.

Somewhere nearer the other end of the spectrum, we find a figure such as Alexander Hamilton. Hamilton was quite familiar with the history and theory of classical republicanism, but he found them of little use: "It is as ridiculous," he said, "to seek for models in the simple ages of Greece and Rome, as it would be to go in quest of them among the Hottentots and Laplanders. . . . We might as soon reconcile ourselves to the Spartan community of goods and wives, to their iron coin, their long beards, or their black broth."[28] The British Constitution, he believed, was a more auspi-

cious starting point for the United States.[29] Of course, the British Constitution could be, and often was, classified as mixed and republican (i.e., as
a limited monarchy or monarchical republic), and Hamilton did not reject
the republican label as such. But he did revise the classical recipe in various ways, starting with its view of human nature: "We must take man as
we find him, and if we expect him to serve the public must interest his passions in doing so."[30] Like Adams, he was no egalitarian: "In every community where industry is encouraged," he believed, "there will be a division of
it into the few & the many." Sounding a more republican note, he argued
that constitutional balance was the only way to maintain liberty: "Give all
the power to the many, they will oppress the few. Give all power to the few,
they will oppress the many. Both therefore ought to have power, that each
may defend itself against the other."[31] Hamilton's thinking started from
classical premises but took them in a proto-liberal direction. He defined
"liberty" in terms of "common privileges" and "natural rights" that must
be protected from government encroachment.[32] He said nothing of self-
mastery—something of which he, personally, possessed little—nor of political participation as a positive good. Rather, he viewed liberty as an out-
let for ambition or a check against tyranny, nothing more. The principal
end of the American republic for him was not active involvement in public
affairs but private "peace and happiness,"[33] and the principal means toward this end was therefore a "common defence" and the "regulation of
commerce." In Hamilton's view, the chief danger to a republic was not corruption, but anarchy[34] and, more specifically, demagoguery, in which an
ambitious man allies with the many against the few.[35] If individual rights
and social stability were two of Hamilton's chief *desiderata*, the third was
national greatness. Alexander Hamilton was the most prominent proto-
liberal—and proto-imperialist—of the revolutionary era.

Jefferson's stance toward classical republicanism was more ambivalent
than Adams's and more ambiguous than Hamilton's, placing him somewhere in the middle of our spectrum. Like Hamilton, Jefferson could be
quite dismissive of the classical tradition. "So different was the style of
society then . . . from what it is now," he proclaimed in one letter, "that
I think little edification can be obtained from [the classics] on the subject of government." The modern theory of "representative democracy," he
concluded, had rendered the ancient theories obsolete.[36] However, he also
believed that knowledge of the classics was an essential part of a proper
civic education, and he recommended the teaching of classical languages
and history.[37] His view of human nature was also quite classical: "Man
was created for social intercourse; but social intercourse cannot be main-

tained without a sense of social justice; then man must have been created with a sense of justice."[38] Active involvement in public affairs was so important to Jefferson that he devoted many of his later years to the promotion of a system of local "wards" or "hundreds," which were intended to be "little republics" and schools of democracy.[39] Nor was this the only area in which his politics bore a republican imprint. He believed that landed property was the best foundation for an independent citizenry, and that excessive inequality was a mortal threat to civic virtue—views that explain his support for the Louisiana Purchase, easy land policies, and partible inheritance laws.[40] While Jefferson certainly held that all people were equal in rights, he did not believe that they were equal in ability much less that they should be equal in power. He agreed with John Adams "that there is a natural aristocracy among men" whose "grounds . . . are virtue and talent."[41] For that reason, Jefferson also advocated a meritocratic educational system such that "the best geniuses would be raked from the rubbish" and into positions of influence.[42] At the same time, he thought the collective moral sense of the common people superior to that of the educated classes and strongly supported popular education in letters and civics as the most effective antidote to tyranny. Like most of the ancients, Jefferson did not believe that nature had outfitted women for politics. Where he went beyond the ancients—or behind them, if you prefer—was in his view that Native Americans and African Americans were also naturally unfit for political life as a result of their supposedly diminished capacities for reason and self-mastery. He thereby helped to reformulate the republican theory of natural inequality in bioracial terms—a fateful move. On balance, then, Jefferson's views were more republican than liberal and, it appears, became increasingly republican in later life.[43]

Let me conclude this brief survey of the political thought of the American founders with an examination of James Madison, Jefferson's partisan ally and presidential successor. Where Jefferson articulated republican themes in a natural rights language, Madison often did the reverse. In *Federalist* No. 10, for example, Madison defined republics in opposition to democracies, rather than in opposition to the three "simple" forms of government (i.e., monarchy, aristocracy, and democracy), and on two grounds: their territorial extent and their use of representation.[44] The implicit contrast here, made explicit in *Federalist* No. 18, is between the (large) Roman Republic and the (smaller) Greek democracies.[45] Responding to his critics, he further amended this definition in *Federalist* No. 39, in which he eschewed recourse to "political writers" and identified popular sovereignty and regular elections as the hallmarks of republicanism.[46] Similar shifts of emphasis are evident in Madison's theory of republican stability. In the classical theory, to recall, the chief remedies for faction and revolution were a balance between the one, the few, and the many; a mixture of monarchical, aristocratic, and democratic institutions; and the moral education of citizens. Madison's remedies were virtuous representation, territorial expansion, and institutional checks and balances. By channeling public debate through elected representatives and opening those elections to all men of talent, it was hoped that the reasoning of the virtuous might cool the passions of the multitudes. Territorial expansion was desirable because it promoted social heterogeneity. And social heterogeneity was desirable because it hindered factionalism by making it difficult to form groups that had the numbers and the resources to take over the government. Checks and balances added a further layer of protection against factionalism by dispersing governmental authority across different institutions. All of Madison's remedies had precursors within the republican tradition, of course. But he reformulated them in novel ways. The crucial point is that insofar as Madison's views were liberal, his liberalism must be seen as continuous with, and indebted to, classical republicanism.

It seems fair to conclude that republican influences were at least as strong as liberal ones among the political leaders of the revolutionary era. The exception who proves the rule is Hamilton. His views on human nature, human freedom, constitutional architecture, economic policy, and standing armies were arguably most distant from the republican tradition and closest to modern liberalism. The other three founders all espoused some version of republicanism, though to varying degrees. Adams could be categorized as a classical republican, Jefferson as a democratic republican, and Madison as a liberal republican.

At this point, the balance between liberal and republican ideas in the revolutionary era might appear to be about fifty-fifty. But American republicanism had biblical as well as classical sources: it was Christian and Hebraic as well as civic. Once these biblical sources are added to the scale, it will tilt definitively in a republican direction, resolving the long-running political and scholarly debate.

CHRISTIAN REPUBLICANISM?

Many intellectual historians and political theorists assume that republicanism and Christianity are fundamentally opposed. Premodern champions of civic republicanism were often of this view as well. Take Machiavelli. In the *Discourses*, he argues that religion is "the most necessary and assured support of any civil society [*vivere civile*]."[47] But he did not believe that traditional Christianity could inspire enough public virtue. In this regard, he says, the Roman religion was quite superior. Whereas Christianity "places the supreme happiness in humility, lowliness, and a contempt for worldly objects," paganism "places the supreme good in grandeur of soul, strength of body, and all such other qualities as render men formidable."[48] Machiavelli believed that the otherworldly orientation of Christianity weakens its capacity to inspire vigorous action in this world, or what he called *virtù*.

Rousseau's essay *The Social Contract* is marked by an even greater hostility toward Christianity. By establishing a "Spiritual Kingdom on earth," he said, Christianity sundered the primordial unity of state and religion, giving rise to "dual power" and "a perpetual conflict of jurisdiction which has made any good polity impossible in Christian states."[49] What sort of religion would suit a republic, then? A simple one capable of inspiring virtue, he argued, one that affirmed "the existence of a powerful, intelligent, beneficent, prescient, and provident Deity, the life to come, the happiness of the just, the punishment of the wicked, the sanctity of the Social Contract and the Laws" and tolerance for those whose "dogmas contain nothing contrary to the duties of the citizen." In other words, a deistic form of civil religion.

An earlier generation of American historians and political theorists agreed with Machiavelli and Rousseau, viewing "Christian republicanism" as a contradiction in terms. Republicanism tended to go together with heterodoxy, they thought, and vice versa.[50] Later generations of scholars disagreed, however.[51] They showed that English republicans of the seventeenth century such as John Milton, John Harrington, and Algernon Sidney had not seen any contradiction between republicanism and Christianity, and it soon became clear that the vast majority of the American revolutionaries of the following century did not either. There were exceptions, of course, like Thomas Paine and Ethan Allen. But they were just that: exceptions.[52] There was no simple correlation between republicanism and heterodoxy.

So the interesting question is not *whether* Christianity and republicanism could go together—they did—but precisely *how*. There is no single answer to that question either, but I will try to give some sense of the varieties of Christian republicanism that existed during the revolutionary era through a closer examination of three men: Jonathan Mayhew, Benjamin Rush, and Timothy Dwight.

Jonathan Mayhew (1720–1766) was a Harvard-trained Congregationalist minister and, for most of his short life, the pastor of Boston's Old West Church. His theology was Arminian (meaning that he believed free will played some role in spiritual regeneration) and possibly even Arian (meaning that he may not have regarded Jesus Christ as wholly divine). He was also an avowed republican and an early opponent of the Stamp Act. At first glance, therefore, he would seem to confirm the old argument about the connection between religious and political heterodoxy. But Mayhew himself would not have accepted this assessment.[53] He argued strongly for the existence of absolute truth in religion and morality, for example,[54] and he located this truth exclusively in the teachings of Christianity.[55] Further, Mayhew preached many sermons emphasizing the providential character of disasters, which he viewed as incitements to "holiness," if not as punishments for sin.[56] Finally, like many American preachers of this era, he was a fervent believer in the truth of biblical prophecy and the doctrine of the Second Coming.[57] Rumors of Mayhew's heresy, then, are greatly exaggerated.

Politically, Mayhew was a revolutionary. This is evident from his "Discourse Concerning Unlimited Submission" (1750). Preached on the hundredth anniversary of the Stuart regicide (the beheading of the English king in 1650) and widely read for years thereafter, it was an exceedingly clever defense of popular resistance to political tyranny that took the *locus classicus* for the doctrine of passive obedience (chapter 13 of Paul's epistle to the Romans) and used it to justify a natural right to resist unjust rule. In Mayhew's interpretation,[58] Paul argues "not in favor of submission to all who bear the *title* of rulers, in common; but only, to those who *actually* perform the duty of rulers, by exercising a reasonable and just authority, for the good of human society."[59] In this way, Mayhew argued that resistance to those who were rulers in title only was wholly legitimate.

Mayhew was also a classical republican. He argued that good government "is a blessing to the world . . . by means of [which], we may both procure, and quietly enjoy, those numerous blessings and advantages . . . unattainable out of society."[60] The British government, moreover, he saw as doubly blessed, insofar as it afforded "civil and religious liberty"[61] through the establishment of a "free constitution" under which "law, and not will, is the measure of the executive Magistrate's power"[62] and citizens are not "subject to the arbitrary pleasure of others."[63]

More than that, Mayhew was a *Christian* republican. He emphasized the contributions of morality and religion to the maintenance of civil and religious liberty, which he viewed as "natural and God-given."[64] While the importance of public virtue was well known to the ancients, he argued, Christians can better achieve such virtue, because "morals have a close connection with religion."[65] If civil and religious liberty go hand in hand, then so do religious and civil tyranny, he continued, with the reign of Constantine marking the loss of both kinds of liberty,[66] and the Protestant Reformation and English Revolution their recovery.[67]

Last but not least, Mayhew was a *Hebraic* republican. He understood Providence in terms of covenant: "Whatever befalls states and kingdoms . . . are in scripture attributed to god's over-ruling providence."[68] In that regard, England, like Israel, had been especially favored. This was the true meaning of the Exodus story and of the Glorious Revolution, when God "delivered the British nations from one popish and arbitrary king" and instituted "a legal and limited monarchy."[69]

In Mayhew's vision, then, covenant theology and classical republicanism were blended together at two points: first, in a grand narrative that connected the loss of liberty to imperialism and popery, and its recovery to republicanism and Protestantism; and, second, in a political theology that linked republican governance to public virtue, and public virtue to Christian conviction.

Our second Christian republican is Benjamin Rush (1745–1813). More than Mayhew, Rush confounds the old claim about the link between religious and political orthodoxy. As a boy, he was much influenced by his minister, Gilbert Tennent, a former circuit rider turned Presbyterian pastor and protégé of George Whitefield, the great English evangelist. As a young man, Rush considered entering the ministry before choosing a career in medicine.[70] After completing his studies at the College of New Jersey (which later became Princeton), where his evangelical faith was confirmed, he spent several years in Edinburgh, Scotland, where he encountered Hume and other luminaries of the Scottish Enlightenment. He then moved to London, where he frequented the Club of Honest Whigs, a circle of republican intellectuals centered around Catherine Macaulay. It was there that he underwent a second conversion—this time to civic republicanism. After returning to Philadelphia, where he established a successful medical practice, Rush soon became involved in agitation against the Stamp Act and later signed the Declaration of Independence. Despite his early years in Britain, his firsthand encounters with skepticism, his subsequent career in science, and his radical political views, Rush never wavered in his commitment to the evangelical Christianity of his youth. In the decades after the revolution, he became engaged in a wide range of reform movements, including temperance, abolition, public education, penal reform, and ecumenical cooperation, anticipating the reformist zeal of nineteenth-century evangelicals more generally.

Like Mayhew, Rush saw Christianity and republicanism as wholly complementary. "Republican forms of government," he argued, "are the best repositories of the Gospel,"[71] because true religion requires liberty, and religious and civil liberty go hand in hand. Conversely, he argued that "a Christian cannot fail of being a republican" because "the Gospel inculcates those degrees of humility, self-denial, and brotherly kindness, which are directly opposed to the pride of monarchy and the pageantry of a court."[72] Like Mayhew, he also laid considerable stress on the role of education and religion in inculcating virtue and morality, and on the importance of virtue and morality in sustaining a republic, and he devoted much energy to educational reform in his later years. "Virtue," he declared, "is the living principle of a republic," and the only means "of rendering a republican form of government durable . . . is by disseminating the seeds of virtue and knowledge" through public education.[73] To Rush, a proper education was in part a moral education, and moral principles had to be rooted in religious belief.[74] In a letter to Noah Webster, he worried that "all our attempts to produce political happiness by the solitary influence of human reason will be . . . fruitless. . . . Reason produces, it is true, great and popular truths, but it affords *motives* too feeble to induce mankind to act agreeably to them. Christianity unfolds the same truths and accompanies them with *motives*."[75] For this reason, Rush believed that republican government could only be fully realized in the Christian era; in the absence of true religion, he thought, the ancients had lacked the necessary virtue. Indeed, in a moment of millennial fervor, he even went so far as to argue that "it is only necessary for republicanism to ally itself with the Christian religion to overturn all the corrupted political and religious institutions of the world."[76] The French Revolution, however, showed that republicanism *without* Christianity, and reason *without* religion, could be dangerous. "The conduct of the French Convention," he observed, "seems intended to prove that human reason alone in its most cultivated state will not make men free or happy without the aid of divine revelation and the influences of the Spirit of the Gospel upon the hearts of men."[77] So close was the connection between religion and virtue for Rush that he "had rather see the opinions of Confucius or Mahomed inculcated upon our youth, than see them grow up wholly devoid of a system of religious principles."[78] Still, Rush remained firmly committed to the American tradition of separating civil and religious authority. "Human governments may receive support from Christianity," he wrote to Thomas Jefferson, "but it must be only from the love of justice and peace which it is calculated to produce in the minds of men."[79] But while he rejected a religious establishment of any kind as contrary to the principles of Christianity, he envisioned a sort of Protestant proto-establishment that would seek to stamp out private and public vice and safeguard the morals of the nation—a vision that was in fact partially realized in the antebellum years.[80] "From the success, or failure, of your exertions in the cause of virtue," he told an assembly of ministers, "we anticipate the freedom or slavery of our country."[81] By "virtue" he meant not only the public virtues praised by the ancients, but also the private ones promoted by the Puritans: temperance, thrift, diligence, and filial piety.

Having looked at the views of one theologian and one reformer, I conclude this examination with someone who was both of these things and more: a child prodigy and a gifted speaker and writer; a state legislator and later chief of the Federalist Party in Connecticut; a Congregationalist minister and eventual president of Yale College; and the grandson of Jonathan Edwards, married to the daughter of a wealthy financier from New York. The only thing that Timothy Dwight (1752–1817) assuredly was not is "heterodox." On the contrary, he was the very embodiment of Federalist orthodoxy and, just as assuredly, a republican. In many ways, his political views were remarkably similar to Mayhew's and Rush's. Like them, he believed that the endurance of a republic depended more on public virtue than on institutional design. "The formation and establishment of knowledge and virtue in the citizens of a Community," he argued, "will more easily and more effectually establish order, and secure liberty, than all the checks, balances and penalties, which have been devised by man."[82] The stability of Sparta and Rome, he contended, was due not only to their balanced constitutions but also to their "heathen virtue."[83] And there were only two sure means of promoting virtue, he added: "Religious Education and Public Worship."[84] Without religion and virtue, liberty and republican government could not long survive: "Religion and liberty are the meat and the drink of the body politic. Withdraw one of them, and it languishes, consumes, and dies."[85] Accordingly, one of the greatest dangers to republican liberty was "atheism," of which he considered deism a form. For Dwight, atheists were the fifth column of the Antichrist, the shock troops of the end times. And Dwight saw other, more homely dangers to liberty as well: besides the Whigs, excessive wealth and luxury, "unlimited" trade and commerce, militarism, and imperialism were also great threats to republican stability.[86] Dwight was also quite orthodox in another respect as well. Much more than Mayhew or Rush, and rather like Adams, he inclined to the view that there was a natural connection between moral and social inequality that gave rise to a natural aristocracy. This belief was, of course, a staple of Federalist ideology and one of the main issues that set Federalists apart from Jeffersonians.

The American Revolution proved Machiavelli and Rousseau wrong: it showed that Christian republicanism is not a contradiction in terms. Mayhew and Rush were living evidence of that. The mirror-image claim that there is an essential connection between "heterodoxy" and republicanism is shown to be equally false, with Timothy Dwight and the New England Federalists providing the decisive counterexample. What probably is true is that republicanism goes together more easily with certain *kinds* of Christianity than others, those that emphasize:

1. Ethical duty rather than religious ritual or mystical experience
2. Religious freedom rather than ritual conformity
3. Social reform rather than divine intervention
4. Collective as well as individual chosenness

No doubt, a Christianity of this sort would have been regarded as unorthodox in many settings. But early America was not one of them.

Still, Machiavelli and Rousseau were not *entirely* wrong. There were tensions between classical republicanism and orthodox Christianity, particularly as regards their philosophies of history. For the Christian, the life of Jesus marked a caesura. Ancient Rome could no longer serve as *the* golden age, as *the* model. There were several possible "solutions" to this problem. One was to portray Sparta and Rome as imperfect realizations of a republican ideal, which could only be fully realized in a Christian society, where public virtue was perfected by spiritual regeneration. That is the solution embraced by Mayhew, Rush, and Dwight. Another was to read the Bible itself through a republican lens, starting with the "Hebrew Republic" of the ancient Israelites.

THE BIBLE AND THE REVOLUTION: MILLENNIALISM, APOCALYPTICISM, AND HEBRAICISM

During the 1960s, the same years when some scholars were first discovering the influence of republicanism on the revolution, others began exploring the influence of "millennialism." Some argued that the Great Awakening stoked a popular millennialism that helped catalyze the revolution. Other saw the French and Indian Wars as the crucial spark that ignited millennial expectations. More recently, some revisionist historians have argued that Hebraicism was more influential than apocalypticism. I believe that the revisionists are right: "civil millennialism" was less central to revolutionary ideology than was Hebraic republicanism. I also believe that their predecessors confused two very different sorts of "millennialism": premillennial apocalypticism and postmillennial progressivism. The latter was far more important to the revolution than the former.

The Great Awakening was a revivalist movement that swept across the northern colonies during the 1730s and 1740s, initially spreading throughout the Middle Colonies but eventually taking firmest hold in New England.[87] It originated in the "Pietist" movements that had arisen in the Netherlands and Germany a few decades earlier.[88] The American movement featured itinerant preachers such as the famous English evangelist George Whitefield and "New Light" ministers such as the great American theologian Jonathan Edwards. Its use of mass revival meetings and emphasis on individual emotional experience fostered a more ecumenical and egalitarian version of Protestantism. At the same time, polemical attacks on lukewarm or "unconverted" ministers and on abstruse and "impractical" theology sparked conflict and divisions within individual congregations and denominations. The revivalists brought not peace, but the sword.

The feeling of religious "awakening"—whether real or just perceived[89]—generated a sense of expectation among many of the movement's participants. In his famous account of the Great Awakening, Jonathan Edwards speculated openly that Christ's reign "will begin in America," and, more specifically, in New England.[90] It could not begin in Europe or England, he reasoned, because God would want to make a fresh start. "When God is about to turn the earth into a paradise, he does not begin his work where there is some growth already, but in the wilderness," Edwards reasoned, as such an achievement would be a more miraculous manifestation of his glory. Further, the fact that "America was discovered about the time of the reformation" Edwards took to be a sign that the millennial Kingdom would first be established in the New World.[91] Citing the book of Isaiah, Edwards concluded that the progression of God's Kingdom had always been from east to west: first from Israel to Rome, and now from Rome to America.[92] "And if we suppose that this glorious work of God shall begin in any part of America," he concluded, then New England "must needs appear the most likely of all American colonies" because of the flourishing state of the churches there.

Edwards's millennialism was not a form of premillennial apocalypticism. It did not cite any of the apocalyptic texts. It did not imply that God's Kingdom would be brought about through supernatural violence. And it presumed that Jesus's return would occur after the millennium. Edwards's worldview was millennial, not apocalyptic.

Not that apocalypticism was absent from the scene. In America, the carnage of war has often summoned up such rhetoric. This was true of both the "Indian wars" of the seventeenth century and the "Seven Years' War" (1756–1763). Indeed, according to one historian's calculations, there were more publications featuring apocalyptic motifs during the 1750s than at any other time in the history of colonial America.[93] In the North American context, the Seven Years' War—which Winston Churchill aptly dubbed the "first world war"[94]—pitted the British Empire and its settler colonies against the French Empire and its native allies in a bloody struggle for global preeminence. Many colonists saw this war through an apocalyptic lens. Appellations once reserved for Rome and the Vatican—"Whore of Babylon," "Scarlet Whore," and "Antichrist"—were now hurled at Paris and Versailles. There was perhaps no other time when the American colonists felt themselves more British.

Often, the rhetoric of premillennial apocalypticism was combined with images of blood sacrifice and supernatural violence. In his 1755 sermon on the "Duty of Christian Soldiers," for example, the Congregationalist minister Solomon Williams declared that "the Antichristian Powers have been many Hundreds of years Persecuting the Church of Christ, have shed Rivers of Blood, which Cries for Vengeance under the Altar."[95] He nonetheless warned his listeners that "you are not design'd to be the Executioners of GOD'S Wrath against the *French* . . . nor are you to go against them as Revengers of the Blood of GOD'S Saints . . . but in Defence of your Country."[96]

In another influential sermon delivered just two years later, Samuel Finley, the president of Princeton University, inveighed against those who invoked Christian ethics to defend their pacifism or neutrality in the conflict, warning that they would suffer the "curse of Meroz"—a city whose inhabitants had refused to take up arms in defense of Israel. Unlike Williams, Finley assured his listeners that they *were* instruments of divine judgment and vengeance, and argued that those who were not with him were against God, for "there can be no ME-DIUM between *not helping* and *opposing him*."[97] When "a true Christian" sees "Fields of Blood, mangled Bodies!—the Earth gorged with the Gore of its Inhabitants!—populous Cities in Heaps!," he assured them, "his Mind will be at Rest, because he see[s] it to be a fit and righteous Thing."[98]

Still, blood rhetoric was rare in the political theology of the period. In fact, it was not even the dominant motif in Finley's sermon, which mainly employed Christian theories of just war and republican arguments about duty and virtue. A systematic study of published sermons from this period concludes that "while . . . holy war themes are marked in the writings of about one-fifth of the ministers, including a number of prominent men, the Revolutionary clergy for the most part presented themselves not as priests of a holy people but as the religious and moral leaders of a body politic fighting what they perceived to be a just war."[99] An analysis of biblical citations in revolutionary sermons comes to exactly the same conclusion: "Wartime ministers rarely preached on Revelation, or on the apocalyptic scriptures from the Old Testament. In the ranking of most popular biblical texts that ministers preached on when addressing war, we do not find an apocalyptic text in the top ten or even the top twenty-five."[100] Nor was this pattern confined to religious works. An exhaustive study of political tracts published between 1760 and 1805 found that the most cited book of the Bible was not Daniel or Revelation, but Deuteronomy. Interestingly, this study also found that Deuteronomy was *the* most cited book of any sort, religious or secular.[101]

This finding would not come as any surprise to intellectual historians who study early modern "political Hebraism."[102] The Christian fascination with the Hebrew scriptures had at least two roots. First, the Protestant credo of *sola scriptura* (by scripture alone) had prompted some Christian scholars to learn Hebrew so that they could read the Old Testament in its original language. This knowledge of Hebrew then enabled them to read the Talmud and other rabbinic commentaries. Second, the (re)invention of the printing press and the Protestant emphasis on Bible reading gave lay Christians the means and the motive to read the Old Testament in the vernacular.[103] For various reasons, this motivation was particularly strong among the sorts of Reformed Protestants who later peopled New England.

Political Hebraicism intersected with civic republicanism during the Dutch revolt against Spain (1566–1648) and the English Civil War (1640–1660). Drawing on a heterodox strand of rabbinic commentary on 1 Samuel 8, Dutch and English republicans argued that monarchy was inherently "idolatrous" and that the "Hebraic constitution" was initially republican.[104] Thus, when the Israelites asked for a king, they were committing a sin, and God granted their request only as a form of punishment.

The emergence of Hebraic republicanism represented a major shift within the republican tradition. Classical and Renaissance republicans had generally not seen any inherent contradiction between monarchy and republicanism. On the contrary, they viewed monarchical institutions as desirable elements of a "mixed constitution." The British Constitution, which mixed government by "the one" (the king), "the few" (the House of Lords), and "the many" (the House of Commons), was the paradigmatic example. In contrast, Hebraic republicanism excluded monarchical institutions from republican constitutions and invoked the "Hebrew Constitution" as its political paradigm. For Hebraic republicans, "the one" could not be a king.

Hebraic republicanism all but disappeared from public discourse in England following the restoration of the monarchy and did not fully reappear until the middle years of the American Revolution. Initially, most American patriots imagined the American Revolution as a "royalist revolution."[105] In this early stage, they appealed for royal aid against parliamentary "tyranny" and invoked the British Constitution in defense of their views. Only later did they turn on the king and embrace "exclusive republicanism." And it was only then that they unearthed the Hebraic republicanism of the mid-seventeenth century.

We can follow this development across three sermons preached by Samuel Langdon (1723–1797). Langdon was a Congregationalist clergyman who served as president of Harvard (1774–1780) during the first half of the revolution. The first sermon examined here was preached in 1760, in the midst of the Seven Years' War, and was a paean of "joy and gratitude" to King George II for Britain's recent victories over the French. Langdon opened this speech by comparing George to David and Solomon. Echoing the royalist thinker Robert Filmer, he then argued that "all government originates" with God and "began in patriarchal authority," which "was gradually improved into more ample power." In the same tract, he also argued that the republic of Israel was not a model for other peoples; it was instead "peculiar to their circumstances."[106]

The second sermon was preached in 1775, shortly after the battles of Lexington and Concord. Here, he adopted the language of the "royalist revolution." The British Constitution, Langdon warned, was being undermined through "the machination of wicked men, who are betraying their Royal Master."[107] He then nodded toward exclusive republicanism, arguing that "the Jewish government" was "divinely established" as a "perfect republic,"[108] and, what is more, that the Hebrew republic "was so far from including the idea of a King, that it was a high crime" to speak of monarchy in Israel.[109] Still, Langdon did not go so far as to claim that monarchy would be inappropriate in other contexts.

The third sermon was preached in 1788 before the New Hampshire legislature as it prepared to vote on the new Constitution. Here, Langdon explicitly argued that the Hebrew constitution "may be considered as a pattern to the world in all ages."[110] He then recounted the Exodus story in terms that transparently recalled the American Revolution and characterized the Mosaic covenant as a political "constitution," complete with its own "President," "Senate," and "Courts."[111] Unfortunately, he warned, the Israelites soon lost their republic: "They neglected their government, corrupted their religion, and grew dissolute in their morals."[112] Their greatest "crime," however, was to demand a king, for "God only was their king," and the consequence was "the total loss of their republican form of government."[113] In Langdon's narrative, Israel was the ur-republic and the only perfect one in history. "It was six hundred years after Moses before the Spartans . . . received a very imperfect" constitution, he declared, and another three hundred years before Athens received her republic. The great defect of both, he said, was that "religion . . . was from the beginning interwoven with the state."[114] Unlike the Israelites, the Athenians had failed to separate religious and political authority. If anyone had not fully appreciated the parallels between the Hebrew and American republics, Langdon rendered them still more explicit by comparing the thirteen states to the twelve tribes, Washington to Moses, and the Constitution to the covenant. Throughout, Langdon deftly wove together the Mosaic covenant and civic republicanism to form a vision of Hebraic republicanism.

He was hardly the first to do so. Thomas Paine had already beaten him to the punch in 1776 with the publication of *Common Sense*, the most popular political pamphlet of the revolutionary era. Those who argue for the influence of Lockean liberalism on revolutionary ideology often include this document in their evidence. And, indeed, the first section of Paine's tract does sound more liberal than republican at times. Consider its opening claim that "society in every state is a blessing, but Government, even in its best state, is but a necessary evil."[115] In the following section, however, Paine trotted out the Hebraic argument for exclusive republicanism. "The will of the Almighty declared by Gideon, and the prophet Samuel expressly disapproves of government by Kings," Paine argued, and the government of Israel remained "a kind of Republic" until "the Jews under a national delusion requested a king."[116] Paine himself did not believe a word of this, of course, as he would later confess in a letter to John Adams. But he knew his audience, and the enormous controversy stirred up by *Common Sense* helped expose the American public to the Hebraic argument.

Where did Paine himself pick up the Hebraic argument? We do not know for certain, but it could actually have been from John Locke. Locke's *Second Treatise* is Exhibit 1 in the case for liberal influence on revolutionary ideology. Revolutionary-era writers did often speak of Locke's "book of government."[117] But it is important to remember that Locke's "book" consisted of two treatises, not one. In the *First Treatise* Locke developed a lengthy—if nowadays little-read—critique of Robert Filmer's *Patriarcha*—which had rooted monarchical authority in fatherly authority—based on a close reading of the Old Testament. And sprinkled through the *First Treatise*, we find allusions to the Hebraic argument. Locke referred to Filmer as "a man who is the great champion of absolute power, and the idol of those who worship it."[118] Later, following a lengthy discussion of the Israelites "judges," Locke noted "that of 1750 years that they were God's peculiar people, they had hereditary kingly government amongst them not one-third of the time." Of course, Locke was not advocating for republican exclusivism here. On the contrary, he was defending the Glorious Revolution that put William III on the English throne. Still, one wonders whether Locke himself had not been touched by the Hebraic argument.

Be that as it may, Lockean liberalism itself was not devoid of Hebraic influences. The purpose of the *First Treatise* was not just to critique Filmer, but also to develop the basic premise of the *Second Treatise*, namely, "natural equality" among men. And, as Jeremy Waldron has convincingly argued, Locke's argument for equality was theological rather than political.[119] Waldron summarizes Locke's argument as follows: "Humans are one another's equals . . . by virtue of their . . . capacity to form and manipulate abstract ideas, which enables a person to reason to the existence of God and to the necessity of finding out what if anything God requires of him."[120] In other words, "all men are created equal"—if not in each other's eyes, then at least in the eyes of God. If so, then "Lockean liberalism" was not a form of "radical secularism," as some scholars have claimed. Were there other sources of radical secularism in the revolutionary era?

RADICAL SECULARISM AND THE AMERICAN REVOLUTION

In chapter 1, I defined "radical secularism" as a synthesis of radical individualism and total separationism. I also distinguished three elements of radical individualism: an atomistic view of society ("there are only individuals"), a libertarian view of liberty ("absence of external restraints"), and a commonsense form of utilitarianism ("happiness equals pleasures minus pains"). The foregoing discussion makes clear that radical individualism was quite rare during the revolutionary era. Classical, Christian, and Hebraic republicans thought in terms of groups, such as classes, orders, and nations; espoused a complex understanding of freedom that included independence, self-mastery, and citizenship; and retained the classical and Christian emphasis on virtue. There were hints of radical individualism: some thought of the polity in terms of a social contract, and the idea of natural rights implied a negative definition of freedom *qua* noninterference. But these were inchoate views.

However, the case for radical secularism in the revolutionary era is normally based on the influence of total separationism, not radical individualism. Proponents of a total separationist reading of the revolutionary legacy typically argue more or less as follows. First, they claim that Jefferson and Madison were both secularists of some sort. Then, they insist that Jefferson and Madison authored the religion clauses of the American Constitution. Finally, they conclude that the religion clauses stipulate a "total separation of religion and politics." But each of these claims is debatable.

The first claim is the strongest. After all, it was Jefferson and Madison who coined the phrases that eventually came to define the American version of radical secularism: "wall of separation" (Jefferson), "line of separation" (Madison), and "total separation" (Madison).[121] Radical secularist judges unearthed these phrases during the twentieth century and used them to justify their own total separationist reading of the Constitution. But the secularists sometimes overstate their case. It is certainly true that Jefferson was a sworn enemy of religious establishments. And it is also true that he became increasingly hostile to clerical interventions in public debate, mainly as a result of the unremitting smear campaign that the Federalist clergy mounted against him in the election of 1800 and throughout his presidency. Still, Jefferson was not hostile to organized religion *per se*. On the contrary, he regularly attended religious services, not only during his years as president, when it would have been politically expedient to do so, but also in his later years at Monticello. Nor was Jefferson always opposed to religious symbolism in the public arena in general. True, as president, he did break with Washington's tradition of proclaiming national days of thanksgiving or fasting. Earlier in his career, however, he had joined with Benjamin Franklin in proposing an Exodus theme for the national seal.

The second claim is a bit weaker. It rests on the connection of a series of texts.[122] The First Amendment's religion clauses are linked to Jefferson's "Virginia Statute for Religious Freedom" (1786), which in turn is linked to Madison's "Memorial and Remonstrance Against Religious Assessments" (1785). Finally, Jefferson's "Letter to the Danbury Baptists" (1802) is used to establish that the original intention of these laws was to effect a "total separation" of church and state. But here is the problem: Jefferson did not help to draft the Bill of Rights, as he was in France at the time; and Madison was centrally involved, but only as one member of a committee who was compelled to compromise with others' views. Would Jefferson and Madison have preferred "total separation"? Perhaps. If so, they did not get it. What they got instead was something less radical and more ambiguous: the prohibition of a national religious establishment on the one hand ("no establishment") and a guarantee of individual religious freedom on the other ("free exercise").

The third claim of the total separationists is the weakest of all. Even Jefferson and Madison spoke only of a total separation of "church and state." This is not the same as a total separation of religion and politics. And even if Jefferson and Madison had intended to establish a total separation of religion and politics, there is no reason we should regard their intentions as authoritative. The words of the religion clauses, after all, are not a direct reflection of their intentions, but the result of a political compromise. Contemporary claims that the U.S. Constitution is founded on a "total separation of religion and politics" are therefore seriously overstated.

Critics of the radical secularist interpretation have generally argued as follows.[123] First, they note that neither the First Amendment, nor the "Virginia Statute," nor the "Memorial and Remonstrance" contain the word "separation," much less the phrase "separation of church and state." By forbidding Congress from enacting any "laws concerning a religious establishment," the Constitution devolved church/state questions to the state governments. Second, the critics note that neither the First Amendment nor the "Virginia Statute" was authored solely by Madison or Jefferson. Both were collectively authored compromise formulations. Last, they note that Jefferson's "Letter to the Danbury Baptists" was a public document written in the context of a vigorously contested electoral campaign.[124]

In my view, the critics have the better argument. The religion clauses of the U.S. Constitution did not dictate a "total separation" of religion and politics, nor did they place government on a "wholly secular" basis.

What they did was far more modest. They forbade Congress from creating a national church—*and* from abolishing established churches in the states. And they forbade Congress—but *not* the states—from passing laws that would abridge individual liberty of conscience. They effected an institutional separation of church and state that applied to the federal government, but not the individual states. It is therefore mistaken to claim that radical secularism was the *dominant* tradition of the revolutionary era, much less *the* founding tradition of the United States. One could surely still argue that the steady increase of religious pluralism in American society has necessitated a sharper separation of church and state. Few, if any, Americans would want to bring back state-level religious establishments today. But that is a political rather than a historical argument.

The American historian Harry Stout rightly concludes that the "differences that would divide 'secular humanists' and 'evangelicals' in the late nineteenth century were . . . still more potential than real" in the early republic.[125] This is not to deny that there were differences. Jefferson's views were certainly not the same as Timothy Dwight's. But that does not make Jefferson a radical secularist *avant la lettre*. Modern-day radical secularists searching for a revolutionary-era hero will have to look to more radical—and more marginal—figures such as Thomas Paine or Ethan Allen.

CONCLUSION

There is a striking degree of continuity between the godly republicanism of the Puritans and the Hebraic republicanism of the revolution. In many ways, the latter is just a deeper version of the former. To the typological interpretation of the covenant narrative, the revolutionaries added the exclusive republicanism of the Talmudic scholars. To the thin republicanism of the Puritans, they added a fuller engagement with the republican tradition developed in the classical, Renaissance, and early modern periods. So there was growth as well as continuity.

Of course, there were also important differences between the Puritan and revolutionary versions of the civil religion. In part, these grew out of the incorporation of liberal ideas and values. The republican idea of fixed social orders was tempered with a liberal emphasis on natural human equality. Adams and Jefferson sought to reconcile these ideas in their vision of a "natural aristocracy" in which all were afforded the same chances but some rose to the top through talent and effort. To be sure, this natural aristocracy was only open to white men. Others were still considered "naturally" unfit to join it. The republican idea of individual independence based on landed property was buttressed by the liberal idea of constitutionally guaranteed individual rights. There was an incorporation of new ideas, not just a development of old ones.

Hebraic republicanism was the dominant ideology of the American Revolution. The Revolutionary War did spark some isolated bursts of religious nationalism, but they never grew into a major conflagration. Perhaps this was because a crucial catalyst was in short supply: premillennial apocalypticism. Civil millennialism was richly present, of course, but it was not volatile enough to sustain the nationalistic flames. Nor was radical secularism very widespread. The U.S. Constitution did bring about a greater separation of church and state, much like that envisioned by Roger Williams a century earlier. But the religion clauses of the First Amendment did not effect the total separation of religion and politics that radical secularists would begin calling for a century later.

Of course, religious nationalists and radical secularists are not the only people who invoke the revolution and the Constitution in defense of their views nowadays; nor are they the only ones who misunderstand the republican legacy. Lately they have been joined by a vocal band of libertarians, who espouse an equally untenable interpretation of the nation's founding. Hoisting their pocket Constitutions into the air like the pocket Bibles of yore, they claim that the revolution was fought for liberty, and for liberty alone. They are right that the revolution was about liberty, but they forget the Declaration, which reminds us that it was also fought for equality. Worse, they are deeply mistaken about the meaning of revolutionary liberty. The republican liberty of the founders was not the "leave me the hell alone" liberty of Ayn Rand; it was instead a complex liberty of independence, self-mastery, and citizenship. The libertarians denounce the "culture of dependency" that has taken hold in the United States. They are right about the culture, but they are wrong about its source. The main source is not the welfare state, but a corporate economy in which the many are subjected to the arbitrary will of the few and to all manner of demagoguery and manipulation. They are, above all, wrong about the very aim of the American project, which was not private pleasure and consumption, but "public happiness" and the "general welfare."

CHAPTER 4

Democratic Republicanism

THE CIVIL WAR

ONE OF THE OLDEST debates in Christian theology concerns the relationship between the Old and New Testaments, between the Hebrew Bible and the Christian *evangelium*. In some respects, it is easy enough to show continuity and consistency between the two sets of books. For example, certain Jewish prophecies are commonly interpreted as prefiguring Jesus's life. In other regards, however, there is considerable tension and discontinuity. The legalism of Leviticus ("the law says . . .") sits uneasily with the antinomianism of Jesus ("but I say unto you . . ."). There is a very long—if increasingly disputed—tradition of reading the Old Testament through the New.

There is a similar debate about the civil theology in antebellum America concerning the relationship between the nation's Old and New Testaments: the Declaration of Independence and the American Constitution. Here, too, it is easy enough to find elements of continuity and consistency. For example, both documents evince a marked distrust of centralized power and a strong desire to protect personal liberties. In this sense, the Bill of Rights simply gives institutional form to the political principles of the Declaration.

Or does it? After all, the Declaration pronounces that "all men are created equal," while the Constitution pronounces a black, male slave to be only three-fifths of a man. Both documents are riven by another tension as well: although both open in the name of the American people in the singular form, they speak elsewhere in the name of the United States in the plural form. According to these political scriptures, Americans are both equal and unequal, both one and many.

The political theologians of the early republic had little trouble squaring these circles. They mostly agreed that a black man was not fully a man, just as they mostly agreed that the sovereignty of the individual states trumped that of the federal government. But by 1830 this consensus was unraveling. An ongoing dispute over tariffs led some Southern leaders, such as John C. Calhoun, to declare that the individual states had the right to ignore or even nullify federal legislation that was not to their liking. And the emerging conflict over chattel slavery led some Northern intellectuals, such as Frederick Douglass, to declare the U.S. Constitution a pact with the devil. By the time Abraham Lincoln was elected president, these two disputes had become so intertwined and intractable that most Southerners viewed the outcome of the election as a declaration of war.

The Union would eventually prevail and, with it, Douglass's and Lincoln's democratic republican reinterpretation of the civil religious tradition, though Calhoun's arguments about "states' rights" would live on through Jim Crow and the civil rights movement right up to the present day. (The Pauls, *père et fils*, have recently dressed them up in libertarian garb.) American religious nationalism was also strengthened by the Civil War and then transformed by Reconstruction into a WASP religious nationalism centered in the Old Confederacy. Too, the postbellum decades witnessed the crystallization of a full-blown version of radical secularism that combined libertarianism, social Darwinism, scientism, and "agnosticism" in varying measures. The emergence of this third tradition would fundamentally and lastingly transform the dynamics of American politics, setting the stage for the political polarization and culture wars of the present era.

JOHN C. CALHOUN

At the time of his death in 1850, John C. Calhoun was one of the most influential political and intellectual figures in antebellum America. That same year, Abraham Lincoln had just returned to the law after serving a single term in the U.S. House of Representatives, and Fredrick Douglass was still the publisher of a small abolitionist newspaper. Calhoun, by contrast, had already spent a full four decades in Washington: four terms in the House, eight years as Monroe's secretary of war, another eight as Jackson's vice president, and three terms as a senator from his home state of South Carolina. He was regarded as one of the most powerful speakers and formidable intellects in the United States.[1] And he was something of a constitutional scholar and political philosopher as well.

Intellectual historians of the mid-twentieth century offered wildly diverging characterizations of Calhoun's politics. Louis Hartz described Calhoun as the *philosophe* of the "Reactionary Enlightenment."[2] Richard Hofstadter dubbed him the "Marx of the master class."[3] Russell Kirk derided him as a halfhearted follower of Edmund Burke.[4]

Calhoun's thinking was highly complex, and there is some truth to each of these interpretations. His efforts to alloy democratic self-government with a hierarchically ordered society can be read as an uneasy amalgam of republican and reactionary ideologies. And his political animus toward the "free labor" system of the North did lead to some piercing prognostications about the growth of social inequality and concentration of industrial wealth that would soon follow. Kirk, too, is right that Calhoun's fear of anarchy and distaste for democracy made him a reluctant revolutionary at best.

But recent interpreters have proposed a different reading: Calhoun *qua* civic republican.[5] Calhoun's writings are replete with republican themes of virtue and corruption, and balance and faction, as well as with classical references to the historical experiences of ancient republics such as Sparta and Rome. There was also a Christian, or at least deist, strand in Calhoun's worldview. He believed strongly in the Providential role of the United States in human affairs. Calhoun's thought can therefore be read as an alternative version of the civil religion, a heretical one that combined reactionary republicanism with pessimistic Providentialism.

This is not the outcome one might have anticipated at the outset of Calhoun's career. As a young man, Calhoun was a Jeffersonian Democrat,[6] and, during his first two decades in Washington, an ardent nationalist. Following the War of 1812, Calhoun proudly proclaimed that "we see everywhere a nationality of feeling. . . . We hear sentiments from every part of the House in favor of Union and against sectional spirit."[7] As Monroe's secretary of war, Calhoun embraced an expansive view of federal powers, advocating the creation of a standing army—a heretical stance in his day—supporting a tariff to fund it, and justifying both measures by invoking the "general welfare clause."

But Calhoun's loyalties underwent a radical transformation during the final two decades of his life. His youthful nationalism gave way to a passionate sectionalism, and his admiration for Jefferson cooled to the point of hostility. At first, Calhoun defended the interests of the South with a Jeffersonian reading of the Constitution: "The General Government emanated from the people of the several States, forming distinct political communities, and acting in their separate and sovereign capacity, and not from all of the people forming one aggregate political community."[8] The United States, in other words, were plural, rather than singular. By the time of his death, however, Calhoun's thinking was fully post-Jeffersonian. This shift was visible in the two major political treatises he composed during the final years of his life. One, "The Disquisition on Government," was a general work of political philosophy. It was intended as an introduction to the second, "A Discourse on the Constitution and Government of the United States."

In the "Disquisition," Calhoun argued that human nature is inherently social and that human flourishing is only possible in society. But, he added, human beings are inherently selfish as well, and that selfishness trumps sociability.[9] One purpose of government is therefore to restrain human rapacity and ensure individuals' physical security. Another is to protect individual liberty and encourage collective progress. Of these two goods, Calhoun argued, security is the more important, because "the existence of the race is of greater moment than its improvement."[10]

Calhoun also modified the classical theory of constitutional balance. He agreed that "power can only be restrained by power—and tendency by tendency."[11] But he also argued that there is a natural tendency for state power to become more and more centralized, and for party coalitions to coalesce in pursuit of electoral majorities. The end result, he contended, is a majority party that uses federal power to tyrannize the minority.

His remedy? The power of the "numerical majority" must be contained through a system of "concurrent majority." Such a system would involve "taking the sense of each interest or portion of the community . . . separately, through its own majority . . . and . . . requir[ing] the consent of each interest, either to put or to keep the government in action."[12] In other words, each "section" would have veto powers over any federal legislation.

Calhoun paid lip service to equality but defined it in the narrowest of terms. Citizens are equal before the law, he said. But they are not equal in any other sense, and any effort to make them so is politically and economically dangerous: politically because some individuals and communities are simply not fit for liberty; economically because inequality breeds competition, and competition brings progress.

While the "Disquisition" set out Calhoun's first principles, the "Discourse" diagnosed the nation's ills. Its constitution was out of balance, he said, perhaps fatally so. The founders had intended to establish a "democratic" and "federal republic": "democratic" in the sense that "classes, orders and all artificial distinctions" are excluded, and "federal" in the sense of a "league" between the states in their role as "free," "independent," and "sovereign" "communities."[13] His evidence? Those passages of the founding documents that conjugated "United States" in the plural.

But what of the preambles, which speak of the United States as a single "people," as in "We, the People"? Or the phrase "of America"? Or the motto, *E pluribus unum*? Calhoun's response was that the English language does not permit a plural form of "people," that the phrase "of

America" was a rhetorical flourish,[14] and that the national motto obtains only in foreign affairs. The "United States" were a plural construct.[15]

But this arrangement had become imperiled in the decades since the founding, he believed. Constitutional limits on federal power had to be restored. The Supreme Court should be stripped of its powers of judicial review, the presidency of its control over patronage, and the Congress of much of its financial power. As well, the constitutional balance between North and South had to be restored by opening the territories to slavery and establishing a dual executive—one president from the North, another from the South. Without these reforms to the nation's founding documents, Calhoun warned, the only alternatives were monarchy or disunion.

As for the Declaration, it was in need of redaction. The phrase "all men are created equal," Calhoun argued, was a blatant falsehood "inserted . . . without any necessity."[16] Adam and Eve excepted, human beings are born, not created. Moreover, they are born dependent, not free: dependent on family, community, and society.

Calhoun himself made little effort to justify slavery. Perhaps he didn't feel the need.[17] But others worked to reconcile slaveholding with republicanism and Christianity. Their task was not difficult.[18] In the ancient world, slavery and republicanism were of a piece. Athens, Sparta, and Rome were all slave states, and classical republicans from Plato to Cicero saw slavery as a natural consequence of human inequality.[19] Pro-slavery thinkers in the South built on the classical legacy, arguing that the labor of the slave underwrote the leisure of the master, freeing him to engage in politics and other higher pursuits; that the management of slaves was a higher calling of sorts that required self-mastery on the part of the slaveholder, providing a solid foundation for civic virtue; and that slavery benefited nonslaveholding Southerners as well, insofar as it freed all white men from onerous forms of labor, thereby ensuring a fundamental social equality and civic solidarity between them.[20] These apologists also critiqued the Northern free-labor system for its striving, materialism, and intraracial inequalities, which they believed inimical to republican virtue.[21]

It was easy to defend slavery in Christian terms, too.[22] The proof texts were ready to hand[23]: the ancient Israelites were permitted to take slaves as spoils of war; Jesus did not criticize slavery in the Gospels; and Paul sanctioned it in the epistles to Philemon and the Corinthians. Southern Christians conceded that certain evils attended the "peculiar institution." But was this not true of all human institutions?

ABRAHAM LINCOLN

Lincoln's early political views were remarkably similar to Calhoun's. The young Lincoln agreed that "the Congress of the United States has no power, under the constitution, to interfere with the institution of slavery in the different States."[24] As late as 1845, Lincoln would insist that it was "a paramount duty of us in the free states . . . to let the slavery of the other states alone."[25] In this, he was simply adhering to the general consensus of the era on the limits of federal power, a consensus that encompassed Whigs as well as Democrats, nullificationists, and even many abolitionists.[26]

Lincoln's interpretation of the Declaration was similar to his reading of the Constitution. For Congressman Lincoln, the "spirit of '76" was first and foremost the right of revolution. In 1847, in the midst of the Mexican-American War, Lincoln argued that "any people anywhere, being inclined and having the power, have the *right* to rise up, and shake off the existing government, and form a new one that suits them better."[27] Was this not a writ for secession? Not until Fort Sumter would Lincoln rethink this argument.

On questions of race, too, Lincoln's early opinions were well within the mainstream. In his pre–Civil War public pronouncements, Lincoln rejected the notion that blacks and whites could ever be "political and social" equals on the grounds that "there is a physical difference between the two" races.[28] Nor was this just political pandering. In private conversation, Lincoln is known to have told racist jokes and used the "n-word."[29]

The similarities between Lincoln and Calhoun extended to more fundamental questions of political philosophy and theology as well. Both men embraced core tenets of civic republicanism. Like Calhoun, Lincoln believed that human freedom requires self-mastery.[30] Also like Calhoun, Lincoln retained a strong belief in divine Providence, in a "Living God" who intervened in human history, albeit in ways that often eluded human reason.

And yet, from the outset, there were also real if subtle differences between the two men, as between the sections and parties they represented. First and foremost, there was the matter of slavery. Lincoln's parents had rejected it, and Lincoln himself learned to abhor it at an early age.[31] There were also differences in political philosophy. Calhoun tended to see differences in property and power as reflective of natural differences of ability—and, by extension, of race. Republican government required the proper organization of these differences. The freedom of the white planter derived from the labor of the black slave and the subordination of propertyless whites. By contrast, Lincoln's civic republicanism was inflected by a liberal individualism that gave considerable weight to hard work. In good Lockean fashion, Lincoln grounded private property in "free labor," a view that probably accorded well with his own experience of social mobility through hard work. For him, wage labor was just a brief stopover on the path toward propertied independence. The slave system completely inverted this schema: it made property (in persons) the source of (forced) labor.

The two men also differed in their attitudes toward federal power. The ardent nationalism of the youthful Calhoun had derived from the imperatives of military defense. Lincoln, however, viewed the federal government as a potential agent of socioeconomic amelioration. He supported public funding for primary schooling and economic infrastructure as a means of promoting social equality and material prosperity and—eventually, if tentatively—of promoting racial equality and social reconstruction as well.

There was, too, a small but crucial difference in the two men's understandings of divine Providence: whereas Calhoun's stance was essentially fatalistic, Lincoln inclined toward a more covenantal view. In the 1850s, Lincoln had warned Americans that God might punish the United States for holding slaves, just as he had done to ancient Egypt.[32] In his Second Inaugural Address (1865), he would set forth a harsh moral arithmetic that required that "all the wealth piled by the bond-man's two hundred and fifty years of unrequited toil . . . be sunk" and "every drop of blood drawn with the lash . . . be paid by another drawn with the sword"[33] in order to settle America's moral accounts.

At the same time, Lincoln also understood the American experiment in republican government in missionary terms, as a "germ which . . . is still to grow and expand into the universal liberty of mankind."[34] In one of his earliest speeches, he even went so far as to propose the establishment of an American "political religion" founded upon the Declaration and the Constitution, "taught in schools, in seminaries, and in colleges," and written in "Primers, spelling books, and in almanacs."[35]

In the final decade of his life, Lincoln's views diverged more and more sharply from Calhoun's. The first turning point for Lincoln was the Kansas-Nebraska Act of 1854, which allowed the establishment of new slave states. At home in Springfield, Lincoln reflected deeply on these events, spending weeks holed up in the state library consulting "the founders' statements about slavery [and] previous congressional debates" on the subject.[36] His conclusion: while the framers had agreed to "tolerate" slavery in order to secure the ratification of the Constitution, they were opposed to its extension and wished for its eventual extinction. He first voiced these objections publicly in 1854, when he argued that the framers "forbore to so much as mention the word 'slave' or 'slavery,'" preferring instead to hide it away, "just as an afflicted man hides away a wen or a cancer, which he dares not cut at once, lest he bleed to death."[37] Slavery, Lincoln continued, was contrary to "the plain unmistakable spirit of that age," which "began by declaring that all men are created equal."[38] Moreover, by insisting that "there is no right principle of action but *self-interest*," contemporary advocates of slavery were threatening the self-sacrificing civic-mindedness that sustains republican government; more than that, they were depriving "our republican example of its just influence in the world."[39] The only remedy for these ills was a return to first principles. "Our republican robe is soiled, and trailed in the dust," Lincoln declared. "Let us repurify it. . . . Let us turn slavery from its claims of 'moral right.' . . . Let us return it to the position our fathers gave it. . . . Let us re-adopt the Declaration of Independence."[40]

Subsequent pronouncements would make clear how narrowly Lincoln still understood the Declaration's promise and the Constitution's terms. Reacting to the *Dred Scott* decision in 1857, Lincoln argued that the authors of the Declaration "intended to include *all* men, but they did not intend to declare all men equal *in all respects*."[41] At this time, he was still not prepared to grant African Americans anything more than the "inalienable rights" to the fruits of their own labor. And yet, there were already hints that Lincoln hoped and aspired to something more. Near the close of his *Dred Scott* speech, Lincoln added that the principal of equality was intended as a "standard maxim for free society . . . constantly looked to, constantly labored for, and even though never perfectly attained, constantly approximated, and thereby constantly spreading and deepening its influence . . . [for] all people of all colors everywhere."[42]

Another major turning point in Lincoln's thinking occurred in 1860, the year of his presidential campaign and of Southern secession. Lincoln responded to these events as he had in 1854: by returning to the founding documents and debates. He presented his conclusions in his First Inaugural Address, which argued, *pace* Calhoun, that the creation of the American nation antedated the ratification of the U.S. Constitution:

> The Union is much older than the Constitution. It was formed, in fact, by the Articles of Association in 1774. It was matured and continued by the Declaration of Independence in 1776. It was further matured, and the faith of all the then thirteen States expressly plighted and engaged that it should be perpetual, by the Articles of Confederation in 1778. And finally, in 1787, one of the declared objects for ordaining and establishing the Constitution was *"to form a more perfect union."* . . . It follows from these views that no State, upon own mere motion, can lawfully get out of the Union.[43]

The Union, in his view, was "perpetual." In short, Lincoln explicitly and forcefully rejected the "compact" theory invented by Calhoun and invoked by Confederate leaders.[44]

As the Civil War progressed, Lincoln would use the word "nation" with increasing frequency. In his 1862 "Message to Congress," he described the American people as "one national family" and the American territory as "our national homestead."[45] A year later, at Gettysburg, he would famously describe the United States as "a new nation, conceived in Liberty, and dedicated to the proposition that all men are created equal."[46] Lincoln's language mirrored a broader shift in Northern sentiment toward a more nationalist understanding of the United States.[47]

At times, Lincoln's nationalism could veer perilously close to religious nationalism. In the Gettysburg Address, for example, Lincoln described the battlefield as "hallowed" ground, "consecrated" by those who gave "the last full measure of devotion."[48] Still, he never used the word "blood." And when he did, as in the Second Inaugural Address, the blood was exacted as a punishment, not given as a sacrifice. Nor did Lincoln imagine that he or his allies were righteous instruments of divine justice in a cosmic struggle between good and evil, as religious nationalists so often do.[49] He came to see the Civil War as a form of divine-punishment-cum-Providential–lesson, in which both North and South were being punished for their complicity in slavery and shown "that there has been a difference of purpose between the Almighty and them."[50] While the South imagined it was fighting for liberty and the North for union, Lincoln concluded that the true purpose of the war had been to abolish the "peculiar institution" and chastise an "almost chosen people." *Almost* chosen, because it had grown arrogant in its material success and self-righteous about the political example it was setting.[51]

Lincoln's revised version of the American civil religion differed sharply from Calhoun's heretical one. In Calhoun's civil theology, the spirit was governed by the letter, and the Old Testament was erased by the New. The singular terms of the preambles—"one people" and "We, the People"—were subordinated to the plural terms of the articles—"The United States are . . ." Similarly, the Declaration's proposition that "all men are created equal" was understood to be superseded by the Constitution's three-fifths clause. Nor to Calhoun were these documents perpetual covenants; rather, they were limited contracts that could be terminated by their signatories at any time. In Lincoln's reading, in contrast, the letter was governed by the spirit, and the realization of that spirit would require time. The nationally focused singulars of the two preambles governed the plurals that followed. And the Declaration's promise of equality was not superseded by the Constitution's compromise with slavery. The fact that the covenant had been broken did not mean that it could not be mended. Lincoln's civil theology presumed that the meanings of American scripture were imperfectly understood by a fallen people and would only gradually be revealed through fearsome lessons imparted by an angry God.

FREDERICK DOUGLASS

In 1832, when John Calhoun was beginning his first year as a U.S. senator from South Carolina, the young Frederick Douglass (1818?–1895) was still enslaved on a Maryland plantation. Having surreptitiously taught himself to read, he had organized a clandestine church, in which he lectured his fellow slaves on the New Testament. For this, his master, Thomas Auld, turned him over to a notorious slave-breaker, who beat Douglass savagely until the young man finally resisted, besting him in a physical confrontation. Douglass attempted to flee several times during these years. He finally succeeded in 1838, with the aid of his future wife, Anna Murray, a free black woman who lived in Baltimore. After their marriage, Murray and Douglass moved north to Massachusetts. There, they were soon drawn into the orbit of the radical abolitionist William Lloyd Garrison. A gifted orator—perhaps the most brilliant of his generation—Douglass lectured widely before abolitionist audiences, recounting the brutalization of slavery and serving as a living testimony to the intellectual capacities of black Americans. In 1845, he published his *Narrative of the Life of Frederick Douglass, a Slave*, the first of three memoirs. Over the next five decades, Douglass worked tirelessly not only for the abolition of slavery and the equality of freedmen, but also for women's rights and the temperance movement.

During the first decade of his freedom, Douglass's views hewed closely to Garrison's. Both men expressed great admiration for the Declaration's affirmation of human equality but roundly condemned the U.S. Constitution as a "covenant with death and an agreement with hell" for its tacit recognition of black slavery. Douglass, however, did not share Garrison's patriotism. "I have not, cannot have, any love for this country, as such," he proclaimed in 1847. "I desire to see its [America's] overthrow as speedily as possible, and its Constitution shivered in a thousand fragments, rather than this foul curse [of slavery] should continue."[52] The framers he regarded as "little better than a band of pirates."[53]

Douglass's views began to change during the late 1840s, partly as a result of his own studies and reflections, and partly as a result of the influence of Gerrit Smith and other like-minded abolitionists, who argued that the Constitution was actually an antislavery document. They read the Constitution through its preamble, with its promises to "promote the General Welfare" and "secure the Blessings of Liberty."[54] In 1851, Douglass publicly announced a "change of opinion": "Interpreted as it ought to be interpreted, the Constitution is a glorious liberty document," he declared. "Read its preamble, consider its purposes. Is slavery among them? Is it at the gateway? Or is it in the temple? It is neither."[55]

If Douglass's views converged with Lincoln's—and diverged from Calhoun's—on this point, they arrived at their destination by rather different routes. For Lincoln, the New Testament of the Constitution had to be read through the Old Testament of the Declaration. This led to a rather minimalistic vision of racial equality *qua* natural equality in civil society—an equality that did not extend to political rights or social relations. For Douglass, however, the New Testament superseded the Old and stood on its own. This led to a more expansive understanding of racial equality *qua* human equality that extended to women as well as to blacks.[56]

This positive revaluation of the founding documents went together with a positive revaluation of national belonging. Just months after announcing his "change of opinion," in 1851, Douglass pronounced that "the free negro's place is in America." "Simultaneously with the landing of the Pilgrims," he pointed out, "there landed slaves on the shores of this continent. . . . We came here when it was a wilderness. . . . *We* leveled your forests; *our hands* removed the stumps from your fields. . . . We have been with you . . . in adversity, and by the help of God will be with you in prosperity."[57] "Why should we not stay here?" he asked. In this way, Douglass insisted upon African Americans' place in the nation's founding.

Douglass had nothing but contempt for Calhoun.[58] And although he did agree with Calhoun on one point—that dependency undermined character[59]—he disagreed about the cause of dependency, maintaining that it was social, not racial.[60] Recalling his sojourn in Ireland at the time of the Great Famine, he argued that the "common people" of Ireland "lacked only a black skin and wooly hair to complete their likeness to the plantation Negro," so similar were they in their physical bearing, "vacant expression," and "petty quarrels."[61] Douglass contended that slavery was degrading to the master as well.[62] Why? Because suppressing the humanity of the slave required suppressing the humanity of the master: "The first work of slavery is . . . to destroy all sense of high moral and religious responsibility."[63] Slaveholding is so morally corrupting, he concluded, "that a slaveholder cannot be a good citizen of a free republic."[64] Too, he saw the institution as socially corrupting: "Slavery, like all other gross and powerful forms of wrong which appeal directly to human pride and selfishness . . . has the ability and the tendency to get a character in the whole network of society surrounding it."[65] In his view, slavery tends to undermine all forms of human liberty, not only free labor, but freedom of speech and the press as well. Douglass stood the classical argument of proslavery republicans on its head: far from encouraging self-mastery and underwriting free institutions, he said, slavery turns masters into brutes, and subordinates political freedom to material self-interest. And once corrupted, a republic cannot persist. "The lesson taught by history is that the preservation or destruction of communities does not depend upon external prosperity," he declared. "They are saved not by art, but by honesty. Not by the gilded splendors of wealth, but by the hidden treasure of manly virtue."[66]

Where Calhoun and Lincoln were more apt to speak the language of civic republicanism than that of covenant theology, the reverse was true of Douglass. At times, Douglass could sound more like Jeremiah than Cicero. He denounced slavery as a "sin," and not just an individual sin that would be punished in the next world, but also a "national sin" that would provoke divine wrath in this world as well. Following the Hebrew prophets, and anticipating liberation theology, he argued that the biblical God is first and foremost a "God of the oppressed."[67] He excoriated America's churches for preaching "a religion which favors the rich against the poor; which exalts the proud above the humble; which divides mankind into two classes, tyrants and slaves; which says to the man in chains, *stay there*; and to the oppressor, *oppress on*."[68] He spoke of a coming "judgment day of slavery" and warned that "prouder and stronger governments than [America's] have been shattered by the bolts of the wrath of a *just God*."[69]

And yet, Douglass's jeremiad was a "progressive jeremiad" rather than a classical one. It called the nation *forward* to a millennial future, rather than back to a golden age. He envisioned a "grand movement" for slavery's "overthrow" that "under God" would attain an unstoppable momentum.[70] American abolitionism he viewed as part of an ongoing "conflict between liberty and slavery" that was "the same in all countries, in all ages and among all peoples,"[71] a conflict that would eventually "release every slave and prepare the earth for a millennium of righteousness and peace."[72] What was the motor behind this movement? The "great law of progress written out by the hand of God on the human soul."[73]

Over time, Douglass's millennial optimism was increasingly tempered with a hard-nosed realism. The *Dred Scott* decision marked a major turning point in his political assessment. It convinced him that the "peaceful annihilation" of slavery was "almost hopeless" and that "the slave's right to revolt is almost perfect."[74] While some abolitionists, such as William Lloyd Garrison, preferred peaceful secession to civil war, Douglass concluded that the Civil War was an "Abolition War" and supported it tirelessly.[75] For Douglass, the road to the millennium was not always a peaceful one.

The closing decades of the antebellum era witnessed a slowly deepening crisis of the American civil religion. Who were "the People"? And in what sense are "all men created equal"? In their efforts to defend slavery, Southern thinkers like John Calhoun drifted toward a heretical version of the civil religion that denied the existence of an American nation and struck human equality from the founding covenant. For them, the "United States" was a plural construct, a compact between "free and independent states." The states themselves were hierarchical societies, premised on "natural" inequalities of race, ability, and property. Calhoun and his allies sought to locate this vision within the civil religious tradition by appealing to Old Testament examples and the slave republics of antiquity. But their civil theology was clearly heretical insofar as it appealed to legalistic texts instead of prophetic principles—to Leviticus rather than Jeremiah—and also insofar as it abjured the founders' vision of basic human equality.

Meanwhile, leading abolitionists and Republicans such as Douglass and Lincoln were actively recovering and reformulating the civil religious tradition. Their new civil theology was premised on a new reading of scripture in which the bodies of the founding documents were governed

by the principles of their preambles. "The People" were the American people, not the people of the states, and the principle of equality trumped
the provisions permitting slavery. Political calculation and lingering racism prevented Lincoln and other Republicans from embracing the consequences of these principles as quickly as they might have; here, radical abolitionists such as Douglass were clearly to the fore. But by war's
end, the radical faction of the Republican Party and many of its Northern
supporters were prepared to defend full equality for the freedmen and
freedwomen—and not just a Lockean right to the fruits of their labor,
but a civic and political equality as well. The Civil Rights Act of 1866 and
the Thirteenth, Fourteenth, and Fifteenth Amendments were the institutional realization of this shift. It comes as no surprise that modern-day
libertarians and religious nationalists now argue for their repeal.

The new version of the civil religion broke with the classical tradition
in two ways. First, it introduced a new understanding of political time.
In classical republicanism, political time was conceptualized in cyclical
terms. By contrast, Lincoln and Douglass *transformed the revival cycle
into a progressive spiral*: the point was not to return to the eternal social
order of a bygone golden age, nor even to recover the original meaning of the founding principles; rather, it was to more fully realize the
moral meaning of those principles, even when that meant abandoning
established interpretations. Second, the new version of the civil religion
broke once and for all with the inegalitarian legacy of classical republicanism. Lincoln and Douglass argued that republican liberty could be
rebuilt on a "free labor" foundation. And there was considerable merit
to this argument at a time when smallholding farmers and independent
artisans were widespread and wage labor was often a stepping-stone to
economic independence. But despite this merit, it was in this area that
Lincoln's and Douglass's political vision was to prove shortsighted. In the
decades that followed, the closing of the frontier and the expansion of
industrial capitalism would transform wage labor from a phase of life to
a way of life, leading progressive and populist thinkers to return anew to
the questions of federal power and civic equality. But that is the subject
of the next chapter.

RELIGIOUS NATIONALISM COMES OF AGE

While the debate over slavery sparked a major rethinking of the civil
religion, the debate over Reconstruction led to a sharper articulation
of its two rivals: religious nationalism and radical secularism. These

viewpoints first emerged in full force in the mid-1840s. Between 1845 and 1848, the United States "annexed" the Republic of Texas, signed the Oregon Treaty with Great Britain, conquered California and New Mexico, and drove the Native Americans out of the Great Lakes region. The concomitant incorporation into the nation of these regions' large non-"Anglo-Saxon" populations greatly increased the salience of "racial" divisions in public discourse and popular consciousness.[76] The first wave of mass immigration from Europe heightened their salience even further. Between 1846 and 1850, the eastern ports were accepting 250,000 new arrivals each year, many of them Catholics from Ireland and Germany. While the Germans could be reckoned to the "Saxons," the Mexicans and the Irish were often lumped together with slaves as "black."[77] The basic elements of American religious nationalism were now assembled: empire, race, ethnicity, and religion. In this vision, the true America was white, Anglo-Saxon, and Protestant and destined to rule the world.

Secession and the Civil War disrupted the development of WASP religious nationalism by splitting the "white Anglo-Saxons" into two rival "nations." "The present conflict is not a *civil* strife, but a war of *Nationalities* . . . a war of alien races,"[78] claimed one Southern writer. The Confederates are an inferior "race" in need of more civilization, countered some Northerners. These "national" divisions were deepened by religious ones. Almost all of the Protestant denominations split along sectional lines. The ruptures were theological, too.[79] Southern clergymen moved during this period toward a more literalistic and fatalistic theology, which appealed to biblical examples of slavery and emphasized human sinfulness, while Northern clergymen moved toward a more contextual and optimistic theology, which appealed to biblical principles of equality and emphasized moral progress.[80] The quarrel between "fundamentalists" and "modernists" was already taking shape.

Northern and Southern Christians also tried to one-up each other politically. Conservative Christians had long complained about America's "Godless Constitution."[81] They argued that the absence of any reference to the Creator was unbefitting of a "Christian nation."[82] The preamble to the Confederate Constitution aimed to remedy this situation by "invoking the favor and guidance of Almighty God." In the North, the newly established National Reform Association proposed that the preamble to the U.S. Constitution be revised to read[83]: "We, the people of the United States, humbly acknowledging Almighty God as the source of all authority and power in civil government, the Lord Jesus Christ as the Ruler among the nations, his revealed will as the supreme law of the land, in order to constitute a Christian government, and in order to form a more perfect union."[84] Some members of the group went even further, pressing for "presidential proclamations and oaths of office that would recognize Jesus Christ" and even for religious tests for political office.[85] Their efforts not only failed but backfired, sparking the crystallization of an American version of radical secularism, as have similar efforts by modern-day Christian nationalists.

The Confederacy also outdid the Union on the ritual front. Confederate president Jefferson Davis declared nine official "Fast and Thanksgiving Days," and Southern state legislatures proclaimed dozens more.[86] Lincoln followed suit by nationalizing the traditional New England Thanksgiving celebration.[87] This was all well within the bounds of the civil religious tradition. But rites for the fallen sometimes devolved into religious nationalism.[88] On both sides of the Mason-Dixon line, battle deaths were constantly celebrated as a form of "blood sacrifice." Battlefields were declared "consecrated" by the blood of the fallen. Blood was seen as having transformed battle relics into sacred objects suitable for public veneration. Fallen soldiers were described as "blood martyrs." Fallen commanders, like Stonewall Jackson, were celebrated as "holy warriors," possessed of supernatural powers and worthy of quasi-religious devotion.

Public rhetoric took an apocalyptic turn as well. Preachers, poets, and politicians portrayed the war as a cosmic struggle between the forces of good and evil, invoking typologies from the books of Daniel and Revelation.[89] The first stanza of the Battle Hymn of the Republic, for example, is rife with apocalyptic imagery—the "coming of the Lord," "the grapes of wrath," "a terrible swift sword"—and might just as easily have served as a battle hymn for the Confederacy.

The new civil religion of democratic republicanism set the tone during the Reconstruction era. Radical Republicans and their followers embraced an egalitarian form of civic nationalism that included non-whites—and excluded unrepentant rebels.[90] In this vision, citizenship flowed from political values rather than skin color. Northern reformers and educators flooded the South, where they worked with the Freedmen's Bureau to provide "uplift" for newly emancipated blacks.[91] They were on a civil religious mission.

But few Southern whites felt the appeal of this mission. Most embraced an updated version of Southern religious nationalism instead: the mythology of the "Lost Cause."[92] This view contained both old and new elements. The emphasis on "states' rights" and the fascination with

ancient Greece were old, as were claims of Southern chosenness and vic-
timhood and the invidious contrasts drawn between a pious Dixieland
and a "heretical" North overrun with "Transcendentalists," "Spiritualists,"
and "Deists." But there were some new elements. One was an appeal to
the chivalry and valor of the Angles and the Saxons, from King Arthur to
Oliver Cromwell. Another was the comparison of the defeated Confederacy with a crucified Christ. Both were seen as having been slain by a brutal pagan empire; both were believed to be destined to rise again.[93] The
heroes and martyrs of the Confederacy—Lee, Jackson, and Davis—were
portrayed not only as Old Testament warriors, but also as Christ figures.
Of course, Christ's pacifism posed a problem for Christian nationalism.
But this difficulty was overcome by appealing to the vengeful Christ of
the apocalyptic texts. That was the solution of the Ku Klux Klan, which
symbolically affixed devil's horns to their conical caps.

The Lost Cause ideology had a ritual dimension as well. There were
seemingly innocent occasions: festive reunions of Confederate veterans,
solemn commemorations of fallen heroes, sermons, lectures, christen-
ings, dedications, parades, and so on. And there were other less innocent
ones, particularly the public lynchings and racial violence that spread
through the South beginning in the 1880s.[94] This Southern development
conformed to a general pattern. Religious nationalism is often accompanied by ritual violence against cultural and racial "others" who are pur-
portedly threatening the patriarchal control of "indigenous" men over
"their" women.[95] Underlying both the peaceful and the violent enact-
ments of the Lost Cause ideology was the same language of blood sacrifice and blood purity.

The language of WASP religious nationalism would also provide a
shared vernacular for sectional reconciliation between North and South,
albeit with somewhat different regional accents.[96] In the South, there
was more stress on "white" than on "Anglo-Saxon" or "Protestant" because most Southern whites were arguably "Anglo-Saxon," while most
blacks were avowedly Protestant. Race was thus the most powerful dividing line.[97] In the North, there was greater stress on religion than on
race because there were far fewer African Americans and far more Catholics, some of whom were arguably Anglo-Saxon (e.g., the Irish and the
Germans).

But when Northerners and Southerners gathered together to com-
memorate the war, as they increasingly did in the wake of Reconstruction, they could drop the regional idioms and join together in celebration
of the commingled blood of "the blue and the gray." Slavery was slowly

omitted from public discussion of the war, and black Americans were slowly excluded from its public commemorations. While Thanksgiving became more and more a "Yankee holiday," Memorial Day took its place as *the* national holiday, a time when the white North and the white South assembled to celebrate their dead. Thus was sectional reunion achieved and national mourning enacted, but at the expense of racial division and collective amnesia. Only within the African American community was the civic narrative of democratic republicanism kept fully alive. It would be one "gift of black folks" to the nation.

RADICAL SECULARISM ARRIVES

The seeds of radical secularism may have been planted during the revolutionary era. But they did not blossom until after Reconstruction, when they sprouted from a rich ideological mulch imported from western Europe whose ingredients included free thought, political economy, and evolutionary theory. Eventually, two distinct varieties of radical secularism arose. One was more secularist than individualist. Its DNA was derived mainly from free thought and cultural evolutionism. I will call this "progressive" secularism. The other variant was more individualist then secularist. Its ideological DNA was derived mainly from political economy and social Darwinism. I will call this "conservative" secularism.

The public embodiment of the progressive version of radical secularism was Robert Ingersoll (1833–1899), a famous lawyer, politician, and orator.[98] Ingersoll was born in the town of Dresden, New York, in the heart of the "burned-over district," so called because of the numerous movements that "burned" through it during the first half of the nineteenth century: the religious revivals of the Second Great Awakening, the millennialism of the "Millerites," the socialist experiments of the Owenites, and the Mormon visions of Joseph Smith, to name only the best known.[99] Ingersoll's father was a Presbyterian minister whose family lineage stretched back to the Massachusetts Bay Colony.[100] He would be driven out of one pulpit after another for his abolitionist convictions. Ingersoll's mother died when he was still a toddler, and he and his four siblings spent their childhoods in a succession of small towns in the lower Midwest. Because of this itinerant lifestyle, Ingersoll had little formal schooling. Like his hero Thomas Paine, he was an autodidact.[101] As a boy, he worked his way through the meager contents of his father's library, consuming the Bible, Calvin's *Institutes*, Milton's *Paradise Lost*, and Bunyan's *Pilgrim's Progress*, among others. This education was enough to alienate him from Christianity for the rest of his life. Ingersoll balked at the violence of the Old Testament, the miracles of the New, the arbitrariness of Calvinist predestination, and the asceticism of the English Puritans. Later, as a young man, he discovered kindred spirits in Shakespeare, the Enlightenment *philosophes*, the Romantic poets, and the Greek atomists.[102]

Following in Lincoln's footsteps, Ingersoll apprenticed in the law, settled in southern Illinois, joined the Republican Party, and fought in the Civil War. He then started a family, built a lucrative legal practice, and worked the campaign trail, eventually earning a short stint as Illinois attorney general. Ingersoll first gained national notoriety when he was tapped to nominate the anti-Catholic nativist James Blaine for president at the Republican National Convention of 1876.

Ingersoll's forensic abilities were legendary. Mark Twain and Walt Whitman both thought him the greatest orator of his generation. His friend Henry Ward Beecher believed he was "the most brilliant speaker of the English tongue . . . on the globe."[103] Capitalizing on this newfound acclaim, Ingersoll moved to a palatial villa in Washington, DC, and then to a brownstone on Gramercy Park in New York. In the final two decades of his life, Ingersoll was the most sought-after stump speaker in the Republican Party, as well as its chief *consigliere*. Along the way, he became a very wealthy man, renowned for his boozy soirees.

When he was not on the campaign trail or in the courtroom, Ingersoll was often on the lecture circuit, preaching his gospel of "free-thought," "agnosticism," and "secularism." He deserves some credit for injecting each of these terms into wider circulation in the United States. All three were borrowed from Great Britain. The term "freethinker" was first coined by the Irish polymath William Molyneux (1656–1698).[104] To be a freethinker, said Ingersoll, was to base one's beliefs on "reason," "observation," "experience," and "self-reliance."[105] And it was to be without religion. "The truth is that what is called religion is necessarily inconsistent with free thought," Ingersoll argued. "A believer is a bird in a cage; a free-thinker is an eagle parting the clouds with tireless wings."[106]

"Agnosticism" was also a neologism imported from the United Kingdom. It was invented by the British naturalist Thomas Huxley (1825–1895) in opposition to the term "gnosis," or knowledge of revealed religion.[107] Ingersoll explained agnosticism as follows: "I use the word 'Agnostic' because I prefer it to the word Atheist. As a matter of fact, no one knows that God exists and no one knows that God does not exist."[108]

The term "secularism" was coined by the liberal activist George Holyoake (1817–1906).[109] Holyoake himself carefully distinguished secularism from the aggressive atheism promoted by Charles Bradlaugh and his followers. At least in tone, the secularism espoused by Ingersoll—a master of sarcasm and polemic who delighted in lambasting religious belief—was closer to that of Bradlaugh than that of Holyoake.

Ingersoll's vision was "progressive" in at least two senses. First, it anticipated the emancipatory concerns of the Progressive movement. Ingersoll was an outspoken champion of civic equality. Having opposed slavery as a young man, he would later champion equal rights for women and workers and even developed a protean defense of animal rights in his attacks on "vivisection." Unlike later progressives, however, Ingersoll also championed laissez-faire economics and opposed redistribution. His egalitarianism was civic, not social.

Ingersoll's vision was also "progressive" in that it located radical secularism within a general theory of historical development. During the late eighteenth century, the great thinkers of the Scottish Enlightenment had argued that history could be divided up into stages. This approach was popularized through the "positive philosophy" of Auguste Comte (1798–1857) and the "social Darwinism" of Herbert Spencer (1820–1903). Additional fodder was provided by European scholars working in the new fields of biblical criticism, social anthropology, and comparative religion. In popular lectures such as "The Gods," Ingersoll skillfully wove these various elements together into an accessible and compelling story that linked scientific progress and human liberation and concluded that secular humanism was the next stage of cultural development.[110]

In what sense, though, was Ingersoll's secular progressivism "liberal"? Interestingly, his collected works include only a handful of references to the canonical figures of modern liberalism,[111] and he used the word "liberal" mainly in reference to liberal religion.[112] However, his speeches and writings fairly bristle with talk of liberty. Still, Ingersoll's liberty was not exactly a libertarian liberty. It was closely connected with "civic," "moral," and "humanitarian duties." And it was grounded in a capacious understanding of individual rights, probably derived from the views of Ingersoll's hero, Thomas Paine.

The same is true at the level of policy. As an active member of the National Liberal League and as president of its successor organization, the National Secular Union, Ingersoll championed "total separation of church and state."[113] At a time when most Americans still understood "separation of church and state" as a synonym for "religious freedom,"

Ingersoll and his allies reinterpreted it as the removal of religion from public life. The platform of the Liberal League included planks that seem radical even today.[114] It demanded the repeal not only of antiblasphemy and sabbatarian laws, public prayers, and Bible reading in public schools, but also of religious holidays and judicial oaths. More than that, it proposed the imposition of a gag order on political speech by religious leaders, the denial of public funds to religious charities doing secular work, the removal of the tax exemption on church properties, and even the abolition of any laws that happened to be in accord with principles of Christian morality. Ingersoll's secularism was thus hardly liberal. To this degree, his liberalism and his secularism were fundamentally at odds.

If Ingersoll was the public embodiment of progressive radical secularism, then Yale social scientist William Graham Sumner (1840–1910) was one of the greatest champions of the conservative variant.[115] Sumner was born to English immigrants of modest means. His parents eventually settled in Connecticut, and, after attending public school in Hartford, Sumner entered Yale. Following graduation, he spent two years studying in Geneva, another two in Göttingen, and one more in Oxford. While the Civil War raged at home, Sumner immersed himself in Hebrew, French, and German, as well as theology and biblical criticism, all in preparation for a career in the ministry. After returning to the United States in 1867, he was ordained in the Episcopal Church and over the next five years occupied pulpits in New Haven, New York, and New Jersey. But his heart was not in it, and he soon began lobbying for a faculty position at his alma mater. He was appointed a professor of political and social science at Yale in 1872, a position that he would occupy until his death almost four decades later. There, he enjoyed a large following among the students. Many joked that their major was "Sumnerology."[116]

In the scholarly literature, Sumner is often classified as a "social Darwinist."[117] Taken literally, the term does not quite fit. While Sumner was clearly much influenced by Spencer, he had little knowledge of Darwin.[118] However, if by "social Darwinism" one means a loose amalgam of laissez-faire economics, Spencerian social evolutionism, and Malthusian demography, then the label fits very well. Consider Sumner's best-known and most controversial book, *What Social Classes Owe to Each Other*.[119] His answer, in a word, was "nothing." Sumner saw wealth as a just reward for self-discipline and hard work. Redistribution, he argued, is counterproductive, because it transfers capital from the "fit" to the "unfit." The only thing that the social classes do owe to one another is to look after their individual self-interests.

What sort of "liberal" was Sumner, then? Not a "Lockean liberal," certainly. Like the British utilitarian Jeremy Bentham, Sumner regarded the doctrine of "natural rights" as "nonsense on stilts." Indeed, he rarely even spoke of rights, and then mostly in reference to what we now call "property rights." Nor did Sumner have any use for the idea of "natural liberty." In his view, such liberty as a person has is a product of civilization—of laws and institutions—and not of nature.[120] As for equality, Sumner sided with Calhoun: he regarded people as naturally *unequal*. And government, he maintained, should not waste resources on social leveling.[121] There was a zero-sum trade-off between liberty and equality, he argued, and liberty should always be given priority.[122] Sumner's understanding of liberty was not libertine, however. On the contrary, he was an ardent advocate of the "bourgeois virtues" of self-discipline, hard work, and frugality.[123] While he wrote little about marriage, family, and sexuality, his views on these subjects also seem to have been quite conventional.[124] In modern terms, then, Sumner was not so much a "libertarian" as a "classical liberal."

Sumner was assuredly not any kind of civic republican, though. Despite his undergraduate training in the old classical curriculum, Sumner betrayed little knowledge of the central principles of classical republicanism. When he did use the term "republican"—which was seldom—it was emptied of its traditional content. He defined a "republican government" as one in which power is conferred by a "temporary or defeasible tenure," and a "democratic republic" as one free of aristocratic titles and forms.[125] His emphasis on self-discipline did have a vaguely republican ring to it. But his understanding of liberty was more liberal than republican.[126] By "liberty," he mostly meant a lack of state interference in the economic activity of individual citizens. Other core concepts of classical republicanism are either absent from his writings (e.g., "mixed constitution," "faction," or "balance") or used in distinctly nonrepublican ways (e.g., "corruption.").[127] In truth, the notion of a *res publica* in the sense of "the common good" or "the public's business" had no place whatsoever in Sumner's worldview. His ethics were starkly utilitarian and his social theory radically atomistic. "To me," he quipped, "the State is only All-of-us," a mere "abstraction" that conceals "a little group of men chosen in a very haphazard way by the majority of us to perform certain services."[128]

Sumner was not an outspoken secularist. He was far more concerned with the "separation of economy and state" than with the separation of church and state.[129] Asked about his religious views in later life, he replied that he had "put them in a drawer" after leaving the ministry, and that when he reopened the drawer, he "found it empty."[130] He still appeared in church from time to time as the occasion demanded, but he also dismissed religion as a "phantasm" when behind closed doors.[131] Like many other secular academics, he believed that religion was fundamentally at odds with science, and that religious belief constituted a major obstacle to scientific progress. But he did not air these views loudly, whether out of prudence or decorum.[132]

In the influential figures of Ingersoll and Sumner, then, we see the rise of two forms of radical secularism: a progressive variant that was more secular than it was liberal, and liberal in a Lockean rather than a utilitarian sense; and a conservative variant that was more secular than it was liberal, and liberal in a utilitarian rather than a Lockean sense. In Ingersoll, we find the seeds of total separationism; in Sumner, those of radical individualism. What we do not find in either, it should be noted, is a genuinely Lockean liberalism that combines an affirmation of natural rights and human equality with a thoroughgoing respect for religious freedom—the sort of liberalism, in other words, that is more in tune with the American project and a potential ally of the civil religion.

CONCLUSION

The American Civil War gave rise to a third version of the civil religious tradition: democratic republicanism. It was "democratic" in the sense of being egalitarian. The ancient republics were slave societies. The Renaissance republics were aristocratic ones. The American Revolution had done away with aristocracy, but not, of course, with slavery. Whether the Declaration's promise of human equality should really apply to "all men"—or, indeed, whether it even applied to anyone—was hotly disputed. To both questions, John Calhoun, William Graham Sumner, and many others answered firmly in the negative. Nor did the Civil War really settle the matter. The disputed election of Andrew Johnson to the presidency marked the end of Reconstruction and the beginning of Jim Crow. In a sad irony, the Democratic Party, long a stalwart defender of the "common man," would soon make a Faustian bargain with the Old Confederacy: Southern votes in exchange for silent complicity in the new system of racial oppression. Though slow to bear fruit at the national level, this bargain would eventually put Woodrow Wilson in the White House. Not that the Republican Party was much better. It may have been notionally committed to Lincolnian principles of racial equality, but it was unwilling to invest any political capital in their realization. For the time being, democratic republicanism remained more aspiration than reality. Still, that aspiration was a bold and noble one. Since antiquity, political philosophers had argued that republics had to be homogeneous and small. The American experiment was an ongoing effort to disprove this received wisdom by forging a stable republic out of a large and diverse citizenry.

The inspiration for that experiment was more religious than philosophical, though. The ancient Israelites had taken a first step toward civic equality during the era of the Hebrew republic. By doing away with rule by a god-king, they had separated divinity from monarchy. The early Christians had taken another major step in this direction when they established their new *ekklesia*, which included both men and women, enslaved and free, and on a purely voluntary basis. It was this egalitarian strand of the Judeo-Christian tradition—and not some version of secular liberalism—that inspired abolitionists like Garrison and Douglass. In other words, it was prophetic religion that first put democratic equality into civic republicanism. Secular liberalism was still too weak a tonic to fortify the egalitarian constitution of the United States—tinged as it was by cultural elitism and social Darwinism. Nor, in truth, has it fully lost this elitist tinge even today.

The Civil War and Reconstruction periods also strengthened and transformed American religious nationalism. The religious nationalist rhetoric of "blood," "sacrifice," and "martyrdom" lent meaning to the death and suffering of war. But such language lingered on in the peacetime rhetoric of national remembrance as well. The Civil War had "killed" the Confederacy as well as its soldiers, and the "Lost Cause" myth lent some meaning to that "death," too. Like Christ, so it was hoped, the South would rise again.

American religious nationalism was doubly transformed during this time. Its sacred center was removed from New England to the Old South, where it arguably still remains—the source of the pervasive militarism, hyperpatriotism, and Christianism that still distinguishes some parts of the South from the rest of the country. Its symbolic core was also transformed. In the Puritan version of religious nationalism, blood sacrifice propitiated an angry God. In the new Lost Cause version, such sacrifice redeemed the nation. In this formula, the nation was quietly set in God's place. Religious nationalism had become wholly idolatrous.

Meanwhile, sectional reconciliation was achieved at the cost of racial exclusion. Yankees could not be full members of the Confederate religion of the Lost Cause. But white Northerners could and did join together with their Southern brothers and sisters in the annual ritual of Memorial Day. White Anglo-Saxon Protestants set sectional divisions aside in the name of a racial and cultural unity that was consecrated by the blood of Union and Confederate soldiers commingled on the battlefield. But blacks, Catholics, Jews, and other suspicious persons were not welcome at the festivities.

Just as fateful in the long run was the crystallization of a third, rival version of American political theology. Since the Puritan era, American politics had oscillated between two poles: the civil religion and its idolatrous cousin, religious nationalism. The crystallization of radical secularism did not immediately alter this dynamic. For the time being, radical secularism had little resonance beyond a small elite within the Republican Party. The seedbeds of secularism, however, were to be found in the new class of knowledge workers: lawyers, journalists, scientists, teachers—in short, those who derived their livelihoods from mastery of some sort of secular expertise.[133] By the mid-twentieth century, this new class had largely displaced the old Protestant elites from the commanding heights of public life: the courts, the media, the universities, and the schools. The trenches of the "culture war" would soon be dug, and the mediating tradition of prophetic republicanism would be pinned down by the crossfire. But that was still far in the future. The Protestant establishment would have a few more words to say before then.

The Civil War era also gave rise to three new forms of historical consciousness, three contrasting frameworks for conceiving of the American story: circular, linear, and spiral. During and after the Civil War, the historical consciousness of American evangelicals moved in two different directions: proto-liberal and proto-literalist. The liberal direction was presaged by the abolitionists, who had increasingly elevated the spirit of Christianity above the letter of Christianity. The literalist direction was presaged by the proslavery clergy, who clung to the letter of scripture even when it was in plain conflict with the spirit of Christianity. But these differences would not fully break out into the open until the "fundamentalist/modernist" controversies of the early twentieth century. Eventually, the literalist approach to Christian doctrine would coalesce with the "originalist" approach to the American Constitution. In this form of historical consciousness, American history consists of a double movement: away from the plain meaning of the sacred texts and then back again. Such a framework was at least as old as the Protestant Reformation, which sought to reclaim the original tenets of early Christianity.

The historical consciousness of radical secularism was governed by the metaphors of "progress," "development," and "evolution." The idea of progress was at least partly inspired by Christian eschatology, the belief that historical time was slowly but surely moving toward some end point or culmination, a kind of secular millennium. But it also owed a significant debt to theories of historical development pioneered by the great thinkers of the Scottish Enlightenment. On this view, history was divided into a series of developmental stages (e.g., traditional vs. modern or agrarian vs. industrial). Moreover, each new stage fully superseded the old, rendering knowledge of and about the past obsolete and antiquarian. In this way of seeing the world, tradition was inherently opposed to progress and all that went with it: science, rationality, and liberation, to name but a few.

The historical consciousness of the civil religion also underwent a fundamental transformation in these decades. The historical consciousness of Douglass and Lincoln was spiral, rather than circular or linear. Like the literalists but unlike the progressives, the civil religionists emphasized the periodic return to sources. They envisioned the future by not only revisiting but also reinterpreting the past: there lay the break with the literalists. Like the progressives and unlike the literalists, the civil religionists also emphasized the possibility of moral progress in human history. But for them, "progress" involved a vindication of the past, a realization of its aspirations, and not simply a break with the past or a supersession of its principles: there lay the break with the radical secularists. In this view, time was neither a line nor a circle, but a spiral, widening upward and outward toward higher principles and greater inclusiveness.

CHAPTER 5

The Progressive Era

EMPIRE AND THE REPUBLIC

IN MANY WAYS, the Civil War was a sort of dress rehearsal for America's not-too-distant future. It revealed the nation's latent military and industrial potential. It sparked (abortive) efforts to achieve greater civic inclusion and social equality. It created the rudiments of an administrative state and a welfare state.[1] And it swept many Americans out of the provincialism of their local communities and into a nationwide political and theological debate. But the costume did not fit just yet, and the nation shed it quickly. The great armies were demobilized, and the munitions factories shuttered. Reconstruction was halted, and Jim Crow took its place. Philosophical and theological debate gave way to a "Gilded Age" of political complacency and material striving.

But over the next half century, the social transformations foreshadowed during the war would gradually come to fruition, though often in unintended and ironic ways. A nation born out of an anti imperial uprising acquired an empire of its own in Cuba and the Philippines.[2] A constitutional amendment intended to secure the civic equality of the freedmen—the Fourteenth—was used to protect the property rights of corporate "persons," thereby laying the legal groundwork for immense concentrations of economic power. Meanwhile, a standing army was reestablished, not to defend Southern blacks against lynch mobs, but to counter "domestic disturbances" caused by striking workers. The ironclad warships of the Civil War spawned the great steamers that ferried millions of European immigrants to American shores. A railroad network initially constructed to shuttle troops and supplies to the battlefront now formed the sinews of a transcontinental economy. The sons and daughters of Protestant clergymen and activists became the vanguard of a secular and bohemian intelligentsia. In short, by the time of the First World War, America had become in reality what it had been only in potential fifty years earlier: an industrial, imperial, and military power with an ever more urban, plural, and worldly culture, governed by an increasingly centralized, regulatory, and administrative state.

Taken together, the massive and interlocking social and cultural transformations of the Gilded Age—the growth of militarism, imperialism, industrialism, corporatism, pluralism, and secularism—posed some very profound questions for the civil religious tradition. Was it possible to be a "light to the nations" as well as a "defender of democracy"—to lead by example but also to rule by force? What would become of the "city on a hill" if it could no longer remain free of "entangling alliances"? Did the closing of the frontier and the growth of the corporation spell the end of "republican virtue"? Indeed, could propertyless "wage slaves" actually become good citizens? How could the "mixed" and "balanced" constitution of classical republicanism be maintained in an era of plutocracy and corporate power? Could the power of "the many" still function as a counterweight to the power of "the few"? Could the *res publica* coexist peacefully with the *res privata*? For that matter, could a self-consciously Protestant culture integrate an increasingly Catholic and Jewish population? Finally, could the civil religion be reformulated in nontheistic terms to accommodate the growing ranks of nonbelievers? In sum, could the civil theology of a geopolitically isolated society of small property-holders of WASP heritage be reformulated for a powerful and pluralistic nation of wage-earners?

On these questions, the leading intellectuals of the Progressive Era were hardly in agreement. Some observers read the times through a linear lens. They would conclude, with Woodrow Wilson, that "the old political formulas do not fit the present problems: they read now like documents taken out of a forgotten age."[3] Others took an originalist position. They would insist, with Teddy Roosevelt, that the Constitution was "a nearly perfect instrument" and that Americans needed only to "keep this Republic true to the principles of those who founded" it.[4] Still others, perhaps even the majority, held fast to the racialist and militarist heresies of WASP religious nationalism. Some would strengthen this toxic brew with an extra measure of apocalyptic religion. And not a few, mostly "cultured despisers of all religion," would turn instead to creeds new and foreign, such as those put forth by Spencer and Nietzsche, to fortify the radical secularism inherited from the Reconstruction era. But there were a few as well—and they are the main focus of this chapter— who would seek to revitalize the civil theology, not simply by returning to the founding documents as Lincoln and Douglass had done, but by returning to the various traditions that stood behind them—to the Hebrew prophets, Greek philosophy, and the Christian Gospels. And there they would find the moral, political, and poetic resources they needed to breathe new life into it. One result, evident in the work of John Dewey and Reinhold Niebuhr, was a "high church" form of the American civil theology, which was much deeper and far more systematic than its Civil War–era predecessor, but also more removed from national ritual and popular discourse. Its strength—intellectual depth—had a corresponding weakness—a shallow appeal. Another result, evident in the work of W.E.B. Du Bois, was a "black church" version of the civil religion, in which the prophetic and especially poetic elements of the tradition were more faithfully preserved. Still another version, exemplified by Jane Addams, was a "low church" form of civil religion and a feminist variant of civil theology.

JOHN DEWEY: FROM CIVIL RELIGION TO PUBLIC PHILOSOPHY AND BACK

A lineal descendant of the New England Puritans, John Dewey (1859–1952) was born and raised in Burlington, Vermont, the kind of self-contained, self-governing New England township about which Tocqueville had written so glowingly in *Democracy in America*. His mother, Lucina, was a pious Congregationalist and, indeed, an old-fashioned orthodox Calvinist.[5] Dewey's father, Archibald, was a small businessman and an ardent Unionist who had enlisted in Lincoln's army. Dewey spent most of his childhood in Burlington and remained there for college as well. His mentor at the University of Vermont was H.A.P. Torrey, a German idealist philosopher of a liberal Protestant persuasion. After graduation, Dewey taught high school for several years before beginning his graduate studies at Johns Hopkins. While there, Dewey came under the spell of the neo-Hegelian philosopher George Sylvester Morris—and not, ironically, of Morris's colleague, the great pragmatist philosopher Charles Sanders Peirce. When Morris left for the University of Michigan in 1884, Dewey followed. While at Michigan, he slowly drifted away from churchgoing, Protestantism, and neo-Hegelianism. His early interest in speculative metaphysics—in "the meaning of Thought, Nature and God, and the relation of one to another,"[6] as he put it—now shifted toward empirical psychology.

In 1894, Dewey moved to the University of Chicago. Much of his energy during these years went into nonacademic projects, such as the creation of his Laboratory School in Hyde Park and the support of Jane Addams's Hull House a few miles north. The intellectual fruits of these labors were harvested in the decades following his subsequent move to New York to teach at Columbia, where he wrote *Democracy and*

Education (1916), *Reconstruction in Philosophy* (1920), *Experience and Nature* (1925), *The Public and Its Problems* (1927), *The Quest for Certainty* (1929), and *A Common Faith* (1934), along with countless essays and lectures. By this time, Dewey was not just a well-known academic philosopher. He was a highly influential public intellectual—"America's philosopher," as some called him.

Like Emerson and Whitman, two of his heroes, Dewey's hopes for American democracy were sometimes positive to the point of pie-eyed. But this optimism was tempered by a rigorous empiricism, which opened Dewey's eyes to the mounting challenges confronting the American project. Dewey saw two dangers, or, rather, three. On the one hand, he worried that a hidebound religious traditionalism was preventing the country from adapting its political culture and democratic institutions to new circumstances. On the other hand, he was concerned that a cynical individualistic materialism might unmoor it from its ethical and political traditions. Most of all, perhaps, he worried that American democracy might be crushed between these two juggernauts. His life's work was to chart a middle course between reactionary forms of fundamentalism and the atomistic strain of liberalism. In this sense, his intellectual project was fundamentally a civil religious one.

What was his contribution? Where Wilson and other Progressives looked to the moderns and dismissed tradition, Dewey turned back to the ancients and used the classical tradition to reimagine modernity. Aristotle particularly influenced him. In that philosopher's writings, he found an integrated system—an interrelated ethics, politics, and metaphysics—that allowed him to move beyond traditional piety and laissez-faire liberalism. Under this influence, he recuperated and reconstructed classical ideas of "virtue" and "flourishing," freedom and balance, and natural law and cosmic purpose. And he developed a nontheistic understanding of "faith" and "religion," what he called the "democratic faith." Dewey's great contribution was to show that the civil religion could be rebuilt on naturalistic foundations.

"Aristotle!?" some scholarly readers might exclaim.[7] They can be forgiven for overlooking the connection. Dewey's remarks about the ancients were often critical. He especially liked to contrast the dynamism and experientialism of his approach to the "stasis" and "intellectualism" of the Greeks. Nonetheless, close readers have long recognized that Dewey had a deep and "genuine affinity to Aristotle, an affinity which his able students saw more clearly than Dewey realized, or perhaps was willing to admit."[8]

Dewey had read the Greeks in his student years[9]—as all young philosophers do—and the Athenian influence was evident in his early writings on pedagogy, particularly in the stress he placed on civic education in the public schools.[10] It was also evident in the ethics textbook that Dewey published in 1908 with his old Chicago colleague James H. Tufts. Together, they developed a neo-Aristotelian ethics of virtue as an alternative to a Kantian ethics of duty ("the categorical imperative") and Bentham's ethics of utility ("the greatest good of the greatest number"). To be sure, they did not speak explicitly of "virtues" or "vices"; they referred instead to "habits of character whose effect is to sustain and spread the rational or common good" and to vices as those "traits of character, which have the opposite effect."[11] In this way, they tacitly combined a Greek notion of virtue *qua* "moral excellence" with a Christian one of "selfless love." Dewey would later define civic or "democratic virtues" as "creative methods of deliberate social decisions and intelligent cooperation."[12]

Aristotle's influence is also evident in Dewey's analysis of happiness. Like Aristotle, he understood "happiness" as "flourishing" rather than as "pleasure." Happiness, he argued, is more than a simple sum of bodily pleasures or positive emotions. It results from the development of human potential.[13] Dewey's definition of human nature could easily have been lifted straight out of Aristotle's *Politics*: "Man is naturally a being that lives in association with others in communities, possessing language, and therefore, enjoying a transmitted culture."[14] However, where Aristotle saw one template for happiness, Dewey saw many. Each individual's path to happiness depended on his or her unique personal abilities and sociohistorical context. In this sense, Dewey's theory of happiness tacitly combined the Greek idea of human purpose (*telos*) with the Christian ideal of personal vocation.

Not surprisingly, Dewey's understanding of freedom was more republican than liberal, and avowedly so. Liberal philosophers generally "thought of individuals as endowed with an equipment of fixed and ready-made capacities," he observed, and understood freedom as the removal of "external restrictions," particularly on commercial activity.[15] But this conception is naïve, he argued, and doubly so. Human capacities must be developed, and their development depends largely on external conditions. To be free, on Dewey's definition, is not simply to get what one wants at the lowest cost, but to engage in "intelligent choice" grounded in "intelligent desires," with "intelligence" connoting something like practical wisdom.[16]

Dewey was also a *democratic* republican. He wanted to democratize freedom. In ancient societies, based on slave economies, freedom was restricted to male citizens. But in modern societies, based on industrial economies, he insisted, freedom can be extended to all—assuming, of course, that material resources and basic rights are extended to all first. That was the task, said Dewey, and the imperative.

That democratic freedom had not been so extended, he argued, was due to a constitutional imbalance in the American polity. In an earlier America—an agricultural America—where property was more equally distributed, the power of the many had been sufficient to counterbalance the power of the few. In the new America—an industrial America—property was so concentrated in the hands of the few that they could ride roughshod over the interests of the many. The only way that the old balance could be restored, Dewey reasoned, was if the many used the power of the state to counterbalance the power of the wealthy. Democratizing freedom would involve tempering the capitalist economy with the powers of the national state.

So Dewey's political theory can be seen as a modernized version of civic republicanism. Was there a prophetic dimension to Dewey's thought as well?[17] Certainly, there was a metaphysical dimension to it. As was his wont, Dewey presented his views as an attempt to reconcile and transcend two opposing positions: an atomistic and deterministic materialism on the one hand, and a supernatural and teleological theism on the other. The result was a naturalistic and democratic world picture that—unsurprisingly—owed much to Aristotle. Dewey insisted that "man" was in and of nature. But he denied the existence of any fixed or final ends in nature itself.[18] In his view, nature is "complex" and "contingent," "pluralistic" and "relational," composed of "individualities" and "qualities." In a word, *nature itself is democratic.* Thus, for Dewey, the democratic project is fundamentally attuned to the very structures of the cosmic order. In this sense, *the democratic project is an inherently spiritual project.*

Dewey did try to incorporate a religious dimension into his worldview. In his 1934 Terry Lectures, he propounded a "common faith" for a democratic America. Once again, he presented his own position as the synthesis of two conflicting stances: supernatural religion and militant atheism.[19] Religious claims to absolute truth, he argued, are relativized by the plurality of religions and the discoveries of science.[20] But the atomistic materialism of militant atheism leaves "man in isolation from the world of physical nature and his fellows."[21] To overcome this divide,

Dewey argued, we must emancipate "the religious" from "religion" and also protect it from a crude materialism. Religion is received "beliefs" and "practices," "dogmas" and "rituals," ensconced in "institutions" and served by "priests." The religious is the "consummatory experience" of the "unification of self" and the "unity of ideals."[22] And "God" or "the divine" is simply the "One word" that we use to denote this experience. Such an "experience" is not outside of nature, Dewey argued; it is part of it. Nature is more than just matter, then. That is what the reductionists fail to see.

Dewey's effort to reconstruct civic republicanism was quite successful. Put briefly, the main components of Deweyan republicanism were:

1. A *virtue ethics* that gave due attention to classical notions of moral excellence as well as Christian ideals of self-sacrificing love while recognizing the plurality of human goods and vocations
2. A theory of *human freedom* that valued both positive and negative liberties but was fully egalitarian and recognized the role of objective conditions in human development, the role of coercion in politics, and the need for balance between groups
3. A *democratic metaphysics* that could underwrite a democratic faith

The weak spot in Dewey's republican vision was an inattention to institutional architecture and social equilibrium. Alas, these weaknesses would eventually be passed on to contemporary liberalism.

Dewey's attempt to incorporate a religious dimension into his vision was less successful, marred as it was by the secularist prejudices of the age. However much Dewey may have opened himself to "the religious" in his latter years, he remained an implacable foe of religion as it was conventionally understood: "The opposition between religious values as I conceive them and religions," he insisted, "is not to be bridged."[23] Dewey's hostility to churchly religion extended to public policy as well. He was an early adopter of the emerging jurisprudence of "total separation," and he lobbied forcefully and repeatedly to exclude religious instruction of any kind—general or particular, mandatory or voluntary—from the public schools on the grounds that it weakened national identity and impeded civic education. This was not only politically imprudent, but also philosophically inconsistent. Dewey's "infinite pluralism" was evidently not elastic enough to accommodate any sort of traditional religion. There was no need to accommodate believers, he felt, because the Christian message had already been incarnated and the Kingdom of God realized in modern democratic institutions, which had exorcised evil and oppression from human society.[24] In this regard, his "democratic faith" proved worryingly naïve. It ultimately impeded, rather than facilitated, the diverse coalitions that would be required to defend and deepen the achievements of American democracy. Addams faced this challenge more squarely than Dewey.

JANE ADDAMS: AMERICAN ACTIVIST

Addams's biography was similar to Dewey's in many ways.[25] They were of the same generation: Addams was born in 1860, less than a year after Dewey. Both grew up in small towns—in Addams's case, the town of Cedarville, in northern Illinois. Addams's father was an ardent member of the Republican Party and a Civil War veteran, just like Dewey's. She, too, aspired to an Ivy League education (Smith College) but was sent to a local college instead (Rockford Female Seminary). Like Dewey, Addams gradually moved away from an orthodox, churchgoing Christianity during early adulthood. Their life trajectories would eventually cross on the South Side of Chicago, where Addams inaugurated her activist career with the opening of Hull House in 1889. Dewey would take up residence a few miles farther south in 1894.

There were biographical divergences, too, of course, some of them consequential. Addams's family was much more prominent and much more prosperous. Her father was a founding member of the Illinois Republican Party and a personal acquaintance of Abraham Lincoln. (Perhaps this is why her writings displayed such profound insight into the inner lives of the rich and powerful.) Addams's father was also a Quaker, which may explain her unconditional pacifism. Her mother died when she was eight years old, and her relationship with her domestically and artistically inclined stepmother was always fraught, which may be one reason that Addams's own "household" at Hull House became a social and moral project. This much is certain, though: the initial establishment of that household would not have been possible without the considerable resources afforded by a sizeable inheritance.

The biggest difference between Dewey and Addams, at least at first glance, was vocational. If Dewey was the archetypical American philosopher, then Addams was the paradigmatic American activist. Still, one should not overdraw the contrast. Just as Dewey's philosophy was deeply grounded in his political activities, so, too, did Addams's political activities bear fruit in her writings. Much of this writing focused on specific causes and argued from concrete examples of human suffering rather than from abstract principles of social justice. But some of it dealt with philosophical questions such as the meaning of democracy and patriotism.[26] Surely, the differences in these two individuals' vocations had as much to do with gender as with inclination.

Because Addams was more of an activist than a scholar, her contribution to the American civil religion was quite different from Dewey's. It was based not so much on a philosophical deepening of the founding traditions as on a direct experience with present realities, particularly the experiences of the "new immigrants" in the American city. Many of these immigrants were neither "Anglo-Saxon" nor Protestant, and this provoked considerable unease among native-born members of the dominant ethnicities. Some advocated legal restrictions on immigrants for the sake of ethnocultural purity, while others favored cultural assimilation into "Anglo-Saxon" ways. Many settlement houses in the United States were dedicated to this program of "Americanization." The presence of refined members of the WASP elite in the midst of slums, so the rationale went, would provide immigrants with opportunities to learn good morals and American folkways.

Addams herself was never a full-blown assimilationist. But in its early years, Hull House did pursue a program of cultural uplift.[27] It offered classes in literature, painting, and other forms of "high culture." But Addams quickly realized that there was much the immigrants could teach *her*.[28] What especially impressed Addams were the "numberless instances of self-sacrifice" that the immigrants performed for one another—far more than the well-to-do, in her observation.[29] Perhaps this was the real meaning of Jesus's first beatitude, she ventured: the poor are blessed because they are given more "opportunities for self-sacrifice."[30]

While she understood this lesson as ethical, other lessons were for her more sociological. Consider her involvement in the great Pullman strike of 1894.[31] In this conflict, Addams publicly advocated for outside arbitration. This, however, the great railroad magnate George Pullman categorically rejected. Why? Why did this man, who "had been dined and feted throughout Europe as the creator of a model town, as the friend and benefactor of workingmen," refuse to negotiate with his employees?[32] The first reason, Addams argued, was that his "benevolence" had been infected with a "pride" that had slowly degenerated into self-righteousness.[33] (Reinhold Niebuhr might have agreed!) The second was that his ethics had failed to "evolve." Pullman's ethics were not yet "social"; they were still "individual," "familial," and "commercial," based on rigid observance of the moral rules of the preindustrial era rather than on the open-minded engagement with other points of view that a more pluralistic society demanded. Ironically, Addams concluded, Pullman's personal probity provided the alibi for his moral imperiousness. (Again, Niebuhr might have agreed.) But the strikers were not blameless either. In Addams's judgment, they had displayed a "fatal lack of generosity in their attitudes toward the company."[34] And while their ethics were incipiently "social," they were still too materialistic. Too often, she charged, organized labor acted "for the sake of the fleshpots, rather than for the [sake of] human affection and social justice."[35] The achievement of a truly "social ethics" would require democratic engagement between the two sides.

Addams wove together these two lessons—the lessons of Hull House and those of the Pullman strike—in *Democracy and Social Ethics* (1902). This work offered a piercing diagnosis of the moral shortcomings impeding the American project. The ethic of the privileged was limited, she argued—first, by an overly narrow understanding of democracy. In general, she said, the "well to do of the community think of politics as something off by itself" and not as "the expression of their social or moral life." Even the reformist elements of the upper classes were "almost wholly occupied in the correction of political machinery and . . . a . . . better method of administration."[36] The second limitation of this ethic was that the privileged worldview was typically based on individual ethics, rather than social ones. Why? Because, Addams noted, "it is always a temptation to assume that the side which has respectability, authority and superior intelligence, has therefore righteousness as well, especially when the same side presents concrete results of individual effort as over against the less tangible results of associated effort."[37] Nevertheless, she concluded, the ethic of the new immigrants was likewise limited in two ways. First, while it was properly social, it was overly materialistic, more concerned with "fleshpots" than genuine "social intercourse." Second, it was insufficiently democratic, because it was too much a hostage to the urban political machines. How could these differences be bridged? By members of the elite who "var[ied] from type" and made democracy "a rule for living" and "a test of faith," she argued.[38] And the crucial sites for that work were the industrial city, where the two classes lived side-by-side, and the settlement house, where they could be brought together.

There were many similarities between Dewey's version of the civil religion and Addams's—above all, their expansive visions of democracy as a way of life and even a kind of faith and as America's historical contribution to civilizational advance. But there were also ways in which Addams's articulations of the civil religion differed from Dewey's and sometimes went beyond them. Where Dewey broke fully with the Christian tradition and sought to develop a fully naturalistic form of ethics, Addams did not. Her civil religion remained firmly rooted in "social Christianity."[39] In her demands for social justice and social activism, Addams frequently appealed to the Hebrew prophets and the words of Jesus. Further, where Dewey simply called for the development of human capacities, Addams catalogued the concrete forms of social dependency that undermined the democratic aims of the American project: of women upon men, of black upon white, of immigrant upon native, of servant upon mistress, of factory hand upon industrial capitalist. She was attuned to the subtle structures of symbolic violence in everyday life in a way that Dewey as a white man simply was not. Addams understood that true democracy required not only a basic level of material resources but also emotional habits of *social recognition*, of really seeing "the other" in his or her experience and particularity. While Addams may never have fully overcome her own sense of sociocultural superiority, and therefore fell short of the lofty ideals of contemporary multiculturalism, she still came far closer to them than almost anyone else of her time and must be accounted one of the most pluralistic thinkers of the Progressive Era. In a nation of nations, she realized, the civil religion must be Janus-faced: it must bridge sacred and secular, tradition and critique. It must be anchored in tradition but open to the present.

As Addams recognized, one of the greatest barriers to American democracy was the smug self-satisfaction and shallow self-righteousness of the privileged races and classes. But stripping away this veil would require sharper rhetorical tools than Addams could muster. It would require a renewed form of prophetic critique. Du Bois and then Niebuhr would take up this task.

AMERICAN SOUL: THE NEW COVENANT
OF W.E.B. DU BOIS

The family resemblances between W.E.B. Du Bois's (1868–1963) life story and those of Dewey and Addams are striking.[40] Like Dewey, Du Bois was born and raised in the heart of New England, in Great Barrington, Massachusetts, and, again like Dewey, he was brought up in the Congregational Church. Like Addams, he lost one of his parents as a child when his father abandoned his mother shortly after his birth. Like Dewey, the young Du Bois was a gifted student with Ivy League aspirations that had to be deferred for financial reasons. Instead, he attended Fiske on a scholarship before realizing his dream, earning a second BA from Harvard in 1890 and a PhD in 1896, the first African American to do so. Like Addams, he began to drift away from the orthodox, churchly Christianity of his youth during his student years. His early ambivalence toward organized religion would eventually harden into a deep animosity in old age. But unlike Dewey, his political ethics remained firmly rooted in the Judeo-Christian traditions of social justice and self-sacrificing love.[41] And unlike Addams, he retained some measure of religious belief, if not in a personal God "who consciously rules the universe for the good of mankind," then at least in a "vague Force, which in some incomprehensible way dominates all life and change" and guides them toward justice.[42]

There was another very important difference between these three thinkers, of course: Du Bois was black. And this simple fact inflected his academic trajectory and intellectual agenda in ways both great and small. His sterling credentials notwithstanding, an appointment at, say, Chicago or Columbia was completely out of the question, just as it was for Addams, by virtue of her sex. After brief stints teaching classics at Wilberforce University and sociology at the University of Pennsylvania, he accepted a position at Atlanta University, where he spent much of his career. The central thrust of all of his writing throughout never changed: to refute racist ideologies that attributed the "backwardness" and poverty of American blacks to biological or moral defects and to document the role that economic interests and racial prejudice had played in their oppression.[43]

How did Du Bois contribute to the civil theology? First, he embarked on a radical rewriting of the old covenant. In the received version, the Puritans were the founders of the covenant, and their descendants its carriers. The temptation that always lurked within this vision was the racialization of the polity. Du Bois countered this danger by writing black Americans into the founding narrative, even suggesting that they and not the Puritans were the real founders. "Your country?" he demanded. "How came it yours? Before the Pilgrims landed we were here."[44] Following in the footsteps of the black abolitionists, he challenged the Puritans' status as a chosen people. Were blacks not more like the Israelites? "Fire and blood, prayer and sacrifice, have billowed over this people, and they have found peace only in the altars of the God of right," Du Bois thundered.[45] Maybe it was the African Americans who were the real saving remnant, he mused. Maybe it was black righteousness that had shielded a white nation from divine retribution: "Generation after generation have pleaded with a headstrong, careless people to despise not Justice, Mercy, and Truth, lest the nation be smitten with a curse."[46]

Two decades later, Du Bois reprised this argument in more secular form. Without the "gifts of black folk," he argued, America would never have become America. Those gifts were threefold: "a gift of story and song," "the gift of sweat and brawn," and "a gift of the Spirit."[47] Black folk music was the basis for American folk music as such, said Du Bois, and the only great contribution the nation had thus far made to the world's musical culture. Black labor had provided the material foundation for Southern civilization and "enabled America to grow economically and spiritually at a rate previously unparalleled anywhere in history."[48] And black spirit was the engine of American democratization. Black Americans had stood (almost) alone in demanding a fully inclusive democracy such as neither Americans nor Europeans had conceived in the eighteenth century, and such as they had not even accepted in the twentieth."[49] Further, he declared, "without the active participation of the Negro in the Civil War, the Union could not have been saved, nor slavery destroyed."[50] Ironically, poor Southern whites had only been enfranchised as an electoral counterweight to the freed black slaves.[51] Last, Du Bois argued that it was American blacks who had actually liberated American whites—from the joyless culture of the "Protestant ethic."[52] Echoing Max Weber—whose lectures he had attended while a student in Berlin in the 1890s and with whom he had extensive contact during and after Weber's 1904 trip to the United States[53]—Du Bois came to see Puritanism as the root of a "disenchanted" relationship to nature and an overly moralistic attitude toward labor. Perhaps, he suggested, the greatest of the spiritual gifts bequeathed by African Americans was a "sensuous receptivity to the beauty of the world" and "the idea of toil as a necessary evil ministering to the pleasure of life" rather than as "a great moral duty."[54] "While the gift of the white laborer made many Americans rich," he concluded, "it will take the psychology of the black man to make it happy,"[55] a sentiment Weber might well have agreed with.

But the prophetic element never really disappeared from Du Bois's thought. Indeed, it is only against the background of black "chosenness" that the meaning of Du Bois's most famous locution—the metaphor of "the veil"—becomes clear.[56] "I have been in the world but not of it," claimed Du Bois; "I have seen the human drama from a veiled corner."[57] In the Hebrew Bible, the veil serves two functions. The first is to mark the Holy of Holies, the place where man encounters God's judgment.[58] The second is to conceal the radiance of Moses's face after he has re-

ceived the Ten Commandments.[59] Thereafter, Moses covers his face with
a veil, which he removes only when listening to God or speaking to the
people—that is, when recording or pronouncing the Law, which is that
element of God's righteousness that humans can comprehend. The apos-
tle Paul gives the veil a new meaning: it covers over the saving truth
of the Gospel from "those who are perishing."[60] For Du Bois, African
Americans were "the ark of testimony" for the sins of America, those
people who were closest to God and his seat of judgment and to whom,
and in whom, the ethics of Jesus had been most fully revealed. They were
also the veil that white Americans used to conceal their own sins from
themselves. Only by removing the veil that separated them from their
black countrymen, Du Bois implied, would white Americans ever come
to know the unflattering truth about themselves. The realization of the
American project therefore depended upon a lifting of the veil and a
"contact of living souls" across the races.

This brings us to Du Bois's second major contribution to the civil
religion: his proclamation of a "new covenant." This covenant appealed
to the Sermon on the Mount and the crucifixion and placed particular
stress on inclusivity and equality and on love and self-sacrifice. The
opening words of his 1904 "Credo" affirmed a "God who made of one
blood all races that dwell on earth . . . differing in no essential particular,
and alike in soul and the possibility of infinite development."[61] Racial
inequality in American political and religious life was not only a violation of the founding documents, but an "utter denial of the very first
principles of the ethics of Jesus Christ."[62] For Du Bois, to "call the practical religion of the nation Christian" was therefore "absurd."[63] Like
Addams, Du Bois regarded selfless love as the highest ideal in Christ's
teachings, an ideal more fully realized in black Christianity than in
white piety: "There has run in the heart of black folk the greatest of
human achievements, love and sympathy, even for their enemies, for
those who despised them and hurt them and did them nameless ill," he
declared. "They have nursed the sick and closed the staring eyes of the
dead. They have given friendship to the friendless, they have shared the
pittance of their poverty with the outcast and nameless; they have been
good and true and pitiful to the bad and false."[64] Above all Americans,
he continued, there "looms the figure of the Black Mammy, one of the
most pitiful of the world's Christs," who herself "was an embodied Sor-
row, an anomaly crucified on the cross of her own neglected children for
the sake of the children of masters who bought and sold her as they
bought and sold cattle."[65]

Du Bois's civil religion was not confined to the genres of political and ethical philosophy. He was acutely aware that a "religion of mere reason and morality will not alone supply the dynamics of spiritual inspiration and sacrifice."[66] This view inspired his many retellings of the crucifixion story, a dozen in total, all penned between 1900 and 1935,[67] and most revolving around a black Christ who (re)appears in modern America.[68] These stories must be read against a triple backdrop: the gradual whitening of iconographic representations of Christ in the nineteenth-century United States[69]; the runaway success of earlier works featuring a white Christ, especially Charles Sheldon's *In His Steps*,[70] the historical progenitor of the contemporary "what would Jesus do" movement; and, finally, the hateful epidemic of lynching, which claimed the lives of at least three thousand black men during the late nineteenth and early twentieth centuries.

Why a black Christ? As Du Bois explained: "Jesus Christ was a laborer and black men are laborers; He was poor and we are poor. He was despised . . . and we are despised. He was persecuted and crucified and we are mobbed and lynched."[71] Not all of Du Bois's recountings of the crucifixion figured black Christs, however. In two of them, "Jesus Christ in Texas" and "Jesus Christ in Georgia," the race of the Christ figure is ambiguous. The white characters initially perceive him as white but then decide he is "mulatto," "even if he did not own the Negro blood." He is described as having hair that "hung in close curls far down the sides of his face and his face was olive even yellow."[72] Du Bois's point in these stories was clear: the whitening of Christ in America had gone so far, and the racial prejudice of white Americans so deep, that they would have been unable and unwilling to recognize a Jewish Jesus even if they met him face to face.

So "what *would* Jesus do?" For Du Bois, the answer was obvious: he would minister to the downtrodden, socialize with "outcasts and tramps," and urge his listeners to "treat other people just like you want to be treated," even to the point of loving their enemies, but also to "rest and sing sometimes," just as he did in the Gospels.[73] But the underlying question was: "How would Americans react?" The answer contained in Du Bois's parables is, again, that privileged white Christians—judges, politicians, dames, and even ministers—would not recognize Jesus if they saw him, nor he them; they were simply too blinded by racial animus.

Du Bois anticipated many of the themes of black liberation theology: not only the idea of a black Christ and a black God, but also the vision of God as the God of the oppressed, and the view that white Christianity badly distorts Christian ethics.[74] Was he therefore guilty of reverse racism, a form of black religious nationalism, as some critics of black liberation theology have suggested?[75] In truth, Du Bois's motives were more polemical than theological. He wished to shore up the morale of African Americans during a period of great disappointment and oppression. And he wanted to shock white Americans into living up to the ethical demands of their religious creed. In doing so, he expanded the homiletic repertoire of the American civil religion by renarrating the crucifixion of Christ in the form of a jeremiad, creating a hybrid form that we might call a "Christomiad" as a minor-key counterpoint to the bombastic melodies of the Southern "Redeemers" who would invoke Christ's name before the lynching tree. Like many prophets, Du Bois was scorned and reviled and eventually driven into exile. White America was not yet ready for a black prophet.

AMERICAN PROPHET: REINHOLD NIEBUHR AND CHRISTIAN REALISM

While John Dewey was often called "America's philosopher," Reinhold Niebuhr was frequently referred to as "America's theologian," though he is perhaps better described as "America's prophet." Nor was vocation the only thing that separated the two. Niebuhr was born in 1892, a full generation after Dewey. His formative years were spent in a small town in rural Illinois, not New England. Nor could Niebuhr claim a Puritan lineage. His father, Gustav, was a Protestant pastor who had emigrated from Germany. His mother, Lydia, was the daughter of a German missionary. One thing he did share with Dewey was a checkered CV. Niebuhr graduated from Elmhurst College in Illinois and from Eden Theological Seminary in Missouri, his father's alma mater, before completing his education at the Yale Divinity School. There, Niebuhr felt like "a mongrel among thoroughbreds."[76] After graduation in 1915, he was called to a church in Detroit. Niebuhr was a powerful preacher, and his congregation grew quickly, but his true vocation was prophetic rather than pastoral. Within a year of his arrival, he had published two articles in the *Atlantic*. By the early 1920s, he was traveling and lecturing throughout the United States and Europe. In 1928, Niebuhr accepted a post at Union Theological Seminary in New York City. There, he was a prophet among priests, a man with a calling but few credentials.

One way of understanding Niebuhr's project is as an effort to recover and reconstruct the Puritan legacy and, in particular, the notion of "covenant" and the practice of "jeremiad." This Niebuhr did by returning to the traditions of which they were a part: the Augustinian understanding of "original sin" and the Hebrew tradition of prophetic critique. Niebuhr believed that modern Americans trivialized sin, albeit in varying ways. Conservative Protestants focused too much on sexual peccadillos; they reduced righteousness to prudery. Religious and secular liberals were too optimistic about education; they greatly underestimated the tenacity of pride and the subtlety of self-love. In Niebuhr's phrase, modern liberals were "foolish children of light."[77]

If we wish to recover an adequate notion of original sin, said Niebuhr, we have to go all the way back to Paul and Augustine. For them, the root cause of human sinfulness was not desire or ignorance; it was a pride or self-love that led human beings to overestimate their powers and ignore their finitude. This view is aptly conveyed in the biblical myth of the Fall.[78] Lucifer's pride leads to his fall; Adam's and Eve's lead to theirs.[79] Anticipating modern-day practitioners of the hermeneutics of suspicion, Paul and Augustine discovered the taint of pride in even the most virtuous acts. This taint could be subtly masked not only from others but from oneself. Those with power and privilege were especially prone to self-deception of this sort.[80]

Where Niebuhr went beyond Paul and Augustine was in his analysis of collective forms of self-love and self-deception. Niebuhr recognized that powerful groups and institutions are more plausible, tempting, and deceptive sources of pride than individual accomplishments, especially for the less privileged members of a society: plausible because groups and institutions have a permanence and a power that the individual does not; tempting because identifying with them provides an escape of sorts from the situation of weakness and finitude that afflicts all human beings, and the feelings of insecurity and anxiety it gives rise to; deceptive because devotion to a group or institution allows personal pride to be masked by a veil of altruism.

One of the most dangerous forms of collective pride, said Niebuhr, is "modern religious nationalisms." What makes them so dangerous is that they conjoin so many different forms of collective pride—not only spiritual and national pride, but race and class pride as well—and then arm them with the power of the modern state. Nation is easily combined with religion because of their shared "aura of the sacred."[81] The masses are easily mobilized because "the man in the street, with his lust for power and prestige thwarted by his own limitations and the necessities of social life, projects his ego upon the nation and indulges his anarchic lusts vicariously"[82] Writing in the closing years of World War II, Niebuhr argued that religious nationalisms are not merely "idolatrous,"[83] but truly "demonic," not only in the theological sense that they involve "the invasion and possession of the self" by a racial and national "spirit" that makes "pretensions of divinity,"[84] but also in the material sense that they can unleash apocalyptic forms of death and destruction. America, Neibuhr contended, has still not exorcised this demon, nor escaped these apocalyptic dangers.

While Niebuhr was likely thinking of fascist forms of political religion in this context, he was equally critical of the American variety of WASP religious nationalism.[85] John Adams had earlier foreseen the danger of such a combination, declaring, "Power always thinks that it has a great soul and vast views . . . and that it is doing God's service when it is violating all His laws."[86] And that danger, Niebuhr observed, had been fully realized in the Spanish-American War, when the "ambition and vanity" of Teddy Roosevelt joined with the "will-to-power of an adolescent nation and the frustrated impulses . . . and martial ardor" of the man in the street in an act of blatant imperialism.[87] It was the ideological culmination of a whole series of collective conceits stretching back to the founding itself.[88] The "Puritans," Niebuhr argued, "gradually shifted from their emphasis upon a divine favor to the nation, to an emphasis upon the virtue which the nation had acquired by divine favor."[89] This conceit further deepened when Americans came to attribute their material prosperity to their moral virtue rather than to the natural endowments of the vast continent they inhabited.[90] These moral conceits were then combined with racial conceits about the "Anglo-Saxon" or "Nordic" peoples *qua* "master race," as the "master organizers," not only of their own destiny, but of the world's. In this way, Niebuhr traced the roots of American religious nationalism to the hidden conceit that lurked deep within the Puritan understanding of covenant: the belief that God had chosen them, not out of his own divine mercy and sovereign grace, but on account of their peculiar individual and collective virtues.

Returning to the "traditional values" of the Puritans was therefore not enough. To undo this conceit, said Niebuhr, one had to reach back further, to the intellectual guardians of the covenant, the Hebrew prophets themselves. Not that they had entirely escaped the sin of spiritual pride or its devolution into national pride. The book of Joel, Niebuhr contended, advanced "a nationalistic interpretation of history" of truly "extravagant proportions." Niebuhr's favorite prophet, his model, was Amos. Unlike Joel, "Amos prophesied judgment upon other nations as well as Israel, on Damascus, Philistia and Ammon."[91] His God was not the God of Israel, but the sovereign of all peoples. Like John Winthrop, Amos knew the covenant to be a source, not only of blessings, but of danger. "You only have I known of all the families of the earth," God said through Amos, "therefore I will punish you for all your iniquities."[92] The Israelites were not to await a political messiah who would bring national glory. "Woe to you who desire the day of the Lord!" Amos warned. "It is darkness and not light, as if a man fled from a lion, and a bear met him."[93] Nor were they to imagine that divine favor could be secured through pious rituals. "I hate, I despise your feasts," thundered Amos's God, "and I take no delight in your solemn assemblies."[94] What God desires, above all, said Amos, is justice: "Take away from me the noise of your songs. . . . But let justice roll down like waters, and righteousness like an ever-flowing stream."[95]

Niebuhr highlighted the continuities between Christ and the prophets. All were fiercely opposed to any form of political idolatry. John the Baptist warned against the racial and national pride of the Israelites, proclaiming that "God is able of these stones to raise up children unto Abraham."[96] Christ's death on the cross at the hands of the Romans put an end to expectations of national deliverance by a political messiah. And Paul's mission to the Gentiles confirmed that God is the God of all peoples.

But there is also an element of discontinuity in this narrative: the new covenant proclaimed by Christ is a covenant not only of justice, but also of love. Not that love and justice are at odds. It is only through selfless acts of love that some measure of justice is even possible. But the self-love of man also means that a politics of love cannot be realized in this world, and this means, in turn, that the fulfillment of history cannot take place within history. All forms of political millenarianism and utopianism, all efforts to realize an end of history or a heaven on earth, of whatever political stripe they may be, must therefore be eschewed as vainglorious attempts at premature escape from the historicity and imperfections of human existence.

Niebuhr's understanding of divine Providence was thus more like Augustine's and Lincoln's than Calvin's or Winthrop's. Niebuhr did not doubt that historical events somehow conform to divine purposes; otherwise history would be meaningless. But he rejected the view that human beings can readily divine these purposes; this would exceed the limits of human reason. We really only know God's purposes when they prove to be at odds with our own. One of the few Americans to fully understand this, he felt, was "our greatest President," Abraham Lincoln, and one of the few texts in which a prophetic understanding of the American project had found its full articulation, he thought, was in Lincoln's Second Inaugural Address. For Niebuhr, Lincoln's greatness lay in his ability to steer a steady course between self-righteousness and sentimentality, between a commitment to justice, insofar as he could apprehend it, and charity, insofar as it could be realized. The spiritual sources of this greatness were two: a "broken spirit and a contrite heart" combined with a "moral resoluteness about the immediate issues" and "a religious awareness of another dimension of meaning and judgment."[97]

Niebuhr believed that a nation under covenant has need of prophets. Not prophets of the millenarian variety, who vainly proclaim the time and place of the Second Coming. Not prophets of a pseudo-Puritan sort, who loudly insist that the American nation return to its "moral values." The task of the prophet, for Niebuhr, is not to stoke millennial expectations or enforce divine contracts. Such a conception represents a fundamental misunderstanding of the nature of prophecy and covenant. A nation under covenant is not a nation under contract, but a nation *under judgment*. And the role of the prophet is to remind the nation of this, to preach an ethos of contrition and humility on the one hand, and to inspire acts of charity and justice on the other.

Thus far, I have focused on Niebuhr's efforts to rethink the Puritan strand of the civil religion. But what about the republican strand? Here, too, Niebuhr made important contributions. Consider his theory of history. In classical republicanism, recall, political history follows a cyclical course of corruption and renewal. In modern progressivism, by contrast, human history follows a linear course of ever-increasing enlightenment and mutuality. Lincoln and Douglass viewed history as a spiral. Niebuhr added that this spiral is continually widening as the scope of human communities expands over time, from the small bands of prehistory to the nation-states of our era.

This expansion of human community is driven by both the "light" and the "dark" sides of human nature: by the light side of animal sociality and human brotherliness, but also by the dark side of animal dominance and human pridefulness. Because human beings are both animals and spirits with both light and dark sides, the widening of human communities brings growing possibilities but also growing dangers. The possibilities include greater opportunities for physical security and social justice, as polities become larger and more inclusive. The dangers include greater opportunities for predatory violence and material exploitation stemming from the concomitant concentration of social power, both political and economic. What is more, the dangers are often realized before the possibilities are achieved, as the world wars sadly showed. History is therefore a *spiral* in the sense that progress often comes through regress.

From a Niebuhrian perspective, then, the classical theory is historically naïve but politically realistic: naïve insofar as it folds historical evolution into an eternal cycle, and realistic insofar as it grasps the role of conflict and corruption in human history. By contrast, the progressive theory is historically realistic but politically naïve. It is realistic to the degree that its "evolutionary" model allows for the contingencies of history and the diversity of societies. But it is naïve to the degree that it envisions enlightenment and education as the driving forces of the evolutionary process. Niebuhr's theory aspired to be both historically and politically realistic, to meld a progressive appreciation of historical change with a classical sensitivity to political corruption.

On corruption, too, Niebuhrian realism suggested a synthetic view. In classical parlance, "corruption" is a quasi-natural process, somewhat akin to the decay of organic matter. There is no remedy for it. For most progressives, on the other hand, corruption is a purely moral phenomenon, the result of bad decisions by bad actors. It can be remedied with education and reform. Niebuhr did not explicitly address the problem of corruption, but his version of Christian realism does suggest an interpretation of corruption that goes beyond classical naturalism and progressive moralism. On this view, even the most virtuous of actions contains a germ of pride that sprouts shoots of self-deception, providing cover for still more expansive and poisonous forms of pride. In this way, the subtle form of spiritual pride that lurked within the covenant theology of the American Puritans led later generations to ignore the role of good fortune in their material prosperity, giving rise to excessive pride in American power more generally and setting the stage for a self-righteous imperialism. For Niebuhr, corruption is inevitable but not natural and results from virtue as much as vice.

To say that it is inevitable, however, is not to say that it is irresistible. Skeptical as Niebuhr was of classical rationalism and Renaissance humanism, his theory of democracy still had a republican ring. Like the ancients, he regarded social and institutional balancing as the best and only safeguard of individual freedom and self-government. And in modern societies, he argued, social balance means class balance. While Niebuhr eschewed the revolutionary strategy of Marxian socialism as dangerously utopian, he applauded the political organization of working people as the only sure remedy against the unchecked greed and self-serving fulminations of the propertied few. As regards political balance within the state itself, he affirmed the Madisonian solution of a separation of powers. Even if he may not have known it, and although he surely would have denied it, Niebuhr's republicanism also had a Machiavellian ring. He was deeply attuned to the importance of myths, and especially of founding myths, in sustaining popular government. In his first major work of political theology, he had gone so far as to argue that democratic politics has need of "dogmas, symbols and emotionally potent oversimplifications."[98] In his mature work, he would develop a noninstrumental theory of myths in the sense of transcendent narratives that falsify the "facts of history, as seen by science, to state its truth."[99] Only myth, he believed, can maintain the necessary tension between the preservation of present goods and the quest for ultimate aims, while safeguarding against attempts to "escape" from history "prematurely" via a utopian politics.

This tension results from the fact that the prophetic value of social justice and the Christian value of sacrificial love must be enacted within history but cannot be realized within history. They are at once imperative and impossible. One of the central tasks of prophetic critique and political theology must therefore be to maintain this tension by resisting all attempts to reduce the transcendent values of justice and love to "historical relativities" such as "social contracts" and "ethical mutuality." Indeed, for Niebuhr, this tension is the distinguishing mark of theological orthodoxy in both Judaism and Christianity, and all theologies that relax it represent corruptions of the faith, whether they take the form of the sacrificialism of preprophetic Judaism, the sacramentalism of medieval Catholicism, or the "Lutheran political ethic" in which an "absolute distinction between the 'heavenly' or 'spiritual' kingdom and the 'earthly' one, destroys the tension between the final demands of God upon the conscience, and all the relative possibilities of realizing the good in history."[100] Tension was also the governing principle of Niebuhr's ethics. In a sly subversion of Aristotle's famous metaphor of the bowman, Niebuhr repeatedly suggested that it may be necessary to overtension the string and overshoot the target in order to actually hit it, because the arrow of moral progress is always shot into the headwinds of human pride and self-love. Thus, while Niebuhr rejected religious nationalisms and secular utopias that collapse the distinction between the religious and the political, he was just as adamantly opposed to sectarian religions or secular materialisms that seek to pry them apart. Where Weber saw the tension between the religious and political spheres as tragic, Niebuhr

viewed it as salutary and, indeed, as the principal source of moral progress in human history and one of the distinguishing features of the Western tradition.

Thus far, I have focused mainly on Niebuhr's interpretation of the
democratic project in American history. Contemporary discussions of
"Christian realism" have focused more on Niebuhr's thinking about international relations and political totalitarianism. Here, too, Niebuhr
sought a middle way between the unconditional pacifism embraced by
much of the American Left after World War I and the full-throated jingoism that came to increasingly dominate the Right. The problem with
modern versions of Christian pacifism, he said, is that they accept the
Renaissance doctrine of human goodness and reject the Christian doctrine of original sin, but the fact of human sin means that "justice can
only be achieved by a certain degree of coercion on the one hand, and
by resistance to . . . tyranny, on the other."[101] Niebuhr was far quicker
than most leftists to realize the tyrannical trajectory of Soviet Communism and Marxian socialism. While he remained critical of the Spanish-
American War, he was an early proponent of American entry into World
War II. Unfortunately, the modern-day left-wing hawks and right-wing
Wilsonians who have invoked Niebuhrian arguments in support of the
"war on terror" and the "battle against Islamo-Fascism" have not proven
as astute as Niebuhr in their political diagnoses of the present conjunc-
ture. Instead, they have fallen prey to the prophetic temptation that confronts any political pundit, the desire to be the watchful sentry who first
espies apocalyptic dangers looming on the horizon. Right-wing acolytes,
meanwhile, have too often forgotten Niebuhr's commitment to social
justice.

If modern-day Christian realists sometimes forget Niebuhr's politics
in favor of his geopolitics, then Niebuhr himself may be accused of emphasizing freedom to the neglect of equality and thereby of neglecting
one of the core principles of the civil religion. Indeed, Niebuhr's recurring and sometimes uncritical usage of the phrase "Anglo-Saxon," as in
"Anglo-Saxon democracies" suggests that he was not wholly immune to
a certain degree of cultural and perhaps even ethnic pride. The same
cannot be said of Jane Addams, much less of W.E.B. Du Bois. For them,
much more than for Niebuhr or Dewey, the tasks of overcoming ethnocultural arrogance and racial inequality were central components of the
democratic project. For others, however, overcoming these inequalities
was as hopeless as the democratic project itself. For this self-styled secular elite, the main task was keeping the ignorant masses at bay.

H. L. MENCKEN: SECULAR HERO?

Two versions of radical secularism sprang up in the decades following the Civil War. The "classic liberalism" of William Graham Sumner was a version of radical individualism, while the militant "agnosticism" of Robert Ingersoll was a form of total separationism. But Sumner's conservative brand of radical secularism was more individualist than secularist, and Ingersoll's version of progressive secularism was more secularist than individualist. It was not until the early twentieth century that these two versions of radical secularism were fused into a comprehensive political ideology.

The public embodiment of this outlook was the journalist and critic H. L. Mencken (1880–1956). Mencken was the scion of a well-to-do Baltimore cigar manufacturer, and his extended family tree included many generations of German intellectuals stretching as far back as the seventeenth century. Though a gifted student, the young Mencken showed little interest in attending college. After graduating from high school at age fifteen, he began working in the cigar business. But he quickly realized that his real vocation was in the other family business—the business of letters. So, in 1899, at age eighteen, he presented himself at the editorial office of the *Baltimore Morning Herald*. Within a year, he was writing a weekly column on the *Herald*'s editorial page. By 1907, he had published his first book, *The Philosophy of Friedrich Nietzsche*. The following year, he became co-editor of the *Smart Set,* a New York literary journal. He was not yet thirty. Mencken's meteoric ascent was briefly interrupted by a wave of public outrage occasioned by his outspoken support for Kaiser Wilhelm during World War I, but it resumed during the 1920s. In 1924, he cofounded a new literary magazine, the *American Mercury*. Then, in 1925, he published his famous dispatches from the Scopes trial. The next year, he completed his *Notes on Democracy*, the first work in a trilogy on politics, religion, and ethics.

Mencken was now at the apogee of his influence. The evening of December 8, 1934, marked an inflection point in his public trajectory. At the annual dinner of the Gridiron Club—a carnivalesque "roast" of the U.S. president by the press corps and vice versa—Mencken delivered a ferocious skewering of Franklin Roosevelt. FDR responded in kind with a verbatim reading from one of Mencken's withering polemics against his fellow journalists. Publicly humiliated before his colleagues, Mencken vowed revenge. This deep personal animus toward Roosevelt now reinforced Mencken's growing misgivings about the New Deal. He lashed out again and again. Suddenly, it was Mencken who seemed out of step. His libertarian denunciations of relief programs seemed mean-spirited instead of clever. His apologetic descriptions of Hitler's Germany appeared naïve instead of radical. Even so, Mencken still had—and still has—many followers. "When I was growing up in Maryland in the 1960s," reports the intellectual historian Jackson Lears, "H. L. Mencken still possessed the status of a demigod."[102] Mencken has many devotees even today. The "Menckenbot" tweets out a line penned by the author every day to some ten thousand followers, and the libertarian liberalism he favored is back in vogue with the "smart set" of a new century. In 2012, University of Chicago biologist Jerry Coyne celebrated Mencken as "the first New Atheist."[103] Wherein lies the appeal?

Part of it surely comes from Mencken's breathlessly sardonic prose style. But another part stems from the sense of knowing superiority in which it invites the reader to partake. One of his biographers christened Mencken "the skeptic."[104] That is true enough, as far as it goes. Mencken certainly did not accept anything on anybody else's authority. But his acidic wit did not dissolve all conviction. He had, to begin with, an unwavering conviction in his own intellectual superiority. And he had, too, a firm belief in the moral superiority of his ancestral homeland.

Both of these tendencies were cemented by Mencken's youthful encounter with Friedrich Nietzsche. Later in life, Mencken would insist that Nietzsche's influence on him had been slight. And that, too, is true enough, insofar as Mencken's comprehension of Nietzsche was also slight. His interpretation of Nietzsche was often confused, at times wildly so, as in his jaw-dropping mischaracterization of Nietzsche's moral theory as "utilitarian." Mencken also had an unfortunate tendency to confuse his own personal prejudices with Nietzsche's philosophy. In his hands, Nietzsche became "an all-American type, a world-improving, can-do go-getter delighted to have seen through the fraud of Christianity and gone beyond good and evil"—in other words, an avatar of Mencken himself.[105]

However shaky his grasp on the fine points of Nietzsche's philosophy may have been, Mencken had a firm enough grasp of the central thrust of Nietzsche's work, at least as it was understood at the time. Nietzsche had divided humanity into two groups: a small elite and a great "herd." The elite sought freedom and beauty. They were noble predators. The herd wanted equality and security; they were lowing sheep. Christianity was the religion of the sheep, and the priests were their cunning shepherds, who tried to fold the elite into the herd as a means of dragging them down and controlling them, all in the name of something called "civilization." But this priestly project was a fundamental misunderstanding of the real sources of civilizational advance. In reality, Nietzsche argued, and Mencken agreed, the elite is the creator of all greatness in life and history, so the inevitable result of Christianity is cultural mediocrity. What was needed, Nietzsche concluded, was a new post-Christian elite.

Where was this new race, Mencken wondered? Where else but in Germany! Writing in the *Atlantic Monthly* in November of 1914, shortly after the outbreak of World War I, Mencken announced that Nietzsche's philosophy had given birth to a "new Germany" that was now leading the world in every creative field: science and medicine, engineering and manufacturing, literature and music, and, of course, philosophy. This progress was "initiated and carried on . . . by a new aristocracy of the laboratory, the study and the shop."[106] This aristocracy was creating a "new democracy," one that was not founded on the "romantic theory that all men were natural equals" but was an "aristocratic democracy in the Athenian sense—a democracy of intelligence, of strength, of superior fitness—a democracy at the top."[107] In other words: a meritocracy. This new elite had shrugged off its religion and dispensed with the Christian God, "providing a substitute—in a helmet!—for the vacancy."[108] Who was the great man in the helmet? The Kaiser? Thor? That was not clear. In any event, the transformation was all due to Nietzsche! "Germany becomes Nietzsche, Nietzsche becomes Germany," Mencken crooned.[109] Needless to say, the article was ill timed and poorly received, and Mencken had to keep his head down for the rest of the war.

Not that the war changed his views. A decade later, in his 1927 volume *Notes on Democracy*, Mencken turned his Nietzschean lens on the politics of his home country. Surveying American democracy, he saw what Nietzsche had seen in European Christianity: the herd's efforts to shackle the elites. Both democracy and Christianity start from the premise that human beings are equal in some sense. This, argued Mencken, is false. "Men are not alike," he insisted, and the difference between the elite and the herd is "qualitative" and not just "quantitative."[110] Really, they are like two different species. While the elite is concerned with freedom and beauty, the herd is moved by fear and envy. Consequently, democratic politics consists of two things: "pursuits of horrendous monsters, most of them imaginary" and hatred "of the fellow who is having a better time of it."[111] The real victims in democratic society, Mencken contended— anticipating the arguments of Ayn Rand's John Galt—are the elites, who are confronted with the ugliness of mass culture and constrained by the strictures of herd morality. Their interests, he concluded, would be better served in an "aristocratic democracy" such as Nazi Germany or an enlightened monarchy such as Frederick the Great's Prussia.

Of course, if one followed Nietzsche's elite/herd distinction to its logical conclusion, it might well lead to out-and-out racism, support for eugenics, and a glorification of war. And in Mencken's case, that is precisely where it did lead. "In any chance crowd of Southern Negroes one is bound to note individuals who resemble apes quite as much as they resemble Modern Man," he wrote in his notebooks.[112] Elsewhere he fumed that: "Despite ten thousand New Deals, nothing whatever can be done in the long run for the man who is stupid and lazy, and has more children than he can care for." Mencken's remedy? Mass sterilization.[113] In a 1933 review of *Mein Kampf*, Mencken described German anti-Semitism as "understandable"; later, he would add that Hitler's annexation of Austria was "sensible."[114] Statements of this sort were by no means rare in Mencken's writings, and even his most sympathetic biographer has reluctantly concluded that Mencken was, among other things, a rabid anti-Semite. Nor did such outbursts end even after the war, when the horrendous crimes of the Nazis against European Jewry were public knowledge.[115]

Nowadays, of course, Mencken is mostly remembered for his blistering dispatches from the Scopes trial. Consider the following description from his obituary of William Jennings Bryan, who had died a few days after the proceedings:

> Bryan was a vulgar and common man, a cad undiluted. He was ignorant, bigoted, self-seeking, blatant and dishonest. His career brought him into contact with the first men of his time; he preferred the company of rustic ignoramuses. It was hard to believe, watching him at Dayton, that he had traveled, that he had been received in civilized societies, that he had been a high officer of state. He seemed only a poor clod like those around him, deluded by a childish theology, full of an almost pathological hatred of all learning, all human dignity, all beauty, all fine and noble things. He was a peasant come home to the dung-pile. Imagine a gentleman, and you have imagined everything that he was not.[116]

Read on its own, this description still seems witty. Read against the background of Mencken's Nietzschean libertarianism and the facts of Bryan's biography, it merely seems vicious. One of Bryan's primary concerns about teaching Darwin was that it might open the door to social

Darwinism. Where Mencken was concerned, this worry was surely not misplaced. The Scopes trial was not just about science and religion. It was also about elitism and egalitarianism.

Is it unfair to focus on Mencken as an exemplar of radical secularism? Perhaps. But Mencken's views do reveal certain underlying tensions within that tradition that are still evident today. There is, to begin with, the tension between liberalism's emphasis on liberty and America's other founding value of egalitarianism. Lockean liberalism grounds human equality in theology. But libertarian liberalism dismisses equality. It sees human beings as naturally unequal and any attempt to maintain equality as an infringement on liberty—or, more than that, as an attempt to violate the rules of nature enshrined in the market. This tension is particularly pronounced in conservative versions of libertarianism that celebrate individual liberty and free markets. In some cases, conservative libertarianism goes hand-in-hand with racial prejudice (as in the case of Ron Paul). Then there is the tension between strong secularism and another of America's founding values: religious freedom. Lockean liberalism grounds religious freedom in liberty of conscience. But strong secularism sees all religion as a form of authority or coercion. For radical secularists, then, "religious freedom" is really an oxymoron. What people need, they argue, is freedom *from* religion. This tension is most evident in progressive versions of libertarianism that celebrate individual creativity and scientific authority. Thus, "new atheists" sometimes oppose religious freedom in the name of freedom itself.

These tensions within radical secularism often give rise to a certain style of public engagement that is at odds with democratic pluralism. There is, first of all, a tendency toward moral superiority and intellectual elitism. Opposing views are dismissed as "backward." In Lockean liberalism, these tendencies are checked by a humbler epistemology that stresses human limitations. In libertarian liberalism, by contrast, they are set free by appeals to scientific authority, while in conservative libertarianism, the appeal nowadays is usually to a laissez-faire version of economic theory. Either way, opponents are routinely dismissed as "stupid."

Our founding values of liberty and equality can be harmonized by various means. They can be harmonized through a theistic liberalism of the Lockean variety, as the theologian Nicholas Wolterstorff has brilliantly shown.[117] They can also be harmonized through a secular republicanism that links civic equality and political freedom. Whether they can be harmonized through a naturalistic liberalism, especially of a libertarian sort, remains to be shown. I, for one, am doubtful.

RELIGIOUS NATIONALISM:
SHIFTS AND TRANSFORMATIONS

During the three decades between the onset of World War I and the conclusion of World War II, American religious nationalism underwent a series of major shifts and transformations. Two events, separated by three decades, illustrate these changes.

First, the fourteenth annual reunion of the United Sons of Confederate Veterans took place in June of 1904 in Nashville, Tennessee.[118] The organizers estimated a total attendance of thirty thousand people, including some ten thousand veterans. Reassembled regiments processed together behind their old battle flags through "an archway of red, white and blue, with the placid features of their beloved Lee" festooned with flags, and then into a spacious "Tabernacle." There, Tennessee governor James B. Frazier addressed the assembled veterans as "the descendants of the men who suffered at Valley Forge with Washington, the greatest rebel the world has ever known," and reminded them that "a Southern man had written the Declaration of Independence, Southern men had dominated the constitutional convention, and a Southern man had written the organic law of the Nation." The "Commanding General," Stephen D. Lee, then assured his charges that "the blood of our race" had not been shed in vain and, indeed, that "without the shedding of blood there is no redemption."

Finally, the keynote speaker, the Rev. Dr. Randolph Harrison McKim (1842–1920) strode up to the stage.[119] Born in Baltimore in the generation before Mencken, McKim was descended from Scots-Irish stock on his father's side and the Jamestown settlers on his mother's. In 1861, he interrupted his studies at the University of Virginia to enlist in the Confederate Army. Over the next three years, he saw heavy fighting and eventually rose to the rank of lieutenant. He spent the final year of the war as an Episcopal chaplain and later earned a doctorate from the College of William and Mary. Following stints in North Carolina, New Orleans, and New York, he accepted a post at the Church of the Epiphany in Washington, DC, in 1888. He remained there until his death. Though theologically conservative, McKim was no "yokel." He read Latin, Greek, French, and German; traveled extensively in Europe; and wrote scholarly studies of biblical criticism and academic histories of the Civil War.[120]

On this day, gazing out over his assembled comrades, McKim offered up a learned defense of Confederate secession worthy of John C. Calhoun combined—paradoxically—with a ringing affirmation of country and flag. "This is now for us an indissoluble Union of indestructible States," he assured his listeners. "We are loyal to that starry banner . . . baptized with Southern blood" during the revolution.[121] Though split apart by the Civil War, by the "providence of God," he maintained, North and South were now "drawn . . . together in bonds of genuine brotherhood. Their blood ha[d] watered the same soil."[122] Not only is "the soil trodden by a patriot . . . holy ground," but the blood spilled by the sons of the South had "transfigured" all present.[123] As for the "Lost Cause," it was not truly lost. The cause of the Confederacy, said McKim, had always been "the cause of Liberty," that "sacred heritage" of the "Anglo-Saxon" race, and liberty had been preserved.[124]

While the spilling of Southern blood in the Spanish-American War had helped to reconcile the "sons of the South" to the cause of the Union, it was World War I that finally transformed the states of the old Confederacy into a bastion of "hyper-patriotism."[125] Here, too, McKim was a leading voice. Preaching from his Washington pulpit just ten days after the *Lusitania* disaster, he drew on the Christian scriptures to develop a critique of pacifism and a case for war. These texts, he argued, contain "innumerable examples of men filled with the Spirit of God" who were also "faithful soldiers."[126] In support, he pointed to Abraham, Moses, Joshua, and even Isaiah: they had all been prophets and warriors, he claimed.[127] If Jesus chose not to fight, it was only because his kingdom was not of this world. "If it had been a worldly kingdom," McKim reassured his listeners, Jesus would not have hesitated to "employ the agency of war."[128] He supported this view by invoking the book of Revelation, which described Jesus as "one whose 'eyes were as a flame of fire,' 'making war in righteousness,' and 'followed by the armies of Heaven.'"[129] In the same vein, McKim concluded that Paul was not speaking figuratively when he told the Ephesians to "put on the whole armor of God."[130] And since "self-sacrifice" is the "supremest virtue inculcated by the Christian religion," the soldier dies the death of a Christian martyr.[131] Once the United States entered the Great War, McKim escalated his religious nationalist rhetoric still further, describing the war as a "holy war" and a "crusade," the Germans as "the embodiment of all evil, all wickedness and all cruelty," the Kaiser as "The AntiChrist," and the battlefield as "Calvary."[132]

The second episode took place a full generation later on the other side of the continent, when the Associated Churches of Los Angeles staged a giant rally at the Shrine Auditorium.[133] The highlight of the evening was a five-act tableau staged by Aimee Semple McPherson, a famous Pentecostal revivalist. Scene one depicted the "Pilgrim Fathers" landing on the "rough and rugged New England coast." Scene two showed the drafting of the U.S. Constitution, "conceived in prayer and executed by Christian gentlemen." Scene three presented Abraham Lincoln "kneeling in prayer" during the Civil War. Scene four showed "alien hands chiseling from off the American dollar the words 'in God we trust'" and using red paint to obscure a line of the national anthem: "Our Father's God to Thee." The climactic fifth scene opened on Miss America asleep on the steps of the U.S. Capitol, with "the flag flying proudly atop the dome."[134] While Miss America dozed, Lucifer snuck onstage and removed the cornerstone of "faith" from the Capitol's foundation. An atheist, who stole the cornerstone of "home," followed him. Then McPherson stepped on stage, clad in her customary white robes, and cried: "AMERICA, AWAKE! An enemy is at your gates! They have penetrated your walls!" Whereupon Miss America sprang to her feet, "unsheathe[d] the sword of Faith," and called for "Uncle Sam." In her closing peroration, McPherson proclaimed, "Never again shall another flat take the place of Old Glory! . . . Our forefathers poured out their blood to protect it!"

The shift from a historical to a mythological register that took place in the transition between scenes three and four was typical of McPherson, who often blurred the boundary between secular and sacred time.[135] Sixteen years earlier, during World War I, for example, McPherson had given a speech on "modern warfare": "The greatest battle the enemy has ever waged is being fought today. This battle is raging between the children of God . . . and every demon in hell. . . . The children of God are called upon by the Holy Spirit to enlist in the Army of King Jesus and fight as good soldiers who are sure of certain victory."[136] Was McPherson urging her listeners to convert or enlist? It was not clear. The same sort of ambiguity ran through an earlier address on "Liberty Loans." "Our King Jesus is calling for LIBERTY LOANS from all His loyal subjects who intend to go 'over there' to rule and reign," McPherson declared.[137] But just where was "over there"? Europe? Or heaven? Was a liberty bond a ticket through the pearly gates? McPherson then presented a roll call of biblical figures from Abraham to Paul who had made liberty loans to the "great struggle," for which they had won great victories—and healthy returns. Again, the meaning was ambiguous: Was the "great struggle" spiritual or earthly?

For McPherson, such questions were meaningless. She viewed historical events through an apocalyptic lens[138] and read the prophetic texts of the Bible in "literalist" fashion. She believed that the "signs of the times" could be seen in contemporary historical events, that the end of the world and the Second Coming of Jesus were imminent, and that his glorious return would bring an end to Satan's reign and initiate an earthly millennium.[139] For decades, McPherson's monthly journal, the *Bridal Call*, ran regular columns on the "signs of the times." Typically, each contained a potpourri of prophetic passages from the Bible and a mixture of worrisome dispatches from around the world reporting on the growth of atheism, communism, anarchism, and licentiousness; the persecution of Christian churches and missionaries at home and abroad; the horrors of military and class warfare; natural disasters; economic downturns; and so on.[140] There was no shortage of bad news during the active years of McPherson's ministry, which ran from the beginning of World War I through the Great Depression to the end of World War II.

The evolution of McPherson's views was part of a broader trend within American Pentecostalism, and, indeed, within conservative Protestantism more generally. Early Pentecostalism was highly populist and relatively apolitical.[141] Pentecostal evangelism focused on the downtrodden and emphasized personal transformation. This was true of McPherson's ministry as well. Following the onset of the Great Depression and then America's entry into World War II, theologically conservative Protestants became increasingly nationalistic and militaristic.[142] McPherson's ministry blazed the trail. McPherson never wavered in her loyalty to FDR and the New Deal, but she did abandon her longstanding commitment to pacifism and embraced the cause of "100% Americanism," with its nativist undertones. This late McPherson prefigured the religious nationalism of the new Christian Right that emerged in the late 1970s. Not coincidentally, its leadership ranks would also include many Pentecostals, including Pat Robertson and, more recently, Sarah Palin.

CONCLUSION

American religious nationalism originated in Puritan New England. By the early twentieth century, it had migrated south and then west. In the process, the increasingly anemic language of Yankee religious nationalism received a massive transfusion of blood rhetoric from Southern ideologues of the "Lost Cause." In the Old South, this new current connected militarism, racism, and nativism; although it was most vociferously manifested in the new Ku Klux Klan, it also was evident in the less strident language of WASP religious nationalism.[143] In Southern California—the birthplace of a sunny Pentecostalism and a center of the defense industry—a slightly different version of religious nationalism took shape. It was less sanguinary but more militaristic.[144] These two currents would eventually flow together in the nationalistic faction of the "Reagan coalition," with its dual bases in the two "Southlands"—Dixie and California—that had since coalesced into a unified "Sunbelt."

American religious nationalism had long been tempered by republican and liberal elements, most notably, the ancient suspicion of standing armies and the Lockean commitment to human equality. But as civic republicanism faded from popular discourse during the early twentieth century and the United States became an empire, popular worries about militarism started to fade as well. During the Cold War, lingering doubts were systematically suppressed in the interests of national security. For many, militarism rather than republicanism was now the litmus test of true patriotism.

Meanwhile, two types of libertarianism challenged egalitarianism. One was a post-Lockean liberalism that drew on classical political economy. Locke had also been concerned with commerce and property, of course, but the post-Lockeans were concerned with nothing else. The other was a Southern-style libertarianism that spoke loudly about individual liberty in order to drown out any talk of racial equality.[145] This type was "libertarian" only in the general sense that it gave absolute priority to individual liberty. What both libertarian currents shared was the claim that liberty was *the* "founding value"—the *only* founding value. Separated by intellectual lineage and sectional origin, these two currents of libertarianism would eventually flow together during the late twentieth century in the populist libertarianism of Ron and Rand Paul and the elitist techno-libertarianism of Silicon Valley.

Earlier versions of American religious nationalism had been tempered by postmillennial optimism. Since Puritan times, belief in prophecy had waxed and waned. In bad times, it leaned toward the premillennial apocalypticism of a Cotton Mather; in good times, it inclined toward the postmillennial optimism of a Jonathan Edwards. By the late nineteenth century, however, Christian postmillennialism was evolving into a secular progressivism—a vague faith in the bounties of technology, the goodness of human nature, and the rightness of the American project.

In that form, it still lives on today within radical secularism and kindred worldviews. But when Christian postmillennialism exited stage left, the dialogue became a monologue dominated by premillennial apocalypticism, with American militarism doing the background vocals.

There was, too, a shift within religious nationalism from a frontier worldview to an imperial one. Until the late twentieth century, the eyes of religious nationalists had been trained westward. By the late nineteenth century, they were turning outward.[146] The old metaphor of "conquering Canaan" was now inadequate, and a new trope rose up in its place: the story of "crusades" and "holy wars." Already evoked by McKim, this rhetoric would only grow in influence in the decades that followed.

The origins of the "culture wars" are usually traced to the Progressive Era struggles between "fundamentalists" and "modernists," with the Scopes trial serving as their dramatic climax.[147] In this narrative, the plot turns on the growing split within American Protestantism and the "war of religion and science." This story is not wrong, but it is incomplete. It gives too little attention to ideological and geopolitical factors. The emergence of Protestant fundamentalism is only one part of the transformation of religious nationalism, in which the injection of blood rhetoric, generic libertarianism, postmillennial apocalypticism, and crusading militarism were at least as crucial. Further, radical secularism cannot be seen merely as a natural outgrowth of science or enlightenment. It was also a political project that joined a post-Lockean liberalism with an aggressive secularism. Finally, the conventional account is also incomplete insofar as the action includes only two dramatis personae: liberalism and conservatism. In my story, of course, there are three actors, and the central plot dynamic is devolution rather than polarization. In my view, it was the late nineteenth-century emergence of a full-blown radical secularism that really undermined the old polarity between civil religion and religious nationalism.

A new polarity had now emerged. The gyre had begun to widen.

CHAPTER 6

The Post–World War II Period

JEW, PROTESTANT, CATHOLIC

WHEN MODERN-DAY conservatives and liberals think back to the 1950s and 1960s, they often perceive them through the lens of the "culture wars" of the late twentieth century. The conservative narrative is "Paradise Lost": the 1950s were a golden age of family, faith, and country; the 1960s a leaden era of, in Nixon's formulation, "acid, amnesty, and abortion." The liberal narrative is "Prometheus Unbound": the 1950s were a reactionary era of conformity, oppression, and exclusion; the 1960s a progressive era of experimentation, freedom, and togetherness.

There is some truth to both of these tales. The first fifteen years of the post–World War II era were characterized by unusually early marriages, high birth rates, and a male breadwinner norm. Moreover, the postwar era did bring an end to the "religious depression" of the 1930s and 1940s. Rates of religious believing, belonging, and building reached levels never seen before or since. Meanwhile, two new wars, one hot (in Korea) and the other cold (with the Soviet Union), generated little opposition or protest.

The next fifteen years did unsettle this conservative Eden. Rates of divorce, abortion, and female labor force participation all increased. Liberal Protestantism entered into a long-term demographic decline. American cities were rocked by protests. But for many Americans, this Eden had never been a paradise in the first place. For Southern blacks living under Jim Crow, for middle-class women involuntarily bound to home and hearth, for working-class boys drafted to fight a war they no longer believed in, and for idealistic college students who wanted more than the "American Dream" of suburban comfort, the 1960s were indeed a period of liberation.

Conservatives and liberals have been arguing about the legacy of the 1960s ever since. This chapter does not attempt to settle that debate. Instead, it tells another story built around a different and more modest frame: not Paradise Lost or Prometheus Unbound, but "Tradition Recovered." The recovery of civic republicanism was primarily the work of secular academics. The leading figure in this movement was Hannah Arendt, a German-born Jewish *émigrée* and political theorist. The recovery of prophetic religion during this period, as in the previous two, was mostly the work of religious intellectuals, particularly black clergymen. The greatest and most influential of these figures was, of course, Martin Luther King Jr. In Arendt and King, we see the two strands of the civil religious tradition unraveling. In the work of the Catholic intellectual John Courtney Murray we see an effort to spin them back together using the Catholic tradition of "natural law." It worked, at least for a time: the civil rights movement brought together a diverse coalition of social reformers that bridged long-standing divides of race and religion as well as the growing chasm between the religious and secular worldviews—the sort of coalition that is needed today to remedy the deepening inequalities and cultural malaise of our own era. For that reason alone, it is worthy of closer study.

HANNAH ARENDT: REPUBLICANISM RECONSTRUCTED

A secular Jew educated in Weimar Germany, Hannah Arendt may at first glance seem an unlikely figure in a study of American civil religion. But Arendt's classics-based education made her an eloquent defender of civic republicanism. One does not have to dig very deep to discover the civic republican foundations of her thought. In her masterwork, *The Human Condition*, Arendt focuses on the Greek ideal of "action."[1] "Action" in this sense refers to collective deliberation within a political community— what is more commonly called "positive liberty." Arendt believed that action had become increasingly devalued over time. Plato's celebration of contemplation had ushered in the autumn of action. The Roman Republic brought an Indian summer. But winter arrived with Christianity, which replaced the political freedom of the citizen with the spiritual freedom of the believer. The secular philosophies of the modern era put public freedom into a deep freeze.

Why should an intellectual such as Arendt put action above contemplation? A vital clue is contained in the preface to *Between Past and Future*, where Arendt reflects on "what four years in the *résistance* had come to mean to a whole generation of European writers and men of letters . . . who as a matter of course had never participated in the official business of the [French] Third Republic. . . . After a few short years they were liberated from what they originally had thought to be a 'burden.' . . . They had lost their treasure. . . . [T]hey had discovered that he who 'joined the Resistance, *found* himself.'"[2] The publicity, spontaneity, and urgency of political action delivered intellectuals from the solitude, self-doubt, and lassitude of the contemplative life. Most likely, Arendt experienced this herself through her own work with the Resistance during World War II.

In a later meditation on the French and American revolutions, Arendt sought to restore America's collective memory of its own "lost treasure." Like the Resistance fighters, the founding fathers had stumbled onto the treasure of freedom almost by accident. John Adams, she noted, had recalled that he and his contemporaries had been "called without expectation and compelled without previous inclination" and had discovered that "it is action, not rest, that constitutes our pleasure."[3] Thomas Jefferson would later refer to this "pleasure" as "public happiness"[4]—suggesting a very different meaning of the "pursuit of happiness" of which he had spoken in the Declaration. What the revolutionary generation had discovered, Arendt argued, is "that public freedom consisted in having a share in public business, and that the activities connected with this business by no means constituted a burden but gave those who discharged them in public a feeling of happiness they could acquire nowhere else."[5] By "the pursuit of happiness," in other words, the American founders had meant something public and collective, rather than something private and individual.

Accidentally rediscovered, this treasure had soon been lost again. Why? In Arendt's words, because "the Revolution had failed to provide a space where this freedom could be exercised. Only the representatives of the people, not the people themselves, had an opportunity to engage in those activities of 'expressing, discussing, and deciding' which in a positive sense are the activities of freedom."[6] Jefferson was one of the few to grasp the implications of this development; his proposed system of local "wards" or "councils" (discussed in chapter 3) was an effort to safeguard and pass on the newly discovered treasure. Of course, another reason for the loss of public happiness Arendt observed was that most Americans were primarily concerned with their private welfare. The fundamental question that had been posed but not answered by the American Revolution was "whether the new government was to constitute a realm of its own for the 'public happiness' of its citizens, or whether it had been devised solely to serve and ensure their pursuit of private happiness more effectively than had the old regime."[7] The mass migration and consumer capitalism of the nineteenth and twentieth centuries—and the concomitant "public relations" campaign by those who profited from them—had pushed public opinion toward a focus on private happiness as the core element of the "American Dream."

Arendt contested this understanding of the American project. The principal goal of the American founders was neither individual liberty nor property rights, she insisted, but public freedom. Nor was the framers' goal the establishment of "limited government," in which power is checked by law, as many libertarians nowadays claim: "Power . . . cannot be checked, at least not reliably, by laws," she maintained.[8] As Montesquieu had discovered, "only power arrests power . . . without destroying it." Arendt's republican reading of the American Revolution was soon vindicated by American historians (see chapter 3), and her work quickly became required reading for young advocates of "participatory democracy" during the 1960s and 1970s.[9]

Like Dewey, Arendt also extended the principle of balance to the relationship between polity and economy. The biggest problem with modern capitalism, she argued, is that it invades the political realm and colonizes the space of public freedom—turning meeting halls into strip malls and town squares into gated communities. Arendt was highly critical of the "pro-market" reading of American history propagated by business interests during the Cold War: "When we were told that by freedom we understood free enterprise, we did very little to dispel this monstrous falsehood," she wrote, "and all too often we have acted as though we too believed that it was wealth and abundance which were at stake in the postwar conflict"; on the contrary, the real divide was not between capitalism and socialism, but between public freedom and totalitarian rule.[10] "Only legal and political institutions that are independent of the economic forces" can contain the relentless expansion of the market, she warned.[11] Thus, it is crucial that the autonomy of the polity be preserved, not just because this will lead to more social justice—though that is probably the case, too—but also because it will preserve a space for action and prevent human life from being consumed by work and labor.

Still, it may be fairly asked whether Arendt's civic republicanism can really be seen as a contribution to the American civil religion. Didn't she see Christianity and republicanism as fundamentally at odds? Wasn't she determined to keep religion—and morality—completely out of politics? Yes, on both counts.

But things are not as straightforward as they seem. The political theologian Carl Schmitt famously quipped that "all significant concepts of the modern theory of the state are secularized theological concepts."[12] Arendt was surely no friend of Schmitt's—nor am I—but his words do fit her "concept of the political." Early on, Arendt argued that the possibility of politics depends on practices of "forgiveness" and "promising." The need for forgiveness arises from the law of unintended consequences. And "the discoverer of the role of forgiveness," she stated, "was Jesus of Nazareth."[13] Her "proof-text" for this statement was Jesus's dying words: "Forgive them Father, for they know not what they do."[14] The importance of promising, Arendt contended, derives from the "unpredictability of the future."[15] Promising is constitutive for republican freedom because it provides the "only alternative" to "domination."[16] And who discovered the role of promising in human affairs? "Abraham, the man from Ur, whose whole story, as the Bible tells it, shows such a passionate drive toward making covenants that it as though he departed from his country for no other reason than to try out the power of mutual promise in the wilderness of the world, until eventually God himself agreed to make a covenant with him."[17] Here, at least, Arendt seems to imply that Athens and Jerusalem are not so far apart after all—indeed, that arriving in Athens requires not one but two journeys through Jerusalem, one to learn the practice of promising, and another to learn the art of forgiveness.

Elsewhere, though, she did insist that the route to Athens must bypass Jerusalem. Echoing Machiavelli and Rousseau, she charged Christianity with being too "otherworldly" to sustain a "love of the world," too focused on individual salvation to motivate civic virtue. (Surprisingly, she seemed altogether unaware of the Christian and Hebraic variants of republicanism that had developed in early modern England and colonial America.) And where did this "otherworldly" and "individualistic" picture of Christianity come from? Augustine is the authority she most often invoked. And yet Arendt's reading of Augustine is surprisingly superficial (though this is perhaps less surprising when one recalls that Arendt wrote her dissertation on Augustine at the age of twenty-two!).[18] For one thing, Augustine saw the "two cities" of Jerusalem and Athens as historically intertwined, rather than metaphysically separated. Jesus, Augustine pointed out, had said, "My Kingdom is not of this world," but he had added that "the Kingdom of God is at hand." While many American Christians construed Jesus's words as a prophecy of his imminent return, Augustine understood them to mean that the Kingdom of God is also *here right now in this world.* If this is the case, an Augustinian Christian cannot simply disengage from "this world." Augustinianism generates an "innerworldly" rather than an "otherworldly" political ethos. [19] An Augustinian Christian will not seek "glory" in politics, much less "immortality," but neither will he or she avoid or deride politics. Augustinianism may not lead to the sort of "authentic politics" that Arendt envisioned, but neither does it lead to the sort of antipolitical otherworldliness that she feared.

Arendt may have been right to worry that certain kinds of love may be at odds with republican politics, to wit, "the love of the religious zealot, the sentimental soul or the romantic embrace."[20] But her worries extended much further than these types, to the neighborly love that is at the heart of the Christian ethic. Neighborly love, she contended, is too strong an emotion for politics; "respect," not love, and "friendship," not "intimacy," was, for her, the proper ethos. While Arendt's defense of the autonomy of the political is understandable, even laudable, George Kateb was right to conclude that Arendt "purges politics of too much": "To purge true politics of love, goodness, compassion, and pity," he observed, "is to purge it of the largest part of moral inhibition."[21] And also, I would add, of one foundation for civic friendship as well. For what can sustain civic solidarity in the imagined community of a large republic other than a generalized love of one's fellow citizens? This, as it turned out, would be one of the central messages of Martin Luther King's ministry.

MARTIN LUTHER KING: PROPHECY REFIGURED

Few historical figures are more deeply ensconced in America's public imagination than Martin Luther King Jr. What Lincoln and his Gettysburg Address were to an earlier generation of Americans, King and his dream are to ours: a civic saint and his last testament.[22] Controversial in his time, King is now embraced by conservatives and progressives alike—though perhaps too easily.

Contemporary conservatives like to invoke King's dictum that we be judged by "the content of our character" rather than "the color of our skin."[23] They portray King as a color-blind egalitarian who would have been fiercely opposed to modern-day policies of affirmative action.[24] But they would find much less to like about the King of 1967 or 1968, a King who strongly opposed the Vietnam War and spoke out for a radical redistribution of wealth to the urban poor.

Contemporary liberals may feel more comfortable with the King of 1968 than their conservative co-citizens.[25] They may feel that the "real King" belongs to them. But what about his religiosity?[26] Was it just a political front, as some "new atheist" authors argue?[27] If so, then what should we make of the evening of January 27, 1956? On this night, King was awakened by a telephone call: another death threat. (It was the early months of the Montgomery bus boycott.) He sat down at his kitchen table to pray. "At that moment," he later recounted, "I experienced the presence of the Divine as I had never experienced Him before. It seemed as though I could hear the quiet assurance of an inner voice saying: 'Stand up for righteousness, stand up for truth; and God will be at your side forever.' Almost at once my fears began to go. My uncertainty disappeared. I was ready to face anything."[28] It seems that King's religiosity cannot be so easily dismissed.

So, just who was Martin Luther King?

To begin with, he was a Christian and a Southerner. As such, he spent much of his life in the bosom of the black church and under the iron fist of Jim Crow. His parents were distinguished. His father, Martin Luther King Sr., was a pastor; his mother, Alberta Williams King, a pastor's daughter. Still, the young King could not evade the stream of racial sleights and insults—the white policeman who addressed his father as "boy"; the white friend who was forbidden from playing with him—that had washed over Southern blacks since time immemorial.

King was also an intellectual and a political prodigy. At age fifteen, he entered Morehouse College, a historically black college in Atlanta. Upon graduation, he entered Crozer Theological Seminary, a liberal Protestant school near Philadelphia. He was a great success there, both socially and academically. His classmates elected him class president. His professors encouraged him to attend graduate school. He followed their advice and enrolled in the doctoral program at Boston University, a major center of "personalist" theology and philosophy. There, King met his future wife, Coretta Scott, herself a preacher's daughter from Alabama, who was studying music at the Boston Conservatory.

Finally, King was a pastor and a preacher. After receiving his PhD at age twenty-five, he opted against an academic career and against remaining in the North. Instead, he accepted a call from the Holt Street Baptist Church in Montgomery, Alabama. Just two years later, in 1956, still only twenty-seven years of age, he became the chief spokesman for the Montgomery bus boycott. From that year on, until his assassination in 1968, the American civil rights movement wholly consumed King's life.

What was King's contribution to the civil religion? King did not explicitly appeal to the civic republican strand of the tradition, in the way that Arendt did. Instead, his main contribution was to elongate and strengthen the tradition's prophetic strand by weaving an older "typological" thread back into its inner fibers and adding a new "personalist" one as well.

King's stance toward the American project, like Lincoln's and Douglass's, was critical but affirming. King was fully aware of the moral rot that had spread through American society as a result of racial prejudice, just as Malcolm X and Stokely Carmichael were.[29] But unlike the latter two, King did not conclude that the American project was beyond redemption, and he rejected calls for racial separatism and violent revolution.

Nor did King ever give up this hope. In his final speech, delivered the night before his assassination, King once more urged his listeners to "make America what it ought to be."[30] In his various "dream" speeches, he urged his followers to recover an older dream, the American dream that "used to be."[31] Such a dream was not the callow postwar dream of material ease,[32] but the nobler one of human equality and national unity that had animated the revolutionary generation. "The substance of the dream is expressed in these sublime words . . . : 'We hold these truths to be self-evident—that all men are created equal,'" he declared. And not "some men," he added, but "all men." King often cited the Constitution and the Declaration in his speeches. Indeed, the only text he cited more often was the Bible.[33]

But King did not just rearticulate the dream that used to be. He also redreamed that dream. His vision of racial equality and national unity went beyond Lincoln's vision of civic equality and political union; it even extended beyond the broader form of social equality and more ambitious program of economic redistribution championed by Douglass. King's version of the American Dream was "a land where men of all races, of all nationalities, and of all creeds can live together as brothers," as members of "the beloved community."

King did not regard this dream as his alone. Echoing the Puritans, he argued that "God somehow called America to do a special job for mankind and the world." "Never before in the history of the world have so many racial groups and so many national backgrounds assembled together in one nation," he declared, a statement even truer now than in King's day. "And somehow if we can't solve the problem in America, then the world can't solve the problem, because America is the world in miniature and the world is America writ large."[34] In this sense, King was an "American exceptionalist." His exceptionalism, however, was not the Christianist and militarist exceptionalism of the early twenty-first century, which sees America as an already-chosen nation, the long arm of divine justice in a godless world, but rather the original exceptionalism of the Puritan era, which saw America as an almost-chosen nation, a people who had been set apart and placed under judgment. Like Winthrop, King hoped that America could serve as an example to the world—and warned of God's wrath should it fail: "The judgment of God is upon us," he said, "and we must either learn to live together as brothers or we are all going to perish as fools."[35] The outcome of that wager is still an open question.

Many of King's critics would dismiss this dream as a "fairy tale," a product of childish naïveté about the hard realities of race relations in American society. But they misunderstood the tough-minded Christian realism that underlay King's politics. It was at Crozer, King later recalled, that he "began to question the liberal doctrine of man," and it was his reading of Niebuhr that made him "aware of . . . the reality of sin at all levels of human existence"—individual, social, and historical.[36] King warned his liberal contemporaries not to be "foolish children of light" who imagined that social progress "rolls in on the wheels of inevitability" without determined action by the oppressed. Appeals to conscience, he concluded, rarely suffice to bring about real change. The rationalizations of the powerful must first be swept away.

This was the real purpose of nonviolent protest. By staging dramatic confrontations with the white power structure, one could reveal the moral evil that underwrote the system of racial apartheid; one could bring the billy clubs, baseball bats, attack dogs, and fire hoses into public view.[37]

King knew that the protesters themselves were not altogether innocent. Hence, the Southern Christian Leadership Conference's training in nonviolent resistance always involved a good deal of individual and collective self-examination.[38] And the SCLC followed Gandhi's practice of collective self-examination and psychological "purification" prior to any nonviolent action.

Like Niebuhr, King was also critical of "foolish children of darkness" who believed that politics was purely a matter of power, that power was solely a function of coercion, and that appeals to conscience were therefore useless. This argument was one of the central critiques he faced, not only from the cynical supporters of Jim Crow in the South, but also from the black power movement in the North. King understood the appeal of black power; he knew it was rooted in the experience of black powerlessness. But he nonetheless rejected the goals of black nationalism for moral, social, and political reasons: moral insofar as the movement gave up on racial integration and doubled down on racial separatism; social insofar as he regarded American blacks as a "hybrid" people, racially and culturally; and political insofar as he regarded strategies of violent revolution as impractical and counterproductive.

In retrospect, King's assessment of power dynamics in the United States and the world now looks more hardheaded than Malcolm X's or Huey Newton's. "No internal revolution has ever succeeded in overthrowing a government by violence unless the government had already lost the allegiance and effective control of its armed forces," King wrote, and "anyone in his right mind knows that this will not happen in the United States." This view would soon be vindicated by scholars of revolution and, of course, by the subsequent course of American history.[39] What is more, King added, "arguments that the American Negro is a part of a world which is two-thirds colored and that there will come a day when the oppressed people of color will violently rise together to throw off the yoke of white oppression are beyond the realm of serious discussion."[40] The fantasy that a "Third World revolution" would topple the "white power structure" was just that: a fantasy. Martin Luther King was a great many things, but politically naïve was surely not one of them. Andrew Young would later reflect that "everything [King] did was formulated much more out of a sense of Christian realism" than most Americans at the time understood.[41]

Still, there were differences between King and Niebuhr. King found Niebuhr's realism a shade too pessimistic. "There is a kind of Christian assurance which releases creative energy into the world," he once wrote, "and which in actual fellowship rises above the conflicts of individual and collective egoism."[42] King also arrived at a somewhat different view of the relationship between love and justice. For Niebuhr, recall, an ethic of love could only be realized within the confines of the church; in the temporal realm, we must settle for justice. King understood the relationship between love and justice in more dialectical terms: "Power without love is reckless and abusive . . . and love without power is sentimental and anemic," he declared. "Power at its best is love implementing the demands of justice. Justice at its best is love correcting everything that stands against love."[43]

So, for King, love and power were not opposites. Like Gandhi, King understood love as a real power in the world, a creative force that could disclose and sometimes achieve new possibilities of human community. In what sense did he intend this word "love" to be understood, though? King distinguished three varieties: *eros*, meaning a romantic or sexual love that unites two people; *philia*, meaning a "reciprocal love" between friends; and *agape*, which he understood as "redemptive goodwill for all men . . . which seeks nothing in return."[44] "Agape," he stated, "is disinterested love. . . . It begins by loving others *for their own sakes*."[45] It is also "love seeking to preserve and create community . . . a willingness to go to any length to restore community."[46] As such, "love is mankind's most potent weapon for personal and social transformation."[47] By distinguishing between these various senses of love, King was able to show that love and justice are better understood as distinct moments in a historical process, rather than as opposing principles of moral action, as Arendt had claimed.

Niebuhr and King also approached the prophetic texts somewhat differently: Niebuhr analogically and King typologically. Read typologically, as one scholar has explained, "the Bible and contemporary experience take the shape of a single, enormous tapestry whose figures are repeated in many locations with a variety of significations."[48] For King, the typological source par excellence was the Exodus narrative. Consider King's 1967 address to the SCLC: "We still have a long, long way to go before we reach the promised land of freedom. Yes, we have left the dusty soils of Egypt, and we have crossed a Red Sea that had for years been hardened by a long and piercing winter of massive resistance, but before we reach the majestic shores of the Promised Land, there will still be gigantic mountains of opposition ahead and prodigious hilltops of injustice."[49] King did not say, "We are *like* the Ancient Israelites" or "Racial equality is *like* the Promised Land." King used typology, not analogy. Why? Because the struggle for freedom and equality is recurring and continuing, both within every individual and within every society. "There is something deep down within the very soul of man that reaches out for Canaan," King explained. "Men cannot be satisfied with Egypt. . . . And eventually they rise up and begin to cry out for Canaan's land."[50] For King, the Exodus narrative was neither a true story nor an inspiring myth; rather, it was a typological narrative that disclosed a deeper truth about human aspirations and historical destiny.

King's understanding of Christian eschatology was also distinctive. For Niebuhr, the eschaton was altogether outside of historical time. The prophecies of Daniel and the Revelation of John were to be understood in purely allegorical terms, and any talk about the end of time was derided as an attempt to "prematurely" escape from the "relativities of history." The eschaton, for Niebuhr, entered into earthly experience solely as a "hope" for justice. In contrast, in contemporary evangelical "prophecy belief," the books of Daniel and Revelation are treated as coded predictions of future events, not references to present travails. King's eschatology sat in between these two extremes. It was more than hope and less than the millennium. For King, the "Promised Land" was something that humankind must always march toward but can never reach. Still, the "Kingdom of God" does come down to Earth from time to time, only to disappear again. It arrives in fleeting experiences of "beloved community," in those numinous moments when we realize "that God made us to live together as brothers and sisters and to respect the dignity and worth of every man."[51] For Coretta Scott King, and perhaps many others, the March on Washington and her husband's "I Have a Dream" speech there was one such epiphany: "At that moment," she would later reflect, "it seemed as if the Kingdom of God appeared. But it only lasted for a moment."[52]Though fleeting, Martin Luther King believed, such moments are recurring and cumulative in their effects.

King's philosophy of history is captured in his famous remark that "the arc of the moral universe is long but it bends towards justice." For King, human history was not an endless cycle, as it had been for the ancients. Nor was it a straight line, as it is for the moderns. Rather, it was a curved arrow. Its initial trajectory was off target, because human beings are prideful creatures; even when they aim for justice, their vision is distorted by self-regard. But "there are moral laws of the universe just as abiding as the physical laws," King countered.[53] And the most important of these, he added, is the "law of love."

Again, in what sense did he intend these terms "love" and "law" to be understood? There was, to begin with, God's love for his creatures and his wrath against those who oppress them. King's God was not the clockwork God of the deists, who wound up the universe and turned his back on it. King's God was the personal God of Abraham and Isaac and Jacob, who walked beside his people and intervened in human history when and where he must. "As you struggle for justice . . . you do not struggle alone," said King. "But God struggles with you. And He is working every day."[54]

How did he do this? Sometimes King's God was an angry God of judgment who issued moral decrees and punished those who transgressed them. "God has injected a principle in this universe," said King. "God has said that all men must respect the dignity and worth of all human personality. 'And if you don't do that, I will take charge. . . . And if you don't stop . . . I'm going to rise up and break the backbone of your power. And your power will be no more.'"[55] At other times, King's God was a forgiving God of mercy, who redeemed the many through the unwarranted suffering of a few out of an unconditional love for all humanity. Here, the law of love trumped the rules of justice, as those who had already suffered involuntarily were required to willingly suffer still more in order to redeem their oppressors. Just as the cross had created the possibilities for a new community, so, too, did other acts of nonviolence. "The aftermath of nonviolence," King argued, "is the creation of the beloved community. The aftermath of nonviolence is redemption. The aftermath of nonviolence is reconciliation."[56] It is the force of God's love, lived out by his people, that slowly "bends" the arc of history and steers it toward justice.

What, then, of injustice? Like all forms of Christian theology, King's philosophy of history generates thorny questions of theodicy: If God is both omnipotent and benevolent, then why does he allow evil and suffering in the world? King gave at least three answers to this problem, all of which had to do with freedom, reason, and redemption. The first argued that because God is free and we are created in his image, we are therefore free as well, at least within the constraints given by the material and social worlds. This means that we are also free to do evil. Of course, God could intervene and prevent us from doing so. But then we would not be free, would we?

This is a fairly standard answer to the theodicy problem within Christian theology. However, it leads to a second conundrum: Why do we choose the evil over the good? King's answer was that "reason is darkened by sin." This does not mean that it is *occluded* by sin. All human beings possess a basic knowledge of right and wrong, regardless of whether or what they believe. But reason is distorted by sin, that is, by self-interest and self-regard.[57] Importantly, for King, evil results from sins of omission as much as from sins of commission. The principal cause of racial injustice, for example, is not the evil actions of a few so much as the continued inactions of the many.

Which brings us to the third and final question: Why is there suffering? Because suffering is redemptive, said King, and unmerited suffering is, or can be, especially redemptive. This is because unmerited suffering can penetrate the veil of self-regarding rationalizations that all too often darkens our moral sensibilities, allowing us to see our fellow human beings as they really are, namely, as fellow children of a loving God, created to be free.

King's version of prophetic religion was also deeply influenced by his personalism.[58] Personalism helped King to develop a distinctive understanding of freedom, equality, rights, and community, the four values that were at the core of his conception of the American Dream. King regarded personality as a fundamental aspect of reality.[59] It is what sets humans apart from both animals and things and what unites them with the divine personality of God. As noted earlier, one characteristic of the divine personality is freedom. God *chose* to create the world *ex nihilo*. He *chose* to sacrifice "His only begotten Son." Consequently, King argued, freedom must also be an essential feature of human personality. "To rob a man of his freedom" is therefore "to rob him of something of God's image."[60] Equality must be understood in the same way. "All men are created equal" insofar as they are created in "the image of God," and consequently, all people "are equal in intrinsic worth."[61] Likewise, it is because each person is inherently sacred that "each of us has certain basic rights that are neither derived from or conferred by the state." And it is because these rights are "God-given" that they are "inalienable." In this way, King reinterpreted the negative rights of the American Constitution in personalist terms.[62]

Personalism is sharply at odds with atomism. The human person "is by nature a societal creature," said King, and a "self cannot be a self without others."[63] Indeed, all human beings "are caught in an escapable network of mutuality," such that the flourishing of each is dependent on the flourishing of all.[64]

Was there a republican strand to King's civil religion? King does not seem to have been especially familiar with the republican tradition, but he shared many basic assumptions with it. He understood human beings as inherently social, for instance, and believed human wellbeing required strong communities. King also valued human freedom very highly, more highly than social order.

Conversely, his views were often at odds with classical liberalism. He did not understand freedom as the absence of restraint; he believed that it involved a certain measure of self-mastery. This is one reason why King was so critical of the sort of libertinism and "riotous living" he often observed in Northern cities—and may have regretted in himself. It is also why he believed that nonviolent protesters had to have a firm command of their passions before they could be politically effective. Nor did King think that legal principles and formal institutions alone were sufficient to expand and preserve freedom and equality. Like Niebuhr, he believed that power always had to be counterbalanced with power. If the many failed to stand up to the few, corruption was the inevitable result.

Still, the lack of explicit engagement with the republican tradition and the general absence of republican concepts in King's works did have consequences. King's words reached a much broader audience than Arendt's. His "Letter from a Birmingham Jail" and "I Have a Dream" speech now serve as a shorter catechism of the civil religious tradition. And because the prophetic voice was the dominant one in King's dream, the prophetic strand of the civil religion now weighs much heavier in our political culture than the republican one does. This is surely one reason why recent attempts to revive the civil religion have often been worryingly one-sided. One hears many prophetic notes: calls to return to the values of the founding, calls for unity and solidarity. But one hears few republican remedies, particularly the need for the power of the few to be counterbalanced by the power of the many. As a result, the civil religious tradition has all too often become a one-legged man, hopping along on the critical leg of the prophetic tradition without the aid of the constructive leg of the republican tradition. It was the Catholic tradition that suggested how that second leg might be reactivated and its movements coordinated with the first.

JOHN COURTNEY MURRAY: AMERICAN CATHOLIC IN A CATHOLIC AMERICA

For the first three centuries of its existence, the American experiment had borne a distinctly Protestant imprint. Catholics had been in North America as long as—indeed, longer than—Protestants. But Protestants had dominated the culture almost from the start, and the relationship between Americanism and Catholicism had always been fraught. "Minions of the Anti-Christ," "enemies of the Republic," "slaves to the Pope," "backward" members of an "inferior culture"—these were just a few of the epithets that Protestants had hurled against "Romanists" over the centuries.

Not that Rome itself did much to discredit these charges. Preoccupied with events in Europe and suspicious of liberal democracy, the Catholic Church's attitude toward the American project ranged from indifference to hostility. Rome held fast to the old ideal of the "confessional state" until well into the twentieth century and opposed the American system of institutional separation between church and state.

That America and Rome eventually began to overcome this distrust was due in no small part to the patient labors of John Courtney Murray.[65] Born in New York City in 1904, Murray joined the Society of Jesus at the age of sixteen. After studying classics and philosophy at Boston College, he spent several years teaching high school in Manila. He then received seven years of advanced theological training in Maryland and Rome before taking up a post at Woodstock College in Maryland.

Nevertheless, Murray's was not the quiet existence of the small-town college professor, but the itinerant life of a well-known public intellectual. From the closing days of World War II until his premature death in 1967, Murray divided his considerable energies among his studies, his church, and his country, variously serving as the editor of a Jesuit journal, a member of the Second Vatican Council, and an outspoken defender of American democracy.

The overarching aim that linked these various projects together was Murray's ambition to demonstrate that the Catholic tradition, far from being at odds with religious freedom, human rights, and liberal democracy, might in fact represent its firmest foundation. His best-known work, *We Hold These Truths*, a defense of the "American proposition," was published the same year that Kennedy was elected president and promptly became a best-seller. Murray's visage graced the cover of *Time* magazine that same year, confirming his status as the Catholic answer to Reinhold Niebuhr. Five years later, Murray was summoned to Rome and asked to draft an affirmation of religious freedom on behalf of the Second Vatican Council.

In developing a Catholic defense of religious freedom, Murray also elaborated a Catholic vision of the American project, one that was historically deeper and geographically wider than its Protestant predecessors. Conversant with the Greek and Roman classics and trained in the methods of the scholastics, Murray was able to articulate a modern version of the Christian form of republicanism that had once animated the American revolutionaries. In so doing, he was also able to point the way toward a more dynamic understanding of tradition itself that overcame the static views of some Catholics and many Protestants.

To understand Murray's argument for religious freedom, we first need to understand the arguments against it. Proponents of the confessional state rejected liberal democracy based on the following assumptions: (1) there is a moral law, (2) that law is known only by revelation, and (3) violation of that law will result in divine retribution. So if the moral law stipulates that marriage is between one man and one woman, for example, and if this law is known to us only through scripture, and if permitting other forms of union will inevitably spark God's wrath, then the personal freedoms allowed by liberal democracy look like a risky bet. On this view, liberal democracy is still preferable to a totalitarian government that represses religion, but it is also worse than an authoritarian government that enforces the moral law. By this logic, the American system would still be preferable to the Soviet one, but a confessional state such as Franco's Spain would clearly be preferable to both. This is exactly why some of Murray's opponents saw liberal democracy as the lesser of two evils, rather than as the best system of government.

Murray firmly acknowledged the existence of a moral law, and he did not deign to address the question of divine wrath. Instead, his critique of the confessional state focused on the second assumption: that the moral law is known only via divine revelation. Unlike his opponents, Murray believed that it could also be known through natural reason. Indeed, on his view, it can be known to anyone possessed of a sound mind. Thus, it should be possible for Christians and non-Christians to achieve a substantial amount of agreement about moral questions by means of rational reflection and reasoned argument.

Murray also advanced two further arguments against state enforcement of public morals. The first concerned proper limitations on state power and was grounded in his opposition to "monism," the view that "absolute sovereignty" over social life should be vested in one institution, be it the church or the state. One of the great achievements of the "Christian revolution," he said, was the separation of the temporal and spiritual realms, resulting in a "dualist" system of rule.[66] Thus, Murray was a firm believer in "separation of church and state" in the sense of an *institutional* separation, though emphatically not in the sense of an institutional *subordination* of the church to the state or of discursive *restrictions* on religious speech.

Indeed, Murray advocated not just dualism, but pluralism. On his view, the Thomist view, human beings are innately social, and their sociality naturally gives rise to various forms of association that are historically and morally prior to the state and have a sacred as well as temporal character. Murray referred to such associations as *"res sacra in temporabilus"*: "The chief example is the institution of the family—the marriage contract, itself, and the relationships of husband and wife, parent and child. Included also are other human relationships in so far as they involve a moral element and require regulation in the interests of the personal dignity of man."[67] For Murray, then, the temporal realm consisted of a variety of distinct but overlapping spheres of human sociability, each with their own laws and dynamisms. Such a view is strongly reminiscent of and perhaps even partly inspired by Max Weber's theory of "value spheres" and "life orders."

Murray's second argument against the public enforcement of morals concerned the dual distinctions between private and public morals and between morality and the law. Many Protestant thinkers fail to make these distinctions, Murray lamented, necessary though they are, and this has had at least two deleterious consequences for American culture. On the one hand, he claimed, this failure has led some Americans to loudly demand that private morals be made into public laws. As examples, Murray pointed to legal bans on the sale of pornography and contraceptives. Murray worried that such laws encroached on the moral autonomy of the person and the family. On the other hand, he argued, the failure to properly distinguish law and morality has misled other Americans into the false belief that whatever is not legally prohibited is therefore morally permitted. Sharp dealings in the business world are the paradigmatic example. The fact that such practices do not violate the law, said Murray, does not mean that they do not violate morality. So what is the proper relationship of law and morality? For Murray, "It is not the function of the legislator to forbid everything that the moral law forbids, or to enjoin everything that the moral law enjoins. . . . Law seeks to establish and maintain only that minimum of actualized morality that is necessary for the healthy functioning of the social order. . . . Beyond this, society must look to other institutions for the elevation and maintenance of its moral standards."[68]

At first glance, this may sound rather like the kind of argument that a secular liberal would make regarding efforts to "legislate morality." However, Murray's defense of liberal democracy diverged from the secularist one in at least three ways. First, it was grounded not just in the inherent dignity and moral autonomy of the individual person, as the radical secularist version was, but in the corporate autonomy of the *res sacra* as well. For Murray, rights were corporate as well as individual. The state must therefore safeguard the rights of families, churches, and firms, and not just those of individuals.

Second, for Murray, the goal of liberal democracy was not to emancipate individuals for the "pursuit of happiness" so much as to embed individuals in the kinds of moral communities that make happiness possible in the first place. Thus, while Murray was quite happy to affirm the negative rights of liberal democracy, his reasons for doing so were not entirely consistent with those given by radical secularists.

Finally, Murray did not espouse a secularist view of the liberal state as morally neutral. In his view, the state must actively protect the *res sacra*, including religious communities. For Murray, liberal democracy was not a means of removing religion from politics; instead, it was a means of reestablishing the dualism and pluralism that were originally instituted by Christianity itself but had been upset by the monist claims of the secular state.

I now turn to Murray's argument for religious freedom, which was simultaneously theological, ethical, and political. Theologically, Murray emphasized the voluntary character of the Christian faith so as to fully undermine any argument for religious coercion. Murray's arguments recalled long-standing Protestant arguments for liberty of conscience originally advanced by thinkers like Roger Williams and John Locke. Ethically, Murray appealed to the dignity of the human person, a dignity grounded in the "inner freedom" of the human personality. Any effort to coerce the "internal religious decisions" of an individual human person, he contended, amounts to an assault on his or her innate human dignity. The proximate source of this argument is personalism, the Catholic version of personalist philosophy Murray first encountered during his studies in Boston. Finally, he advanced the political argument, the argument from limited government. A state that attempts to enforce religious orthodoxy, Murray said, is necessarily making theological judgments about right doctrine. In doing so, it exceeds its authority as well as its competence. Only the church has the right and the ability to make these determinations. A church may decide that a particular view is heterodox. It may also exclude the heterodox from membership. That is all quite within its rightful powers. What it may not legitimately do is enlist the civil authorities in this mission or impose civil penalties on its followers.

It should perhaps be stressed that Murray's understanding of religious freedom was an expansive one that went beyond simple liberty of conscience. The inner freedom of the individual person may be a necessary condition of religious freedom, Murray argued, but it is not a sufficient one. Religious freedom in the full sense is also external and corporate. It entails the right to practice one's faith in public and to join together with one's coreligionists. This stance put him at odds not only with radical secularists, who wished to confine religion to the sacristy, but also with Catholic proponents of the confessional state, who were loath to grant religious freedom of this sort to non-Catholics.

Some of Murray's opponents claimed that his arguments for liberal democracy and religious freedom were really just apologies for the American experiment. But such a critique is unfair. Whatever one thinks of Murray's reasoning, there was a method to it. It was very close to the sort of "critical hermeneutics" that Paul Ricoeur has referred to as *ressourcement*. By *ressourcement* (literally, "re-sourcing"), Ricoeur meant a critical reappropriation of the textual sources that define a particular tradition.[69] Reappropriation is necessary because the full meaning of the textual sources is not immediately evident at the moment of "revelation";

rather, it is gradually disclosed over historical time. Consider the idea of "religious freedom." Until recently, Murray argued, many Christians believed that this concept referred to a purely inner freedom. However, historical experience has slowly taught us that inner freedom requires external freedom as well. It has become clear that the limited sort of religious freedom afforded to Christians in a totalitarian state or to dissenters in a confessional state is really no freedom at all.

Another reason why a return to the sources is required from time to time, Murray contended, is that the application of a tradition to a particular historical situation can result in a distortion of its general meaning. Consider Pope Leo XIII's theory of the confessional state. Looking back, it is clear that Leo XIII was reacting to the political overreach of an aggressively monistic vision of liberal democracy in some parts of Europe. Unfortunately, Murray argued, what had begun as a polemic was then transformed into a doctrine—a doctrine, moreover, that was deeply at odds with a proper understanding of the Catholic tradition itself, which had long prescribed some form of "dualism" or "diarchy" that could distinguish temporal and spiritual authority. Ironically, then, the ambitions of liberal monists helped to spawn the mistake of confessional monists.

Murray applied this method not only to the Catholic tradition, but also to the American tradition, or what he referred to, echoing Lincoln, as the "American proposition." It, too, was in need of *ressourcement* because it, too, had become increasingly distorted, so much so that its core meaning was in danger of being lost altogether. According to Murray, the sources of danger were three: "idiocy," "barbarianism," and "tribalism." These were not vague epithets for Murray; each term had a very concrete meaning.

First, Murray understood the term "idiocy" in the ancient Greek sense as referring to someone who had not been educated into the life of the citizen and did not partake in the government of the polis. In ancient Athens, an "idiot" was a private citizen who shunned public life. Contemporary "idiocy," in Murray's sense, was somewhat like "individualism" in Tocqueville's: "A mature and calm feeling, which disposes each member of the community to sever himself from the mass of his fellows and to draw apart with his family and his friends, so that after he has thus formed a little circle of his own, he willingly leaves society at large to itself." A republic of idiots, said Murray, cannot persist for long.

For Murray, the family tree of contemporary idiocy extends back through modern utilitarianism to classical liberalism. "In the state of nature" envisioned by Hobbes and Locke, he argued: "Man appears with complete suddenness as a full-grown individual, a hard little atom in the midst of atoms equally hard, all solitary and self-enclosed, each a sociological monad. The idea of man, therefore, is that of an individual who is "absolute lord of his own person and possessions, equal to the greatest and subject to nobody."[70] By this logic, Murray continued, "society is not the product of nature but of artifice."[71] It is not difficult to imagine what Murray would have thought of the dumbed-down version of classical liberalism propounded by modern libertarians such as Ayn Rand: he would have regarded it as the *non plus ultra* of idiocy. And he would have been particularly appalled by Catholic apostles of Rand, such as Paul Ryan, who seem strangely unaware of the deep incompatibility of their religious and political commitments.

Murray (rightly) rejected this atomistic view of the human person. On the classical view, which he affirmed, human beings are innately social beings who can only achieve genuine happiness in society with others. Like Leo XIII's notion of the confessional state, Murray concluded, Locke's vision of the social contract had originally been conceived for polemical purposes in a very specific historical context. "He was not searching for a generalized theory that would make society right," Murray concluded, "but simply for a theory that would make it right for England to have resisted an autocratic king."[72] Alas, this theory then hardened into a more general—and fundamentally mistaken—account of natural law.

Murray did not trace the "American proposition" to "Lockean liberalism," however. Rather, he explicitly situated it within the ancient tradition of civic republicanism.[73] Genuine freedom, he argued, is only possible within human society. Indeed, it is precisely the "web of restraints" woven by civilization "which deliver man from a host of slaveries" and enable him or her to live a genuinely human life guided by love, reason, and faith.[74] Thus, republican self-mastery is only possible in a system of ordered liberty.

If an idiot is someone who does not understand public life, then a "barbarian," in Murray's terms, is someone who rejects public reason, that is, "the traditional role of reason and logic in human affairs." The present-day barbarian, said Murray, is someone "who reduces all spiritual and moral questions to the test of practical results or to an analysis of language or to decision in terms of individual subjective feeling." Surveying the social landscape of post–World War II America, Murray identified four different species of barbarians: "relativists," "technocrats," "positivists," and "pragmatists."[75] Relativists do not believe that there are any public ends, only private ones. Technocrats focus on the efficiency of means to the exclusion of ends. Positivists believe that science is the only source of knowledge. And pragmatists believe that results are the only criterion of truth. What makes the modern barbarians so dangerous, said Murray, is they are clad not in furs and skins but in a "Brooks Brothers suit" or an "academic gown."

Finally, the third danger to American proposition that Murray perceived was "tribalism." Tribalists (mis)understand the polity as a form of kinship and thereby confuse the state with the family. This leads to excessive solidarity with one's fellow citizens and excessive hostility toward other nations. "The unity of the tribe . . . is based on kinship . . . and the enemy tribe is the stranger," said Murray. "No matter who the stranger is, as a stranger, he is the enemy. The tribe seeks security in sheer solidarity, a solidarity that is absolutely intolerant of anything alien to itself."[76] A properly ordered political society is not based on imaginary family or kinship ties, Murray argued. Rather, it is based on civic friendship, which is "a special kind of moral virtue" involving "the discipline of passion, prejudice, and narrow self-interest." Such a relationship "has nothing to do with the cleavage of a David to a Jonathan, or with the kinship of the clan."[77]

The most dangerous form of tribalism that Murray saw at work in his own era was anticommunism. Murray himself was quite critical of communism, of course. But he worried that the United States would be "driven into a unity based simply on negation" rather than on a commitment to a set of positive "propositions."[78] His worries were not misplaced.

Nor would Murray have had any truck with the contemporary version of religious nationalism that sails under the flag of "American exceptionalism." As a member of a church whose borders extend well beyond those of the United States, Murray said, the American "Catholic may not, as others do, merge his religious and his patriotic faith, or submerge one in the other."[79] Unfortunately, some of his fellow Catholics were so anxious to demonstrate their patriotic bona fides that they fell prey to this temptation. Some still do.

The sort of civic friendship that Murray advocated should not be confused with ideological consensus, however. Civic friendship, for Murray, was based on rational argument or, better yet, on reasoned *dis*agreement about shared values. For example, there may be general agreement about the value of religious freedom, even if there is vociferous debate about giving public monies to parochial schools. Or there may be a public consensus about human dignity but heated controversy about the personhood of the fetus and the permissibility of abortion. The crucial point is that rational disagreement necessarily presumes some deeper level of substantive agreement. (It also presumes a modicum of goodwill and a minimum of political civility.)

The problem with tribalism is that it demands more. It is not satisfied with rational disagreement but demands ideological unanimity instead. It says: "You're either for us, or against us." But complete unanimity is neither possible nor desirable. It is not possible because of human moral and intellectual limitations, and it is not desirable because rational debate helps to disclose the full meaning of a political tradition. In contrast, the problem with barbarianism is that it demands less. It is not interested in rational debate about shared ends. Instead, it focuses on other ends, such as subjective preferences (relativism) or practical results (pragmatism), or on the most efficient or powerful means to achieve those ends (technocracy and scientism). And finally, the problem with idiocy is that it demands nothing of the citizen *qua* citizen.

Murray referred to the subjective agreement that underlies civic friendship as the "public consensus." The term is not entirely felicitous and is easily misunderstood. "Consensus" to Murray did not mean unanimity. Nor did it rule out dissent. On the contrary, said Murray, the public consensus *presupposes* dissent as its vital principle. Similarly, "public" was not intended to mean everybody, or even the majority. The public consensus may even be at odds with "public opinion" in the pollster's sense of majority opinion.

So just what is the "public consensus"? And in what sense is it "public" and a "consensus"? By "consensus," Murray seems to have meant something like "core values." Most people will disagree about the meaning of those values, and a few will not share them at all. Nonetheless, those values will serve as the focal point of the "civic conversation." By "public," Murrays appears to have meant those citizens who are actively engaged in this conversation. Some (the barbarians) will find the conversation pointless and will choose to speak of other things. Others (the idiots) will find it uninteresting and will prefer to focus on their private affairs. Still others (the tribalists) will be too busy shouting to participate.

Why refer to an argument that may only engage a minority as a "public consensus"? Again, Murray was not as explicit on this point as he might have been. But there would appear to be two reasons for embracing the term. First, the public consensus was the consensus of the founders, who set out the basic terms of the civic conversation. Second, this consensus constituted the Americans as a people and continues to do so today. The public consensus is the beginning of political debate, and it is through continued debate that a people continues to exist *qua* a people.

CONCLUSION: "CIVIC RELIGION"
OR "PUBLIC CONSENSUS"?

As some readers will have no doubt guessed, the title of this chapter alludes to the title of Will Herberg's brilliant study of religion and civic life in postwar America, *Protestant, Catholic, Jew* (1956).[80] The starting point for Herberg's analysis, and the inspiration for his title, was a short article by Ruby Jo Reeves Kennedy, a young sociologist from Yale. Kennedy's doctoral dissertation focused on marriage patterns in New Haven from 1870 to 1950. She found that Protestants, Catholics, and Jews married within their religious communities but across ethnic lines. "Protestant British-Americans, Germans, and Scandinavians intermarry," she discovered, as do "Catholic Irish, Italians and Poles," and Jews from various regions of Europe. Kennedy referred to this pattern as the "triple-melting-pot."[81]

The second source of inspiration for Herberg's analysis was *The Uprooted*, Oscar Handlin's seminal study of American immigration from the colonial era up through the early twentieth century. One of the distinctive features of the assimilation process in America, Handlin noted, was the pivotal role of religious communities. It was in the congregation, the parish, and the synagogue that recent immigrants became ethnic groups, that Swabians and Hessians became "Germans," that Neapolitans and Sicilians became "Italians," and that Berliners and Viennese became "Ashkenazi Jews." Kennedy's findings suggested a further second-order effect in which these ethnic identities were melted down and reformed into religious ones.

In his own work, Herberg reflected on the consequences of this dynamic for America's civic culture. His central thesis was that "to be a Protestant, a Catholic, or a Jew are today the alternative ways of being an American."[82] Under this new dispensation, he added, "not to identify oneself and be identified as either a Protestant, a Catholic or a Jew is to somehow not be an American."[83] This was both the achievement and the limitation of the civil religious tradition circa 1960, when the Protestant-dominated civil religion at last gave way to a more inclusive "Judeo-Christian" one. This new vision of a "tri-faith America" was manifested in many ways: in a groundswell of "interfaith dialogue," in tri-faith chaplaincies in public institutions, and even in popular culture. There was, for example, the famous story of the "four chaplains" in the U.S. Navy—two Protestants, one Catholic, and one Jew—who gave their life vests to four young soldiers when their ship was sunk by a German Uboat in 1943, a story that was retold and memorialized numerous times in the decade that followed.[84] Given the depth and virulence of anti-Catholic and anti-Semitic sentiments that had long prevailed among many American Protestants and were still alive even in the 1960s, the "Judeo-Christian" version of the American civil religion must be seen as a large step forward. As wide as this expanded circle was, however, it still excluded the sorts of nonbelievers who had been so central to the progressive civil religion. So two steps had been taken forward and then one step back. Even now, there is considerable reluctance among some American Christians to take that step again and include nonbelievers.

Herberg was highly critical of the Judeo-Christian vision, however, not only because it excluded "the old-time 'village atheist,'" but also because it diluted religion itself.[85] Herberg worried that national unity was being achieved at the cost of religious authenticity. The search for a lowest common denominator across the three faith traditions was robbing them of their "uniqueness" and "distinctiveness." In this new "civic religion," this "American culture religion," Herberg charged, there was nothing to have faith in but "faith itself."[86] "What should reach down to the core of existence, shattering and renewing," he lamented, "merely skims the surface of life, and yet succeeds in generating the sincere feeling of being religious."[87] Religion, he believed, had lost its prophetic content: "The God of judgment has died."[88] In his place, Americans had enthroned a divine therapist and life coach who would help them achieve the American Dream of material ease without threatening their "peace of mind." What's more, he argued, this shallow faith was all too easily coopted and manipulated by cynical political and economic elites. It "comes to serve as a spiritual reinforcement of national self-righteousness and a spiritual authentication of national self-will," Murray contended,[89] and the "power of positive thinking" becomes little more than a tool for employers seeking to enhance the bottom line. The inspiration for this line of argument was none other than Reinhold Niebuhr, whom Herberg had encountered in the early 1950s.

Was Herberg right or wrong? Both, as it turns out. He was certainly right that American elites were invoking the Judeo-Christian tradition to justify the "American way of life," sometimes to the point of equating the two, and that this robbed religion of its prophetic bite. But he was also wrong to overlook the many countercurrents that were already swirling around him. Arendt's *Human Condition* appeared the same year as *Protestant, Catholic, Jew*. By the time the two books went into production, the Montgomery bus boycott was already in full swing, and Murray had completed his historical studies of the confessional state in Catholic thought and was hard at work on his defense of the American proposition. Taken together, Arendt's, King's, and Murray's work went a long way toward addressing Herberg's various concerns. Arendt showed that the American project also had secular roots in the civic republican tradition. King's resuscitation of the prophetic tradition demonstrated that the "God of judgment" was far from dead. And Murray demonstrated how the two strands of the civil religious tradition could be woven back together again. All three showed that the civil religious tradition could be expanded beyond its Protestant origins in a way that was not philosophically or theologically shallow.

This is not to say that Arendt, King, and Murray were in full agreement with one another on all points. Far from it. Among other things, they disagreed about the nature of the civic bond, the relationship between love and justice, the reliability of human reason, and the possibilities of mass politics. King envisioned the civic bond as analogous to the family bond, although not in the sense of a biological family, but according to the model of the Christian church, whose members were urged to love one another as sisters and brothers. He thereby united the two senses of *ekklesia*, the original Greek sense of "political community" and the later Christian sense of religious community. This was what he meant by the "beloved community." By contrast, Arendt and Murray conceived of the civic bond in terms of the model of friendship, and, specifically, a friendship between equals. To the degree that love entered into civic relationships, it took the form of *philia* rather than *agape*. Its source was mutual respect, not God's love. *Philia* might have been strong enough to hold together a small and homogeneous citizenry, such as that of Athens, King might have argued, but is it powerful enough to hold together a large and diverse citizenry such as America's? Perhaps not, Arendt might have replied, but isn't selfless love too powerful an emotion to inject into politics? Murray might have backed her up, asking: Shouldn't it be confined to our relations in civil society? Of course, King did not imagine that a political community could long remain a "beloved community." Instead, he contended that the moral progress of a political community required occasional injections of self-sacrificing love. Only then could it achieve justice. Arendt and Murray certainly agreed that justice must be one of the ends toward which a political community strives. But they were confident that reasoned debate was a sufficient means to this end. King was skeptical. With Niebuhr, he believed that reason was darkened by pride and sin, or, in more secular terms, that it was clouded by narcissism and self-interest. Sometimes, self-sacrificing love was the only means of opening people's eyes to their complicity in social injustice. Perhaps, Arendt might have replied, but nonviolent resistance would not have stopped Hitler or Stalin—about that, Niebuhr was surely right! Nonviolent tactics are only effective in open societies that allow public debate. Of course, Murray might have added, not everyone is able or willing to be part of the civil conversation. Surely, King might have interjected, but who decides? White men legally excluded blacks from public debate for over two and a half centuries in the North and for almost three and a half in the South. Women had not fared much better. Friendship versus brotherhood, reason versus emotion, love versus justice, elitism versus egalitarianism—these are perennial debates in Christian theology and political philosophy that stretch back to the nation's founding and beyond. As such, they are the ethical core of our "public philosophy" and the shared focus of our "civic conversation." These questions unite us, not because we have reached agreement on them, but because we have agreed to argue about them.

EPILOGUE: RELIGIOUS NATIONALISM
AND RADICAL SECULARISM

Like other wars before it, World War II fanned the flames of sacrificial apocalypticism, that specifically American form of Christian nationalism. But the rhetoric did not melt away into metaphor after the shooting subsided, as it had done in previous wars. Instead, the red-hot rhetoric fanned by the Cold War tempered and hardened apocalypticism into a durable peacetime ideology that has endured to the present day. On its surface, the new religious nationalism seems similar to the old, perhaps because it is composed of the same elements, namely, the rhetoric of blood sacrifice and that of violent apocalypse. On closer inspection, however, one discovers important differences.

For one thing, the basic ingredients are in different proportions: over time, the balance shifted—and still continues to shift—from sacrifice to apocalypse. Why? There were at least two reasons. One was the development of nuclear weapons, which made the fiery imagery of the end times suddenly seem realistic, even scientific. The other was the continued spread of "premillennial dispensationalism" among American Protestants. In this interpretation of Christian eschatology, which was dominant among postwar evangelicals, the Second Coming would be ushered in by the "tribulation," a period of horrific war and natural disasters.

There were sociological differences between the old and new religious nationalisms as well. The old version had been championed by leading members of the Protestant establishment like Shailer Mathews, who had applauded World War I as a Christian crusade. By contrast, the leading spokesmen of the new religious nationalism were more often conservative evangelicals, like Billy Graham. Indeed, the new religious nationalism served as a useful testament to their patriotic bona fides.

A third difference concerned the character of the religious "other." Since the American Revolution, sacrificial apocalypticism had had a confessional and ethnic element that pitted an "Anglo-Saxon" and Protestant America against a southern European and Catholic "element" and sometimes also a Jewish "radical." The struggle against fascism and then communism gave birth to both a new "them" and a new "us." The new "them" was a "secular" or "political religion," that is, "paganistic" fascism and "Godless Communism" *qua* ersatz religions. The new "us" was Protestants, Christians, and Jews, or, more broadly still, the Judeo-Christian tradition. The ironic result was a more "ecumenical" type of sacrificial apocalypticism.

The fourth and final difference, but perhaps also the most important one, was the sacralization of the military. Fond as they may have been of martial metaphors, for most of their history Americans had viewed the military as a necessary evil at best. The long-standing tradition of American antimilitarism had two main sources: the pacifistic strand within Christianity and the republican suspicion of standing armies. Even in the years immediately after World War II, there was intense popular pressure for a rapid military demobilization and a return to "normalcy." This changed during the Cold War. The passage of the National Defense Act in 1947 laid the institutional foundations of the modern security state, and the Truman and Eisenhower administrations taught Americans to love the military. Seen against this historical backdrop, the nonviolence of the civil rights movement and the movement against the Vietnam War appear not as a violation of America's national traditions or a rejection of traditional understandings of patriotism but as a reassertion of them.

On the traditional account, the chief dangers to republican government are standing armies and commercial prosperity, which undermine liberty and virtue, respectively. On this the American founders agreed with the republican theorists of classical antiquity, Renaissance Italy, and the North Atlantic. For nearly two centuries, the American republic had been shielded from these twin dangers by its geographical isolation from "old Europe" and the great agricultural expanses of its western frontier.

If the Cold War brought standing armies—and with them a more militaristic form of religious nationalism that legitimated a burgeoning national security state—then the postwar boom brought commercial prosperity and a more technocratic form of secular liberalism that absolved the citizenry of all civic duties save mass consumption. It may seem peculiar to characterize the 1950s as a liberal era. Today, this decade is usually remembered as a conservative period. But that is not how the 1950s were understood by the leading intellectual observers of the time. In *The Liberal Imagination*, for example, which was first published in 1950, the New York literary critic Lionel Trilling famously remarked that "in the United States at this time liberalism is not only the dominant but even the sole intellectual tradition. For it is the plain fact that nowadays there are no conservative or reactionary ideas in general circulation." In *The Liberal Tradition in America*, published just five years later, the political scientist Louis Hartz went further still, arguing that "Lockean liberalism" had *always* been the dominant tradition in American life. But however shortsighted or astigmatic Trilling's political prognostications and Hartz's historical vision would prove to be, ignoring as they did the role of republicanism, religion, and race in American history, they were not altogether wrong about their own era. Something like a "Lockean liberalism" certainly was highly influential during the 1950s, if by this we mean a political theory in which the primary purpose of the political order is to ensure negative liberty or, to put it more plainly, to protect individual rights.

And yet this characterization is still not quite right either, and not only because so many individuals' rights were still being so grossly and systematically violated. It is also wrong because it misses the important changes that occurred in the political and economic order of mid-twentieth-century America. During the war, big government and big business had gotten bigger still—gigantic, even—and their relationship had grown closer than ever, to the point of open embrace. The iconic figures of the age were not the yeoman farmer and the country gentleman of Lockean lore, but the "organization man" and the "Eastern Establishment."

The religious order had grown more liberal as well, if by "liberal" we mean ecumenical and tolerant. It had not necessarily grown more "liberal" in the generic political sense of the term, however. Quite the opposite: the religious best-sellers of this age were not *Christianity and the Social Crisis* (Rauschenbusch) or even *In His Steps* (Sheldon), both books that evinced liberal social concern; they were *The Power of Positive*

Thinking (Peale) and *Peace of Mind* (Liebman), works that promised material success and psychological wellbeing. Increasingly, the prophetic and public version of liberal religion was giving way to a therapeutic and private one, a development that the Belgian sociologist Karel Dobbelaere would later characterize as "internal secularization."[90]

Meanwhile, the social order was undergoing structural transformations that shrank the public sphere further still. The small towns and big cities of the prewar era had both contained physical spaces where diverse citizens could and did regularly encounter one another, whether they wanted to or not. By contrast, the suburban settlements of the postwar era contained less public space and a less diverse citizenry, as sprawling lawns replaced busy street corners, and shopping centers replaced town halls. In short, suburbanization made democratic politics that much more difficult and improbable.

And let us be honest: that may be just what most members of the "Greatest Generation" wanted. And maybe we should not be too judgmental of that desire either: after the material privations and political exertions of the Depression and the war, the frisson of consumerism and the joys of private life were surely a welcome change. But neither should we be surprised that some members of the Baby Boom generation regarded the new "American way" of mass consumption and private contentment as thin gruel and longed for the richer taste of civic engagement and public freedom. Seen against this background, many of the movements of the 1960s were revolts not just against the cultural conservatism of the 1950s but also, and perhaps above all, against the technocratic and therapeutic liberalism of the mid-twentieth century.

CHAPTER 7

From Reagan to Obama

TRADITION CORRUPTED AND
(ALMOST) RECOVERED

IN THE SPAN of one short decade, the entire liberal era came undone. That decade was not the 1960s, but the "long" 1970s, stretching from 1968 to 1980. These years signaled the end not only of America's postwar boom but of its industrial preeminence. American economic competiveness had been slipping as that of its rivals increased, and the "oil shocks" erased any remaining advantage. The era of neoliberal "downsizing" and "offshoring" had begun. Suddenly, the old verities of the Protestant ethic seemed uncertain. It was no longer enough to "work hard and play by the rules."

The long 1970s were also a decade of geopolitical shocks. The United States' ignominious retreat from Vietnam was soon followed by other embarrassments, with the Soviet invasion of Afghanistan, the Sandinista revolution in Nicaragua, and the Iranian hostage crisis being the most discomfiting. Some Americans wondered if America should try to police the world, others doubted whether it could. Pumped up by its victories in the world wars, America's ego now underwent a painful deflation. Some tried to compensate for this shrinkage with bluster and hot air, others by pressing for a new round of imperial adventures.

The unraveling of the liberal consensus also had domestic origins. Its hidden inner spool—the liberal Protestant mainline—was getting smaller and looser. Many of the younger generation no longer saw the point of organized religion; they sought salvation elsewhere. Some still did see the point, but they often looked to evangelical and charismatic forms of religion. The old mainline split in two directions: "bourgeois bohemianism" to the left and "conservative evangelicalism" to the right. Meanwhile, those who remained in the pews often felt estranged from those who occupied the pulpits. Pushed by the social movements of the 1960s and pulled by the nascent counterculture, the liberal Protestant leadership tacked quickly to the left, leaving its parishioners behind.

Something similar happened in American politics. Nixon's "Southern strategy" and politics of resentment set off a slow-moving exodus of white Christians—both evangelical and Catholic—from the Democratic Party. This realignment would be cemented in the "Reagan coalition" of 1980 and 1984. Meanwhile, the "red states" of the Northeast were becoming bluer as the old WASP establishment and the new urban professionals moved left on social issues and re-registered as Democrats. At the same time, the massive influx of big money into national politics was slowly opening up another split in the electorate, one between the people and the elites. This growing divide would later fuel the anti-establishment backlashes that followed the 2008 financial crisis: the Tea Party on the right and Occupy Wall Street on the left. The polarization by this time was not just between Left and Right, but between top and bottom—between the people on the one side and the politicians and the donor class that funded them on the other. Democracy was degenerating into aristocracy, and aristocracy into oligarchy.

As the vital center flew apart, so did prophetic republicanism. Republican freedom landed on the left. But one of its core elements was badly damaged in the crack-up: self-mastery, which had been hammered to bits by the counterculture. Left on its own, the third element of republican freedom—nondependency—all too quickly devolved into a radical individualism that was incompatible with the second element of active citizenship; and, with the addition of a little antireligious sentiment, this new version of individual freedom was easily transformed into radical secularism. The commercialized counterculture lite of *Jonathan Livingston Seagull* initiated the first shift; the "new atheism" of the early 2000s catalyzed the second.

Meanwhile, prophetic religion flew toward the right. Many deemed its core elements—particularly the doctrine of original sin—outmoded and old-fashioned. Some replaced it with "positive thinking"; others with sexual prudery. Retrofitted with these downgraded internal guidance systems, prophetic religion drifted off in the direction of moral denunciation or, worse, crusader nationalism. Ronald Reagan and Jerry Falwell would initiate this shift. Pat Robertson and George W. Bush would complete it.

The dissolution of the civil religion brought an escalation of the culture wars. The growth of radical secularism confirmed religious conservatives' worst fears about secular liberalism. And the growth of religious nationalism confirmed secular progressives' worst fears about conservative religiosity. Many—most, even—were caught in the middle. Some—a small minority—simply exploited the situation. There was money to be made from the culture wars, after all. Many media personalities and political consultants profited handsomely from the rapidly expanding culture wars–industrial complex of talk radio, cable news, direct mail, and attack ads. In the process, they polluted American culture on a grand scale by injecting anger, division, and resentment into the country's political lifeblood. Not since Reconstruction had the American people been so bitterly divided. This division eventually translated into congressional gridlock, which then fed further recriminations and divisions.

One of the few places where the memory of the old-time civil religion still survived during these decades—perhaps even the only one— was the pews of the black church. It was there that a young adult convert named Barack Obama first learned to preach its cadences. His national debut became the emotional highpoint of the 2004 Democratic National Convention. To many, his presidential campaign four years later felt like a religious revival, a *civil* religious revival. There were great crowds, happy tears, and even "holy rolling" amid the rousing rhetoric and call-and-response chants of "Yes We Can." But for all its hope and promise, the Obama revival remained partial and one-sided: it was more prophetic than republican—much more. And therein lay its fatal weakness.

The story of this chapter, then, is of a tradition corrupted and then recovered—but only *partly* recovered. It is the story of a two-legged tradition limping along on one leg. It is a story that is still unfolding today.

FROM NIXON TO REAGAN

Richard Nixon was arguably the first president of the "new right."[1] But he can also be seen as the last representative of the postwar "liberal consensus." He was, after all, the architect of affirmative action, the man who instituted the comprehensive "wage and price controls" of the early 1970s and even proposed a government-guaranteed basic income for all Americans. The language of Nixon's first inaugural address was unmistakably liberal. "The second third of this century," he said, "has been a time of proud achievement. . . . We have shared our wealth more broadly than ever. We have learned at last to manage a modern economy."[2] He went on to reaffirm the government's role in a wide range of areas: achieving "full employment, better housing, excellence in education"; "rebuilding our cities and improving our rural areas"; "protecting our environment and enhancing the quality of life." Ultimately, he concluded, "in all these and more, we will and must press urgently forward."³ Can anyone imagine a Republican candidate giving such a speech now? Or any time soon? Nixon's language was also strikingly secular. He did not close his address with the now-customary benediction "God bless America." That tradition was introduced by Ronald Reagan.

Consider *his* first inaugural address. Reagan insisted—and not for the first time—that "government is not the solution to our problem." Rather, he argued, "our present troubles . . . result from unnecessary and excessive growth of government." These troubles had nothing to do with the failings of the American people, he emphasized, for "the citizens of this blessed land" were "heroes," every one. Gone was any mention of "sharing the wealth" or "managing the economy." Mentions of God, on the other hand, were plentiful indeed. In one shout-out to his evangelical supporters, Reagan noted that "tens of thousands of prayer meetings are being held on this day" and proposed that "each Inauguration Day . . . should be declared a day of prayer." He closed his speech with a personalized benediction: "God bless you," a departure from his by then customary "God bless America."

On first hearing, this sounded like a conservative version of the civil religion. And Reagan did occasionally invoke notions of covenant and renewal and often spoke of evil—but always and only with reference to communism and the Soviet Union. Where the American people and the United States were concerned, he invariably gushed about their "goodness" and "greatness." Far from warning about the dangers of an excessive national pride, Reagan positively encouraged it. This watered-down version of the civil religious tradition left out the bitter salt that had given the prophetic stance its sting: the notion of collective sin. And therein lay one of Reagan's greatest, least noted, and most fateful innovations.

Gone, too, were the old Puritan and republican anxieties about the corrupting potential of excessive luxury and wealth. For Reagan, wealth was good, and unambiguously so. The only real source of corruption in American life, he thought, was the state—especially the *welfare* state. By punishing hard work and rewarding indolence, he believed, the welfare state threatened not only America's affluence but its moral virtues as well. The other culprit was the regulatory state, which, by stifling innovation and entrepreneurship, was blocking the wellsprings of American prosperity. Unplug them, Reagan argued, and a rising tide would lift all boats. In fact, if the welfare and regulatory states were not reined in, he warned, they would soon succeed in killing off the Protestant ethic as well. Virtue had to be rewarded—in cash. Redistributing this re-ward—"sharing the wealth"—was tantamount to theft.

Secular progressives might be tempted to conclude that Reagan's rhetoric was just another acting role. But that is too cynical. It is true that Reagan was not exactly a frequent churchgoer in his later years. But it would be wrong to conclude that he was personally irreligious. The question is not whether he had a theology, but what kind of theology he had.

Not a Falwellian kind. That much is clear. Reagan's religious views are better seen as Emersonian.[4] Like Emerson. Reagan flatly rejected any notion of original sin. In a 1951 letter, he wrote that "my personal belief is that God couldn't have created evil so the desires he planted in us are good."[5] This is why he saw no need for government to restrain our desires. Left to their own devices, human beings are essentially good. Like Emerson, Reagan also believed in the inherent goodness of creation. This belief took root in his childhood and was regularly replenished by adult experiences of the sublime beauties of the natural world. Again, like Emerson, Reagan did not draw a sharp line between God and nature. When his daughter Maureen asked him whether she could "reach up high enough" to "touch God," Reagan replied: "You don't have to reach up. God is everywhere, all the time, all around us."[6] Reagan's theology was not Augustinian. It bordered on Pelagianism and pantheism.

Where Reagan parted ways with Emerson was in his view of Providence. Emerson had a personal acquaintance with tragedy, while Reagan's philosophy of history was almost Panglossian. God has a plan for everyone, he believed, and everything always works out for the best. Setbacks are really just opportunities in disguise. Reagan's view of America's role in the world was not especially Emersonian either. That the United States had been set apart by God as an instrument for spreading freedom throughout the world he had no doubt. While Reagan was clear-eyed about the brutal realities of communist rule, he proved astonishingly naïve about his allies in the anticommunist crusade, particularly the authoritarian regimes of Latin America and South Africa. How far Reagan's perspective was from Lincoln's and Niebuhr's! In Reagan's comic political theology, there was little room for tragedy or irony.

The post-Augustinian character of Reagan's worldview is also evident in his use of "American scripture."[7] Consider, for example, his (mis)use of Winthrop's *Arbella* speech. Addressing the Conservative Political Action

Committee in January 1974, Reagan quoted most of the speech's key passage verbatim: "We shall be as a city upon a hill. The eyes of all people are upon us, so that if we deal falsely with our God in this work . . . we shall be made a story and a byword throughout the world." Removing the prophetic sting from his words, he immediately added that "we have not dealt falsely with our God" and omitted Winthrop's insistence, a few sentences earlier, that "wee must be willing to abridge ourselves of our superfluities, for the supply of others' necessities." Naturally, he made no mention of either the introductory passage in which Winthrop warned that "the riche must not eat up the poore" or the Puritan's radical suggestion that "there is a time when a Christian must sell all and give to the poor." Announcing his candidacy for the presidency five years later, Reagan again quoted this same passage, this time followed by his own personal interpretation, which was wholly individualistic and Emersonian. On Reagan's reading, Winthrop's covenant entailed a commitment to "the principles of self-reliance, self-discipline and morality, and—above all—responsible liberty for every individual." Of course, nothing could have been further from Winthrop's actual meaning, which involved mutual aid, communal discipline, collective morality, and, not least, a limited liberty. It was in this speech, too, that Reagan first spoke of America as a "shining city upon a hill." This was an especially redolent rephrasing at the close of the 1970s, a decade of rising energy costs that had led President Carter to recommend turning off the lights. In later speeches, Reagan dropped the original quote for the paraphrase, which he would attribute to Winthrop and enclose in quotation marks. Thus was Winthrop's "Model of Christian charity" transformed into a paean to libertarian liberties.

The anti-Augustinian premises of Reagan's vision were also evident in his invocations of the other founders of the revolutionary generation. His favorite founder was not the dour Adams, the stoic Washington, or the orthodox Henry, but that scourge of conservative Federalists, the optimistic bon vivant and deist Thomas Jefferson. After Margaret Thatcher, his favorite "cousin," meanwhile, was not Edmund Burke or Benjamin Disraeli, but the iconoclastic firebrand Thomas Paine, whose millenarian reading of the American project—"we can begin the world over again"—he frequently cited. Reagan's fondness for Paine foreshadowed a fundamental shift in American conservatism. Burkean caution was being supplanted by a revolutionary and unbridled optimism about the power of free markets and American arms to usher in an earthly millennium that would be the "end of history" and the beginning of peace and prosperity for all. Of course, some of Reagan's allies had a very different understanding of the millennium and the means by which it would be effected.

FROM GRAHAM TO ROBERTSON

Polling legend Lou Harris once concluded that "Reagan would have lost the [1980] election by one percentage point without the help of the Moral Majority."[8] The Moral Majority, launched by Jerry Falwell, was the first in a series of omnibus activist organizations that coordinated the diffuse movement known as the "New Christian Right." Next came the Christian Coalition hatched by Pat Robertson and Ralph Reed; then, the Family Research Council created by James Dobson and Tony Perkins. The Moral Majority defined itself as prolife, profamily, procapitalist, and pro-American and, conversely, as anti-abortion, antigay, anticommunist, and antimultilateralist. And its successors mainly stuck to that script.

How new was the New Christian Right? It displayed plenty of continuities with an older religious conservatism. But there was something genuinely "new" about it too. A brief comparison of Jerry Falwell and Billy Graham will help to bring out some of the key contrasts. Graham was just as firmly opposed to abortion and gay marriage as Falwell, for example. But on other key issues, the two were very far apart. Graham was an early convert to the cause of civil rights, a vocal defender of Martin Luther King, and a strong supporter of Lyndon Johnson's "war on poverty." Eventually he soured on the war in Vietnam and became more and more circumspect about American interventionism in general. Falwell, by comparison, was a late convert to the cause of racial integration and publicly dismissed King as a communist agitator. He was a vehement opponent of "welfarism" and a fervent devotee of free-market fundamentalism à la Milton Friedman. He blamed the Vietnam debacle on backstabbing liberals and cheered American intervention in Grenada and Iraq. In sum, Graham was squarely within the liberal consensus of the mid-twentieth century, while Falwell stood entirely outside of it.

The differences were theological as well as ideological. Graham's style was "churchly" in the sociological sense of that term: he preferred a big tent that would accommodate as many people as possible, and he allowed for a certain measure of disagreement. He preached a spare theology of "saving grace" and eschewed doctrinal controversies and political litmus tests. He even soft-pedaled "wedge issues" such as abortion and gay rights, particularly in the second half of his career. Falwell's approach was "sectarian" in the sociological sense: he wanted a pure community that was restricted to the right thinking, even if that meant leaving some people out in the rain. He liked to draw clear, sharp lines between heterodoxy and orthodoxy and between wrong and right. He did not shy away from controversy but used it as a means of keeping his followers in line. What really "revived" during the 1970s, then, was not "conservative Christianity" per se but rather its fundamentalist and sectarian variant, which would increasingly set the agenda and the tone for American Christianity as a whole.

At first glance, Falwell's frequent imprecations against America's "national sins" might seem to be classical jeremiads that fit neatly into the civil religious tradition. If the American people did not repent for feminism and hedonism and, above all, for abortion and homosexuality, Falwell warned, they would lose God's favor and face his wrath. His most (in)famous jeremiad was delivered on Pat Robertson's television show, *The 700 Club*, three days after the 9/11 attacks: "The pagans, and the abortionists, and the feminists, and the gays . . . , the ACLU, People for the American Way—all of them who have tried to secularize America—I point the finger in their face and say 'you helped this happen'."

On closer inspection, though, Falwell's jeremiads do not fit the Puritan mold after all. There were six major differences. Unlike the Puritans, Falwell emphasized sexual sins to the exclusion of social justice. Indeed, Falwell rarely ever mentioned greed, selfishness, corruption, or imperialism—the sorts of offenses that the Hebrew prophets most often denounced—except to deny that they were unjust in the first place.

So it is perhaps not surprising—and this is the second major difference—that Falwell's prophetic denunciations rarely invoked the Hebrew prophets themselves.[9] Indeed, he cited Milton Friedman far more often than Jeremiah, while Amos and Isaiah received no mention in his rhetoric at all. And on those occasions when Falwell did quote from the Old Testament, he mostly invoked the legal injunctions of Deuteronomy and Leviticus or the moral maxims of Proverbs.

The Hebrew prophets had directed their jeremiads at the Israeli people and their rulers. Puritan jeremiads followed this pattern as well. But Falwell's jeremiads were mostly aimed at the "Gentiles," that is, at non-fundamentalists. There were occasions when Falwell chided the Christian churches. He typically accused them of being too politically "passive" in their responses to the nation's sins. But he did not blame them for the nation's plight. Rather, he laid the lion's share of the blame for America's problems at the feet of "secular humanism."[10] That is the third difference.

The fourth is that for the Hebrew prophets, the national covenant was a living covenant with an evolving God. Again and again, the covenant between the Israelites and their God was renegotiated, and each iteration was more socially inclusive and more ethically universal than the last. The historical development of America's civil religion had followed a similar pattern. In the Falwellian dispensation, however, the national covenant is a fixed agreement with an unchanging God. Following the Mormon political theologian and John Birch Society leader W. Cleon Skousen, Falwell and other leaders of the New Christian Right argued that the U.S. Constitution is a divinely inspired document containing immutable political truths.[11] Not ethical truths concerning human freedom, equality, and happiness, but *institutional* truths concerning the proper form of government. On their reading—which echoed John C. Calhoun's—the core truths of the founding documents are contained in the articles rather than the preambles. To alter this architecture, they contended, is to court disaster.

This led as well to a very different understanding of prophetic time—the fifth difference. In the Hebraic tradition, time is spiral: "wandering" eventually brings progress, and disorientation leads to discovery. In the fundamentalist vision, wandering serves no purpose. When you're lost, you're just lost, and the best thing to do is return to your starting point. As the liberal Protestant theologian William Sloane Coffin once perceptively remarked, there was no forward in Falwell's theology, only "back, back, back" to the moral and political "absolutes" of Christianity and the Constitution.

The sixth and final difference between the Falwellian jeremiad and the American civil religion concerns the nature of good and evil and what human beings can know about it. In the Augustinian tradition the forces of evil are invisible and immaterial and only partially and imperfectly known to human beings. In theological principle, Falwell might well have affirmed these distinctions, but in rhetorical practice, he tended to run roughshod over them. Again and again he identified particular individuals as literal agents of the devil. Some of the targets were predictable enough, as in his decades-long crusade against the Clintons. Others were less so: on one occasion, Falwell went so far as to describe Billy Graham himself as "the chief servant of Satan in America." This rhetoric of demonization was often extended to entire groups. Falwell sometimes suggested that secular humanists were "satanic emissaries" who had physically occupied the United States. Likewise, after 9/11, Falwell argued that Islam was "satanic" and once described Muhammad as a "terrorist."

But what has the Lynchburg of Falwell to do with the Santa Barbara of Reagan? Were there any real affinities between Falwell's fundamentalism and Reagan's Emersonianism? To outsiders, it may seem an unlikely union, one born entirely of political expediency rather than ideological or personal affinity. But that would be a superficial judgment, as judgments of other people's relationships often are. In some ways, the worldviews of Reagan and Falwell were surprisingly complementary. Both saw free markets as the institutional foundation of personal freedom and moral order, and the welfare state as a slippery slope toward personal dependency and moral chaos. So, too, did their life stories coincide. Like many Americans of their era, Reagan and Falwell grew up in small towns during the Great Depression and enjoyed great success in the boom years following World War II. As a result, both were inclined to see a strong connection between the conservative values of their childhoods and the material successes of their adult years—and thereby to overlook the importance of social and historical context to their personal experiences of rapid upward mobility.

There were other still-deeper affinities as well. Both viewed American history through a simple "golden age" lens. Reagan and Falwell did not wish to *recover* America's founding ideals; they wished to *restore* the *status quo ante*—before the counterculture, before the New Deal—the "real" America, as they had understood and lived it in the small-town America of the mid-twentieth century. For them, the founding documents were not so much a set of political ideals to which the nation should aspire as a set of social blueprints to which the nation must adhere, not just because they had proven useful or were part of tradition, but because they were in fact *divinely inspired*, written in stone and handed down to the founders like the Ten Commandments to Moses on Mount Sinai. Thus, their philosophy of history was straightforwardly circular, rather than spiral.

Furthermore, both men inclined toward a literalist approach to religious and political "scripture" in which the meaning of texts such as the Bible and the Constitution was plainly evident to the common sense of the untutored mind. For them, the learned interpretations of the "cultural elites"—be they social scientists or lettered theologians—were inherently suspect. Indeed, to them, interpretive disagreements of any kind suggested veiled ambitions or defective character. Thus did the New Right belatedly develop its own "hermeneutics of suspicion."

But the most fateful parallel between the two men concerned their basic understanding of the nature of good and evil. Both were inclined to paint the world in black and white. Neither saw much gray, the sorts of inscrutabilities and "relativities" that had so troubled and preoccupied Lincoln and Niebuhr. For Reagan and Falwell, moral truths were few and simple. Both men also tended to draw moral boundaries *between* persons and nations, rather than *through* them. Evil was embodied in particular persons ("liberals," "homosexuals") and localized in specific collectivities ("communists," "feminists"), as was good ("Christians," "patriots"). What is more, they understood such boundaries as slippery slopes. A single step away from unfettered capitalism, for example, was a fateful step toward Soviet-style communism. Likewise, a single step away from fundamentalist Christianity was a fateful step toward "secular humanism." In this moral schema there was no middle ground, no such thing as a "mixed economy" or a "liberal Christianity." These were just flat-out contradictions. The world could be neatly divided into two camps. On one side, the good side, lay "Christian America" and its devoted allies. On the other side, the evil side, lay most everyone else.

And therein lay the decisive mistake. A civil religion that locates all evil outside of itself and claims certain knowledge of divine Providence quickly mutates into self-worship and self-benediction—in a word, into religious nationalism. While some thoughtful conservatives did warn of this danger, the movement as a whole eventually succumbed to it. The crucial turning point was 9/11. This was no accident: the temptations of religious nationalism are particularly great in times of war, when the ultimate sacrifice must be made by a few and then rendered meaningful to those left behind, and greatest of all when the enemy is a religious other. In democratic polities, the temptation may be further heightened by electoral politics, particularly during closely contested elections, when the margin of victory hinges on turning out "the base" and the most effective means of doing so is overheated rhetoric suffused with anger and fear. And thus it was that the conservative civil religion so rapidly devolved into the crude religious nationalism now known as "American exceptionalism." But this was not to take place until after a brief intermezzo led by another generation, one that still put civic duty ahead of party politics.

BUSH REDUX

Historical time does not always move in straight lines; sometimes, it circles back on itself. Such was the case in 1988, when Ronald Reagan passed the torch to George Bush Sr. Chronologically, Bush was a half generation younger than Reagan; culturally, he was a half generation older. While Reagan did not become politically engaged until the post-war boom years, for Bush, the war was politically formative. Where Reagan was rooted in the future strongholds of the GOP—the small towns of the "heartland" and the big cities of the Sun Belt—Bush still had one foot in the tony towns of the Northeast that represented the old stronghold of the party. He was very much a product of the "Northeastern establishment"—of the classrooms and playing fields of Andover and Yale—and this was clearly reflected in his political views, which were on the right-hand side of the "liberal consensus." In foreign policy, the elder Bush was very much a realist, more concerned about protecting America's "national interests" than about spreading its "democratic faith." He was also a multilateralist who preferred to work through international institutions and placed great faith in the transatlantic alliance. Thus, in his prosecution of the First Gulf War, Bush Sr. patiently assembled a broad international alliance around a narrow strategic end: driving Iraq out of Kuwait. In economic policy, too, the elder Bush was very old school: a pragmatic fiscal conservative, not a laissez-faire ideologue. As the candidate of the post-Reagan GOP, he obediently mouthed the new supply-side orthodoxy—which he had earlier denounced as "voodoo economics." But as president, he quickly reverted to type: confronted with rising deficits, he reneged on his "read my lips, no new taxes" campaign pledge. In social policy, his views were really more Goldwater than Falwell. Publicly, he toed the line on abortion. But his private views were more pragmatic. The elder Bush was part of that now-extinct species, the "liberal Republican."

Bush's civil theology was also more Episcopalian than Emersonian. It acknowledged sin but without equating it to sex. In his acceptance speech at the 1988 Republican National Convention, for example, Bush equated sin with self-seeking. "There's graft in city hall, the greed on Wall Street; there's influence peddling in Washington and the small corruptions of everyday ambition," he declared.[12] Speaking before a group of World War II veterans, Bush acknowledged one of the nation's collective sins: the wartime internment of Japanese Americans. [13] Apparently, "apology" was not yet a dirty word in the GOP lexicon. Too, Bush defined success in terms of service rather than income. After taking the oath of office on a Bible opened to the Beatitudes, Bush began his inaugural address with this awkward prayer: "Heavenly Father . . . write on our hearts these words: 'Use power to help people.' ."[14] During his tenure in office, he spoke often of "the honor of public service."[15] Unlike Reagan, he did not imagine that free markets could fully translate vice into virtue—that we help others simply by helping ourselves. Nor did he ever claim that the United States was a special instrument of divine justice or pretend to any foreknowledge of divine Providence. Speaking in the midst of Operation Desert Storm, Bush eschewed arguments about national greatness and national chosenness. Instead, he laid out a careful argument in terms of Augustine's doctrine of just war. Nor did he resort to apocalyptic imagery. Instead, he concluded with Lincoln's words: "My concern is not whether God is on our side, but whether we are on God's side."[16] In short, Bush Sr.'s civil theology is easily understood as a right-of-center version of the civil religious tradition—and, as such, an example that some American conservatives might consider revisiting.

The same cannot be said of his son's political theology, which quickly devolved into religious nationalism following the 9/11 attacks. In retrospect, this divergence between father and son is somewhat surprising. The *cursus honorum* of the younger Bush was a carbon copy of the elder's, albeit a smeared one: an undistinguished academic and athletic career at Andover and Yale, a failed stint as a fighter pilot in lieu of military service in Vietnam, and a checkered business career bankrolled by family friends. It was this failure to launch that would eventually drive Bush to the bottle. But then came a midlife redemption: a fortunate marriage, a sobriety pledge, newfound faith, and, finally, political successes that arrived faster and rose higher than had the father's.

For a time at least, it appeared that the apple had not fallen so far from the tree. As governor of Texas, the younger Bush was known as a pragmatic reformer and a bipartisan conciliator. As a presidential candidate, too, his positions often echoed his father's. He promised a "humble" (read: realist) foreign policy. He advocated a new brand of "compassionate conservatism" that recalled his father's "kinder, gentler" America. Finally, he proclaimed himself a "uniter, not a divider," a pragmatist who could reach across the aisle. His early pronouncements signaled a civil theology in the paternal mold. In his acceptance speech at the Republican National Convention in 2000, he insisted that the "American founders . . . never saw our nation's greatness in rising wealth or advancing armies, but in small unnumbered acts of caring and courage and self-denial." And in his first inaugural address, he presented the "American story" as the "story of a flawed and fallible people."

Like his father, Bush seemed to lack "the vision thing." And then came 9/11, and with it a new vision. That vision didn't come right away. When Bush first received news of the terrorist attacks, he was at an elementary school in Florida. A video recording taken of the classroom that morning shows him perched atop a child's chair looking paralyzed, disoriented, panicked, and much too small for the task ahead.

That appearance was not deceptive—but the vision soon arrived. Speaking from the altar of the National Cathedral just three days later, Bush was clearly a changed man, or least a coached man: resolute, calm, and controlled. He delivered a brief civil homily that began with a short remembrance of the dead and an eloquent consolation to the living. Shifting focus toward the end, Bush then promised revenge against the perpetrators and provided a brief interpretation of their deeds: "In every generation," he contended, "the world has produced enemies of human freedom. They have attacked America because we are freedom's home and defender, and the commitment of our Fathers is now the calling of our time."

Over the next seven years, through the ups and downs of two wars and two terms in office, Bush would hold fast to this basic interpretation of the 9/11 attacks: they were aimed at freedom itself and at its greatest champion, the United States. Again and again the president would stumble down the slippery slope from civil religion to religious nationalism. The first missteps were taken in the special address he delivered before a joint session of Congress on September 20. Bush did not go so far as to frame the new war as a religious war. (Of course, many of his supporters were not quite so circumspect.) Instead, he argued that the 9/11 attackers were "enemies of freedom" and also "traitors to their own faith." Bush's transgressions against the civic creed were of a somewhat subtler sort. Many of his critics focused on his statement that "every nation, in every region, now has a decision to make. Either you are with us, or you are with the terrorists." But there were other less often noticed parts of the speech that were just as troubling. At times, Bush seemed to conflate America with God, as in his promise that "justice will be done," a subtle echo of a line from the Lord's Prayer, "Thy will be done." Toward the end of the speech, perhaps in an effort to project confidence, Bush again overreached: "The course of this conflict is not known, yet its outcome is certain. Freedom and fear, justice and cruelty, have always been at war, and we know that God is not neutral between them." Bush's words subtly embedded the new war in the cosmic struggle between good and evil, and strongly implied that God was on America's side. In so doing, he fell prey to the very temptations against which Niebuhr—and his own father—had so strenuously warned: pretensions to providential foreknowledge and moral innocence. His Manichean worldview and unreflective nature blinded him to the "relativities" and "corruptions" to which his prideful imprecations would soon give rise. Alas, his "vision" would not improve over time; indeed, it would grow ever blurrier. In fact, the clearer it seemed, the blurrier it really was.

Bush sought to draw sharp lines between good and evil. But, like Falwell and Reagan, he often implied that the line ran between people and nations rather than through them. "We are in a conflict between good and evil," he proclaimed at West Point in 2002, "and America will call evil by its name." Nor was this the only point on which apparent clarity masked deep confusion. Bush's justifications for the war on terror and the war in Iraq were simple and unchanging: the purpose of these wars, he said, was to defend "freedom" and oppose "evil," to take the fight to the terrorists so that the terrorists would not take the fight to America. But if he was clear about America's purposes and power, he continually confused them with those of God. Certainly, one of America's founding purposes was to institutionalize individual freedom. For Bush, this was also one of God's main purposes. "God has planted in every human heart the desire to live in freedom," he once said.[17] Thus, to him, America's purposes and God's purposes were one: "Freedom is not America's gift to the world," he argued, "it is God's gift to all humanity."[18] Americans, he claimed, have "been called to a unique role in human events."[19] In defending freedom, then, America was simply acting on God's behalf, perhaps in his stead.

Bush succumbed to a similar confusion about God's powers. For the believing Christian, these powers include the power to deliver the world from evil. But on more than one occasion, Bush imputed such powers to the United States. In his 2002 State of the Union address, for example, he assured his fellow Americans that "we can overcome evil with greater good." Later that year, in a speech delivered in New York City on the first anniversary of 9/11, Bush suggested that "the greatness of America" itself would "deliver" the American people from evil. In his concluding peroration, he then assured his listeners, in blankly biblical language, that "this ideal of America is the hope of all mankind. . . . That hope still lights the way. And the light shines in the darkness. And the darkness will not overcome it." Because America is always on the side of the good and because it wields such immense power, he maintained, it need not and must not ever ask for a "permission slip" for its "missions" and "crusades." This was a curious theology indeed, one that made individual freedom the central message of the Christian gospels and claimed for one nation the power to overcome evil.

Still, one must resist the temptation to caricature. Elsewhere, often before smaller audiences, Bush sometimes used more measured terms. In a 2004 speech, for example, he plainly stated that "there is a dividing line in our world, not between nations, and not between religions or culture, but a dividing line separating two visions of justice and the value of life." Americans, he insisted, do not "consider themselves a chosen nation; God moves and chooses as He wills."[20] And yet, in Bush's case, the careful qualifications were often followed by bold pronouncements about good and evil, missions and crusades, rather than the other way around.

During the Reagan years, the conservative movement elaborated a heterodox version of the civil religious tradition that was composed of two strands. Reagan himself wove the first. In the orthodox tradition of civic republicanism, "freedom" involved self-government, and in two senses: government of one's desires and active citizenship in pursuit of the common good. In the American version of civic republicanism, the nation's political compass also had a second lodestar: equality. Freedom was not to be restricted to an elite of white property-holding males, as it had been in the ancient world and the antebellum South; it was to be extended to all. In Reagan's heterodox version of civic republicanism, by contrast, freedom was subtly but radically redefined. The only desires that really needed governing were sexual ones. All other desires were essentially good, particularly the desire for wealth and luxury, which civic republicans had traditionally seen as the principal source of moral corruption. The real fount of personal "dependency," Reagan argued, was politics, not economics. A welfare recipient was dependent; a wage earner was not. In other words, the true domain of human freedom was the marketplace, not the public square. And because the marketplace rewarded virtues, especially diligence and daring, the redistribution of wealth was fundamentally immoral. Equality meant equality before God and the law and nothing more.

Protestant conservatives like Falwell and Robertson wove the second strand of the heterodox civil religion. In the orthodox tradition of prophetic religion, the terms of the national covenant included not only the commands of the Decalogue but also the protection of the weak. In this vision, the chosen people were neither singled out for special blessings nor commissioned for divine crusades; rather, they were exhorted to live according to a higher set of standards, to serve as a "light to the world." The prophetic voice of the jeremiad was therefore directed at the people themselves, and especially at the powerful among them. In the heterodox vision of Falwell and company, prophecy too was subtly but radically redefined. The national covenant was recast around "family values." Conservative Christians were urged to exercise "dominion" over American society, and to embark on "crusades" to spread freedom. And the targets of the new jeremiad were not the chosen or the powerful, but the goyim and the downtrodden. What is more, prophecy became increasingly focused on the apocalypse rather than the Promised Land. From the apocalyptic perspective, America's problems were not the result of its moral failings; they were due to Satan himself and the enemies of the New Christian Right in their capacity as his corporeal agents. Viewed through Robertson and his contemporaries' literalistic hermeneutics, the prophetic books became a sort of skeleton key that unlocked the secrets of divine Providence. In this way, the fallibility of human reason—a staple of Calvinist theology—was superseded by charismatic means.

The two strands of the conservative civil religion were intertwined along two axes. The first, and most obvious, was sexual morality, particularly a categorical opposition to abortion and homosexuality. Interestingly, opposition to divorce, once a mainstay of conservative morality, was generally downplayed, perhaps because it was just as prevalent among conservative evangelicals as other segments of the American population, not so easily concealed as abortion or homosexuality, and likely to cramp the freewheeling lifestyles of the men in the pulpits. The second, and less obvious, connection between the two strands was an ethos of "personal responsibility." Liberal observers often wonder how libertarian economics and Christian ethics can be combined—how, to put it more pointedly, Friedman's *Free to Choose* can be reconciled with Jesus's Sermon on the Mount. The lynchpin of the synthesis that was forged between libertarianism and Christianity in these years was an ethic of "individual accountability" or "personal responsibility." In Arminian theology, as in laissez-faire economics, an individual's fate is determined by his or her choices, both in this world and in the next.

FROM MONDALE TO OBAMA

During the very years when conservatives were busy elaborating this new version of religious nationalism, liberals were moving in the direction of a secular liberalism. Consider Walter Mondale's acceptance speech at the Democratic National Convention in 1984. Despite the fact that Mondale was a preacher's son, his rhetoric was wholly devoid of religion, civil or otherwise. It contained no verses from the Bible, no allusions to the Founders, not even a token reference to the Declaration or the Constitution. Instead, Mondale focused on social class, social programs and civil rights. He excoriated the Republicans as the party of privilege and promised to defend Social Security and Medicare. In short, it was an utterly generic speech and could just as easily have been given by a Northern European social democrat. Reading the speech with the benefit of hindsight, and contrasting it with Reagan's paean to "morning in America," one can hardly be surprised at Mondale's thumping at the polls the following November.

Now fast-forward four years to Dukakis's 1988 acceptance speech at the Democratic National Convention in Atlanta. It contained a few cursory gestures toward the civil religious tradition. Early on, Dukakis spoke of his immigrant father's "deep and abiding faith in the promise of America," and near the end, he spoke of a "pledge," a "covenant" sworn by the "people of Athens." But the only sustained engagement with the tradition came midway through his declamation. In a subtle jab at Reagan, which was no doubt lost on all but a few, Dukakis quoted a few phrases from the part of John Winthrop's "Model of Christian Charity" that immediately preceded the section on Reagan's beloved metaphor of the "city upon a hill"; specifically, Dukakis drew on the passages in which Winthrop urged his listeners to "delight in each other" and "be knit together as one." But the master frame of Dukakis's speech was the consumerist version of the American Dream. And with the American economy firing on all cylinders, most voters felt that that dream was already within their reach. At the polls, voters delivered the third Republican landslide in a row.

It was not until the "man from Hope" took the stage in New York during the next election cycle that the Democratic Party really began to get back its civil religion. Bill Clinton spoke not only of "hope" but of "faith" and "vision" and "values" as well. He warned that the "American ethic" of "hard work" and "fair play" was threatened by "greed." He justified "equality" in religious terms and quoted scripture not once but twice, once drawing on the Old Testament (Proverbs 29:18), once on the New (1 Corinthians 2:9). The master trope of his acceptance speech was the notion of "the New Covenant, a solemn agreement between the people and their government based not simply on what each of us can take but what all of us must give to our Nation." "We offer our people a new choice based on old values," he continued. "We offer opportunity. We demand responsibility. We will build an American community again." He then offered a series of policy proposals. Some, such as universal health care, were long-standing goals of the Democratic Party. Others, like "ending welfare as we know it," signaled a shift to the right. All were presented in a call-and-response format more typical of a Baptist sermon.

Then came Barack Obama's 2008 presidential bid. Throughout his campaign, in moments both light and dark, Obama sought to retrieve and rearticulate the orthodox civil religious tradition by returning to some of its deepest sources and weaving its strands together into a coherent vision of the American project.

Few Americans were better equipped to do so. Obama had begun reading the canonical works of the African American tradition—Douglass, Du Bois, King—when he was still in high school. During his college years at Occidental and then Columbia, he was initially interested in political philosophy but eventually focused on international relations.[21] At Harvard Law School, he acquired a deep knowledge of the founders and the Constitution and was exposed to civic republicanism, American pragmatism, and virtue ethics—all foci of renewed academic interest during the late 1980s. Following graduation, he spent three years working as a community organizer just a few miles south of Jane Addams's Hull House. It was through this work that he was directly exposed to the black church tradition for the first time. Following his conversion to Christianity in the late 1980s, Obama heard the modern-day jeremiads of Jeremiah Wright and delved deeply into Niebuhr and Augustine. In short, if one were putting together a course of study in America's civil religious tradition, the reading list would look a lot like Obama's own intellectual biography.

While Obama's ability to retrieve these sources has much to do with his formal education, his drive to resynthesize them probably has more to do with his personal history. In his autobiographical writings and campaign speeches, Obama has presented this history as deeply and even uniquely American, a blend not only of black and white but of native-born and immigrant, city and country, the heartland and the coasts. "I stand here knowing that my story is part of the larger American story," he proclaimed in 2004, "and that, in no other country on earth, is my story even possible."

Meanwhile, Obama's critics have presented this biography as utterly foreign. They have focused instead on his father's roots in Kenya, Obama's own childhood years in Indonesia, his adolescent ones in the antipodes of American culture in Hawaii, and his East Coast education at Columbia and Harvard, thereby building a composite of a man who is very definitely part of the "liberal elite," quite possibly a Muslim, and probably not born in the United States. One Republican charged that Obama still needs to "learn to be American."

"Birther" nonsense to one side, Obama's critics do make an important point: he probably did need to "learn to be American" in a way that most other native-born Americans do not. However, in Obama's case, this seems ultimately to have led to an *over-* rather than underidentification with American culture[22]—and not just because he grew up around the edges of that culture, but also because he did not comfortably fit into the existing compartments of race, ethnicity, region, or class. So his biography is indeed "uniquely *American*" in the sense that it would not have been possible in any other country. But it is also "*uniquely* American" in the sense that it does not conform to any stock type. It is American society in miniature, a cultural composite that defies easy classification. This meant that Obama's efforts to achieve a coherent personal identity necessarily involved reflections on America's collective identity.

Obama's synthesis is not a radical secularist one. Obama flatly rejects the conventional argument that religious arguments must be kept out of the public square. "If we scrub language of all religious content," he warned a group of left-leaning Christians, "we forfeit the imagery and terminology through which millions of Americans understand both their personal morality and social justice. Imagine Lincoln's Second Inaugural Address without reference to 'the judgments of the Lord.' Or King's I Have a Dream speech without reference to all of 'God's children.' Their summoning of a higher truth helped inspire what had seemed impossible, and move the nation to embrace a common destiny."[23]

But Obama's reservations about radical secularism are not premised solely on a political calculation. They are also rooted in personal experience and theological conviction. When religious liberals "abandon the field of religious discourse—when we ignore the debate about what it means to be a good Christian or Muslim or Jew . . . others will fill the vacuum," he has argued. "And those who do are likely to be those with the most insular views of faith, or who cynically use religion to justify partisan ends."[24] In short, if some citizens choose to make religious arguments in the public square, then other citizens are entitled and perhaps even obligated to respond with religious counterarguments.

But while Obama is not a radical secularist, neither is he a Christian nationalist who thinks appeals to the "Judeo-Christian tradition" are themselves sufficient to justify a public policy. Because of the "increasing diversity of America's population," he has argued, "we are no longer just a Christian nation"—if, indeed, we ever were—but "also a Jewish nation, a

Muslim nation, a Buddhist nation, a Hindu nation, and a nation of non-believers." So while religious arguments should not be banned from the public square, religious citizens should try to "translate their concerns into universal, rather than religion-specific values." "I may be opposed to abortion for religious reasons," he has declared, "but if I seek to pass a law banning the practice, I cannot simply point to the teachings of my church or evoke God's will. I have to explain why abortion violates some principle that is accessible to people of all faiths, including those with no faith at all."[25] The same standard holds for religious liberals who favor social programs for the less fortunate, he maintains. They may open by citing Matthew 5, which instructs Christians to care for "the least of these." But they should also try to make their case in more secular terms—by appealing to the Golden Rule, say.

Obama's acceptance of public religiosity may seem at odds with his demands for "translation" and "accessibility," but it is not. Our approach to church–state issues, Obama argues, cannot be based on some hard-and-fast rule (e.g., "Religion must be kept strictly private" or "America is a Christian nation"). Rather, it must be guided by a "sense of proportion" that weighs competing goods against one another: "Not every mention of God in public is a breach to the wall of separation," he has argued. "It is doubtful that children reciting the Pledge of Allegiance feel oppressed or brainwashed as a consequence of muttering the phrase 'under God.' I didn't. Having voluntary student prayer groups use school property to meet should not be a threat, any more than its use by the High School Republicans should threaten Democrats." In short, Obama is just as wary of secularist fundamentalism as he is of Christianist fundamentalism.

Between these two extremes, Obama contends, lies a *via media* that brings together the secular and theistic elements of American culture into a unified worldview that can be embraced by believers and nonbelievers alike. "Alongside my own deep personal faith," Obama has said, "I am a follower, as well, of our civic religion."[26] Elsewhere, and often, he has spoken of a civic "faith," "creed," "ideal," or "ethic" that is shared by all Americans and underwrites national unity. "Being an American," he said in a speech on immigration reform, "is not a matter of blood or birth. It's a matter of faith. It's a matter of fidelity to the shared values we all hold so dear."[27] The civic faith, in other words, is separate from religious faith in the strict sense of the term and undergirds the nation's sense of common purpose.

What is the content of this creed, as Obama understands it? Generally speaking, Obama's vision pulls most forcefully on the prophetic tradition, including its oldest strand, covenant theology. Obama's speeches and writings often present condensed versions of the American story, stories of covenants made, broken, and remade. In the "More Perfect Union" speech, delivered in March 2008 in the midst of the Jeremiah Wright scandal, Obama opened with the first sentence of the preamble to the Constitution: "We the people, in order to form a more perfect union." Covenant made. But many Americans, he immediately added, were completely excluded from this union—women, of course, but, even more harshly, black slaves. Covenant broken. The Civil War was fought to right this grievous wrong. Covenant remade. Then came Jim Crow. Covenant broken again. Not until the civil rights movement was Reconstruction really completed. Covenant remade again.

How does Obama understand the content of this covenant? Obama acknowledges the importance of individual freedom in the American tradition, but he also emphasized the ideals of social equality and national unity as well. Similarly, while he nods to the conservative virtues of temperance and restraint, he places greater weight on social justice and Christian charity. His proof-texts are the preambles to the Declaration and the Constitution, alongside the Hebrew prophets and the Christian gospels. Reflecting on what he himself prays for at the National Prayer Breakfast in 2011, for instance, Obama said that "justice and mercy and compassion to the most vulnerable" topped his list, which was grounded in the "urgency of the Old Testament prophets."[28] Three years earlier, at CNN's Compassion Forum, Obama went so far as to argue that "the core value of all religions," including Christianity, is that "I am my brother's keeper, I am my sister's keeper."

Obama's rearticulation of the civil religion also owes a considerable debt to the Augustinian variant of prophetic Christianity as developed by Reinhold Niebuhr. In a conversation with David Brooks, Obama described Niebuhr as one of his "favorite philosophers." When Brooks asked Obama what he took away from Niebuhr, he responded: "I take away the compelling idea that there's serious evil in the world, and hardship and pain. And we should be humble and modest in our belief we can eliminate those things. But we shouldn't use that as an excuse for cynicism and inaction. I take away . . . the sense that we have to make these efforts knowing they are hard, and not swinging from naïve idealism to bitter realism."[29] Asked about the existence of evil in a nationally televised forum with Pastor Rick Warren the following year, Obama gave a similar response: "Evil does exist."[30] But, in an obvious allusion to the younger Bush, he quickly added that we should not imagine that we can "erase evil from the world. That is God's task." Speaking to a class of graduating cadets at West Point, he urged them to have "no illusions": "We know that a world of mortal men and women will never be rid of oppression and evil."[31] However, he declared, this knowledge does not excuse us from confronting evil when we see it. Realism about evil should not lead to cynicism about our fate: "We do not have to live in an idealized world to still reach for those ideals that will make it a better place." Instead, as Obama urged in his Nobel Address, "let us reach for the world that ought to be—that spark of the divine that still stirs within each of our souls. . . . We can admit the intractability of deprivation, and still strive for dignity. . . . We can understand that there will be war, and still strive for peace."

What exactly does Obama mean, both here and elsewhere, by "evil"? This is a crucial question, because the American civil religion can quickly degenerate into a crude religious nationalism when specific people or faiths or nations are unqualifiedly categorized as good, and others as evil. Obama has scrupulously avoided this slippery rhetorical slope. When he has used the word "evil," it has always been in relation to specific acts or categories of acts, such as the genocide in Darfur or the physical abuse of children. And even when speaking of the most patently evil acts, he has always been careful to separate them from the actors themselves. In dedicating the new 9/11 memorial at the Pentagon, for example, Obama described the terrorists as "perpetrators" of evil, and Al Qaeda as "a small band of murderers" that "perverts religion." Nowhere did he hint that members of this group were demonic agents of satanic forces. More than that, he reminded his listeners of the scriptural injunction to "get rid of all bitterness, rage and anger, brawling and slander."[32] And if Obama did not categorize America's enemies as unqualifiedly evil, neither did he view America as unqualifiedly good. "We must be willing to acknowledge our failures, not just trumpet our victories," he emphasized.[33] The greatest of these failures, or at least the one Obama mentions most often, is "the original sin of slavery." But it is certainly not the only failure that America has experienced. During his 2008 campaign, Obama often described the use of torture in the war on terror as a moral failing, a flagrant violation of American ideals.[34]

This willingness to own up to America's failures has led many conservatives to charge that Obama does not believe in "American exceptionalism." George W. Bush's top political adviser, Karl Rove, led this charge. In an op-ed published in the *Wall Street Journal* in April of 2009, shortly after Obama's first major trip abroad as president, Rove accused Obama of conducting an "apology tour," of "confessing the nation's sins" in the vain hope that other nations would do likewise. Other conservative commentators quickly piled on, arguing that Obama did not see America as unique, that he saw it as a country just like any other. For a time, it looked as if the GOP was going to stake its 2012 campaign on the idea of American exceptionalism. Mitt Romney's campaign book was entitled *No Apology.* Newt Gingrich's was called *A Nation Like No Other: Why American Exceptionalism Matters.*[35]

Are the critics right? Does Obama see America as "just another nation"? Certainly, Obama rejects the legal theory of American "exemptionalism" advanced by some conservative scholars, which asserts that America's hegemonic status places it above international law. "We cannot stand up before the world and say that there's one set of rules for America and another for everyone else," Obama has declared. He also rejects the view that America is always and everywhere a force for good in the world; likewise, the notion that the American military is an instrument of divine justice. "No Holy War can ever be a just war," Obama has argued. "For if you truly believe that you are carrying out divine will, then there is no need for restraint."[36] But that does not mean that he sees America as "just another nation." "The United States has been one of the greatest sources of progress the world has ever known," he has insisted. "We were born out of revolution against an empire. We were founded upon the ideal that all are created equal, and we have shed blood and struggled for centuries to give meaning to those words—within our borders, and around the world. We are shaped by every culture, drawn from every end of the Earth, and dedicated to a simple concept: *E pluribus unum*: 'Out of many, one.' " Elsewhere, he has insisted that "ours is a story of optimism and achievement and constant striving that is unique upon this earth."[37] Obama is indisputably an American exceptionalist of a certain sort, just not the sort that religious nationalists prefer.

Why not? Mainly for theological reasons. At least since Emerson, American progressives have inclined more and more toward the view that all human beings are basically or essentially good. Since Reagan, many American conservatives have come to a similar conclusion (except, of course, where sexual desire of a nonmarital or nonheterosexual sort is concerned). Obama categorically rejects this Pollyannaish view. Like Augustine and Niebuhr, he is a firm believer in original sin. Indeed, the doctrine of original sin is arguably the central pillar of Obama's entire theology. Asked whether he believed in sin in an interview about his faith, he answered with a simple and unequivocal "yes." Obama sees original sin much as Niebuhr did: not as a "dogma" premised on divine revelation, but as a brute fact of human nature that is easily verified. His understanding of the deeper sources of human sinfulness is also remarkably similar to Niebuhr's. In his Nobel Address Obama traced evil to "the imperfections of man" and the "limitations of reason." Of what does he think these imperfections consist? Of the "temptation of pride, and power." But he clearly does not see sin solely in individualistic terms. In his 2006 Sojourners speech, for instance, Obama defined sin in terms of "societal indifference" as well as "individual callousness." Four years later, in an on-air exchange with best-selling author and megachurch pastor Rick Warren, Obama suggested that sin is a matter of "fundamental selfishness."[38] Obama's understanding of original sin is not exclusively Niebuhrian, however. In his view, sin often involves a lack of empathy, an inability to recognize ourselves in another. Conversely, "progress comes when we look into the eyes of another and see the face of God."[39] Overall, Obama's view of human sinfulness is perhaps best seen as a combination of Niebuhr's Christian realism and Addams's social gospel.

As we have seen, another perennial pitfall of the prophetic tradition, which is deepened by the allures of biblical literalism, is to be found in "prophecy belief" of the Robertsonian variety, which claims to unlock the providential significance of mundane events and casts contemporary personages as actors in a cosmic drama. Obama has been careful to sidestep this pitfall as well. To be sure, he has often expressed the belief that human history has a certain shape. He has approvingly quoted Martin Luther King's claim that "the arc of the moral universe is long but it bends toward justice." And, in a nod to Reagan and Bush, he has argued that "experience shows that history is on the side of liberty."[40] But Obama retains a Lincolnian skepticism regarding human claims to special foreknowledge of God's will. At the National Prayer Breakfast in 2011, for instance, he reminded his audience that "God's plans for us may not always match our short-sighted desires."[41] Consequently, politicians should not claim to have a divine mandate or to act in God's name. And what applies to our personal lives applies *a fortiori* to external events. In a speech given a few months later in Joplin, Missouri, following a devastating tornado that leveled the entire town, Obama acknowledged that "the question that weighs on us at a time like this is: Why? Why our town? . . . We do not have the capacity to answer."[42] Note the sharp contrast between this sentiment and Falwell's and Robertson's prophetic interpretations of 9/11 and Hurricane

Katrina. Ironically, in his hesitation to claim to know the ways of God, Obama is actually much closer to the historical Puritans than are their self-proclaimed heirs.

And yet, for all his mastery of the prophetic tradition, President Obama sometimes seems bereft of the prophetic voice that defined his 2008 campaign. His soaring oratory seemed to fall an octave or two after the election. The pundits found his first inaugural address too somber, even a little flat, and his presidential briefings and speeches too "wonkish" and "professorial." Why? There are many reasons, of course. One is Obama's skill set. Mario Cuomo once quipped to the president, "You campaign in poetry; you govern in prose." And Obama's poetry is generally better than his prose. He often seems to lack a rhetorical "middle register" that can connect policy and poetry (a register in which Bill Clinton excelled). A second reason for the disjuncture is Obama's underlying philosophy of governance: it is deeply pragmatic, not in the folk sense of "flexible," but in the properly philosophical sense of "deliberative." Obama seems genuinely to believe that democratic dialogue eventually leads to the common good, even in a hyperpartisan culture such as twenty-first-century Washington. Whether this approach is naïve is an open question. (Niebuhr might have thought so.) Still, it is principled and not pusillanimous, as some of Obama's progressive critics have charged. But there is also a third reason for the disjuncture, one that is of particular relevance to us, namely, the "performative contradiction" between prophecy and the presidency. One role of the prophet—although not the only one—is speaking truth to power. But what happens when the prophet *becomes* the power? Prophets are mainly concerned with higher principles—with divine commands. Rulers must also attend to consequences—earthly ones. Of course, as Max Weber reminded us, the best rulers try to give both their proper due. They use power to pursue ideals, and they use ideals to generate power. And that is certainly what Obama has tried to do. But this task is easier if there are prophetic voices that speak from outside the halls of power, voices like those of Douglass, Addams, Niebuhr, and King. It is not clear that such voices exist today. Thus, Obama confronts a much sharper "performative contradiction" than Lincoln, Wilson, Roosevelt, or Johnson did. He is compelled to juggle the roles of prophet and president to a degree that they were not.

How does civic republicanism fit into Obama's vision? Obama is certainly aware of this strand of the tradition. His year in law school coincided with a revived interest in civic republicanism among English-speaking intellectuals. Still, Obama pulls more gently on this tradition than on its prophetic counterpart. One finds no references in his speeches and writings to Aristotle or Cicero or Machiavelli or Milton alongside those to Isaiah and Matthew and Niebuhr and King. Nonetheless, a careful listener can detect some distant echoes of the republican tradition in Obama's rhetoric.

I say "echoes" because Obama does not often use the classical terminology, preferring modern equivalents instead. Where the ancients might have spoken of humanity's innate "sociality," for example, Obama speaks of its deep need for "community." It is a need he has felt and acted on himself. During his years as a community organizer, he has recounted, "I came to realize that without a vessel for my beliefs, without an unequivocal commitment to a particular community of faith, I would be consigned at some level to always remain apart, free in the way that my mother was free, but also alone in the same ways that she was ultimately alone."[43] And what was true for him personally, he has argued, has generally been true of American society as well: "Our individualism has always been bound by a set of communal values, the glue upon which every healthy society depends."[44] Without some sense of community, he implies, we cannot be happy as individuals or healthy as a society. We are sociable creatures whose individual and collective wellbeing is dependent upon communal integration.

If Obama imparts a communitarian spin to human sociality, he proposes a pragmatist vision of self-government when he invokes the ideal of "deliberative democracy." By this, he means a system "in which all citizens are required to engage in a process of testing their ideas against an external reality, persuading others of their point of view, and building shifting alliances of consent."[45] In essence, Obama defends the classical ideal of collective self-government as an open-ended "conversation" between rational citizens who are oriented toward rational truth and the common good. It is worth noting that many American progressives regard such an ideal as unrealistic. Some see representative democracy as little more than a political market, a means of "aggregating preferences" about policy. Others see it as just a clash of competing interests or a battle of sovereign wills. American conservatives generally espouse an equally cynical view but come to a very different conclusion: let the market sort it out.

Unlike many American liberals, Obama does not shy away from talking about "values" and even "virtues." And unlike many American conservatives, he understands these terms in a broader sense that goes beyond "family values" or Victorian prudery. In his view, a healthy society requires a good deal of civic virtue: the willingness of citizens to make personal sacrifices for the sake of a common good. At the same time, he recognizes that virtues can also devolve into vices when they are practiced in excess. As he has wisely observed: "Self-reliance and independence can transform into selfishness and license, ambition into greed and a frantic desire to succeed. . . . We've seen patriotism slide into jingoism. . . . We've seen faith calcify into self-righteousness."[46]

Obama's understanding of individual freedom is also fairly republican, particularly when compared to the liberal understandings that currently predominate on both the left and the right. In the liberal tradition, the primary meaning of "freedom" is the absence of external restraint. About this much at least, contemporary liberals and conservatives are in tacit agreement.[47] Obama acknowledges the centrality of "negative liberty" in the American tradition. "But," he adds, "we understand our liberty in a more positive sense as well," one that is realized in "those homespun virtues" that "help us realize opportunity." Among other virtues, he names "self-improvement," "discipline," "temperance," "thrift," and "self-reliance."[48] On this point, then, Obama hews very close to the classical republican view that genuine freedom requires self-restraint—the government of the passions by reason.

One can also detect some distant echoes of the other major themes of classical republicanism in Obama's political rhetoric. For example, one can read Obama's concern with rising economic inequality as a concern over danger to the constitutional balance and a potential source of corruption. As "the few"—the "1 percent"—claim an ever greater share of the nation's resources, they also gain an ever greater influence over the political process. This is all the more true following the Supreme Court's decision in *Citizens v. United*, which allows unlimited political donations by corporations and the wealthy and may lead the upper class to place its private interests ahead of the public good. Obama's unusually strong reaction to the *Citizens v. United* decision, delivered during a State of the Union address with the justices present, seems to have been sparked by this worry. His concern with expanding the middle class—"the many"—can be understood in a republican fashion as well. Like Tocqueville, Obama understands a large middle class to be a crucial bulwark of American democracy. Finally, Obama's criticisms of excessive partisanship in Washington echo long-standing republican concerns with the potentially corrupting effects of political "factions," concerns that go back well beyond the founders to the Florentines and the ancients themselves. Still, all in all, these echoes are faint at best, even for those with the ears to hear them.

CONCLUSION

Progressive observers sometimes imagine that the culture wars are just a political spectacle carefully stage-managed by business interests to distract the white working class from its "true interests"—a boisterous circus that quells a gnawing hunger for bread. In this ring, the televangelists! In that ring, the shock jocks! Conservative observers take a slightly longer view. They mostly blame the 1960s. Sexual liberation, feminism, gay rights—*that* was the beginning of the great unraveling. There was no more right or wrong. Suddenly, everything was permitted.

There is some truth to both of these interpretations—but not much. If the preceding chapters have shown anything, it is that the roots of our culture wars are very, very deep. The religious nationalist script was not penned by Jerry Falwell in the 1970s; it was written by Cotton Mather in the 1700s. The radical secularist script was not dreamed up by Jane Fonda in the 1960s; it was put together by Robert Ingersoll after the Civil War. This, alas, is the price of historical amnesia: being an actor in an old scene and thinking it's opening night.

The election of Barack Obama in November of 2008 brought a brief respite from the shouting. But it was a very brief respite indeed, lasting just two short months, from Election Day until Inauguration Day. Then came the Tea Party and the Occupy movement, which were diametrically opposed on many policies but tacitly united in their populism. Both argued that American democracy had been taken hostage by a small elite. The Tea Party's ire was directed at the political leaders of the two parties. The Occupy movement's anger targeted economic elites in business and finance.

The culture wars are now conjoined with class war. And if we do not end the culture wars soon, we will surely lose the class war in the end.

CHAPTER 8

The Civil Religion

CRITICS AND ALLIES

I HAVE TRIED to give religious nationalism and radical secularism their proper dues. But I have not pretended to be neutral toward them. I have argued that they are historically inaccurate, morally incoherent, and sociologically implausible. I have shown that the United States was not founded as a Christian nation or a secular republic, but as a prophetic republic. I have shown that religious nationalism is irreligious and that radical secularism is illiberal. And I have contended that neither provides a plausible foundation for a nation as diverse and metaphysical as the Americans. There is yet another reason for rejecting them, however: they do not offer coherent accounts of democratic tradition either.

DEMOCRACY AND TRADITION REVISITED

When modern-day religious nationalists in the United States talk about "tradition," they imagine it as something fixed and unchanging, a pure spring that issues into a polluted river. To move away from the spring is to risk death by poisoning. This understanding of tradition is deeply indebted to a certain kind of biblical literalism—what Christian Smith refers to as "Biblicism." Key assumptions of biblicism include:

- *Divine Writing.* "The Bible . . . consists of . . . God's very own words written inerrantly in human language."
- *Complete Coverage.* "The divine will about all of the issues relevant to Christian belief and life are contained in the Bible."
- *Commonsense Interpretation.* "Any reasonably intelligent person can read the Bible in his or her own language and correctly understand the plain meaning of the text."
- *Internal Harmony.* "All related passages of the Bible on any given subject fit together almost like puzzle pieces into single, unified, internally consistent bodies of instruction."[1]

On this account, a pure tradition is a fixed tradition, while a dynamic tradition is a polluted one.

There is a close link between evangelical-style biblicism and Tea Party–style constitutionalism. Many evangelicals and Tea Partiers now believe that the Constitution is "divinely inspired" (a claim originally advanced only by a fringe group within the Mormon Church). Indeed, a popular painting by the "patriotic" artist Jon McNaughton depicts Jesus Christ presenting the U.S. Constitution to a transhistorical assembly that includes the founding fathers, ordinary Americans, and representatives of the various branches of the U.S. military. The practice of memorizing, citing, and carrying the text of the U.S. Constitution, which is *de rigueur* in Tea Party circles, simply mimics long-standing practices of Bible-toting and "proof-texting." In addition to such claims of "divine writing," contemporary religious nationalists often assert the principle of "complete coverage" as well. They argue that the U.S. Constitution, as originally written, is fully adequate to meet all the demands of the present day and, indeed, of any day. Many argue that the original text has been marred by subsequent additions and propose the repeal of various amendments. It is further assumed that the U.S. Constitution is a transparent text that can be readily understood by any well-meaning reader, much as the Bible is presumed to be fully "self-explicating" for the average Christian. The idea that there are any internal contradictions within the U.S. Constitution is also rejected—and must of course be rejected if the document is really a product of "divine writing."

Smith argues that biblicism is sociologically implausible and hermeneutically "impossible." It is sociologically implausible because if it were true, there would be no important theological differences among Americans. And it is hermeneutically impossible because the Bible cannot be interpreted without recourse to external sources (e.g., the Christian creeds) and concepts (e.g., the Trinity) that are not found in the texts themselves. These same objections apply *a fortiori* to Tea Party constitutionalism. Constitutional literalism is implausible because if it were true, there would be no disputes about constitutional interpretation (e.g., those between proponents of "originalism" and the "living Constitution"). And it is "impossible" because the interpretation of the written Constitution necessarily relies on appeals to what legal scholar Akhil Amar calls "the unwritten Constitution," namely, various external texts and terms such as *The Federalist Papers* and "the separation of powers."[2]

If contemporary religious nationalism is a kind of traditionalistic antitraditionalism that claims to speak in the name of tradition but lacks a coherent notion of tradition, then radical secularism is a variety of anti-traditionalistic tradition that loudly ushers tradition out the front door and then quietly smuggles it in through the back door. While radical secularism has long defined itself in opposition to tradition, it has been unable to dispense with the idea.

Consider the work of political philosopher John Rawls, arguably the most influential liberal thinker of the late twentieth century. Even he could not dispense with the idea of tradition entirely. In *A Theory of Justice*, his first major work, Rawls spoke often of various philosophical "traditions" ("utilitarian," "contractarian," "Marxian," and so on).[3] And in the closing pages, one finds a passage that could easily have been written by a philosopher of tradition: "To say that man is a historical being is to say that the realizations of the powers of human individuals living at any one time takes the cooperation of many generations (or even societies) over a long period of time. It also implies that this cooperation is guided at any moment by an understanding of what has been done in the past as it is interpreted by social tradition."[4] But this passage is the exception that proves the rule: the idea of tradition did not occupy any important place in Rawls's early work, which attempted to construct a theory of justice on a foundation of pure reason.

But the idea of tradition did find its way into his revised theory of justice, smuggled back in via the concept of "public reason." In his first book, Rawls had advanced a comprehensive theory of justice that he believed would be compelling for any rational person. That belief proved false: many did not find his account the least bit compelling. So, in his next major work, *Political Liberalism* (1993), Rawls advanced a much more limited theory of *political* justice. He began from the premise that "constitutional democracies" that guaranteed the "basic liberties" of thought, expression, and association would inevitably give rise to a variety of "comprehensive worldviews." Given basic freedoms, he reasoned, people would arrive at different opinions. But while citizens might not be able to agree on a "comprehensive doctrine" of justice, Rawls believed they might nonetheless reach agreement on more limited questions of *political* justice. To do so, however, they would first have to set aside their "comprehensive doctrines" of justice and address one another in the language of "public reason." By this he meant reasoning by the public, conducted in public, and based on shared premises.

Many critics objected that "public reason" was just another term for "secular reason," that the comprehensive worldviews he was most interested in excluding from the public sphere were religious ones. Rawls sought to address these criticisms a few years later in an influential essay entitled "The Idea of Public Reason Revisited." There, he conceded that "democratic societies will differ in the specific doctrines that are influential and active within them."[5] In effect, he redefined public reason as the democratic traditions of specific nations. By way of example, he pointed to the "political values . . . mentioned in the preamble to the United States Constitution: a more perfect union, justice, domestic tranquility, the common defense, the general welfare and the blessings of liberty for ourselves and our posterity."[6]

Rawls's final theory of public reason comes very close to the idea of political tradition developed in this book. Still, the American civil religion as I understand it is not quite identical to Rawlsian public reason. There are at least two crucial differences. The first concerns content. Where public reason is composed solely of abstract values (especially freedom and equality), civil religion includes historical narratives and exemplary figures, public poetry and civic heroism, as well as public reason. And not without, well, reason: "public reason" lacks motivational force. It is not capable of mobilizing and unifying citizens around common purposes on its own. The second major difference concerns sources. Rawls saw political liberalism as a philosophical response to the "reasonable pluralism" that arose in the wake of the Protestant Reformation and the collapse of Western Christendom. In this sense, political liberalism is exclusively secular in its origins. Not so the civil religion, of course, which draws heavily on prophetic discourse. On my reading, prophetic religion is actually an integral part of the American version of public reason. Indeed, it is one of the historical taproots—arguably, the most important one—of those very values to which Rawls devoted his life, namely, justice and equality.

THE CIVIL RELIGIOUS TRADITION:
CRITIQUES AND REJOINDERS

The civil religious tradition has also been subjected to various criticisms. One is that civil religion demands too little. Let us call this the "cosmopolitan critique." It addresses the civil religion understood as a form of critical patriotism. In a much-discussed essay entitled "Patriotism and Cosmopolitanism," the philosopher Martha Nussbaum argued that our primary allegiance should be to humanity, rather than to country.[7] Why? Because "nationality" is a "morally irrelevant characteristic." Our moral duties, she said, are duties to other persons *qua* persons and not (just) to our fellow citizens. Furthermore, "patriotic pride" is morally dangerous: it creates an us/them divide that constricts our moral vision. Becoming a cosmopolitan, Nussbaum concluded, is a bit like growing up, in that it involves a high degree of moral autonomy, whereas patriotism is a kind of infantilism that clings to "an idealized image of a nation as surrogate parent who will do one's thinking for one."[8]

The cosmopolitan critique seems compelling. Don't we have moral duties to humanity? Hasn't national pride led to great evil? Surely. But one can answer both these questions in the affirmative without accepting Nussbaum's argument in toto. Take the question of duties. If an "ought" presumes a "can," then surely our moral duties cannot be to "humanity" as such; this plainly exceeds our individual physical and psychological capacities. Rather, our moral duties are to those persons whom we are actually capable of helping. But there are many persons whom we cannot easily help because we do not have the necessary knowledge and skills to do so. (Think of an idealistic but inexperienced American aid worker or missionary stationed in a crisis zone far from home.) For this reason, we may in fact have a special duty to help those who are more physically or culturally proximate to ourselves, such as our families or neighbors or fellow citizens. Further, our duties are not exclusively moral; they may be political as well. If we have the good fortune to live in a constitutional democracy, we arguably have a duty to defend and uphold our national traditions and institutions, because they are a source of positive good not only to ourselves, but also to others, including future generations, and perhaps also a source of aid or inspiration to those who have the misfortune to live under nondemocratic regimes. Finally, many of the greatest moral challenges that presently confront humanity, such as economic inequality and climate change, can only be fairly and effectively addressed via democratic institutions. Individual-level efforts are necessary but not sufficient. We have to defend the institutional means to our greater ends. For all these reasons, it is not clear to me why cosmopolitanism should always trump patriotism.

What about the argument that patriotism is always a source of harm? If by "patriotism" one means the sort of national pride that is blind to national sins, that sees prosperity as the just deserts of piety and virtue and military power as a divine sword that God has entrusted to his people—if, in short, one subscribes to the sort of religious nationalism nowadays known as "American exceptionalism"—then surely the moral harms of patriotism have been, and continue to be, quite considerable. But that is hardly the only possible form of patriotism. Conversely, if patriotism comes in both benign and malign forms, and if it behooves us to know the difference between them, then can't the same be said of cosmopolitanism? Can't Jacobinism or Stalinism be understood as forms of cosmopolitanism? And can't seemingly benign forms of cosmopolitanism also be a source of great harm, as when they underwrite feelings of moral indifference and cultural superiority among jet-setting members of the global elite?[9] Such an ethic might legitimate the moral expatriation of global capital from the democratic state or motivate misguided top-down strategies of economic development.[10] Cosmopolitanism has frequently aided and abetted such injustices and miscalculations.

A second possible critique of the American civil religious tradition is that it demands too much. The political theorist George Kateb has elaborated such a critique.[11] Kateb is a libertarian of sorts. On his view, the social world is composed solely of individuals. He regards nations as "abstractions" sustained by "fictions" and defines patriotism as a "love of one's country" that is "most importantly shown in a readiness . . . to die and to kill for one's country." Putting these two claims together, Kateb concludes that patriotism is ultimately really nothing but "a readiness to die and to kill for an abstraction: nothing you can see . . . or feel as you feel the presence of another person, or comprehend."[12]

Kateb's critique is not without moral force. One thinks of a young soldier who has become cannon fodder in an unjust war. One recalls John Kerry's question about the Vietnam War: "How do you ask a man to be the last man to die for a mistake?" Uncritical patriotism can quickly devolve into unreflective militarism, with individual lives as "collateral damage." If patriotism means "My country, right or wrong," then it must be rejected.

Still, Kateb's premises are questionable. Consider the claim that groups are fictions and abstractions, while individuals are real and tangible. He is, of course, right that that all group identities are at least partly sustained by shared (or, better, overlapping) narratives. However, these narratives need not be mere "fictions"; they may contain historical truth. Nor, for that matter, are actual fictions always false. As Paul Ricoeur reminds us, fictional narratives can reveal certain truths to their readers.[13] This is one reason why people read novels and watch movies. It should also be added that narratives help to sustain *individual* identities. Arguably, what individuates a person *qua* person is a particular history understood in a particular way and oriented in a particular direction—that is, an ongoing and open-ended self-narration. What is more, as Charles Taylor emphasizes, individual narratives are dependent upon and embedded within cultural ones.[14] We only are who we are in relationship to, and dialogue with, those who came before us and those who share our lifeworld.[15] Identity is inherently social. Finally, Kateb's claim that one

can "see," "feel," and "comprehend" an individual but not a group is surely
overdrawn. Of course, one can "see" and "feel" another person's *body* with
one's eyes and hands. But that does not mean that one has really "seen"
or "felt" that person *qua* person, much less "comprehended" him or her.
Do we ever really "comprehend" anyone fully, including ourselves, any
more than we "comprehend" the various groups we are a part of, with
their peculiar histories and cultures? I am not so sure. Kateb's claim that
individuals are readily comprehensible while nations are mysterious abstractions is not as self-evident as he claims.

Kateb also seriously misunderstands the relationship between patriotism and individualism in the United States. No doubt, there have
been, and still are, forms of patriotism that are anti-individualistic (e.g.,
those that envision the nation as an organism). But American patriotism
in almost all of its varieties—civil and uncivil, critical and uncritical—is
surely not one of them. The current version of American hyperpatriotism—namely, "Tea Party patriotism"—is nothing if not hyperindividual-
istic. Witness the recent spectacle of rural libertarians brandishing guns
and flags from atop their horses and ATVs as they squared off against the
Bureau of Land Management and federal law enforcement in Oregon.
For them, American patriotism just *is* radical individualism. What such
"patriots" seem not to understand is that individual rights can only be
durably secured through legal principles and political institutions such
as one finds in constitutional democracies. The real conflict, then, is between patriotism and libertarianism, not patriotism and individualism.
When rightly understood, individualism necessarily leads to a certain
measure of patriotic devotion to constitutional democracy, rather than a
categorical dismissal of constitutional patriotism or a foolish rejection of
democratic institutions.

The foregoing critiques of the civil religion concern the proper ethical relationship between the individual and the nation. Others concern
the relationship between religion and politics. One insists that politics
should be kept out of religion; the other that religion should be kept
out of politics. I will refer to them as the "sectarian" and "secularist" critiques, respectively.

Let me first be clear about what I mean by "sectarian." Max Weber
and Ernst Troeltsch both defined "sects" in opposition to "churches."[16]
Weber emphasized the voluntary character of sects: one entered a church
by birth, a sect by conversion. Troeltsch highlighted the tension between
the sect and the world: a church accepts the secular order as a means
to its ends, while a sect rejects the secular order as a danger to its inner

purity. [17] I will be using the term "sectarian" in a Troeltschian rather than a Weberian sense.

Today, the most influential version of the sectarian critique can be found in the political theology of Stanley Hauerwas.[18] On Hauerwas's view, the American churches have become Troeltschian churches. They have overaccommodated themselves to the ethical and political order of the United States—so much so that they have effectively ceased being Christian churches at all but instead mainly function as cheerleading squads for American democracy. As if this weren't bad enough, Hauerwas adds, American democracy is hardly worth cheering for. The American state is a state just like any other, he argues, with an inherent and ineluctable tendency to expand into and encroach upon all aspects of life, not least the life of the churches. Indeed, from a Christian perspective, as Hauerwas wrote in the mid-1980s, there is really no meaningful difference between liberal democracy and communist totalitarianism, since "democracies . . . can be just as tyrannical in their claims on the loyalties of their citizens as totalitarian alternatives."[19] Conversely, totalitarian regimes may be as religiously free as liberal democratic ones: "Hitler never prevented the church from worshipping freely."[20] Nor should this contention surprise us, because democratic and totalitarian regimes both spring from the same root: "The modern bureaucratic states, American and Soviet, are both creatures . . . of liberalism."[21] The only real difference between such regimes, Hauerwas continues, is that liberal forms of oppression are more subtle and sinister than totalitarian ones. For example, freedom of religion "has tempted Christians in America to think that democracy is fundamentally neutral and, perhaps, even friendly toward the church."[22] In reality, he counters, "no state, particularly the democratic state, is kept limited by constitutions."[23] At the end of the day, Hauerwas concludes, Christians are but "resident aliens" in whatever polity they inhabit, and Christian theology provides no grounds for preferring one sort of polity to another—constitutional democracy to communist totalitarianism, say.[24] On this question, he argues, the scriptures are silent. He thus urges American Christians to stop putting so much faith in the possibilities of politics. Indeed, they should even stop worrying so much about the future of the human species as such, because the concern for nuclear disarmament betrays a lack of faith in the promises of God. Hauerwas's political theology displays all of the hallmarks of Troeltschian sectarianism: an overriding concern about the inner purity of the churches, a deep anxiety about accommodating the world, and a radical pessimism about the possibility of social melioration.

What does Hauerwas recommend the churches do? In essence, they should become Christian churches again. Specifically, they should (1) stop trying to influence the American polity and become their own polities because the church is the only "true polity" the Christian "will know in this life"[25]; and (2) stop trying to translate their message into a public language, as the "church's social task is first of all its willingness to be a community formed by a language the world does not share."[26] In short, when Hauerwas says that "the church should be the church"—and he says this often; it is perhaps his most famous phrase—he means that American churches should become Troeltschian sects. They should stop accommodating themselves to a liberal system that is fundamentally corrupt.

Taken at face value, Hauerwas's analysis is highly problematic, and it has been fiercely criticized from both the left and the right.[27] In this context, I can only highlight a few difficulties. The moral equivalence Hauerwas draws among liberalism, communism, and even Nazism is plainly indefensible and betrays a worrisome lack of political judgment, just as the claim that Christians were as free under Hitler and Stalin as under, say, Reagan or Clinton lacks all sense of ethical proportion. Further, if the preceding pages have any merit, then Hauerwas's breezy equation of liberal democracy and the American project is also unconvincing.[28] Nor is it clear that "church polities" are any less susceptible to the kinds of all-too-human corruptions that afflict their secular counterparts. It would be easy—all too easy—to cite counterexamples. Consider the pedophilia scandals in the Catholic Church. Hauerwas's sectarian tendencies can be, and have been, criticized from a Christian perspective as well. One criticism concerns religious language and public reason. Hauerwas is certainly right that Christian language has become a foreign tongue to increasing numbers of Americans. However, Catholic theories of natural law and the Calvinist doctrine of common grace both imply that Christians and non-Christians have a shared moral sense that can serve as a starting point for civic debate.[29] A second criticism concerns Christian doctrine and political rule. Is Hauerwas right to argue that there is no connection between the two? I am not so sure. Building on the arguments of early modern republicans such as Milton and Sydney that are based on 1 Samuel 8, one could argue that monarchies—and, indeed, autocratic regimes of all sorts—lead to worship of the ruler or the state, that is, to forms of political idolatry that people of faith should resist. Second, building on the doctrine of the Trinity, and on the principle that divine government provides a model for worldly government, one could argue (with John Courtney Murray and against Carl Schmitt) that Christianity favors a system of divided rather than unitary sovereignty. For these reasons and others, it seems to me that one can make a scriptural argument for at least two core features of republican government: representative institutions and the separation of powers.

There are plenty of reasons for American Christians and other people of faith to reject the "sectarian temptation." Some are political. Republican theories of countervailing powers suggest that religious citizens must actively assert and defend their religious freedoms, and that they should not rely solely on the Constitution and the courts to do so for them. Political disengagement endangers the very thing the sectarian values most: the freedom of religion. Other reasons are religious. The Christian religion and, indeed, all of the Abrahamic creeds are ethical faiths that command their followers to seek worldly justice as well as otherworldly salvation. This imperative will inevitably lead religious believers to enter into the public realm from time to time, whether for better or for worse.

Where sectarians are concerned that religion not be corrupted by politics, secularists have the reverse concern: they are worried that religion may somehow creep into politics. Unfortunately, there is no (genuinely liberal) means of preventing this. It is simply not possible to effect a total separation between the two realms, at least not in the context of a democratic polity that respects individual rights. Why? Because, as Jocelyn Maclure and Charles Taylor have shown, there is an inherent tension between religious freedom and civic equality.[30] For example, protecting the religious freedom of minority religions may sometimes involve granting them special protections that are not afforded to other faiths, protections of the sort that have been granted to Jehovah's Witnesses and the Amish. Conversely, ensuring that nonreligious citizens are not coerced into participating in religiously laden rituals may require some restrictions on the religious freedom of other citizens, such as a judge who wishes to say prayers in court. The question then becomes how one properly balances religious freedom and civic equality across different settings. This means that citizens and the judges and legislators who represent them must generally proceed on a case-by-case basis while attending to social context and legal tradition.

The broader question, then, is not whether invoking the civil religious tradition violates the "separation of church and state," but whether *it endangers the civic equality of secular citizens*. I am not convinced that it does, and for at least two reasons. The first is that the civil religion contains a nontheistic strand—civic republicanism—that can be, and often is, understood in purely secular terms. The second is that the religious strand of the tradition can also be understood in nonreligious terms. The Exodus narrative can be read as an inspiring story of emancipation and deliverance; it has been read this way by liberation movements throughout the world.[31] Similarly, the jeremiads of the Hebrew prophets can be understood as a kind of moral poetry, one that reminds us of our duties to the less fortunate. In a recent reflection on the place of religion in the public sphere, the German philosopher Jürgen Habermas has argued that religious traditions contain "untapped semantic resources" that still remain valuable, even in a "post-metaphysical age."[32] As if to vindicate Habermas's thesis, a number of prominent social theorists have recently offered secular reinterpretations of key biblical texts, including the parables of the Gospels, the books of Job and Romans, and writings on monastic life and Pauline theology. [33] One might also point to the recent surge of interest in political theology among political theorists.[34] So there is no reason to assume that secular citizens cannot learn from, or be inspired by, religious texts or theological works.

Of course, some religious citizens may find such reinterpretations offensive or even blasphemous. Likewise, they may have strong reservations about the civic republican strand of the civil religious tradition. They may worry that it grants too much authority to the state and prefer a more libertarian style of politics. Or they may worry that its picture of human possibility is too optimistic and prefer a less "perfectionist" vision of ethics. In short, they may prefer some version of radical secularism to the civil religion. They may feel just as burdened by the civil religious tradition as some secular citizens do. In other words, there are also sectarian arguments for embracing radical secularism.

For all these reasons, then, I am not convinced that public invocations of the civil religious tradition represent any particular threat to the civic equality of nonreligious citizens.

CIVIL RELIGION: NEIGHBORS AND ALLIES

I now want to consider two rational and reasonable positions that are closely related to the civil religious tradition: "constitutional patriotism" (as described by Habermas) and "liberal nationalism" (as described by Tamir and Kymlicka). Both wrestle with the same question that I am trying to address: What sort of loyalty can, and must, a democratic polity reasonably expect of its citizens today, given the increasing cultural diversity that has resulted from immigration, secularization, and, indeed, democratic freedom itself? While the answers these positions give are not identical to mine, in part because they have arisen out of different national contexts, these very differences cast a good deal of light on the Americanness of the American civil religion.

The concept of "constitutional patriotism" (*Verfassungspatriotismus*)[35] was originally invented by Dolf Sternberger, an influential political scientist in post–World War II West Germany.[36] For obvious reasons, patriotism was a highly and, indeed, uniquely fraught concept in that context. The horrors of National Socialism and the crimes of the Holocaust had cast a long, dark shadow over German history. Nor could Germans hearken back to a successful democratic revolution or a long history of constitutional governance in the way that, say, the French or English could. They could not even claim credit for the postwar constitution itself; it had been drafted and imposed by the Allied powers following the defeat of National Socialism.

Habermas first embraced the idea of constitutional patriotism during the so-called Historians' Debate (*Historikerstreit*) of the mid-1980s.[37] This concept was catalyzed by the efforts of the West German chancellor, Helmut Kohl, to turn the page on the Nazi era and reclaim a "normal" form of national identity for West Germany, one based on a shared history and culture. In this, he was supported by some German historians but criticized by many others. Habermas intervened in this disagreement as well, reviving the idea of "constitutional patriotism," which he understood as a form of political allegiance that affirmed the democratic project of the postwar era while also accepting Germany's responsibility for Nazi crimes.

Over the next two decades, Habermas continued to elaborate this concept, ultimately expanding it into a general account of the kind of "postnational" political solidarity that was appropriate not only to a newly unified Germany but also to other diverse democratic societies.[38] Habermas's theory is embedded in a historical account of the European nation-state.[39] He contends that the concept of the nation took on a "double coding" during the nineteenth century: on the one hand, it referred to an ethnocultural group that was imagined as a community of descent (the "nation"); on the other hand, it referred to a political association based on a social contract between equal citizens (the "state"). In this way, he suggests, ethnic solidarity helped launch republican government. Today, Habermas argues, it is both possible (conceptually) and imperative (morally) that republican values be divorced from ethnic loyalties.

Now that political liftoff has been achieved, he reasons, the republican rocket must shed its nationalist engine if it is to continue along its current trajectory toward a "post-national constellation" without veering off in the direction of ethnic exclusion.

Habermas does not offer any specific legal or institutional proposals about how to achieve this divorce—he is a philosopher, after all. But he does offer a few general principles that can serve as navigational aids. First, building on Rawls, he argues for a sharp distinction between a shared political culture and the various subcultural communities it encompasses. It is reasonable to expect citizens to affirm the basic constitutional principles of a liberal democratic polity. But it is not reasonable to insist that all citizens embrace the dominant or majority culture. Citizens can be asked to uphold and defend a constitution, broadly understood, but they cannot legitimately be expected to "assimilate," culturally or otherwise. "Constitutional patriotism" in this way circumscribes the legitimate objects and necessary limits of postnational political allegiance. Second, Habermas argues that republican constitutions should be seen as "historical projects." The central values enshrined in such constitutions are never fully realized, and, insofar as societies are continually changing, they probably never can be. In Habermas's terms, there is a fundamental tension between the "facticity" of a political order and its "validity," or, more plainly, between what a polity is and what it purports to be.[40] What is more, the meaning of a particular constitution is something that only becomes clear over time. Third, and finally, Habermas embeds his theory of constitutional patriotism within a general theory of "deliberative democracy." The central premise of his account is that political decisions in a diverse democracy cannot be legitimated substantively by appealing to impersonal principles or shared values. Instead, they must be legitimated procedurally, by democratic deliberation itself. In a democracy, he concludes, a political decision is legitimate only if and insofar as it is the result of rational debate among all affected parties. Putting these three principles together, we see that constitutional patriotism involves allegiance to a set of *political* values that can only be realized *across time* and that are legitimated via an *inclusive, rational and open-ended debate.*

As should be evident, Habermas's vision of constitutional patriotism is similar to my account of civil religion in a number of respects. First, both involve allegiance to the founding values of a specific polity, rather than to the culture of a dominant ethnos or a catalog of universal rights. Instead of valuing the particular or the universal, they value *the univer-*

sal in the particular. Second, both recognize that the realization of these political values is a historical project, because their full meaning is only gradually elaborated and their implementation inevitably meets political resistance. Republican government is an aspiration, not an achievement. Third, both insist on the importance of civic inclusion as a prerequisite of democratic legitimacy. In a pluralistic republic, inclusion becomes a precondition of freedom and equality.

Of course, there are also some subtle and not-so-subtle differences between the two in vocabulary, emphasis, and tone. For example, where Habermas speaks of constitutional patriotism as a historical project, I speak of civil religion as a political tradition. Where constitutional patriotism mostly looks forward, civil religion also glances backward. As a staunch defender of the Enlightenment, Habermas is evidently less comfortable with the tradition concept than I am. Indeed, early in his career, Habermas launched a fierce polemic against Gadamer's understanding of tradition, claiming that it was opposed to rational critique.[41] In a subsequent intervention, Paul Ricoeur would show that this opposition was overdrawn, and that tradition could in fact be rational and even critical.[42] In the meantime, the tradition concept has found its way back into Habermas's own prose, if not into his core terminology. Further, while Habermas's understanding of constitutional patriotism does contain a civic republican strand, it does not include a prophetic one. Habermas's intention, like Rawls's, was to develop a wholly secular theory of politics. As with Rawls, however, we can observe a gradual lowering of the wall of separation between religion and political discourse, and even an acknowledgement, touched on earlier, that religious discourse may contain "untapped semantic potentials." That said, the two founding moments of modern Germany—the creation of the Federal Republic in 1949 and the reunification of East and West Germany in 1990—were far more secular moments than the three founding moments I have focused on in this book—the founding of the Bay Colony in 1628, the revolutionary era of 1776–1787, and the early Reconstruction period of 1865–1869. Thus, there are good reasons why prophetic religion would be more central to the ethical and political culture of the United States than it would to that of Germany. It must also be added, however, that Habermas's account of the German founding completely ignores the influence of Catholic social teachings and political theology, which were arguably considerable, especially in West Germany.[43] Be that as it may, the third and most significant difference between constitutional patriotism and civil religion concerns their contents. To be sure, my understanding of civil religion *qua* intellectual tradition gives little attention to civic rituals. To this degree, it is comparatively rationalistic. But it is by no means as rationalistic as Habermas's vision of constitutional patriotism, with its focus on the procedures of rational argumentation and debate. While the civil religion as I understand it does encompass a small number of rational and perhaps even universal values—namely, freedom, equality, solidarity, and inclusion—I take these values to be (imperfectly) embodied in specific persons, events, places, and stories. More than that, I take these embodiments to be the real *core* of the civil religion, its primary source of motivational force and ethical direction. Where constitutional patriotism follows political liberalism in prioritizing the right over the good, the civil religion follows civic republicanism and prophetic religion in seeing the two as concretely conjoined.

"Liberal nationalism" is another neighbor and ally of civil religion. It too is quite different from radical secularism. In the first chapter of this book, recall, I characterized "radical secularism" as a combination of libertarian liberalism and total separationism. I have argued in the following chapters that total separationism is unreasonable because it places an unfair burden on religious citizens: the burden of translating religious convictions into secular language. Let me now explain why I regard libertarian liberalism as unreasonable. This will make it easier to see why I do not regard liberal nationalism as unreasonable. The first problem with libertarian liberalism is that it is premised on an asocial model of the human person in which the individual is abstracted from any relationships with other persons, what Michael Sandel has aptly called an "unencumbered self."[44] A human animal lacking ties to other human animals—that is, a *feral* human—is still a human *animal*, of course. But he or she is not a human *person*.[45] Among other things, a human person has an identity and a language. And identity and language are inherently social and intersubjective, that is, they necessarily involve social relations. Since Wittgenstein, we know that a "private language" is an oxymoron[46]; human language is necessarily social and public. Likewise, we know from George Herbert Mead, and, indeed, from Hegel before him, that there is no such thing as a "personal identity" without social relations.[47] For both these reasons, an "agent" abstracted from social relations may be a useful heuristic device for the social scientist, but it should be not be confused with a human person in civic debate.[48] Second, libertarian liberalism is premised on a flawed view of human ethics—flawed insofar as it conceives of human wellbeing in terms of private consumption, particularly of material goods, leaving little room for immaterial and/or collectively generated goods (e.g., play, art, intimacy, conversation, friendship, commensality, etc.). That this view *is* flawed is by now no mere matter of personal opinion but is backed up by robust findings from across the social and biological sciences.[49] Once bodily necessities and physical security have been secured, additional income contributes little to individual wellbeing: wellbeing is not a linear function of material consumption.[50] Many of the most important human goods are neither material nor consumable. Third, libertarian liberalism is philosophically flawed insofar as it rests on an overly metaphysical understanding of human freedom and its relationship to social equality. Human freedom involves more than the absence of external restraints on the individual "will."[51] It also involves the integrity, development, and exercise of an individual person's human capacities. And if we understand freedom in terms of capacities, then freedom requires more than negative rights; it also requires a basic level of resources.[52] A commitment to freedom therefore entails a commitment to equality that goes beyond a narrow vision of "equality of opportunity" (i.e., equality before the law or the absence of discrimination). Fourth, libertarian liberalism is politically flawed insofar as it advances a model of the polity that is plainly unsustainable. It is unsustainable because economic markets cannot function without state regulation (e.g., enforcement of contracts and property rights), and states quickly become corrupt and/or predatory in the absence of a reasonably organized and virtuous citizenry.[53] Fifth, and finally, libertarian liberalism is historically flawed insofar as it is premised on an abstract and hyperrationalistic narrative of political development. Treating the social contract as a philosophical "representation" only partially corrects this error. I could, of course, say much more about the fatal flaws of libertarian liberalism, but I will refrain from doing so because my purpose here is actually fairly limited: to distinguish between reasonable and unreasonable forms of liberalism. My conclusion is simple: libertarian liberalism does not belong to the family of reasonable liberalisms.

Liberal nationalism does. By combining a reasonable form of liberalism ("egalitarian liberalism") with a reasonable form of nationalism ("civic nationalism"), liberal nationalists are able to overcome most if not all of the various defects of libertarian liberalism to which civic republicans usually object and to develop a justification of national loyalties that is adequate to the realities of diverse modern democracies. How so? First, liberal nationalists emphasize that human persons are embedded within, and formed by, "national cultures." By "national cultures," it should be noted, liberal nationalists mean a shared language and history, not the culture of the dominant ethnic group. Second, they acknowledge that human wellbeing may be greatly enhanced by "cultural membership," including national membership, insofar as cultures can provide important models of, and resources for, the life well lived. In other words, liberal nationalists are fairly cold toward the libertarian ideal of the radical chooser, for whom a rejection of custom and tradition as such is a defining feature of the good life. Third, because liberal nationalists are committed to an egalitarian version of liberalism, rather than a libertarian one, they believe that human freedom requires some kind of "civic minimum," not only for reasons of justice, but because freedoms are worth little if they cannot be exercised.[54] For example, freedom of expression is cheapened if citizens are deprived of education. Fourth, liberal nationalists recognize that the protection of negative rights requires the exercise of positive liberty: liberal democracy needs an active and virtuous citizenry in order to survive and thrive. Good institutions are not enough; good citizens are also necessary. Fifth, and finally, liberal nationalism begins from the premise of actually existing nations, rather than from that of abstract social contracts. This premise employs rational reflection as a means of moral evaluation, rather than of "political construction" à la Rawls.

As I noted earlier, this combination of egalitarian liberalism and civic nationalism removes most of the objections that civic republicans have raised against liberalism. By moving in a more republican direction, however, liberal nationalists also open themselves up to the sorts of concerns that liberals often have about "communitarianism," namely, that its idea of a unitary citizenship places excessive burdens on minority cultures. Liberal nationalists have addressed these issues by elaborating a model of "liberal multiculturalism." The Canadian political theorist Will Kymlicka has developed the most influential version of this argument.[55] It hinges on two distinctions, a sociological one and a philosophical one. The sociological distinction is between "national" and "immigrant" minorities. By "national minorities," Kymlicka means "groups who formed functioning societies on their historical homelands prior to being incorporated into a larger state," such as the indigenous peoples of North America or Oceania. The philosophical distinction is between "external protection" of group rights and "internal restrictions" on group members. Kymlicka's version of liberal multiculturalism allows for external protections of group rights for national minorities but not for immigrant minorities, and it forbids internal restrictions on group members for all minorities. Specifically, Kymlicka proposes that national minorities be allowed, and even encouraged, to maintain their own distinctive "societal culture," described as "a territorially-concentrated culture, centered on a shared language which is used in a wide range of societal institutions, in both public and private life (schools, media, law, economy, government, etc.)." But he argues that national minorities not be permitted to abridge the individual rights of their members (e.g., the right to leave the group).

While liberal nationalism and prophetic republicanism are close kin, they are not identical twins. There are several areas of difference and disagreement that are worth highlighting. Most of the leading liberal nationalists exhibit the typical liberal insensitivity to the claims of religion—despite the fact that religious communities often have many of the hallmarks of national minorities (sacred spaces and places, a specific language and history, and a well-developed "societal culture") and consequently might also be entitled to the same sorts of group rights to which national minorities are entitled, namely, external protections but not internal restrictions. Also worrisome is the tendency of some leading liberal nationalists to slip from a civic nationalist register into an ethnic nationalist one, as when the British philosopher David Miller says that we "inherit an obligation to continue [the] work" of our "forbears" because they "have toiled and spilt their blood to build and defend the nation," or when he emphasizes "military victories and defeats" as the central events in the collective memory of the national community.[56] Further, while the liberal nationalist conception of the human good is much "thicker" than the libertarian liberal one, insofar as it gives human sociality its proper due, some civic republicans may still find it too "thin" to the degree that it denies human biology its proper due. Following Martha Nussbaum, civic republicans, including myself, may instead prefer a "thick but vague" conception of the human good that attends more closely to the specifically human capacities that are part of our shared evolutionary heritage.[57] While acknowledging that these capacities are multiply realizable across persons and cultures, such republicans may also insist that they are not infinitely elastic either. If so, then not every vision of the good life is equally good. Such a conclusion will lead to more of an emphasis on positive enablement and less of an emphasis on negative rights. Finally, the prophetic republican will likely regard the liberal nationalist conception of language as too thin and vague, aspiring instead to a shared language of public debate that is not just a "shared vernacular" in the narrow sense (e.g., American English, Quebecois French), but a shared dialect, rich in poetry and metaphor, that touches the "mystic chords" of popular memory.

CONCLUSION

One of the great wagers of the American experiment is that it is possible to forge a nation of nations and a people of peoples, to incorporate an ever more diverse stream of immigrants into an already diverse collection of citizens. That wager does not allow for the traditional solution developed in Central Europe, namely, a democratic state founded on an ethnocultural nation. This is not to deny that America has a distinctive culture, or that Americans' values and mores are different from, say, those of the Chinese or Argentinians. It is simply to insist that one cannot speak of an American people conjoined by blood lineage or immemorial tradition even to the—in truth, very limited—degree that one can in Europe.

Religious nationalism represents an alternative solution to the problem of political identity in a plural society. For blood lineage, it substitutes blood sacrifice; for the blood that flows through our veins, the blood that is spilt in battle. Likewise, for immemorial tradition, it inserts "orthodox" religion (however that may be defined). But this means that the sustenance of national identity requires recurrent infusions of blood and a continual policing of religious orthodoxy. In principle, the blood can be symbolic, supplied by ritual invocations of past sacrifices on behalf of the nation. In practice, however, the blood has too often been quite real, generated by imperial adventures in foreign lands. And the electoral gains that might be extracted from yet another phony war make such adventures a perennial temptation for American politicians. But imperial adventurism of this sort stands in flagrant contradiction to America's founding ideals. John Winthrop urged his fellow Puritans to "be a city on a hill," not to "storm the hill" like Teddy Roosevelt's "rough riders." The Puritans sought to lead by example, not force, even if they often employed violence in fact. As for the founders, none other than George Washington warned the early republic against imperial adventures and entangling alliances of this sort. And virtually all of the founders shared his deep suspicion of standing armies, which was born partly out of a commitment to republican principles and partly out of the experience of colonial oppression. Alas, at least since World War II, that suspicion of military establishments has been gradually transformed into adulation, with vocal support of "the troops" and zealous defense of military expenditures now a litmus test of true patriotism even in left-of-center political circles. This is not to advocate geopolitical isolationism or unconditional pacifism. It is merely to remind the reader that the American project was originally conceived as a democratic project, and not an imperial one.

Perhaps it is obvious that recurring efforts to enshrine a religious tradition—Protestant, Christian, Judeo-Christian, Abrahamic, or whatever—as the national culture are also fundamentally at odds with the American project. In this vein, it is worth emphasizing that persistent claims that the United States was "founded as a Christian nation" or that the U.S. Constitution is "premised on Judeo-Christian values" are neither historically accurate nor politically harmless. They are quite pernicious insofar as they imply that Christians enjoy a different and higher form of national and civic belonging than do non-Christians (with American Jews nowadays incorporated into a kind of "halfway covenant"). This is not to deny the plain sociological fact that Christianity always was and still is the majority religion in the United States. Nor is it to deny that a certain kind of Protestant Christianity exerted a shaping influence on American political thought and institutions. About that, the religious nationalists are quite right. Rather, the point is that America was founded as a *civic* nation, premised on a certain set of political ideals, and that acceptance of these ideals was and is the only legitimate criterion of national belonging and civic rights. About this much, John Rawls and other political liberals were always right.

So who are we as Americans? What binds us together? What do we owe one another? And what should our public conversation be about? Radical secularism, religious nationalism, and prophetic republicanism give very different answers.

On the radical secularist account, we are just so many individuals sharing a space for a time, like passengers on a train, a bus, or a plane. We are all on our own personal journeys, and our itineraries just happen to overlap a little. All we owe one another is a minimum of courtesy. In this version of the American imaginary, there really is no "we" other than "these people, right here, right now." We are not connected by a common history and culture so much as contained by a protective shell around a shared space. Nor do we owe one another anything much, other than respect for one another's space, one another's rights. So, best to stick to neutral topics or, better yet, to just keep quiet. We can all put on our headphones and retreat into our inner lives. American conservatives are right to reject this individualistic and ahistorical understanding, to yearn for something thicker and deeper. That is why many of them gravitate to religious nationalism.

On the religious nationalist account, we are a fearsome clan defending its sacred homeland, knit together by blood and soil. We have spilled blood together before—always for righteous causes, of course! And we will do so again, in defense of our freedom, and to spread the gift of freedom to others, whether they like it or not. We did not choose these missions, these crusades; we were chosen for them, by God or by Fate, whichever you prefer. Why were we thus chosen? For our piety, our courage, and, not least, our generosity. (There have been other candidates, of course, but they have failed the historical tests.) In the evenings, around the fires, we remember the fallen, cajole our comrades, and watch for the enemy, lest he slip silently into the ranks. In this version of the American imaginary, the bonds of the "we" are so strong as to constitute the "I." "Born in the USA!" "Proud to be an American!" "These colors don't run!" Not conversation, then, so much as chanting: "U-S-A! U-S-A!" American progressives are right to reject this prideful and jingoistic vision. They want a quieter and more respectful nation. That is why many of them are pulled toward radical secularism.

On the third account, finally, the civil religious discourse, we are, or at least aspire to be, a sovereign and democratic people. We are part of a collective, multigenerational project, an ongoing effort to realize a set of universal political ideals—above all, freedom and equality—from within the confines of a particular historical trajectory. Some of us are thrown into this project by birth; others enter into it by immigration. We are part of an ever-expanding river flowing through historical time toward an uncertain horizon. Our civic conversation concerns those who have entered and exited the stream before us, and the course that we hope to steer into the future. It is a dialogue in which quiet conservatives and open-minded progressives might become reengaged.

There is no doubt which of these three accounts is the noblest. Which will prevail, alas, is another question.

The Righteous Republic

Let America be America again.
Let it be the dream it used to be. . . .

O, let America be America again—
The land that never has been yet—
And yet must be . . .
America never was America to me,
And yet I swear this oath—
America will be! . . .

—LANGSTON HUGHES

IN ORDER FOR America to be America again, said Langston Hughes, Americans must do four things. They must remember the dream that used to be—and remember it rightly. They must understand that the dream has never been fully realized—and never can be. They must acknowledge that many have been excluded from that dream—and still are. And they must try to redeem the dream for themselves and their posterity—knowing full well that they are ultimately destined to fail. About all this, Hughes was right.

The dream that used to be is the dream of a righteous republic, a dream that is too often misremembered, when it is not wholly forgotten. That dream was never fully realized—not by the Puritans, not by the revolutionaries, not during Reconstruction, and not by later generations. Nor will it ever be, by this generation, the next, or any other, because the American republic is built with the crooked timber of a fallen humanity, just like any other polity. Still, each generation of Americans is responsible for trying to build out its walls and make them straight, to the best of its abilities.

REMEMBERING THE DREAM

The dream of the righteous republic is the dream of a free people governing themselves for the common good. The Puritans imagined it as a city upon a hill knit together by Christian charity. The founders envisioned it as a Christian republic modeled on its Hebrew and Roman predecessors. Lincoln spoke of a government of the people, by the people, and for the people. Addams dreamed that democracy would pervade the American way of life. King's preferred metaphor was the beloved community. The notion of the righteous republic is an attempt to translate these dreams into the present era.

A righteous republic is based on a certain vision of the common good—and not just any vision, but a vision that draws deeply on prophetic religion. That is what makes it "righteous" rather than just "moral." What is the difference? The prophetic ethic of righteousness is a social as well as an individual ethic. It demands that the political community protect the weak and downtrodden from the high and mighty. The prophetic ethic is also an egalitarian ethic. It insists that there are no gods among us, nothing human or material that deserves our worship; all are equal before God and one another. At the core of prophetic religion, then, is an ethic of social justice and human equality that requires that we be willing to abridge ourselves for the sake of others.

A righteous republic is also based on a certain vision of the political community—and again, not just any vision, but one rooted in the republican tradition, rather than its liberal rival. What is the difference between the two? The republican tradition is both more realistic and more idealistic: more realistic because it regards liberal institutions (e.g., rights, elections, and checks and balances) as necessary but insufficient safeguards of the common good and balance between social groups as crucial, and more idealistic insofar as it regards civic virtue as a necessary condition for the continued survival of popular government. Within this tradition, self-interest alone is never enough.

MISREMEMBERING THE DREAM

Today, too many Americans misunderstand the righteousness of the righteous republic. Some understand it too narrowly, as *individual* righteousness, or more narrowly still, as *sexual morality*. To be sure, the prophetic ethic is not a libertine ethic. Some measure of personal and sexual morality is important for a well-ordered society, just as some form of family life is a *sine qua non* for the reproduction of any form of social life—even if *which* form that should be is up for debate. Still, righteousness should not be confused with "personal accountability," much less with mere prudery. Accountability and prudery are often just salves for the too-easy conscience. Genuine righteousness is far more demanding than that.

Many Americans also confuse righteousness with self-righteousness. To be sure, the prophetic ethic is not an anything-goes ethic; it is not based on moral relativism. With King, it presumes that there are laws of justice that are every bit as real and universal as the laws of physics. But it does not pretend to have perfect knowledge of those laws, much less to perfectly embody them either individually or collectively. A spirit of humility and charity always tempers its righteousness.

Too many Americans also misunderstand the values of the republic. Indeed, many reduce those values to just one—freedom—and then misunderstand that as well. The Declaration and the Constitution both speak of other values besides freedom. Equality is especially prominent in the nation's values because of its place in the preamble and in the nation's history. Also important are national solidarity ("We, the People, in order to form a more perfect union"), the common good (or "general welfare"), and active citizenship ("the pursuit of happiness" in the sense of "public happiness"). Civic inclusion and recognition should perhaps be added to our national creed as well.

Too, many Americans misunderstand the kind of freedom that a republic promises—and demands. They conceive of it too narrowly as mere *absence of restraint* or, more narrowly still, as the absence of *governmental* restraint. This is a liberal or libertarian vision of freedom, not a republican one. As such, it is a very grave misunderstanding not only of America's founding traditions but also of the very nature of human freedom.

Republican freedom is more complex than liberal freedom. It means being subject to the rule of general laws rather than the arbitrary will of other persons. For the republican, the relationship of law and freedom is not zero-sum, as it is for the liberal.

Republican freedom also means being the master of one's passions. People who cannot order and govern their own desires are not in control of themselves. They are dominated—tyrannized—by their own passions. Republican freedom also involves active participation in collective self-government. Participation in national politics is not the only possible venue; people may also be virtuous members of their communities or churches or schools. "Idiots," in Murray's sense of the word, are neither virtuous nor free.

The republican understanding of freedom is also more realistic than the liberal one. For the liberal, deliberation and choice are everything. But being free to swim involves more than being allowed to jump in the water. To equate the two is to confuse swimming with drowning. Swimming requires lessons and practice. The same logic applies to the core freedoms of the liberal tradition. How much freedom of expression do I really have if I am illiterate, or if I have no access to books or the Internet? Freedom requires skill, not just will. And a free society is one that affords its citizens opportunities and resources to discover and develop their talents.

We are not "born free"; rather, we become free. We do so by becoming masters of ourselves and becoming active citizens. We are only "born free" in the sense that we may be born into a free society that affords us the opportunity to attain freedom. And that is a matter of good fortune rather than moral virtue.

In sum, true freedom involves more than "being left alone" and "doing what I want." That is not freedom; it is idiocy. So why do so many Americans now confuse the two? Because the republic has been corrupted.

THE DREAM CORRUPTED

Traditions can be corrupted in various ways, and the corruption of the American understanding of freedom has taken several forms. In the first, private interests are dressed up as the public good. Most often, the interests of private property are made to masquerade as the public interest. Politically, this theater has been the work of a small number of wealthy individuals and large business interests and the myriad lobbyists and politicians who are their paid stagehands and public faces. Their latest money lines include "Taxation is theft!" and "Regulation kills jobs!" Their script doctors are neoclassical economists and their libertarian understudies. The moral of their story is unchanging: taxation and regulation are inherently "inefficient." From time to time, they all join hands for a rousing chorus of an uplifting folk tune called "A rising tide lifts all boats!" Of course, anyone with his or her eyes open can see that in the meantime, the big boats have become enormous yachts, while the little boats have been stuck on dry ground for decades.

The second and more subtle form of corruption to the American understanding of freedom was first identified by John Courtney Murray. It occurs when a historical particular is mistaken for a political universal. In the United States, republican freedom is often confused with anti-statism. The roots of this confusion are deep, likely going back to the revolution. The American republic began as a local rebellion against the arbitrary power of the British Crown. But some people mixed up the two; they understood the revolution as a rebellion against state power per se, rather than against *arbitrary* power more generally. In an agrarian society of small property-holders, such as New England or the western frontier, to be sure, there was not much daylight between these two views. Strong property rights did provide sufficient security against arbitrary power under these circumstances. But with the onset of large-scale industrialization, this confusion began to have corrupting consequences. As more wealth was concentrated in fewer hands, and as the majority of Americans began working for wages, private property was just as often a source of arbitrary power as a bulwark against it, and the state constituted one potential means of counterbalancing the power of the few, as Dewey realized. It was not the only one, of course: churches, unions, and other forms of civic association provided other potential sources of balancing. Still, in this context, antistatist and laissez-faire conceptions of freedom were used to delegitimize the efforts of the many to rein in the arbitrary power of the few. What looked like a defense of freedom was actually an attack on freedom. The freedom of the many was being sacrificed for the freedom of the few.

The republican tradition has also fallen prey to another corrupting influence: viciousness. By "viciousness" I mean the opposite of virtuousness, especially the civic kind. There is no way around it: civic virtue is morally demanding. It involves self-discipline and self-sacrifice. The American founders rightly worried that it might be *too* demanding for the citizens of the young nation. "What sort of government shall we have?" Benjamin Franklin was reportedly asked at the Constitutional Convention. "A republic—if you can keep it!" he warned.

One of the great attractions of libertarian liberty is that it is morally undemanding. It requires little more than belligerence and bluster: "Mind your own business!" "Get off my lawn!" "It's a free country!" "I know my rights." Libertarian liberty is a lazy person's freedom. But, then again, many people *are* lazy. Whence comes the appeal.

So why bother? Because libertarian liberty is also self-undermining. Popular government must be defended—and not just from "the terrorists" or by force of arms. Often enough, its real enemies are draped in the flag and carry a briefcase. Without a certain measure of civic virtue, even the Bill of Rights is ultimately nothing but a scrap of parchment.

The fourth and final form of corruption is forgetfulness. Like a piece of fruit, civic virtue has a tendency to wither and shrivel, or so the classical republicans believed. Renaissance republicans like Machiavelli demurred; they believed that civic decay could be halted if the spirit of the citizenry was periodically nourished with the waters of memory. The founts of memory were to be refilled through civic education and civic ritual.

In the United States, these founts have run dry—or, rather, they have been plugged up with detritus from the culture wars. The secular Left champions a version of American history that is true but uninspiring, a tale of victims without any heroes, while the Religious Right prefers one that is inspiring but untrue, a tale of heroes that leaves out the victims. Obviously, what is needed is a version that is true *and* inspiring, one that includes the victims as well as the heroes and is critical but hopeful.

Meanwhile, America's civic holidays, like so much of its public life, have been gradually colonized by consumer capitalism. Nowadays, Memorial Day, Independence Day, and Thanksgiving are mostly occasions for binging on food, drink, television, and other commodities with family or friends. There is little space for public reflection or civic celebration amid all these distractions.

Seen through a republican lens, the source of our ills is easily diagnosed: American democracy is suffering from a severe case of oligarchy, the principal symptom of which is corruption.[1] More and more, the many are being dominated by the arbitrary power of the few[2], who rail against the state while quietly using it to protect their own interests.[3]

Republican theory predicts that a sociopolitical imbalance of this sort will lead to all manner of moral corruption, and that self-dealing, nepotism, and rent-seeking on a grand scale by "the few" will lead to similar behaviors on a smaller scale by the many. Does anyone doubt that this has happened—that corruption has penetrated deep into our body politic?

COUNTERACTING CORRUPTION

The political corruption that has infected the United States is more than a "few bad apples" that can be pruned from the tree; it is a sign that the tree itself is badly diseased. Remedying these ills will require more than a little trimming; it will require replenishing the republic's taproots. Here are a few possible antidotes to contemporary corruption.

1. *Banish big money* from the political process. The "marketplace of ideas" cannot work properly if some people are allowed to buy giant bullhorns that enable them to shout down everyone else or rent private suites where they can cut secret deals with the people's representatives. The cynics are right that money is like water: it will always seep through cracks in the law. But this is

hardly an argument for opening the floodgates, as the Supreme Court so foolishly did in *Citizens v. United*. The absurd reasoning behind that decision—that money is speech and corporations are people, so corporate donations are a form of free speech—provides a textbook illustration of the self-undermining character of the liberal conception of freedom: free speech absolutism and knee-jerk antistatism have provided the intellectual rationale for undermining the people's control over their government. No one who understands what a republic is would ever be hoodwinked by such a specious argument. That five of the most learned people in the United States could not see through this veil of distortions—and that they hoisted that veil so high—is a pitiful testimony to the intellectual bankruptcy of our political culture.

2. *Make civic holidays into holidays again.* Not too long ago, within living memory, stores, restaurants, and bars were closed on civic holidays. No one was forced to remember the fallen, celebrate the Declaration, or give thanks for their blessings, of course. But neither were they distracted from doing so by holiday sales, happy hours, or sporting events. Over time, this space for civic reflection and celebration has been gradually and systematically eroded for the sake of commerce. These "antibusiness," "un-American," and "unconstitutional" restrictions were removed in the name of freedom itself, misunderstood as the freedom to buy, binge, and cheer. Once again, the freedom of the market was allowed to trump the freedoms of the republic. In truth, little harm would be done to American commerce if holiday closings were reinstated, and much good might be done for its civic spirit.

3. *Make character education a part of civic education.* Like the United States, the United Kingdom has a serious problem with public unruliness and incivility, and perhaps for similar reasons—the dominance of a libertarian and libertine misunderstanding of freedom. Unlike the United States, however, the United Kingdom has decided to address this problem by introducing a program of character education in its public schools. This program is based on research done by the Jubilee Center at the University of Birmingham, and its purpose is to instill basic civic virtues such as honesty, courage, and generosity in British schoolchildren. The program is not compulsory. Parents who view it as a waste of their children's time or a violation of their individual rights are free to enroll their children in private schools. There is no reason why

local school districts in the United States could not experiment with programs of this sort.

4. *Establish a universal system of national service.* Many countries require their citizens to perform national service of some kind. In the past, American men were subject to military conscription, but this requirement was effectively eliminated following the Vietnam War. Perhaps it is time to institute a new system, one that includes both men and women, and military as well as civil service. Such a policy could have a number of salutary effects. First, if a wider swath of American families had children in the military, it would put a political brake on imperial adventurism; at present, American soldiers are disproportionately drawn from certain segments of the population. Second, such a system would counteract the increasing segregation of the nation's citizens into homogeneous enclaves sorted by class, race, religion, and politics, giving young Americans some first-hand experience with the nation's diversity. Finally, it would instill an ethic of service in the young.

Further ideas for reform might be gleaned from the republican tradition itself. Oligarchy is not a new problem, after all. As political theorist John McCormick has recently shown, the city republics of Renaissance Italy employed a variety of institutional mechanisms to check the power of "great men."[4] He advances three radical proposals for the present-day United States. First, citizens earning more than $150,000 in income or belonging to households with more than $350,000 in net wealth would be relieved of all tax burdens but in exchange "would give up their right to vote, to stand for office, or to contribute funds to political campaigns."[5] Second, because elections inevitably tend to favor the affluent, who are then overrepresented in government, some political representatives would be chosen by lot rather than election. Third, a people's tribune, composed of fifty-one citizens selected by lot from across the nation and "empowered, upon majority vote, to veto one piece of congressional legislation, one executive order, and one Supreme Court decision in the course of their one-year term," would be created.[6] Taken together, these proposals surely would provide significant checks on the political power of the wealthiest Americans, and without resorting to confiscatory taxation or radical redistribution.

I know that these are radical proposals. Perhaps McCormick really intends them as provocations. Be that as it may, they serve as a useful reminder that the institutional history of civic republicanism extends well beyond 1787 and that this history includes many ideas that ultimately landed on the cutting-room floor of the Constitutional Convention. All too often, the political imaginations of American conservatives do not extend back beyond the "Reagan Revolution" of 1980, while those of American progressives stop at the New Deal. Perhaps modern-day civic republicans should spend a little more time studying political history and political philosophy and a little less time reading social and economic theory.

ASSESSING THE RECOVERY

How would we even know if these remedies worked? What would a republican recovery really mean? What it assuredly would *not* mean, at least not in the first instance, is a recovery of the American economy, as measured in GDP, average income, or some other indicator. While a certain measure of material security surely is a basic social precondition of stable republican government, a high level of material affluence can actually pose a threat to civic virtue, because it attracts too much popular energy into the making of money and the pursuit of luxury. The best foundation for republican government has always been a large and frugal middle class. And one of the surest ways to undermine such a government is to sow greed and envy among the citizens, which is how a large number of Americans now make their living.

Nor would a republican recovery mean a recovery of "American greatness," as measured in military budgets or "power projection." While republican theorists have long extolled the civic virtues of the citizen soldier, they have always been suspicious of standing armies. Similarly, while most republican theorists have also been geopolitical realists, they have typically seen imperialism as a mortal threat to republicanism.[7] Economic prosperity and military strength have not usually been seen as the key indicators of civic health. Rather, republican theorists have emphasized public-spiritedness and political participation.

Of course, in a large polity such as the United States, terms like "public-spiritedness" and "political participation" mustn't be defined too narrowly, in terms of government service or electoral institutions. Properly understood, they would also include many organizations and activities that take place within "civil society," the whole range of "voluntary associations" and "intermediate institutions" emphasized by Tocqueville and his modern-day followers.[8] In some cases, their reach might extend into the economy itself, or at least those segments of it that have collegial governance structures that facilitate collective deliberation (e.g., tech startups, college faculties, cooperative retailers, etc.).

Another measure of civic health might be the density and accessibility of public spaces, modern-day "fora" where citizens can meet and deliberate. Once again, it is important that "public" not be defined too narrowly *qua* "public buildings" or "public facilities." As scholars of political life have long known, public deliberation often occurs in "private" spaces, such as coffeehouses, bars, and, nowadays, even fast-food restaurants. Likewise, the advent of social media means that public spaces need not be physical places in the traditional sense. At the same time, the commercialization and securitization of physical and virtual spaces must be regarded as a serious threat to civic health, as when shopping malls replace town squares, gated communities replace traditional townships, or media companies attack net neutrality in an effort to "monetize" the Web.

For many today, the American Dream is nothing more than property and prosperity. A renewal of the republic would put freedom and equality back into that dream.

REBUILDING THE VITAL CENTER

In order to reclaim the American Dream—the *original* dream of the righteous republic—we will first need to rebuild the vital center. By "we," to be clear, I mean some of us, not all of us. Many Americans have no interest in helping out.

Some will refuse on principle. Religious and secular nationalists will be more interested in another imperial adventure and will denounce the dream of the righteous republic as a craven betrayal of "American greatness." Religious fundamentalists will be far too certain of their own convictions and much too fretful about their own moral purity to reach their hands across the religious/secular divide. Radical secularists will be too jealous of their individual autonomy to commit to anything and will caricature the righteous republic as a form of theocratic oppression. Enlightenment fundamentalists will insist that science has all the answers and will not deign to enter into dialogue with the great unwashed. Nothing much can be expected of these groups.

Others will refuse out of self-interest. There are many who profit from our polarization. The richest rewards accrue to the political performance artists who populate cable news and AM radio, and those who hire them. These individuals use broadcast media to turn anger and invective into paychecks and ad buys. The smaller profits accrue to the partisan trolls who inhabit the nether reaches of the blogosphere. They use social media to turn their personal frustration into fleeting feelings of self-righteousness and moral superiority. And, of course, there are profits, too, for the partisan demagogues who ride this tidal wave of mutual recrimination into elected office or, failing that, into speaking tours, book contracts, and television shows. Nothing can be expected from any of them either.

That leaves the rest of us: those of us who don't confuse democracy with empire, who don't think we have a monopoly on truth or morality, who don't believe that religion is always a source of oppression, and who don't think that science has all of the answers. Or, in positive terms, those of us who are committed enough to the dream of the righteous republic to talk and maybe even walk across the deep trenches that were dug during the culture wars.

Rebuilding the vital center will not be easy. But it is imperative. Our constitutional system cannot function without a vital center. It is not a winner-take-all system, such as Great Britain has. It protects the rights of the minority. It allows for divided government. It establishes a system of judicial review. In a word, it requires compromise.

The vital center must be rebuilt from within civil society. Our party system is a hostile environment for the vital center. Its first-past-the-post rules in which there is no second prize, encourages candidates to pull out all the stops—rhetorical, ideological, financial, and even legal—in a no-holds-barred effort to win. There is a deep tension between our constitutional and electoral systems. This is why we cannot rely on professional politicians to do the job. We must do it ourselves.

If we fail to rebuild the vital center, it will mean the end not only of American democracy—what is now left of it, anyway—but of the American creed itself: *e pluribus unum*. And that would be a disaster, not only for the United States, but for the world. There are many who would like to see the American project fail, not only because they hate our freedoms—and some of them really do—but also because they fear our pluralism. They have placed their wager on cultural homogeneity, on the total unity of the race, the nation, the faith, or the party. The American proposition, our wager, is that they are wrong.

America may not be the last hope for democracy anymore. But it may well be the best hope for a pluralistic democracy in a world that grows more pluralistic by the day.

The eyes of the world are still upon us. And if we should fail, the God of history will not deal kindly with us.

NOTES

INTRODUCTION.
PROPHETIC REPUBLICANISM AS VITAL CENTER

1. Arthur M. Schlesinger Jr., "Not Left, Not Right, but a Vital Center," *New York Times*, April 4, 1948; Arthur Meier Schlesinger, *The Vital Center: The Politics of Freedom* (Boston: Houghton Mifflin Co., 1949).
2. Max Weber and Edward Shils, *The Methodology of the Social Sciences* (New York: Free Press, 1949), 90.

CHAPTER 1. THE CIVIL RELIGIOUS
TRADITION AND ITS RIVALS

1. José Casanova, *Public Religions in the Modern World* (Chicago: University of Chicago Press, 1994).
2. Some rightly noted that Bellah himself had actually stopped using the term "civil religion" during the 1980s, partly because it provoked so much animosity and misunderstanding. See, for example, Robert N. Bellah, "Public Philosophy and Public Theology in America Today," in *Civil Religion and Political Theology*, ed. Leroy S. Rouner (Notre Dame, IN: University of Notre Dame Press, 1986). See also the appendix on public philosophy in Robert Neelly Bellah, *Habits of the Heart: Individualism and Commitment in American Life* (Berkeley: University of California Press, 1985).
3. Bellah originally advanced this argument in his essay "Civil Religion in America," *Daedalus* 96 (1967). A more fully developed version of the argument may be found in Robert Neelly Bellah, *The Broken Covenant: American Civil Religion in Time of Trial*, 2nd ed. (Chicago: University of Chicago Press, 1992). He also wrote various essays defending the idea, most of which are contained in Robert Neelly Bellah and Steven M. Tipton, *The Robert Bellah Reader* (Durham, NC: Duke University Press, 2006).
4. The notion of "public philosophy" originates with Walter Lippmann, *The Public Philosophy* (New Brunswick, NJ: Transaction Publishers, 1989). See also the book by Bellah's collaborator in the *Habits* project: William M. Sullivan, *Reconstructing Public Philosophy* (Berkeley and Los Angeles: University of California Press, 1986). This concept has also been championed by Catholic intellectuals as an alternative to, or translation of, the idea of "natural law." See, for instance, Richard John Neuhaus, "From Civil Religion to Public Philosophy," in Rouner, *Civil Religion and Political Theology*; and idem, *American Babylon: Notes of a Christian Exile* (New York: Basic Books, 2009).
5. On the role of self-transcendence in the emergence of values, see especially Hans Joas, *The Genesis of Values* (Cambridge: Polity Press, 2000). On the inescapability of moral reasoning, see Charles Taylor, *Sources of the Self: The Making of the Modern Identity* (Cambridge, MA: Harvard University Press, 1989).

6. David Foster Wallace, *This Is Water: Some Thoughts, Delivered on a Significant Occasion, about Living a Compassionate Life* (New York: Little Brown, 2009).

7. Recent studies include Martha Craven Nussbaum, *Liberty of Conscience: In Defense of America's Tradition of Religious Equality* (New York: Basic Books, 2008); Andrew R. Murphy, *Conscience and Community: Revisiting Toleration and Religious Dissent in Early Modern England and America* (University Park: Pennsylvania State University Press, 2001). See also the classic study by Edmund Sears Morgan, *Roger Williams: The Church and the State* (New York: Harcourt, 1967).

8. On the connection between Hebraicism and republicanism, see especially Eric Nelson, *The Hebrew Republic* (Cambridge, MA: Harvard University Press, 2010).

9. Bellah, "Civil Religion in America," 42.

10. Robert Neelly Bellah, *The Broken Covenant: American Civil Religion in Time of Trial* (New York: Seabury Press, 1975), 3. Bellah's later reflections on the civil religion controversy may be found in Bellah and Tipton, *Robert Bellah Reader*.

11. In this, it is more Rousseauian than Durkheimian (which is somewhat ironic, given that Bellah himself was more Durkheimian than Rousseauian).

12. Bellah, "Civil Religion in America," 40.

13. Marcela Cristi, *From Civil to Political Religion: The Intersection of Culture, Religion and Politics* (Waterloo, ON: Wilfrid Laurier University Press, 2001); Carolyn Marvin and David W Ingle, "Blood Sacrifice and the Nation: Revisiting Civil Religion," *Journal of the American Academy of Religion* 64, no. 4 (1996).

14. For alternative readings that are more compatible with a civil religious perspective, see, for instance, J. Nelson Kraybill, *Apocalypse and Allegiance: Worship, Politics, and Devotion in the Book of Revelation* (Grand Rapids, MI: Brazos Press, 2010).

15. Paul S. Boyer, *When Time Shall Be No More: Prophecy Belief in Modern American Culture*, Studies in Cultural History (Cambridge, MA: Harvard University Press, 1992).

16. My understanding of prophetic religion is largely inspired by Walter Brueggemann, *Prophetic Imagination*, rev. ed. (Minneapolis, MN: Fortress Press, 2001); William T. Cavanaugh, *Torture and Eucharist: Theology, Politics, and the Body of Christ* (Oxford: Blackwell, 1998); Robert N. Bellah, *Religion in Human Evolution: From the Paleolithic to the Axial Age* (Cambridge, MA: Harvard University Press, 2011).

17. On covenant and law in the Hebrew scriptures, see, for instance, Michael Walzer, *Exodus and Revolution* (New York: Basic Books, 1985); David Novak, *The Jewish Social Contract: An Essay in Political Theology* (Princeton, NJ: Princeton University Press, 2009); Delbert R Hillers, *Covenant: The History of a Biblical Idea* (Baltimore: Johns Hopkins University Press, 1969). I note for the record that I am much less persuaded by Walzer's more recent claim that the Hebrew Bible is a fundamentally apolitical document, as it rests on an anachronistic definition of the "political." See Michael Walzer, *In God's Shadow: Politics in the Hebrew Bible* (New Haven, CT: Yale University Press, 2012).

18. By combining Genesis 9 with passages from other books that are not usually included in the Christian Bible (e.g., the book of Jubilees), Talmudic scholars arrive at a total of seven commandments, rather than just two.

19. The Abrahamic covenant is often said to consist of a series of three covenants, contained in Genesis 12, 15, and 17. The reading I give here stresses the third in the series, the so-called "covenant of circumcision" contained in Genesis 17.

20. Exodus 12, 15, and 17. As should be clear, I read the Abrahamic covenant as conditional.

21. Indeed, I would argue that the importance of blood sacrifice also decreases within and across the covenants. Abraham's final covenant seems to replace blood offerings with the circumcision rite. Moses's final covenant replaces the bloody ritual of circumcision with the "circumcision of the heart." Conversely, the importance of covenant keeping expands within and across the covenants. The number of ritual and legal obligations increases enormously from Noah to Abraham to Moses, expanding from a few sentences to many pages. A similar trend may be observed across the Pentateuch, or Torah, as a whole. Whereas the book of Leviticus fairly drips with blood, Deuteronomy is far less sanguinary. This trend continues with the "later" prophets, though for reasons that will become clear, I do not consider the earlier prophets to belong to the prophetic tradition proper.

22. Of course, there are other prophets, like Joel, who develop the Joshuaic narrative that conjoins blood sacrifice and national greatness.

23. Isaiah 1:11–13.

24. Micah 6:6, 8.

25. Amos 5:22, 24.

26. Jeremiah 22:13–15.

27. Matthew 26:28.

28. Hebrews 6:22.

29. Thus the long genealogical lists that appear in various parts of the Hebrew Bible, such as Genesis 5, 10, 11, 22, 25, 36, 46; Numbers 3, 26; Ezra 7; Nehemiah 11; and 1 Chronicles 1–9.

30. For a general overview, see Frank H. Gorman, "Sacrifices and Offerings," in *The New Interpreter's Dictionary of the Bible*, ed. Katharine Doob Sakenfeld, Sameuel E. Balentine, and Brian K. Blounk (Nashville, TN: Abingdon, 2009).

31. For discussion, see William K Gilders, *Blood Ritual in the Hebrew Bible: Meaning and Power* (Baltimore: Johns Hopkins University Press, 2004).

32. James W. Watts, *Ritual and Rhetoric in Leviticus: From Sacrifice to Scripture* (New York: Cambridge University Press, 2007).

33. Revelation 5:13, 8:8.

34. Revelation 8:7.

35. For a cross-civilizational overview, see Eugen Weber, *Apocalypses: Prophecies, Cults, and Millennial Beliefs Through the Ages* (Cambridge, MA: Harvard University Press, 2000). On the Jewish background, see John Joseph Collins, *The Apocalyptic Imagination: An Introduction to Jewish Apocalyptic Literature* (Grand Rapids, MI: Wm. B. Eerdmans Publishing, 1998). For an overview of Christian apocalyptics, see part I of Boyer, *When Time Shall Be No More*. The authoritative text on premodern popular apocalyptic movements in Europe remains Norman Cohn, *The Pursuit of the Millennium* (Fairlawn, NJ: Essential Books, 1957). However, it should be read in conjunction with the more judicious work by Bernard McGinn, *Visions of the End: Apocalyptic Traditions in the Middle Ages* (New York: Columbia University Press, 1998). A helpful introduction to the vast literature on apocalypticism in the Reformation is Irena Dorota Backus, *Reformation Readings of the Apocalypse: Geneva, Zurich, and Wittenberg* (New York: Oxford University Press, 2000). For a general overview of New England Puritanism and apocalyptic literature, see Avihu Zakai, *Exile and Kingdom: Reformation, Separation, and the Millennial Quest in the Formation of Massachusetts and Its Relationship with England, 1628–1660* (Baltimore: Johns Hopkins University Press, 1982).

36. For a pithy overview of the history and historiography of millennialism and Puritanism, see especially Jeffrey K. Jue, "Puritan Millenarianism in Old and New England," in *The Cambridge Companion to Puritanism*, ed. John Coffey and Paul C. H. Lim (New York: Cambridge University Press, 2008).

37. For a general introduction to the key figures and themes of civic republicanism, see Iseult Honohan, *Civic Republicanism* (New York: Routledge, 2003).

38. Marcus Tullius Cicero, *Cicero: On the Commonwealth and on the Laws* (Cambridge and New York: Cambridge University Press, 1999), I, 24.

39. Aristotle, *The Politics* (New York: Penguin, 1982), I, ii; 1253a1–53a7.

40. The obvious exception to this generalization is the "moral sentiments" approach that one finds, for instance, in Hume's philosophy.

41. Readers familiar with the recent literature will recognize that my understanding of republican freedom has been much influenced by the works of the Cambridge School that formed around Quentin Skinner. See especially Quentin Skinner, *Hobbes and Republican Liberty* (Cambridge: Cambridge University Press, 2008); idem, *Liberty Before Liberalism* (Cambridge and New York: Cambridge University Press, 1998); Philip Pettit, *Republicanism: A Theory of Freedom and Government*, Oxford Political Theory (New York: Oxford University Press, 1997). However, I am skeptical of Philip Pettit's recent efforts to define republican freedom in singular and purely negative terms as "nondependence," which strikes me as much too influenced by the epistemic value that analytical philosophy places on conceptual parsimony. See Pettit, *Just Freedom: A Moral Compass for a Complex World* (New York: W. W. Norton, 2014).

42. For an excellent and subtle discussion of this point, see Jonathan Lear, *Aristotle: The Desire to Understand* (Cambridge and New York: Cambridge University Press, 1988).

43. For Hobbes's understanding of freedom, see Thomas Hobbes, *Leviathan* (Harmondsworth: Penguin, 1968), I, 5; Thomas Hobbes, John Bramhall, and Vere Chappell, *Hobbes and Bramhall on Liberty and Necessity* (Cambridge and New York: Cambridge University Press, 1999).

44. John Locke, *An Essay Concerning Human Understanding* (London: Penguin, 1997), XI, 21.

45. This may sound like a prejudicial example, but it has occupied some of the leading minds of modern economics. See the seminal article by Gary S. Becker and Kevin M. Murphy, "A Theory of Rational Addiction," *Journal of Political Economy* 96, no. 4 (1988).

46. A brief introduction to the virtue concept in ancient ethics may be found in Richard Parry, "Ancient Ethical Theory," in *The Stanford Encyclopedia of Philosophy*, ed. Edward N. Zalta (Stanford, CA: Stanford University Press, 2014). Key texts may be found in Roger Crisp and Michael A. Slote, *Virtue Ethics*, Oxford Readings in Philosophy (Oxford and New York: Oxford University Press, 1997). Key texts in the twentieth-century revival of virtue ethics include Gertrude E. M. Anscombe, "Modern Moral Philosophy," *Philosophy* 33, no. 124 (1958); Iris Murdoch, *The Sovereignty of Good* (London: Routledge, 2013); Alasdair MacIntyre, *After Virtue* (Notre Dame, IN: University of Notre Dame Press, 1984); and Philippa Foot, *Natural Goodness* (New York: Oxford University Press, 2001).

47. On this, see especially Bryan Garsten, *Saving Persuasion: A Defense of Rhetoric and Judgment* (Cambridge, MA: Harvard University Press, 2009).

48. A brief introduction may be found in Athanasios Moulakis, "Civic Humanism," in *The Stanford Encyclopedia of Philosophy*, ed. Edward N. Zalta (Stanford, CA: Stanford University, 2002). The seminal text in this historiography is Hans Baron, *The Crisis of the Early Italian Renaissance; Civic Humanism and Republican Liberty in an Age of Classicism and Tyranny*, rev. 1 vol. ed. (Princeton, NJ: Princeton University Press, 1967).

49. The liberal notion of constitutional balance *qua* institutional balance between the various branches of government is typically attributed to Charles Montesquieu, *The Spirit of the Laws*, trans. Basia Miller Anne Cohler, and Harold Stone (Cambridge: Cambridge University Press, 1989).

50. For the ancients, the ideal was a tripartite balance between "the one, the few, and the many," which is to say, the monarchic, aristocratic, and popular elements of society. For Machiavelli, on the other hand, it was a bipolar balance between the aristocratic and popular elements.

51. Some republicans, like Cicero, thought that the *demos* was the greater danger; they feared ochlocracy, or "mob rule." Others, like Machiavelli, worried more about the nobility; they feared oligarchy. But all agreed that corruption affected the entire polis, not just particular persons. I owe this insight to John P. McCormick, *Machiavellian Democracy* (Cambridge and New York: Cambridge University Press, 2011); Pettit, *Republicanism*.

52. Or so Kant claimed in his essay on "Perpetual Peace." See Immanuel Kant, *Political Writings*, trans. H. B. Nisbet (Cambridge: Cambridge University Press, 1991), 123. Kant is often identified as a republican. On this point, however, he uncharacteristically agreed with Hobbes, whose dismal view of human nature he shared.

53. Bernard Mandeville and E. J. Hundert, *The Fable of the Bees and Other Writings* (Indianapolis: Hackett, 1997).

54. Polybius, *The Rise of the Roman Empire*, trans. Ian Scott Kilvert (London: Penguin, 1981), part VI, section 9; part VI, section 9.

55. On the mixed constitution, see David E. Hahm, "The Mixed Constitution in Greek Thought," *A Companion to Greek and Roman Political Thought* 32 (2009); James M. Blythe, *Ideal Government and the Mixed Constitution in the Middle Ages* (Princeton, NJ: Princeton University Press, 2014); Gerhard Jean Daniël Aalders, *Die Theorie der gemischten Verfassung im Altertum* (Amsterdam: Adolf M. Hakkert, 1968).

56. In addition to the already cited works of Quentin Skinner, and Philip Pettit, one must also mention Gordon Wood, *The Creation of the American Republic, 1776-1787* (Chapel Hill: University of North Carolina Press, 1969); Bernard Bailyn, *The Ideological Origins of the American Revolution* (Cambridge, MA: Belknap Press of Harvard University Press, 1967); Michael J. Sandel, *Democracy's Discontent: America in Search of a Public Philosophy* (Cambridge, MA: Belknap Press of Harvard University Press, 1996); Cass R. Sunstein, "The Enduring Legacy of Republicanism," *A New Constitutionalism: Designing Political Institutions for a Good Society* 38 (1993); idem, "Beyond the Republican Revival," *Yale Law Journal* 97, no. 8 (1988).

57. Ira Katznelson and Andreas Kalyvas, *Liberal Beginnings: Making a Republic for the Moderns* (Cambridge and New York: Cambridge University Press, 2008). The *locus classicus* is Benjamin Constant's essay "The Liberty of the Ancients Compared with That of the Moderns." See Benjamin Constant, *Constant: Political Writings* (New York: Cambridge University Press, 1988).

58. See, for example, Stephen Macedo, *Liberal Virtues: Citizenship, Virtue, and Community in Liberal Constitutionalism* (Oxford: Clarendon Press, 1990); James T. Kloppenberg, *The Virtues of Liberalism* (New York and Oxford: Oxford University Press, 1998); Richard Dagger, *Civic Virtues: Rights, Citizenship and Republican Liberalism* (New York and Oxford: Oxford University Press, 1997); Michael P. Zuckert, *Natural Rights and the New Republicanism* (Princeton, NJ: Princeton University Press, 1994); Joyce Oldham Appleby, *Liberalism and Republicanism in the Historical Imagination* (Cambridge, MA: Harvard University Press, 1992).

59. In truth, Thatcher was more Burkean than Randean, as can be seen from the full quotation: "There is no such thing as society. There is living tapestry of men and women and people and the beauty of that tapestry and the quality of our lives will depend upon how much each of us is prepared to take responsibility for ourselves and each of us prepared to turn round and help by our own efforts those who are unfortunate." However, American libertarians are much more Randean than Burkean, so the abbreviated quotation fits their views quite well. In my experience, even mainstream American liberals lean toward the Randean view.

60. This view originates with Thomas Hobbes, who was much influenced by the views of ancient atomists, such as Epicurus, who believed that the world consisted solely of tiny particles. On the connection between ancient atomism and early modern liberalism, see Catherine Wilson, *Epicureanism at the Origins of Modernity* (New York: Oxford University Press, 2008); Stephen Gaukroger, *The Emergence of a Scientific Culture: Science and the Shaping of Modernity, 1210–1685* (Oxford: Oxford University Press, 2006), part IV.

61. For a devastating portrait of the personal and cultural pathologies that attend such an understanding, see Jonathan Franzen, *Freedom* (New York: Farrar, Straus & Giroux, 2010).

62. I am aware that there are other, more philosophically sophisticated, versions of utilitarianism than this, which is why I refer to such views as "commonsense" utilitarianism.

63. For a trenchant analysis of radical secularism, see Peter Berger, "Two Modest Victories for Common Sense," *American Interest*, December 11, 2013.

64. For the sake of brevity and accessibility, I have chosen not to burden my discussion of tradition with a synoptic review of the philosophical debate. The view of tradition that I defend here draws heavily on discussions in Hans Georg Gadamer, *Truth and Method*, 2nd rev. ed. (New York: Crossroad, 1989); Georgia Warnke, *Gadamer: Hermeneutics, Tradition, and Reason*, vol. 1 (Stanford, CA: Stanford University Press, 1987); Owen Chadwick, *From Bossuet to Newman: The Idea of Doctrinal Development* (Cambridge: Cambridge University Press, 1957); Paul Ricœur, *Time and Narrative*, paperback ed., 3 vols. (Chicago: University of Chicago Press, 1990); Alasdair C. MacIntyre, *Three Rival Versions of Moral Enquiry: Encyclopedia, Genealogy, and Tradition: Being Gifford Lectures Delivered in the University of Edinburgh in 1988* (Notre Dame, IN: University of Notre Dame Press, 1990); Robert Piercey, "Ricoeur's Account of Tradition and the Gadamer–Habermas Debate," *Human Studies* 27, no. 3 (2004); John Henry Newman, *An Essay on the Development of Christian Doctrine*, vol. 1 (London: W. Blanchard and Sons, 1846); Yves Congar, *The Meaning of Tradition* (San Francisco: Ignatius Press, 2004); Jaroslav Pelikan, *The Vindication of Tradition* (New Haven, CT: Yale University Press, 1986); Jeffrey Stout, *The Flight from Authority: Religion, Morality, and the Quest for Autonomy* (Notre Dame, IN: University of Notre Dame Press, 1981); idem,

Democracy and Tradition (Princeton, NJ: Princeton University Press, 2009); Akhil Reed Amar, *America's Unwritten Constitution: The Precedents and Principles We Live By* (New York: Basic Books, 2012); Jack M. Balkin, *Living Originalism* (Cambridge, MA: Harvard University Press, 2011); idem, *Constitutional Redemption* (Cambridge, MA: Harvard University Press, 2011). My views are probably closest to the theory of *ressourcement* developed by Ricoeur in volume 3 of *Time and Narrative*. I am highly critical of constructionist and pragmatist accounts of traditions, such as those found in Richard Rorty, *Contingency, Irony, and Solidarity* (Cambridge and New York: Cambridge University Press, 1989); Eric Hobsbawm and Terence Ranger, eds., *The Invention of Tradition* (Cambridge: Cambridge University Press, 1992). On the fallacies of literalist views of tradition, see especially Christian Smith, *The Bible Made Impossible: Why Biblicism Is Not a Truly Evangelical Reading of Scripture* (Ada, MI: Baker Books, 2012); Vincent Crapanzano, *Serving the Word: Literalism in America from the Pulpit to the Bench* (New York: New Press, 2000). MacIntyre's theory of tradition seems to have been at least partly inspired by Kuhn's theory of paradigms. See Alisdair MacIntyre, "Epistemological Crises, Dramatic Narrative and the Philosophy of Science," *Monist* 60, no. 4 (1977); Thomas S. Kuhn, *The Structure of Scientific Revolutions* (Chicago: University of Chicago Press, 1962).

65. The seminal study of this subject is, of course, Maurice Halbwachs, *On Collective Memory* (Chicago: University of Chicago Press, 1992). A helpful overview of subsequent literature may be found in Jeffrey K. Olick and Joyce Robbins, "Social Memory Studies: From 'Collective Memory' to the Historical Sociology of Mnemonic Practices," *Annual Review of Sociology* 24, no. 1 (1998). Here, I build on the theory of "cultural memory" developed in Aleida Assmann, *Erinnerungsräume: Formen und Wandlungen des kulturellen Gedächtnisses* (Munich: CH Beck, 2006); Jan Assmann and Tonio Hölscher, *Kultur und Gedächtnis*, rev. ed., Suhrkamp Taschenbuch Wissenschaft (Frankfurt am Main: Suhrkamp, 1988).

66. On this, see especially Dale K. Van Kley, *The Religious Origins of the French Revolution: From Calvin to the Civil Constitution, 1560–1791* (New Haven, CT: Yale University Press, 1996); Timothy Tackett, *Religion, Revolution, and Regional Culture in Eighteenth-Century France: The Ecclesiastical Oath of 1791* (Princeton, NJ: Princeton University Press, 1986); Caroline C. Ford, *Creating the Nation in Provincial France: Religion and Political Identity in Brittany* (Princeton, NJ: Princeton University Press, 1993); Suzanne Desan, *Reclaiming the Sacred: Lay Religion and Popular Politics in Revolutionary France* (Ithaca, NY: Cornell University Press, 1990).

67. John Richard Bowen, *Why the French Don't Like Headscarves: Islam, the State, and Public Space* (Princeton, NJ: Princeton University Press, 2007).

68. For a provocative interpretation of their views, see Matthew Stewart, *Nature's God: The Heretical Origins of the American Republic* (New York: W. W. Norton, 2014).

CHAPTER 2. THE HEBRAIC MOMENT:
THE NEW ENGLAND PURITANS

1. James Sleeper, "Our Puritan Heritage," *Democracy Journal*, Summer (2015).

2. The seminal work in this line of interpretation is of course Perry Miller, *The New England Mind; the Seventeenth Century* (New York: Macmillan Company, 1939).

3. On godly or Christian republicanism, see Michael P. Winship, "Godly Republicanism and the Origins of the Massachusetts Polity," *William and Mary Quarterly* 63, no. 3 (2006). On Christian republicanism, see also Mark A. Noll, *America's God: From Jonathan Edwards to Abraham Lincoln* (Oxford and New York: Oxford University Press, 2002); E. Brooks Holifield, *Theology in America: Christian Thought from the Age of the Puritans to the Civil War* (New Haven, CT: Yale University Press, 2003); Richard P. Gildrie, *Profane, the Civil, and the Godly: The Reformation of Manners in Orthodox New England, 1679–1749* (University Park: Penn State University Press, 2004).

4. Here, I follow a line of interpretation initiated in James F. Maclear, "New England and the Fifth Monarchy: The Quest for the Millennium in Early American Puritanism," *William and Mary Quarterly: A Magazine of Early American History* 32, no. 2 (1975).

5. On typology, see especially Sacvan Bercovitch, *Typology and Early American Literature* (Amherst: University of Massachusetts Press, 1972); idem, *The American Jeremiad* (Madison: University of Wisconsin Press, 1978); Thomas M. Davis, "The Exegetical Traditions of Puritan Typology," *Early American Literature* 5, no. 1 (1970). On Puritan biblical interpretation more generally, see also Noll, *America's God*.

6. Thus, while the first generation of New England Puritans saw only rough typological parallels, later generations worked them out in exquisite detail. Compare John Cotton, *God's Promise to His Plantations: As It Delivered in a Sermon* (London: W. Jones, 1630); Cotton Mather, *Magnalia Christi Americana* (London: T. Sowle, 1702).

7. For a helpful overview, see William R. Hutchison and Hartmut Lehmann, *Many Are Chosen: Divine Election and Western Nationalism*, Harvard Theological Studies 38 (Minneapolis, MN: Fortress Press, 1994).

8. For an overview of the English case, see P. Gorski, "Premodern Nationalism: An Oxymoron? The Evidence from England," in *Sage Handbook of Nationalism*, ed. Gerard Delanty and Krishan Kumar (New York: Russell Sage, 2006). On France, see especially Colette Beaune and Fredric L. Cheyette, *The Birth of an Ideology: Myths and Symbols of Nation in Late-Medieval France* (Berkeley: University of California Press, 1991). For a general overview of religion and Western nationalism, see Adrian Hastings, *The Construction of Nationhood: Ethnicity, Religion, and Nationalism* (Cambridge and New York: Cambridge University Press, 1997). On the biblical prototypes, see especially Steven Elliott Grosby, *Biblical Ideas of Nationality: Ancient and Modern* (Winona Lake, IN: Eisenbrauns, 2002).

9. The seminal study is William Haller, *The Elect Nation; the Meaning and Relevance of Foxe's* Book of Martyrs (New York: Harper & Row, 1963). Also helpful are Christopher Hill, *God's Englishman: Oliver Cromwell and the English Revolution* (New York: Dial Press, 1970); and Richard Helgerson, *Forms of Nationhood: The Elizabethan Writing of England* (Chicago: University of Chicago Press, 1992). For an entrée into the more recent literature, see especially Linda Colley, *Britons: Forging the Nation, 1707–1837* (New Haven, CT: Yale University Press, 1992); Colin Kidd, *British Identities Before Nationalism: Ethnicity and Nationhood in the Atlantic World, 1600–1800* (Cambridge and New York: Cambridge University Press, 1999).

10. See, for example, Donald H. Akenson, *God's Peoples: Covenant and Land in South Africa, Israel, and Ulster* (Montreal: McGill-Queen's University Press, 1991); Gary S. Selby, *Martin Luther King and the Rhetoric of Freedom: The Exodus Narrative in America's Struggle for Civil Rights*, Studies in Rhetoric and Religion (Waco, TX: Baylor University Press, 2008).

11. Walzer, *Exodus and Revolution*; Philip Gorski, "Calvinism and Revolution: The Walzer Thesis Re-Considered," in *Meaning and Modernity: Religion, Polity and Self*, ed. Richard Madsen, Ann Swidler, and Steven Tipton (Berkeley and Los Angeles: University of California Press, 2001); Robert M. Kingdon, "The Political Resistance of the Calvinists in France and the Low Countries," *Church History: Studies in Christianity and Culture* 27, no. 3 (1958).

12. Hugh J. Dawson, "John Winthrop's Rite of Passage: The Origins of the 'Christian Charitie' Discourse," *Early American Literature* 26, no. 3 (1991).

13. "'Christian Charitie' as Colonial Discourse: Rereading Winthrop's Sermon in Its English Context," *Early American Literature* 33, no. 2 (1998).

14. On Winthrop more generally, see Edmund Sears Morgan, *The Puritan Dilemma; the Story of John Winthrop*, Library of American Biography (Boston: Little, 1958); Francis J. Bremer, *John Winthrop: America's Forgotten Founding Father* (New York: Oxford University Press, 2005).

15. David D. Hall, *Puritans in the New World: A Critical Anthology* (Princeton, NJ: Princeton University Press, 2004), 169.

16. Ibid.

17. Loren Baritz, *City on a Hill: A History of Ideas and Myths in America* (New York: Wiley, 1964).

18. Hall, *Puritans in the New World*, 169.

19. On covenants and covenant renewal, see Charles E. Hambrick-Stowe, *The Practice of Piety: Puritan Devotional Exercises in Seventeenth Century New England* (Chapel Hill: University of North Carolina Press, 1982); David D. Hall, *Worlds of Wonder, Days of Judgment: Popular Religious Belief in Early New England* (Cambridge, MA: Harvard University Press, 1990).

20. In addition to the previously cited works, see Perry Miller, *The New England Mind, from Colony to Province* (Cambridge, MA: Belknap Press of Harvard University Press, 1983), 53–64. Contemporary discussions include John Cotton, *The Way of the Churches of Christ in New-England, or, the Way of Churches Walking in Brotherly Equality, or Co-Ordination, Without Subjection of One Church to Another. Measured and Examined by the Golden Reed of the Sanctuary, Containing a Full Declaration of the Church-Way in All Particulars*, Early English Books (London: Matthew Simmons, 1645); Richard Mather, *Church-Government and Church-Covenant Discussed: In an Answer of the Elders of the Severall Churches in New-England to Two and Thirty Questions, Sent over to Them by Divers Ministers in England, to Declare Their Judgements Therein: Together with an Apologie of the Said Elders in New-England for Church-Covenant, Sent over in Answer to Master Bernard in the Yeare 1639: As Also in an Answer to Nine Positions About Church-Government* (London: R. O. and G.D. for Benjamin Allen, 1643).

21. The most accessible and authoritative study remains Edmund S. Morgan, *Visible Saints: The History of a Puritan Idea* (Ithaca, NY: Cornell University Press, 1965).

22. The authoritative study of Puritan conversion remains Charles Lloyd Cohen, *God's Caress: The Psychology of Puritan Religious Experience* (New York: Oxford University Press, 1986). See also Patricia Caldwell, *The Puritan Conversion Narrative: The Beginnings of American Expression* (New York: Cambridge University Press, 1983); Murray G. Murphey, "The Psychodynamics of Puritan Conversion," *American Quarterly* 31, no. 2 (1979); Thomas Shepard and Michael McGiffert, *God's Plot: The Paradoxes of*

Puritan Piety; Being the Autobiography and Journal of Thomas Shepard (Amherst: University of Massachusetts Press, 1972).

23. Williston Walker, *The Creeds and Platforms of Congregationalism* (Boston: Pilgrim Press, 1960), 116.

24. Ibid., 117–118.

25. David A. Weir, *Early New England: A Covenanted Society*, Emory University Studies in Law and Religion (Grand Rapids, MI: W. B. Eerdmans, 2004), 154.

26. Walker, *Creeds and Platforms of Congregationalism*, 143.

27. Morgan, *Visible Saints*.

28. See especially Cohen, *God's Caress*.

29. T. H. Breen, *The Character of the Good Ruler; a Study of Puritan Political Ideas in New England, 1630–1730*, Yale Historical Publications Miscellany 92 (New Haven, CT: Yale University Press, 1970); Morgan, *Puritan Dilemma*, 85–86.

30. John Winthrop, *Winthrop Papers, 1498–1649*, 5 vols. (Boston: Massachusetts Historical Society, 1929), 3:423.

31. Weir, *Early New England*, 74.

32. Ibid., 105 (emphasis added). See, more generally, Kenneth A. Lockridge, *A New England Town: The First Hundred Years: Dedham, Massachusetts, 1636–1736* (New York: Norton, 1970).

33. Weir, *Early New England*, 103.

34. A detailed discussion of the rituals surrounding church covenants and covenant renewal may be found in Hambrick-Stowe, *Practice of Piety*. See also Gildrie, *Profane, the Civil, and the Godly*.

35. Colin W. Williams, Sydney E. Ahlstrom, and Charles William Powers, *The Changing Nature of America's Civil Religion* (New York: Aspen Institute for Humanistic Studies, 1973), 75–76.

36. Weir, *Early New England*, 74.

37. See the relevant entry in the Oxford English Dictionary Online.

38. George Lee Haskins, *Law and Authority in Early Massachusetts: A Study in Tradition and Design* (Hamden, CT: Archon Books, 1968).

39. Edmund Sears Morgan, *Roger Williams; the Church and the State* (New York: Harcourt, 1967), 70; Aaron B. Seidman, "Church and State in the Early Years of the Massachusetts Bay Colony," *New England Quarterly* 18, no. 2 (1945): 215, n. 6.

40. See David D. Hall, *A Reforming People: Puritanism and the Transformation of Public Life in New England* (Chapel Hill: University of North Carolina Press, 2012).

41. John Cotton, *A Discourse about Civil Government in a New Plantation Whose Design Is Religion* (Cambridge, MA: Samuel Green and Marmaduke Johnson, 1663), 5.7. Emphasis in original.

42. Ibid., 17.

43. Walker, *Creeds and Platforms of Congregationalism*, 237.

44. Hall, *Puritans in the New World*, 174.

45. Bruce T. Murray, *Religious Liberty in America: The First Amendment in Historical and Contemporary Perspective* (Amherst: University of Massachusetts Press and Foundation for American Communications, 2008), 17.

46. Winship, "Godly Republicanism."

47. Markku Peltonen, *Classical Humanism and Republicanism in English Political Thought, 1570–1640*, vol. 36 (Cambridge and New York: Cambridge University Press,

2004); Andrew Hadfield, *Shakespeare and Republicanism* (Cambridge and New York: Cambridge University Press, 2008); Andrew Fitzmaurice, *Humanism and America: An Intellectual History of English Colonisation, 1500–1625* (Cambridge and New York: Cambridge University Press, 2003).

48. Breen, *Character of the Good Ruler*; Gildrie, *Profane, the Civil, and the Godly.*

49. Nathaniel Bradstreet Shurtleff and Massachusetts General Court, *Records of the Governor and Company of the Massachusetts Bay in New England* (New York: AMS Press, 1968), 1:16.

50. Winship, "Godly Republicanism," 448.

51. It may be objected that the Renaissance republics were "secular" rather than "godly." But while there certainly were some important differences between the republics of the Old and New Worlds, they are not captured by this concept. Recall that most European cities: (1) originated as sacred bodies bound together by religious oaths (John Frederick Wilson, *Religion and the American Nation: Historiography and History*, George H. Shriver Lecture Series in Religion in American History 1 [Athens: University of Georgia Press, 2003]); (2) had civic rituals that were explicitly religious, if not necessarily 100 percent Christian (David J. F. Crouch, *Piety, Fraternity, and Power: Religious Guilds in Late Medieval Yorkshire, 1389–1547* [Woodbridge, Suffolk, and Rochester, NY: York Medieval Press, 2000]; Nicholas Terpstra, *Lay Confraternities and Civic Religion in Renaissance Bologna*, Cambridge Studies in Italian History and Culture [Cambridge and New York: Cambridge University Press, 1995]); and (3) excluded "heretics" and "sectarians" from at least some of the benefits of citizenship, with some even making full citizenship dependent upon membership in a guild or confraternity—bodies that were themselves quasi-religious in nature (Margaret R. Somers, "Rights, Relationality, and Membership: Rethinking the Making and Meaning of Citizenship," *Law and Social Inquiry* 19, no. 1 [1994]). In short, early modern city-states were (still) no more secular than their New England offspring.

52. Bradford's portrait of Morton and Morton's portrait of himself may seem contradictory, but they were not. In the unreformed folk Christianity of which Morton was a paradigmatic representative, maypole feasts and Easter Eucharist were simply two sides of the same coin. The project of the Puritans and other would-be reformers of popular culture was to remove the pagan elements with which European Christianity had been alloyed since late antiquity. The classic English-language accounts of "popular religion" in Reformation Europe are Peter Burke, *Popular Culture in Early Modern Europe* (Burlington: VT: Ashgate Publishing, 2009); Keith Thomas, *Religion and the Decline of Magic: Studies in Popular Beliefs in Sixteenth and Seventeenth-Century England* (London: Penguin UK, 1991).

53. Separatists, or Brownites, as they were also known, believed that the saints must separate from the Church of England. Most of the Plymouth colonists were Separatists. The majority of Puritans, however, including the founders of the Bay Colony, were not.

54. On natural law and Reformed Protestantism during the early modern era, see especially Stephen John Grabill, *Rediscovering the Natural Law in Reformed Theological Ethics* (Grand Rapids, MI: Wm. B. Eerdmans Publishing, 2006).

55. On this, see especially Gildrie, *Profane, the Civil, and the Godly.*

56. See, for instance, Noah Feldman, *Divided by God: America's Church-State Problem—and What We Should Do About It* (New York: Farrar, Straus and Giroux, 2005);

Timothy L. Hall, *Separating Church and State: Roger Williams and Religious Liberty* (Champaign-Urbana: University of Illinois Press, 1998).

57. For a fine-grained analysis of Hutchinson's sympathizers, see chapter 1 in Louise A. Breen, *Transgressing the Bounds: Subversive Enterprises among the Puritan Elite in Massachusetts, 1630–1692* (Oxford and New York: Oxford University Press, 2001).

58. A brief overview of the vast literature on this subject may be found in Charles E. Hambrick-Stowe, "Practical Divinity and Spirituality," in Coffey and Lim, *Cambridge Companion to Puritanism*.

59. On the Ancient and Honorable Artillery Company, see chapter 1 of Breen, *Transgressing the Bounds*. For the European background and a Dutch example, see John Christopher Grayson, "The Civic Militia in the County of Holland, 1560–81. Politics and Public Order in the Dutch Revolt," *BMGN-Low Countries Historical Review* 95, no. 1 (1980). For a critical assessment of the relationship between citizen militias and civic republicanism, see R. Claire Snyder, *Citizen-Soldiers and Manly Warriors: Military Service and Gender in the Civic Republican Tradition* (Lanham, MD: Rowman & Littlefield, 1999).

60. On the covenanted militias, see Timothy Hall Breen, *Puritans and Adventurers: Change and Persistence in Early America* (New York: Oxford University Press, 1980).

61. On this shift, see Thomas S. Kidd, *The Protestant Interest: New England after Puritanism* (New Haven, CT: Yale University Press, 2004).

62. The seminal studies remain Perry Miller, "The Half-Way Covenant," *New England Quarterly* 6, no. 4 (1933); Robert G. Pope, *The Half-Way Covenant: Church Membership in Puritan New England* (Princeton, NJ: Princeton University Press, 1969).

63. See David M. Scobey, "Revising the Errand: New England's Ways and the Puritan Sense of the Past," *William and Mary Quarterly* 41, no. 1 (1984).

64. For events and analysis, see Jill Lepore, *The Name of War: King Philip's War and the Origins of American Identity* (New York: Vintage Books, 1999); Alfred A. Cave, *The Pequot War* (Amherst: University of Massachusetts Press, 1996).

65. Samuel Nowell, *Abraham in Arms; or the First Religious General with His Army Engaging in a War for Which He Had Wisely Prepared, and by Which, Not Only an Eminent Victory Was Obtained, but a Blessing Gained Also* (Boston: John Foster, 1678).

66. Harry S. Stout, *The New England Soul: Preaching and Religious Culture in Colonial New England* (New York: Oxford University Press, 1986), 83.

67. On the racialization of Puritan–Native American relations, see especially Richard A. Bailey, *Race and Redemption in Puritan New England* (New York: Oxford University Press, 2011). On the demonization of the Native Americans, see also David S. Lovejoy, "Satanizing the American Indian," *New England Quarterly* 67, no. 4 (1994). On both subjects, see the indispensable James Axtell, *The Invasion Within: The Contest of Cultures in Colonial North America* (Oxford: Oxford University Press, 1985).

68. General overviews of Puritan eschatology may be found in Joy Gilsdorf, *The Puritan Apocalypse: New England Eschatology in the Seventeenth Century* (New York: Garland Publishing, 1989); Stephen J. Stein, "Transatlantic Extensions: Apocalyptic in Early New England," in *The Apocalypse in English Renaissance Thought and Literature*, ed. C. A. Patrides and Joseph Anthony Wittreich (Ithaca, NY: Cornell University Press, 1984); Avihu Zakai, "Puritan Millennialism and Theocracy in Early Massachusetts," *History of European Ideas* 8, no. 3 (1987); idem, "Reformation, History, and Escha-

tology in English Protestantism," *History and Theory* 26, no. 3 (1987); Maclear, "New England and the Fifth Monarchy."

69. On Eliot, see James Holstun, "John Eliot's Empirical Millenarianism," *Representations* 4, no. 4 (1983). On the place of "Indian missions" in Puritan eschatology, see also Neal Salisbury, "Red Puritans: The 'Praying Indians' of Massachusetts Bay and John Eliot," *William and Mary Quarterly* 31, no. 1 (1974); Amy H. Sturgis, "Prophesies and Politics: Millenarians, Rabbis, and the Jewish Indian Theory," *Seventeenth Century* 14, no. 1 (1999).

70. See Nathan O. Hatch, "The Origins of Civil Millennialism in America: New England Clergymen, War with France, and the Revolution," *William and Mary Quarterly* 31, no. 3 (1974); Ruth H. Bloch, *Visionary Republic: Millennial Themes in American Thought, 1756–1800* (Cambridge and New York: Cambridge University Press, 1988).

71. On this, see especially chapter 4 in Breen, *Transgressing the Bounds.*

72. On Increase Mather's eschatology, see chapter 8 in Robert Middlekauff, *The Mathers: Three Generations of Puritan Intellectuals, 1596–1728* (Berkeley: University of California Press, 1999).

73. On Cotton Mather's eschatology, see chapter 18 in ibid.

74. Ibid., 328.

75. On this, see especially George McKenna, *The Puritan Origins of American Patriotism* (New Haven, CT: Yale University Press, 2008); Eran Shalev, *American Zion* (New Haven, CT: Yale University Press, 2013).

76. Stephen Foster, *The Long Argument: English Puritanism and the Shaping of New England Culture, 1570–1700* (Chapel Hill: University of North Carolina Press, 1996).

77. On the comparatively participatory and egalitarian character of the Puritan polities, see especially Hall, *A Reforming People*; Michael P. Winship, *Godly Republicanism: Puritans, Pilgrims, and a City on a Hill* (Cambridge, MA: Harvard University Press, 2012). By contrast, the Jamestown Colony more closely mirrored the social hierarchy and forced labor systems of England, a point emphasized even in friendly treatments such as Karen Ordahl Kupperman, *The Jamestown Project* (Cambridge, MA: Harvard University Press, 2009).

78. See, for instance, the almost hagiographical treatment of Williams in John M. Barry, *Roger Williams and the Creation of the American Soul: Church, State, and the Birth of Liberty* (New York: Penguin, 2012).

CHAPTER 3. HEBRAIC REPUBLICANISM:
THE AMERICAN REVOLUTION

1. I do not mean to suggest that *all* Christian conservatives are Christian nationalists. That is decidedly not the case. The autodidact historian David Barton is probably the most influential advocate of this view, and certainly the most prolific. See, for instance, David Barton, *America's Godly Heritage* (Aledo, TX: WallBuilders, 1992). The claim that the U.S. Constitution was directly inspired by God seems to have Mormon roots and has been popularized by the conservative media personality Glenn Beck, who often recommends W. Cleon Skousen, *The Five Thousand Year Leap* (Franklin, TN: W. Cleon Skousen, 2009). Similar claims are also advanced by a small group of conservative neo-Calvinists under the banner of "reconstruction theology." The seminal text for this

movement is Rousas John Rushdoony, *The Nature of the American System* (Nutley, NJ: Craig Press, 1965).

2. For a compendium of quotations from the founders, see David Barton, "A Few Declarations of Founding Fathers and Early Statesment on Jesus, Christianity and the Bible," http://www.wallbuilders.com/LIBissuesArticles.asp?id=8755. For an example of constitutional proof-texting, see FaithFacts, "The Bible and Government. Biblical Principles: Basis for America's Laws," http://www.faithfacts.org/christ-and-the-culture/the-bible-and-government.

3. Again, I do not mean to suggest that *all* liberals and progressives espouse this view. Recent examples include Isaac Kramnick and R. Laurence Moore, *The Godless Constitution: A Moral Defense of the Secular State* (New York and London: Norton, 2005); Brooke Allen, *Moral Minority: Our Skeptical Founding Fathers* (Chicago: Ivan R. Dee, 2006); Stewart, *Nature's God*; Susan Jacoby, *Freethinkers: A History of American Secularism* (New York: Metropolitan Books, 2004).

4. For more balanced overviews of the recent literature, see Thomas S. Kidd, *God of Liberty: A Religious History of the American Revolution* (New York: Basic Books, 2012); Steven Waldman, *Founding Faith: Providence, Politics, and the Birth of Religious Freedom in America* (New York: Random House, 2008).

5. This point is rightly emphasized in Kidd, *God of Liberty*.

6. For a balanced and nuanced overview, see especially Lance Banning, "Jeffersonian Ideology Revisited: Liberal and Classical Ideas in the New American Republic," *William and Mary Quarterly* 43, no. 1 (1986).

7. Most American historians speak of "Christian republicanism." See, for instance, Noll, *America's God*; Nathan Hatch, *The Sacred Cause of Liberty: Republican Thought and the Millennium in Revolutionary New England* (New Haven, CT: Yale University Press, 1977). Their interpretation is anticipated by Alexis de Tocqueville, *Democracy in America* (New York: HarperPerennial, 1988). In speaking of "Hebraic republicanism" instead, I have been especially influenced by Eric Nelson, *The Hebrew Republic* (Cambridge, MA: Harvard University Press, 2010); Shalev, *American Zion*; Nathan R. Perl-Rosenthal, "The 'Divine Right of Republics': Hebraic Republicanism and the Debate over Kingless Government in Revolutionary America," *William and Mary Quarterly* 66, no. 3 (2009).

8. For a general overview, see Caroline Winterer, *The Culture of Classicism: Ancient Greece and Rome in American Intellectual Life, 1780–1910* (Baltimore: Johns Hopkins University Press, 2004). For the revolutionary era in particular, see Carl J. Richard, *The Founders and the Classics: Greece, Rome, and the American Enlightenment* (Cambridge, MA: Harvard University Press, 1994). On the Roman influence in particular, see M.N.S. Sellers, *American Republicanism: Roman Ideology in the United States Constitution*, Studies in Modern History (Houndmills, Basingstoke, Hampshire: Macmillan, 1994); Eric Nelson, *The Greek Tradition in Republican Thought*, Ideas in Context 69 (Cambridge and New York: Cambridge University Press, 2004). On the revolutionary era as a whole, a thorough summary may be found in Eran Shalev, *Rome Reborn on Western Shores: Historical Imagination and the Creation of the American Republic* (Charlottesville: University of Virginia Press, 2009).

9. On this point, one might begin with Perl-Rosenthal, "'Divine Right of Republics.'"

10. This point is well argued in Shalev, *American Zion*.

11. For a trenchant, if overstated, version of this argument, see Steven M. Dworetz, *The Unvarnished Doctrine: Locke, Liberalism, and the American Revolution* (Durham, NC: Duke University Press, 1989).

12. On this point, see especially Jeremy Waldron, *God, Locke, and Equality: Christian Foundations in Locke's Political Thought* (Cambridge and New York: Cambridge University Press, 2002).

13. On this, see especially Rogers M. Smith, *Civic Ideals: Conflicting Visions of Citizenship in U.S. History* (New Haven, CT, and London: Yale University Press, 1997).

14. The definitive work remains Bloch, *Visionary Republic*.

15. Hatch, "Origins of Civil Millennialism in America."

16. On this point see especially Stewart, *Nature's God*.

17. Succinct overviews of the debate may be found in the appendix of Garrett Ward Sheldon, *The Political Philosophy of Thomas Jefferson* (Baltimore: Johns Hopkins University Press, 1991); Robert E. Shalhope, "Republicanism and Early American Historiography," *William and Mary Quarterly* 39, no. 2 (1982); Daniel T. Rodgers, "Republicanism: The Career of a Concept," *Journal of American History* 79, no. 1 (1992).

18. On the "liberal consensus view," see Carl Becker, *The Declaration of Independence: A Study in the History of Ideas* (New York: Harcourt, Brace, 1922); Louis Hartz, *The Liberal Tradition in America: An Interpretation of American Political Thought since the Revolution* (New York: Harcourt, 1955); Merle Curti, "The Great Mr. Locke: America's Philosopher, 1783–1861," *Huntington Library Bulletin* 11 (1937); Vernon L. Parrington, *Main Currents in American Thought* (New York: Harcourt Brace, 1930). Left-leaning authors often accepted the "liberal consensus" view and took it as a starting point for more critical assessments. See, for instance, C. B. Macpherson, *The Political Theory of Possessive Individualism* (Oxford: Clarendon Press, 1962).

19. This view was first announced in Robert E. Shalhope, "Toward a Republican Synthesis: The Emergence of an Understanding of Republicanism in American Historiography," *William and Mary Quarterly* 29, no. 1 (1972).

20. Some contended that liberal influences predominated; others doubled down on republicanism. Some proposed "liberal republicanism" as a compromise formulation; others preferred "republican liberalism." Some argued that the Constitution marked a turning point from republicanism to liberalism; others insisted that republicanism lived on as an oppositional tradition.

21. For example, these ideas survived in the form of the classics-based curriculum at American universities, "labor republicanism" among American workers, and "republican motherhood" in American households. On nineteenth-century classicism, see Winterer, *Culture of Classicism*; Shalev, *Rome Reborn on Western Shores*. On labor republicanism, the seminal work is Eric Foner, *Free Soil, Free Labor, Free Men: The Ideology of the Republican Party Before the Civil War* (Oxford and New York: Oxford University Press, 1971). For a more recent evaluation, see Alex Gourevitch, "Labor and Republican Liberty," *Constellations* 18, no. 3 (2011). On republican motherhood, see Linda Kerber, "The Republican Mother: Women and the Enlightenment—an American Perspective," *American Quarterly* 28, no. 2 (1976); Linda K. Kerber, *Women of the Republic: Intellect and Ideology in Revolutionary America* (Williamsburg, VA: Institute of Early American History and Culture, 1980).

22. John Adams, *The Portable John Adams* (New York: Penguin, 2004), 225.

23. Ibid., 339.

24. Ibid., 234.

25. Adams scoffed at the radical egalitarianism of the French revolutionaries. "We are told that our friends, the National Assembly of France, have abolished all distinctions. But be not deceived. . . . Impossibilities cannot be performed." Ibid., 375.

26. Ibid., 292.

27. Ibid., 219, 40.

28. "Continentalist no. IV," in Alexander Hamilton, *Writings*, vol. 129 (New York: Library of America, 2001), 115.

29. "Speech in Convention," in ibid., 156, 64.

30. Quoted in Paul Rahe, *Republics Ancient and Modern*, 3 vols. (Chapel Hill: University of North Carolina Press, 1994), 3:115.

31. "Speech in Convention," in Hamilton, *Writings*, 129, 156.

32. Ibid., 100, 30.

33. Ibid., 161.

34. "Tully no. III," in ibid., 830.

35. Ibid., 794.

36. Thomas Jefferson, Joyce Oldham Appleby, and Terence Ball, *Thomas Jefferson, Political Writings*, Cambridge Texts in the History of Political Thought (Cambridge and New York: Cambridge University Press, 1999), 217–218.

37. Ibid., 258, 89.

38. One sees the influence of moral sense philosophy on Jefferson in this passage as well. Ibid., 143; see also 253.

39. The echo of James Harrington is unmistakable. Ibid., 183.

40. Here, we clearly see the influence of Harrington's concern with landed property. Ibid., 106, 108, 87.

41. Ibid., 187.

42. Ibid., 257; see also 56.

43. On Jeffersonian republicanism in general, see Lance Banning, *The Jeffersonian Persuasion: Evolution of a Party Ideology* (Ithaca, NY: Cornell University Press, 1980). On the evolution of Jefferson's views in a more republican direction, see Sheldon, *Political Philosophy of Thomas Jefferson*.

44. James Madison, *Writings*, Library of America 109 (New York: Library of America, 1999), 164.

45. Ibid., 174.

46. Ibid., 211–212.

47. Niccolò Machiavelli, Harvey Claflin Mansfield, and Nathan Tarcov, *Discourses on Livy* (Chicago: University of Chicago Press, 1996), book 1, 11.

48. Ibid., book 2, 2.

49. Jean-Jacques Rousseau and Victor Gourevitch, *The Social Contract and Other Later Political Writings*, Cambridge Texts in the History of Political Thought (Cambridge and New York: Cambridge University Press, 1997), 4:8, 145.

50. Felix Raab, *The English Face of Machiavelli* (New York: Routledge, 2013 [1936]); Alan Heimert, *Religion and the American Mind* (Cambridge, MA: Harvard University Press, 1933); Judith N. Shklar, "Ideology Hunting: The Case of James Harrington," *American Political Science Review* 53, no. 3 (1959).

51. K. Alan Snyder, "Foundations of Liberty: The Christian Republicanism of Timothy Dwight and Jedidiah Morse," *New England Quarterly* 56, no. 3 (1983); Noll, *America's*

God; Nathan O. Hatch, *The Sacred Cause of Liberty: Republican Thought and the Millennium in Revolutionary New England* (New Haven, CT: Yale University Press, 1977); Stout, *New England Soul*; Mark Goldie, "The Civil Religion of James Harrington," *Languages of Political Theory in Early Modern Europe* 198 (1987); William Gribbin, "Republican Religion and the American Churches in the Early National Period," *Historian* 35, no. 1 (1972).

52. For an analysis of their views, see Stewart, *Nature's God*. As should be obvious, I do not agree with his broader claims about the religious heterodoxy of the founders, which are greatly overstated and often strained, particularly as regards Thomas Jefferson.

53. Jonathan Mayhew, *A Defence of the Observations on the Charter and Conduct of the Society for the Propagation of the Gospel in Foreign Parts: Against an Anonymous Pamphlet Falsly Intitled, a Candid Examination of Dr. Mayhew's Observations, &C. And Also Against the Letter to a Friend Annexed Thereto, Said to Contain a Short Vindication of Said Society* (Boston: R. and S. Draper, Edes and Gill, and T. & J. Fleet, 1763); idem, *A Letter of Reproof to Mr. John Cleaveland of Ipswich, Occasioned by a Defamatory Libel Published under His Name, Intitled, an Essay to Defend Some of the Most Important Principles in the Protestant Reformed System of Christianity, &C.—Against the Injurious Aspersions Cast on the Same* (Boston: R. and S. Draper, Edes and Gill, and T. & J. Fleet, 1764), http://opac.newsbank.com/select/evans/9737.

54. Idem, *Seven Sermons Upon the Follow Subjects; Viz. The Difference Betwixt Truth and Falshood* (Boston: Rogers and Fowlse, 1749), 5–6.

55. Idem, *Striving to Enter in at the Strait Gate Explain'd and Inculcated; and the Connexion of Salvation Therewith, Proved from the Holy Scriptures. In Two Sermons on Luke Xiii. 24* (Boston: Richard Draper, Edes & Gill, and Thomas & John Fleet, 1761).

56. Idem, *A Discourse Concerning Unlimited Submission and Non-Resistance to the Higher Powers with Some Reflections on the Resistance Made to King Charles 1. And on the Anniversary of His Death: In Which the Mysterious Doctrine of That Prince's Saintship and Martyrdom Is Unriddled: The Substance of Which Was Delivered in a Sermon Preached in the West Meeting-House in Boston the Lord's-Day after the 30th of January, 1749/50* (Boston: D. Fowle and D. Gookin, 1750), http://galenet.galegroup.com/servlet/ECCO?c=1&stp=Author&ste=11&af=BN&ae=W030792&tiPG=1&dd=0&dc=flc&docNum=CW121078547&vrsn=1.0&srchtp=a&d4=0.33&n=10&SU=0LRF&locID=29002; idem, *God's Hand and Providence to Be Religiously Acknowledged in Public Calamities: A Sermon Occasioned by the Great Fire in Boston, New-England, Thursday March 20, 1760, and Preached on the Lord's-Day Following* (Boston: Richard Draper, Edes and Gill, and Thomas and John Fleet, 1760), http://opac.newsbank.com/select/evans/8665.

57. Idem, *The Expected Dissolution of All Things, a Motive to Universal Holiness: Two Sermons Preached in Boston, N.E. On the Lord's Day, Nov. 23, 1755; Occasioned by the Earthquakes Which Happened on the Tuesday Morning, and Saturday Evening Preceeding* (Boston: Edes & Gill and R. Draper, 1755); Jonathan Mayhew, Benjamin Edes, and John Gill, *A Discourse on Rev. Xv. 3d, 4th. Occasioned by the Earthquakes in November 1755: Delivered in the West-Meeting-House, Boston, Thursday December 18* (Boston: Edes & Gill and R. Draper, 1755).

58. Mayhew's reading recalls Aquinas's. He rehearses the standard arguments concerning the three forms of corruption and locates their causes in the pursuit of "private interest" over the "common good," having earlier noted that "individual interests and the common good are not the same" (*De regimine principum* I, 1); see Thomas Aquinas,

Political Writings, trans. R. W. Dyson (Cambridge: Cambridge University Press, 2002), 7; However, whenever "government is directed not towards the common good but towards the private good of the rule, rule of this kind will be unjust and perverted" and "such a ruler is called a tyrant" (see *De regimine principum* I, 2, in ibid., 8). In such cases, resistance and even regicide may be legitimate, provided that the tyranny is severe and prolonged, and that the judgment is carried out by "public persons."

59. Mayhew, *Discourse Concerning Unlimited Submission and Non-Resistance*, 12.

60. Idem, *A Sermon Preach'd in the Audience of His Excellency William Shirley, Esq; Captain-General, Governor and Commander in Chief, the Honourable His Majesty's Coucil, and the Honourable House of Representatives, of the Province of the Massachusetts-Bay, in New-England. May 29, 1754. Being the Anniversary for the Election of His Majesty's Council for the Province* (London: G. Woodfall, 1754), 7, http://find.galegroup.com/ecco/infomark.do?contentSet=ECCOArticles&docType=ECCO Articles&bookId=1432102100&type=getFullCitation&tabID=T001&prodId =ECCO&docLevel=TEXT_GRAPHICS&version=1.0&source=library&user GroupName=29002.

61. Ibid., 23.

62. Ibid., 20.

63. Quoted in Bernard Bailyn, "Religion and Revolution: Three Biographical Studies," *Perspectives in American History* 4 (1970), 118.

64. Jonathan Mayhew, *The Snare Broken. A Thanksgiving-Discourse, Preached at the Desire of the West Church in Boston, N.E. Friday May 23, 1766*, 2nd ed. (Boston: R. & S. Draper, Edes & Gill, and T. & J. Fleet, 1766), 2; idem, *Sermon Preach'd in the Audience of His Excellency William Shirley*, 7.

65. Ibid., 10.

66. Idem, *Popish Idolatry: A Discourse Delivered in the Chapel of Harvard-College in Cambridge, New-England, May 8, 1765. At the Lecture Founded by the Honorable Paul Dudley, Esquire* (Boston: R. & S. Draper, 1765), 22–23.

67. Ibid., 23, 29.

68. Idem, *Snare Broken*, 13.

69. Idem, *A Discourse Occasioned by the Death of George II* (Boston: Edes & Gill, 1761), 29–30.

70. Donald J. D'Elia, "Benjamin Rush: Philosopher of the American Revolution," *Transactions of the American Philosophical Society* 64, no. 5 (1974): 10.

71. Letter to Elhanan Winchester, November 12, 1791, in Benjamin Rush and L. H. Butterfield, *Letters*, Memoirs of the American Philosophical Society (Princeton, NJ: Princeton University Press, 1951), 1:611.

72. Benjamin Rush, *A Plan for the Establishment of Public Schools and the Diffusion of Knowledge in Pennsylvania: To Which Are Added Thoughts upon the Mode of Education, Proper in a Republic. Addressed to the Legislature and Citizens of the State* (Philadelphia: Thomas Dobson, 1786), 16.

73. Idem, *An Inquiry into the Influence of Physical Causes Upon the Moral Faculty. Delivered Before a Meeting of the American Philosophical Society, Etc.* (Philadelphia: Haswell, Barrington and Haswell, 1839), 40

74. Idem, *Plan for the Establishment of Public Schools*, 15.

75. Letter to Noah Webster, July 20, 1798, in Rush and Butterfield, *Letters*, 2:799.

76. Letter to Thomas Jefferson, August 22, 1800, in ibid., 2:821.

77. Letter to James Kidd, November 25, 1793, in ibid., 2:746].
78. Rush, *Plan for the Establishment of Public Schools*, 15.
79. Letter to Thomas Jefferson, October 6, 1800, in Rush and Butterfield, *Letters*, 2:824–825.
80. Benjamin Rush, Noah Webster, Robert Coram, Simeon Doggett, Samuel Harrison Smith, Amable-Louis-Rose de Lafitte du Coutreil, and Samuel Knox, *Essays on Education in the Early Republic*, ed. Frederick Rudolph (Cambridge, MA: Belknap Press of Harvard University Press, 1965), 123, http://hdl.handle.net/2027/heb.07492.
81. Ibid., 114.
82. Timothy Dwight, *The True Means of Establishing Public Happiness: A Sermon, Delivered on the 7th of July, 1795, Before the Connecticut Society of Cincinnati, and Published at Their Request* (New Haven, CT: T. & S. Green, 1795), 33.
83. He continued: "Beyond most, perhaps beyond all, the heathen nations, they feared their gods, reverenced an oath, and believed in a providence, which rewarded the good, and punished the evil." Ibid., 28.
84. Ibid., 35.
85. Idem, *The Duty of Americans at the Present Crisis: Illustrated in a Discourse, Preached on the Fourth of July, 1798* (New Haven, CT: Thomas and Samuel Green, 1798), 18.
86. Idem, *True Means of Establishing Public Happiness*, 5–8.
87. For a recent overview, see Thomas S. Kidd, *The Great Awakening: The Roots of Evangelical Christianity in Colonial America* (New Haven, CT: Yale University Press, 2007).
88. The best general overview of the European movements is Martin Brecht, Johannes van den Berg, Klaus Deppermann, Johannes Friedrich Gerhard Goeters, and Hans Schneider, *Geschichte des Pietismus*, vol. 1 (Göttingen: Vandenhoeck & Ruprecht, 1993). In English, see the essays in Jonathan Strom, Hartmut Lehmann, and James Van Horn Melton, *Pietism in Germany and North America 1680–1820* (Farnham, England, and Burlington, VT: Ashgate Publishing, 2009).
89. For skeptical evaluations, see Frank Lambert, *Inventing the "Great Awakening"* (Princeton, NJ: Princeton University Press, 2001); Jon Butler, "Enthusiasm Described and Decried: The Great Awakening as Interpretative Fiction," *Journal of American History* 69, no. 2 (1982).
90. Jonathan Edwards, "Thoughts Concerning the Present Revival of Religion in New England," in *The Works of Jonathan Edwards*, ed. Edward Hickman (London: Ball, Arnold and Co., 1840 [1742]), 381.
91. Ibid., 382.
92. Ibid., 382–384.
93. Kerry A. Trask, *In the Pursuit of Shadows: A Study of Collective Hope and Despair in Provincial Massachusetts During the Era of the Seven Years' War, 1748–1764* (Minneapolis: University of Minnesota Press, 1971), 199.
94. Winston Churchill, *A History of the English-Speaking Peoples*, 4 vols. (London: Cassell, 1956), vol. 3, chapter 5.
95. Solomon Williams, *The Duty of Christian Soldiers* (New London: T & J Green, 1755), 26.
96. Ibid., 28.
97. Samuel Finley, *The Curse of Meroz* (Philadelphia: Chattin, 1757), 8.
98. Ibid., 21.

99. Melvin B. Endy, "Just War, Holy War, and Millennialism in Revolutionary America," *William and Mary Quarterly* 42, no. 1 (1985): 10.

100. James P. Byrd, *Sacred Scripture, Sacred War: The Bible and the American Revolution* (New York: Oxford University Press, 2013), 145.

101. Donald S. Lutz, "The Relative Influence of European Writers on Late Eighteenth-Century American Political Thought," *American Political Science Review* 78, no. 1 (1984): 192.

102. For a general introduction, see Kalman Neuman, "Political Hebraism and the Early Modern 'Respublica Hebraeorum': On Defining the Field," *Hebraic Political Studies* 1, no. 1 (2005).

103. The classic study remains Elizabeth L. Eisenstein, *The Printing Press as an Agent of Change*, vol. 1 (Cambridge: Cambridge University Press, 1980).

104. Petrus Cunaeus and Clement Barksdale, *Petrus Cunæus of the Common-Wealth of the Hebrews* (London: T. W. for William Lee, 1653); John Milton, *John Milton Prose. Major Writings on Liberty, Politics, Religion, and Education* (Oxford: Wiley-Blackwell, 2013).

105. Eric Nelson, *The Royalist Revolution: Monarchy and the American Founding* (Cambridge, MA: Harvard University Press, 2014); idem, "Patriot Royalism: The Stuart Monarchy in American Political Thought, 1769–75," *William and Mary Quarterly* 68, no. 4 (2011).

106. Samuel Langdon, *Joy and Gratitude to God for the Long Life of a Good King* (Portsmouth, NH: Daniel Fowle, 1760).

107. Idem, *Government Corrupted by Vice, and Recovered by Righteousness* (Watertown, MA: Benjamin Edes, 1775), 9.

108. Ibid., 11.

109. Ibid., 12.

110. Idem, *The Republic of the Israelites an Example to the American States* (Exeter, NH: John Lamson and Henry Ranlet, 1788), 7.

111. Ibid., 9.

112. Ibid., 10.

113. Ibid., 25.

114. Ibid., 15–16.

115. Thomas Paine, *Collected Writings* (New York: Library of America, 1995), 6.

116. Ibid., 12–13.

117. Steven M. Dworetz, "See Locke on Government: The Two Treatises and the American Revolution," *Studies in Eighteenth-Century Culture* 21, no. 1 (1992).

118. John Locke, *Two Treatises of Government* (New York: Cambridge University Press, 1988), chapter 1, section 2.

119. Of course, some scholars have argued that Locke was a closet atheist or even a radical Spinozist. The seminal text is Leo Strauss, *Liberalism Ancient and Modern* (Chicago: University of Chicago Press, 1995). For the Spinozan claim, see, for instance, Stewart, *Nature's God*. I am more persuaded by John Dunn, *The Political Thought of John Locke* (London: Cambridge University Press, 1969).

120. Waldron, *God, Locke, and Equality*, 83; Banning, "Jeffersonian Ideology Revisited."

121. I say "coined" because Jefferson and Madison did not invent them. Roger Williams had already spoken of a "wall or hedge of separation" between church and state well over a century before Jefferson used the phrase in his famous "Letter to the Dan-

bury Baptists." See Daniel L. Dreisbach, "Sowing Useful Truths and Principles: The Danbury Baptists, Thomas Jefferson, and the Wall of Seperation," *Journal of Church and State* 39 (1997). Earlier writers, including John Calvin and Richard Hooker, had also used the wall metaphor, which they took from the creation story, to describe the separation between civil and religious authority. See Philip Hamburger, *Separation of Church and State* (Cambridge, MA: Harvard University Press, 2002), 21ff.

122. Recent examples include Steven K. Green, *The Second Disestablishment: Church and State in Nineteenth-Century America* (Oxford and New York: Oxford University Press, 2010); Kramnick and Moore, *Godless Constitution*.

123. For criticisms, see Hamburger, *Separation of Church and State*; David Sehat, *The Myth of American Religious Freedom* (New York: Oxford University Press, 2011); Feldman, *Divided by God*; Steven D. Smith, *The Rise and Decline of American Religious Freedom* (Cambridge, MA: Harvard University Press, 2014).

124. On this point, see especially Daniel L. Dreisbach, *Thomas Jefferson and the Wall of Separation Between Church and State* (New York: New York University Press, 2002).

125. Harry Stout, "Rhetoric and Reality in the Early Republic: The Case of the Federalist Clergy," in *Religion and American Politics: From the Colonial Period to the 1980s*, ed. Mark Noll (New York: Oxford Universtiy Press, 1990), 65.

CHAPTER 4. DEMOCRATIC REPUBLICANISM:
THE CIVIL WAR

1. Merrill D. Peterson, *The Great Triumvirate: Webster, Clay, and Calhoun* (New York: Oxford University Press, 1987).

2. Louis Hartz, *The Liberal Tradition in America: An Interpretation of American Political Thought since the Revolution* (New York: Harcourt, 1955).

3. Richard Hofstadter, *The American Political Tradition and the Men Who Made It* (New York: Vintage Books, 1989).

4. Russell Kirk, *The Conservative Mind, from Burke to Santayana*, 2nd rev. ed. (Chicago: H. Regnery, 1953).

5. Zoltán Vajda, "John C. Calhoun's Republicanism Revisited," *Rhetoric & Public Affairs* 4, no. 3 (2001); Lacy K. Ford, "Republican Ideology in a Slave Society: The Political Economy of John C. Calhoun," *Journal of Southern History* 54, no. 3 (1988); idem, "Recovering the Republic: Calhoun, South Carolina, and the Concurrent Majority," *South Carolina Historical Magazine* 89, no. 3 (1988); Pauline Maier, "The Road Not Taken: Nullification, John C. Calhoun, and the Revolutionary Tradition in South Carolina," *South Carolina Historical Magazine* 82, no. 1 (1981).

6. Irving H. Bartlett, *John C. Calhoun: A Biography* (New York: W. W. Norton & Co., 1993), 45–47.

7. John C. Calhoun, *The Papers of John C. Calhoun*, ed. Robert L. Meriwether (Columbia: University of South Carolina Press, 1959), 1:288.

8. John C. Calhoun and H. Lee Cheek, *John C. Calhoun: Selected Writings and Speeches*, Conservative Leadership Series (Washington, DC: Regnery Publishers, 2003), 318.

9. In this sense, his political philosophy was squarely within the revolutionary tradition of Christian republicanism in its Madisonian dispensation. Ibid., 3.

10. Ibid., 31.

11. Ibid., 8.

12. Ibid., 15.

13. Ibid., 63, 68–69.

14. Ibid., 72–74.

15. Ibid., 111.

16. Ibid., 681.

17. Ibid., 692.

18. William J. Cooper, *Liberty and Slavery: Southern Politics to 1860* (New York: Knopf, 1983); Stephanie McCurry, "The Two Faces of Republicanism: Gender and Proslavery Politics in Antebellum South Carolina," *Journal of American History* 78, no. 4 (1992); Larry E. Tise, *Proslavery: A History of the Defense of Slavery in America, 1701–1840* (Athens: University of Georgia Press, 1987); George C. Rable, *The Confederate Republic: A Revolution Against Politics*, Civil War America (Chapel Hill: University of North Carolina Press, 1994); Drew Gilpin Faust, *The Ideology of Slavery: Proslavery Thought in the Antebellum South, 1830–1860*, Library of Southern Civilization (Baton Rouge and London: Louisiana State University Press, 1981).

19. Peter Garnsey, *Ideas of Slavery from Aristotle to Augustine*, W. B. Stanford Memorial Lectures (Cambridge: Cambridge University Press, 1996).

20. James Henry Hammond, *Selections from the Letters and Speeches of the Hon. James H. Hammond of South Carolina* (New York: J. F. Trow & Co., 1866).

21. Faust, *Ideology of Slavery*; Charles F. Irons, *The Origins of Proslavery Christianity: White and Black Evangelicals in Colonial and Antebellum Virginia* (Chapel Hill: University of North Carolina Press, 2008).

22. Eugene D. Genovese and Elizabeth Fox-Genovese, "The Religious Ideals of Southern Slave Society," *Georgia Historical Quarterly* 70, no. 1 (1986); Elizabeth Fox-Genovese and Eugene D. Genovese, *The Mind of the Master Class: History and Faith in the Southern Slaveholders' Worldview* (Cambridge and New York: Cambridge University Press, 2005); idem, "The Divine Sanction of Social Order: Religious Foundations of the Southern Slaveholders' World View," *Journal of the American Academy of Religion* 55, no. 2 (1987); Mark A. Noll and William A. Blair, *The Civil War as a Theological Crisis*, Steven and Janice Brose Lectures in the Civil War Era (Chapel Hill: University of North Carolina Press, 2006); George C. Rable, *God's Almost Chosen Peoples: A Religious History of the American Civil War*, Littlefield History of the Civil War Era (Chapel Hill: University of North Carolina Press, 2010).

23. Thornton Stringfellow, *A Brief Examination of Scripture Testimony on the Institution of Slavery in an Essay, First Published in the Religious Herald, and Republished by Request, with Remarks on a Review of the Essay* (Richmond, VA: Religious Herald, 1841), microform.

24. Abraham Lincoln, *Selected Speeches and Writings* (New York: Vintage, 1992), 9.

25. Abraham Lincoln and Roy P. Basler, *Collected Works*, Contributions in American Studies (New Brunswick, NJ: Rutgers University Press,1953), 1:347–348.

26. Eric Foner, *The Fiery Trial: Abraham Lincoln and American Slavery* (New York: W. W. Norton, 2010), 42.

27. Lincoln, *Selected Speeches and Writings*, 61; see also 42.

28. Ibid., 149.

29. Foner, *Fiery Trial*, 120.

30. In an 1842 speech to the Springfield Temperance Society, for example, he expressed longing for that "happy day, when, all appetites controlled, all passions subdued, all matters subjected, *mind,* all conquering *mind,* shall live and move the monarch of the world." Lincoln, *Selected Speeches and Writings,* 43.

31. In later years, he described a youthful riverboat journey alongside "ten or a dozen slaves, shackled together with irons" as "a continual torment." Ibid., 103.

32. Lincoln and Basler, *Collected Works,* 2:126–132.

33. Lincoln, *Selected Speeches and Writings,* 450.

34. Ibid., 42.

35. Ibid., 17.

36. Foner, *Fiery Trial,* 85.

37. Lincoln, *Selected Speeches and Writings,* 96–97.

38. Ibid., 97–98.

39. Ibid., 94.

40. Ibid., 98–99.

41. Ibid., 120.

42. Ibid., 121.

43. Ibid., 286–287.

44. Daniel A. Farber, *Lincoln's Constitution* (Chicago: University of Chicago Press, 2003), 79.

45. Lincoln, *Selected Speeches and Writings,* 356–358.

46. Ibid., 465.

47. Melinda Lawson, *Patriot Fires: Forging a New American Nationalism in the Civil War North,* American Political Thought (Lawrence: University Press of Kansas, 2002).

48. Lincoln, *Selected Speeches and Writings,* 405.

49. Mark Juergensmeyer, *The New Cold War?: Religious Nationalism Confronts the Secular State,* Comparative Studies in Religion and Society 5 (Berkeley: University of California Press, 1993).

50. Lincoln, *Selected Speeches and Writings,* 451.

51. Lincoln and Basler, *Collected Works,* 6:156.

52. Frederick Douglass, Philip Sheldon Foner, and Yuval Taylor, *Frederick Douglass: Selected Speeches and Writings* (Chicago: Lawrence Hill Books, 1999), 78.

53. Ibid., 137.

54. Frederick Douglass and Philip Sheldon Foner, *The Life and Writings of Frederick Douglass,* 4 vols. (New York: International Publishers, 1950), 2:49–54.

55. Douglass, Foner, and Taylor, *Frederick Douglass,* 204.

56. Ibid., 102.

57. Ibid., 177.

58. Ibid., 60, 97, 106, 302.

59. "To be dependent," he insisted, "is to be degraded." Ibid., 120.

60. He argued that "the *well* or *ill* condition of any part of mankind, will leave its mark on the physical as well as on the intellectual part of man." Ibid., 285.

61. Ibid., 294–295.

62. "The white man's happiness cannot be purchased by the black man's misery," he argued. "It is evident that white and black 'must fall or flourish together.'" Ibid., 149.

63. Ibid., 167.

64. Ibid., 461.

65. Ibid., 462.
66. Ibid., 361.
67. Ibid., 156.
68. Ibid., 201.
69. Ibid., 148–149.
70. Ibid., 97.
71. Ibid., 496.
72. Ibid., 500.
73. Ibid., 118.
74. Ibid., 344.
75. Ibid., 367.
76. Reginald Horsman, *Race and Manifest Destiny: The Origins of American Racial Anglo-Saxonism* (Cambridge, MA: Harvard University Press, 1981).
77. Thomas R. Hietala, *Manifest Design: Anxious Aggrandizement in Late Jacksonian America* (Ithaca, NY: Cornell University Press, 1985); Matthew Frye Jacobson, *Whiteness of a Different Color: European Immigrants and the Alchemy of Race* (Cambridge, MA, and London: Harvard University Press, 1998); David R. Roediger, *The Wages of Whiteness: Race and the Making of the American Working Class*, Haymarket Series (London and New York: Verso, 1991); Alexander Saxton, *The Rise and Fall of the White Republic: Class Politics and Mass Culture in Nineteenth Century America* (London and New York: Verso, 1990).
78. Edward J. Blum, *Reforging the White Republic: Race, Religion, and American Nationalism, 1865–1898*, Conflicting Worlds (Baton Rouge: Louisiana State University Press, 2005), 5.
79. Noll and Blair, *Civil War as a Theological Crisis*; Rable, *God's Almost Chosen Peoples*.
80. To a remarkable degree, then, the "theological crisis" of the Civil War foreshadowed and set in place the divisions between "fundamentalists" and "modernists" that would emerge again during the twentieth century.
81. Kramnick and Moore, *Godless Constitution*.
82. Green, *Second Disestablishment*.
83. Steven Keith Green, "The Rhetoric and Reality of the 'Christian Nation' Maxim in American Law, 1810–1920" (PhD diss., University of North Carolina, 1997); Gaines M. Foster, *Moral Reconstruction: Christian Lobbyists and the Federal Legislation of Morality, 1865–1920* (Chapel Hill: University of North Carolina Press, 2002).
84. William Addison Blakely, *American State Papers Bearing on Sunday Legislation* (New York: National Religious Liberty Association, 1891), 341–343.
85. William R. Hutchison, *Religious Pluralism in America: The Contentious History of a Founding Ideal* (New Haven, CT: Yale University Press, 2003), 80.
86. Randall M. Miller, Harry S. Stout, and Charles Reagan Wilson, "Introduction," in *Religion and the American Civil War*, ed. Randall M. Miller, Harry S. Stout, and Challes Reagan Wilson (New York: Oxford University Press, 1993), 5.
87. James W. Baker, *Thanksgiving: The Biography of an American Holiday* (Durham, NH: University Press of New England, 2009), 70.
88. Harry S. Stout, *Upon the Altar of the Nation: A Moral History of the American Civil War* (New York: Viking, 2006); Terrie Dopp Aamodt, *Righteous Armies, Holy Cause: Apocalyptic Imagery and the Civil War* (Macon, GA: Mercer University Press, 2002).

89. Philip Smith, *Why War?: The Cultural Logic of Iraq, the Gulf War, and Suez* (Chicago: University of Chicago Press, 2005).

90. Rogers M. Smith and NetLibrary Inc., *Civic Ideals: Conflicting Visions of Citizenship in U.S. History*, (New Haven, CT: Yale University Press, 1997), 286ff.

91. Eric Foner, *A Short History of Reconstruction, 1863–1877* (New York: Harper & Row, 1990); James M. McPherson, *The Struggle for Equality: Abolitionists and the Negro in the Civil War and Reconstruction* (Princeton, NJ: Princeton University Press, 1964).

92. Charles Reagan Wilson, "The Religion of the Lost Cause: Ritual and Organization of the Southern Civil Religion, 1865–1920," *Journal of Southern History* 46, no. 2 (1980); idem, *Baptized in Blood: The Religion of the Lost Cause, 1865–1920* (Athens, GA: University of Georgia Press, 1983); Gary W. Gallagher, *Jubal A. Early, the Lost Cause, and Civil War History: A Persistent Legacy*, Frank L. Klement Lectures 4 (Milwaukee, WI: Marquette University Press, 1995).

93. Geneviève Zubrzycki, *The Crosses of Auschwitz: Nationalism and Religion in Post-Communist Poland* (Chicago: University of Chicago Press, 2006); Michael Sells, *The Bridge Betrayed: Religion and Genocide in Bosnia* (Berkeley and Los Angeles: University of California Press, 1998).

94. Amy Louise Wood, *Lynching and Spectacle: Witnessing Racial Violence in America, 1890–1940* (Chapel Hill: University of North Carolina Press, 2011); James H. Cone, *The Cross and the Lynching Tree* (Maryknoll, NY: Orbis Books, 2011).

95. In Roger Friedland's apt summary: "Religious nationalist movements are patriarchal masculinist projects. . . . These movements struggle to defend and purify the collectivity, to re-form and defend both individual and collective bodies, human and political nation-states. [They] arise under conditions of actual or threatened penetration by alien powers, both military and cultural, territorial and symbolic, in reaction to the dual threat of subordination and section." Roger Friedland, "The Institutional Logic of Religious Nationalism: Sex, Violence and the Ends of History," *Politics, Religion & Ideology* 12, no. 1 (2011): 18.

96. David W. Blight, *Race and Reunion: The Civil War in American Memory* (Cambridge, MA: Belknap Press of Harvard University Press, 2001); Blum, *Reforging the White Republic*.

97. This locution is borrowed from Pierre Bourdieu, "Social Space and Symbolic Power," *Sociological Theory* 7, no. 1 (1989).

98. The best treatment remains Clarence Henley Cramer, *Royal Bob: The Life of Robert G. Ingersoll* (Indianapolis: Bobbs-Merrill, 1952). See also Susan Jacoby, *The Great Agnostic: Robert Ingersoll and American Freethought* (New Haven, CT: Yale University Press, 2013).

99. Whitney R. Cross, *The Burned-over District: The Social and Intellectual History of Enthusiastic Religion in Western New York, 1800–1850* (Ithaca, NY: Cornell University Press 1950); Michael Barkun, *Crucible of the Millennium: The Burned-over District of New York in the 1840s* (Syracuse, NY: Syracuse University Press, 1986).

100. Cramer, *Royal Bob*, 19.

101. On Ingersoll's reading habits, see ibid., 27–28.

102. "The Great Infidels," in Robert G. Ingersoll, *The Works of Robert G. Ingersoll*, 12 vols. (Dresden, NY: Dresden Publishing Company, 1912), vol. 3.

103. Cramer, *Royal Bob*, 100.

104. Molyneux first used this term in a letter to John Locke contending that the tenets of Christianity were acceptable only insofar as they were in accord with natural reason. "Mr. Molyneux to Mr. Locke," April 6, 1697, in John Locke, *Works of John Locke*, 12th ed., 9 vols. (London: C. and J. Rivington, 1824), vol. 8.

105. "My Belief and Unbelief," in Ingersoll, *Works of Robert G. Ingersoll*, vol. 8.

106. "Individuality," in Robert Green Ingersoll, *The Gods and Other Lectures* (Peoria, IL: C. P. Farrell, 1889).

107. Thomas Henry Huxley, *Collected Essays* (New York: Macmillan, 1893), 1:195.

108. "Should Infidels Send Their Children to Sunday School?," in Ingersoll, *Works of Robert G. Ingersoll*, vol. 11.

109. On British secularism, see Edward Royle, *Radicals, Secularists, and Republicans: Popular Freethought in Britain, 1866–1915* (Manchester: Manchester University Press, 1980). On American secularism, see James Turner, *Without God, Without Creed: The Origins of Unbelief in America* (Baltimore: Johns Hopkins University Press, 1985).

110. Ingersoll, *Gods and Other Lectures*.

111. More precisely, they contain no mentions of Smith or Mill and only two of Locke, both of which are to Locke's epistemology, rather than his political philosophy.

112. Based on a search for "liberal" in an electronic version of his works.

113. On this, see Hamburger, *Separation of Church and State*, 193–268.

114. Harry Houdini Collection, *The Truth Seeker Collection of Forms, Hymns, and Recitations: Original and Selected* (New York: D. M. Bennett, Liberal and Scientific Publishing House, 1877), 19–21.

115. Sumner has been the subject of several biographies, none of them entirely satisfactory. See Bruce Curtis, *William Graham Sumner*, Twayne's United States Authors Series (Boston: Twayne, 1981); Harris E. Starr, *William Graham Sumner* (New York: H. Holt and Company, 1925); John K. Dickinson, "William Graham Sumner, 1840–1910: Eine Biographische Und Theoretische Untersuchung Zur Frühen Amerikanischen Soziologie" (inaugural diss., Phillips-Universität, 1963). See also Sumner's own "Autobiography" in William Graham Sumner, *Essays* (New Haven, CT: Yale University Press, 1913), 3–8. The best short introduction to his views is still Robert Green McCloskey, *American Conservatism in the Age of Enterprise: 1865–1910: A Study of William Graham Sumner, Stephen J. Field and Andrew Carnegie* (Cambridge, MA: Harvard University Press, 1951).

116. "'Sumnerology'—the Social Philosophy of Prof. W. G. Sumner," *New York Times*, April 17, 1910.

117. The label was first affixed to him in Richard Hofstadter, "William Graham Sumner, Social Darwinist," *New England Quarterly* 14, no. 3 (1941).

118. Robert Bannister, *Social Darwinism: Science and Myth in Anglo-American Social Thought* (Philadelphia: Temple University Press, 2010), chapter 5.

119. William Graham Sumner, *What Social Classes Owe to Each Other* (New York: Harper & Brothers, 1883).

120. For Sumner's views on this subject, see especially his series of essays on liberty in Sumner, *Essays*.

121. See "On State Interference" in Sumner, *War, and Other Essays* (New Haven, CT: Yale University Press, 1919).

122. See "Earth Hunger" in ibid.

123. See especially the title essay in William Graham Sumner, *The Forgotten Man, and Other Essays*, ed. Albert Galloway Keller (New Haven, CT: Yale University Press, 1918).

124. Sumner, *War, and Other Essays*, 129–228.

125. "Republican Government," in William Graham Sumner *On Liberty, Society, and Politics: The Essential Essays of William Graham Sumner*, ed. Robert C. Bannister (Indianapolis, IN: Liberty Foundation, 1992), 81. On "democratic republicanism," see also "Social War in Democracy" in Sumner, *Essays*.

126. See "Discipline" in Sumner, *On Liberty, Society, and Politics*.

127. For Sumner's use of "corruption," see "The Conflict of Plutocracy and Democracy" in Sumner, *Essays*.

128. See "Introduction" in Sumner, *What Social Classes Owe*.

129. See "Separation of State and Market" in Sumner, *Essays*.

130. Michael O'Brien, "The American Experience of Secularisation," in *Religion and the Political Imagination*, ed. Ira Katznelson and Gareth Stedman Jones (New York: Cambridge University Press, 2010), 148.

131. See "The Scientific Attitude of Mind" in Sumner, *Essays*.

132. On Sumner and Carnegie, see Patrick Allitt, *The Conservatives: Ideas and Personalities Throughout American History* (New Haven, CT: Yale University Press, 2009), chapter 5.

133. Christian Smith, *The Secular Revolution: Power, Interests, and Conflict in the Secularization of American Public Life* (Berkeley: University of California Press, 2003).

CHAPTER 5. THE PROGRESSIVE ERA:
EMPIRE AND THE REPUBLIC

1. Richard Franklin Bensel, *Yankee Leviathan: The Origins of Central State Authority in America, 1859–1877* (Cambridge and New York: Cambridge University Press, 1990); Stephen Skowronek, *Building a New American State: The Expansion of National Administrative Capacities, 1877–1920* (Cambridge and New York: Cambridge University Press, 1982); Theda Skocpol, *Protecting Soldiers and Mothers: The Political Origins of Social Policy in the United States* (Cambridge, MA: Belknap Press of Harvard University Press, 1992).

2. Julian Go, *American Empire and the Politics of Meaning: Elite Political Cultures in the Philippines and Puerto Rico During U.S. Colonialism*, Politics, History, and Culture (Durham, NC: Duke University Press, 2008).

3. Woodrow Wilson, *The New Freedom: A Call for the Emancipation of the Generous Energies of a People* (Garden City, NY: Doubleday, Page & Company, 1913), 3.

4. John Patrick Diggins, "Republicanism and Progressivism," *American Quarterly* 37, no. 4 (1985): 575.

5. According to this doctrine, some were destined to damnation and others to salvation by an eternal—and arbitrary—decree that antedated Creation itself. While there might be earthly signs of one's eternal status, that status could not be altered by good works or even by religious faith.

6. Robert B. Westbrook, *John Dewey and American Democracy* (Ithaca, NY: Cornell University Press, 1991), 15.

7. Over the years, a number of scholars have noticed the influence of ancient philosophy on Dewey's thinking. See Frederick M. Anderson, "Dewey's Experiment with Greek Philosophy," *Internatioal Philosophical Quarterly* 7, no. 1 (1967); John P. Anton, "John Dewey and Ancient Philosophies," *Philosophy and Phenomenological Research* 25, no. 4 (1965); J. J. Chambliss, *Educational Theory as Theory of Conduct: From Aristotle to Dewey* (Albany: State University of New York Press, 1987); idem, "Common Ground in Aristotle," *Educational Theory* 43, no. 3 (1993); idem, *The Influence of Plato and Aristotle on John Dewey's Philosophy*, Mellen Studies in Education 10 (Lewiston, NY: E. Mellen Press, 1990); Nicholas Pagan, "Configuring the Moral Self: Aristotle and Dewey," *Foundations of Science* 13, no. 3/4 (2008); John H. Randall, "Dewey's Interpretation of the Philosophy of History," in *The Philosophy of John Dewey*, ed. Paul Arthur Schilpp and Lewis Edwin Hahn (LaSalle, IL: Open Court, 1939); John Herman Randall, *Aristotle* (New York: Columbia University Press, 1960); Melvin L. Rogers, *The Undiscovered Dewey: Religion, Morality, and the Ethos of Democracy* (New York: Columbia University Press, 2012).

8. Anton, "John Dewey and Ancient Philosophies," 484.

9. Dewey's early philosophical works contain copious (if sometimes rather ill-informed) references to Plato and Aristotle. For example, see his puzzling claim that "Aristotle completely severs ethics from politics." John Dewey, *The Early Works, 1882–1898* (Carbondale: Southern Illinois University Press, 1967), 4:138.

10. In an 1897 essay on pedagogy, for instance, Dewey argued that the ultimate aim of education must be "the formation of a certain character as the only genuine basis of right living." The true purpose of the public school is civic, he argued; it lies in "forming habits of positive service." Ibid., 5:94.

11. Idem, *The Middle Works, 1899–1924*, 15 vols. (Carbondale: Southern Illinois University Press, 1976), 4:273.

12. Ibid..

13. John Dewey and Jo Ann Boydston, *The Later Works, 1925–1953*, 17 vols. (Carbondale and London: Southern Illinois University Press and Feffer & Simons, 1981), 2:243.

14. Ibid., 12:26. As we will see in the concluding chapter, Dewey's view of democratic community was therefore very close to that of contemporary "liberal nationalists."

15. Ibid., 3:99.

16. Ibid., 3:111.

17. Steven C. Rockefeller, *John Dewey, Religious Faith and Democratic Humanism* (New York: Columbia University Press, 1991).

18. Dewey and Boydston, *Later Works*, 1:47.

19. Ibid., 9:3.

20. Ibid., 9:6, 4:36.

21. Ibid., 9:18.

22. Ibid., 9:14, 294.

23. Ibid., 9:20.

24. Rockefeller, *John Dewey, Religious Faith and Democratic Humanism*, 193.

25. The scholarly biographies include Jean Bethke Elshtain, *Jane Addams and the Dream of American Democracy: A Life* (New York: Basic Books, 2002); Louise W. Knight, *Citizen: Jane Addams and the Struggle for Democracy* (Chicago: University of Chicago Press, 2005); *Jane Addams: Spirit in Action* (New York: W. W. Norton, 2010); Jane

Addams, *Twenty Years at Hull-House, with Autobiographical Notes* (New York: Macmillan Co., 1910).

26. Elshtain, *Jane Addams and the Dream*; Jonathan M. Hansen, *The Lost Promise of Patriotism: Debating American Identity, 1890–1920* (Chicago: University of Chicago Press, 2003).

27. Rivka Shpak Lissak, *Pluralism and Progressives: Hull House and the New Immigrants, 1890–1919* (Chicago: University of Chicago Press, 1989).

28. Jane Addams, *Democracy and Social Ethics*, John Harvard Library (Cambridge, MA: Belknap Press of Harvard University Press, 1964), 16.

29. Ibid., 20.

30. Jean Bethke Elshtain, *The Jane Addams Reader* (New York: Basic Books, 2002), 118.

31. Pullman, Illinois, was a company town located on the South Side of Chicago, and its denizens were all employees of the Pullman Palace Car Company, whose works were nearby. The owner of the company, George Pullman (1831–1897), had built it as a private social experiment. The moral life of the town was strictly regulated—there was no alcohol or dancing allowed, for instance—and residents were watched over by company spies, whether in the service of God or mammon it was not clear. The Panic of 1893 and the recession that followed took a deep bite out of Pullman's profits. In an effort to cut costs, he slashed wages and raised rents, pushing many Pullmanites to the brink of starvation. The subsequent strike at the Pullman works escalated into a nationwide railway strike led by Eugene V. Debs, the head of the American Railway Union. Grover Cleveland eventually sided with Pullman and sent in the National Guard, but the strike was not broken until the fall of 1894, when Debs was arrested on trumped-up charges and sent to prison for six months.

32. Elshtain, *Jane Addams Reader*, 166.

33. Ibid., 167.

34. Ibid., 173.

35. Ibid., 174.

36. Addams, *Democracy and Social Ethics*, 222.

37. Ibid., 175.

38. Ibid., 159, 6.

39. Victoria Brown, *The Education of Jane Addams*, Politics and Culture in Modern America (Philadelphia: University of Pennsylvania Press, 2004).

40. David L. Lewis, *W.E.B. Dubois—Biography of a Race, 1868–1919* (New York: H. Holt, 1993).

41. Edward J. Blum, *W.E.B. Du Bois: American Prophet*, Politics and Culture in Modern America (Philadelphia: University of Pennsylvania Press, 2007); Jonathon Samuel Kahn, *Divine Discontent: The Religious Imagination of W.E.B. Du Bois* (Oxford and New York: Oxford University Press, 2009).

42. W.E.B. Du Bois and Herbert Aptheker, *The Correspondence of W.E.B. Du Bois* (Amherst: University of Massachusetts Press, 1973), 3:223.

43. Booker T. Washington and W.E.B. Du Bois, *The Negro in the South, His Economic Progress in Relation to His Moral and Religious Development Being* (Philadelphia: G. W. Jacobs & Company, 1907); W.E.B. Du Bois, *The Suppression of the African Slave-Trade to the United States of America, 1638–1870*, Harvard Historical Studies 1 (New York and London: Longmans, Green and Co., 1896); idem, *The Philadelphia Negro: A Social Study* (Boston: Ginn & Co., 1899); idem, *The Negro Church; Report of a Social Study Made under the Direction of Atlanta University; Together with the Proceedings of the*

Eighth Conference for the Study of Negro Problems, Held at Atlanta University, May 26th, 1903, Atlanta University Publications (Atlanta: Atlanta University Press, 1903); idem, *Black Reconstruction: An Essay Toward a History of the Part Which Black Folk Played in the Attempt to Reconstruct Democracy in America, 1860–1880* (New York: Harcourt, Brace and Co., 1935).

44. W.E.B. Du Bois, *The Souls of Black Folk: Essays and Sketches* (Chicago: A. C. McClurg & Co., 1903), 262, http://www.aspresolver.com/aspresolver.asp?BLTC;S7884.

45. Ibid., 263.

46. Ibid.

47. Ibid., 263.

48. Idem, *The Gift of Black Folk: The Negroes in the Making of America* (Boston: Stratford Co., 1924), 13, http://www.aspresolver.com/aspresolver.asp?BLTC;S7881.

49. Ibid., 57.

50. Ibid.

51. Ibid., 116.

52. Ibid., 159.

53. Lawrence A. Scaff, *Max Weber in America* (Princeton, NJ: Princeton University Press, 2011), 98–116, 81–82.

54. Du Bois, *Gift of Black Folk*, 13, 26.

55. Ibid., 27.

56. Blum, *W.E.B. Du Bois*, 80–81.

57. W.E.B. Du Bois, *Darkwater Voices from Within the Veil* (New York: Harcourt, Brace and Howe, 1920), vii, http://www.aspresolver.com/aspresolver.asp?BLTC;S7888.

58. Exodus 30:7.

59. Exodus 34:29.

60. 2 Corinthians 4:3.

61. W.E.B. Du Bois and David L. Lewis, *W.E.B. Du Bois: A Reader* (New York: Henry Holt and Company, 1995), 105.

62. Washington and Du Bois, *Negro in the South*, 174.

63. Ibid., 186.

64. Du Bois, *Gift of Black Folk*, 337.

65. Ibid., 338.

66. Kahn, *Divine Discontent*, 5.

67. Ibid., 107.

68. Edward J. Blum, "'There Won't Be Any Rich People in Heaven': The Black Christ, White Hypocrisy, and the Gospel According to W.E.B. Du Bois," *Journal of African American History* 90, no. 4 (2005).

69. Stephen R. Prothero, *American Jesus: How the Son of God Became a National Icon* (New York: Farrar, Straus and Giroux, 2003), 87–90.

70. Charles M. Sheldon, *In His Steps: "What Would Jesus Do?"* (Chicago: Advance, 1897).

71. W.E.B. Du Bois and Phil Zuckerman, *Du Bois on Religion* (Walnut Creek, CA: AltaMira Press, 2000), 99.

72. Du Bois and Lewis, *W.E.B. Du Bois: A Reader*, 497.

73. Du Bois and Zuckerman, *Du Bois on Religion*, 184.

74. James H. Cone, *A Black Theology of Liberation*, C. Eric Lincoln Series in Black Religion (Philadelphia: Lippincott, 1970); idem, *Risks of Faith: The Emergence of a Black Theology of Liberation, 1968–1998* (Boston: Beacon Press, 1999).

75. S. P. Fullinwider, *The Mind and Mood of Black America: 20th Century Thought*, Dorsey Series in American History (Homewood, IL: Dorsey Press, 1969).

76. Richard Wightman Fox, *Reinhold Niebuhr: A Biography* (New York: Pantheon Books, 1985), 28.

77. Reinhold Niebuhr, *The Nature and Destiny of Man: A Christian Interpretation*, Gifford Lectures (New York: Charles Scribner's Sons, 1948), 2:200–3.

78. Ibid., 1:179–181.

79. The Pelagians, for example, believed that human beings could and should aspire to moral perfection in this life, while the Gnostics insisted that Christians could attain something like perfect knowledge.

80. "Man loves himself inordinately," Niebuhr observed. "Since his determinate existence does not deserve the devotion lavished upon it, it is obviously necessary to practice some deception. . . . [I]ts primary purpose is to deceive, not others, but the self." Niebuhr, *Nature and Destiny of Man*, 1:203.

81. Idem, *Moral Man and Immoral Society: A Study in Ethics and Politics* (New York and London: C. Scribner's, 1932), 96–97.

82. Ibid., 93.

83. Idem, *Children of Light and the Children of Darkness: A Vindication of Democracy and a Critique of Its Traditional Defence* (New York: Charles Scribner's Sons, 1944), 82.

84. Idem, *Nature and Destiny of Man*, 2:111.

85. Reinhold Niebuhr and D. B. Robertson, *Love and Justice: Selections from the Shorter Writings of Reinhold Niebuhr* (Gloucester, MA: P. Smith, 1976), 59.

86. Quoted in Reinhold Niebuhr, *The Irony of American History* (New York: Scribner, 1952), 21.

87. Niebuhr, *Moral Man and Immoral Society*, 11.

88. Idem, *Irony of American History*, 24.

89. Ibid., 52, 70.

90. Ibid., 50–51.

91. Idem, *Nature and Destiny of Man*, 2:23; Amos 1:3–5, 13–15; 2:1–3.

92. Amos 5:19.

93. Amos 5:18–19.

94. Amos 5:21–2.

95. Amos 5:23–24.

96. Matthew 3:9.

97. Niebuhr, *Irony of American History*, 171–172.

98. Idem, *Moral Man and Immoral Society*, xv–xvi.

99. Idem, *An Interpretation of Christian Ethics* (New York: Harper & Brothers, 1935), 8.

100. Ibid., 19.

101. Reinhold Niebuhr and Robert McAfee Brown, *The Essential Reinhold Niebuhr: Selected Essays and Addresses* (New Haven, CT: Yale University Press, 1986), 109.

102. J. Lears, "The Sophomore," *New Republic* 228, no. 3 (2003).

103. Jerry Coyne, "H. L. Mencken: The First New Atheist," in *Why Evolution Is True*, May 19, 2012, https://whyevolutionistrue.wordpress.com/2012/05/19/h-l-mencken-the-first-new-atheist/.

104. Terry Teachout, *The Skeptic: A Life of H. L. Mencken* (New York: HarperCollins, 2003).

105. Ibid., 82.

106. Henry L. Mencken, "The Mailed Fist and Its Prophet," *Atlantic Monthly* 114 (1914), 602.

107. Ibid., 603.

108. Ibid.

109. Ibid., 607.

110. Henry Louis Mencken, *Notes on Democracy* (New York: Random House, 2013), 164–165.

111. Ibid., 220, 351.

112. Idem, *Minority Report* (Baltimore: Johns Hopkins University Press, 2006), sect. 379.

113. Ibid., sect. 321.

114. H.L. Mencken, "Hitlerismus," *American Mercury* (December 1933).

115. For an unsparing critique, see Lears, "Sophomore."

116. H. L. Mencken, "Bryan," *Baltimore Evening Sun*, July 27, 1925.

117. Nicholas Wolterstorff, *Justice: Rights and Wrongs* (Princeton, NJ: Princeton University Press, 2010).

118. On the proceedings, see United Confederate Veterans, *Minutes UCV* (New Orleans: United Confederate Veterans, 1909).

119. For McKim's biography, see Randolph Harrison McKim, *A Soldier's Recollections: Leaves from the Diary of a Young Confederate, with an Oration on the Motives and Aims of the Soldiers of the South* (New York: Longmans, Green, and Company, 1910); "Randolph Harris Mckim (1842–1920)," in *Encyclopedia of Virginia Biography*, ed. Lyon Gardiner Tylor (New York: Lewis Historical Pub. Co., 1915).

120. Randolph Harrison McKim, *The Numerical Strength of the Confederate Army: An Examination of the Argument of the Hon. Charles Francis Adams and Others* (New York: Neale Publishing Company, 1912); idem, *Problem of the Pentateuch: An Examination of the Higher Criticism* (New York: Longmans, Green, 1906).

121. Idem, *The Motives and Aims of the Soldiers of the South in the Civil War* (New Orleans: United Confederate Veterans, 1904), 21:4.

122. Ibid., 28.

123. Ibid., 32.

124. Ibid., 33.

125. On this point, see especially Wilson, *Baptized in Blood*; Gaines M. Foster, *Ghosts of the Confederacy: Defeat, the Lost Cause, and the Emergence of the New South, 1865 to 1913* (New York: Oxford University Press, 1987).

126. Randolph H. McKim, *For God and Country, or the Christian Pulpit in War* (New York: E. P. Dutton & Company, 1918), 4.

127. Ibid., 6.

128. Based on a rather tortured reading of Jesus's reaction to the Roman soldiers who arrested him, as recounted in John 18:36. See ibid., 3.

129. Ibid., 9.

130. In Ephesians 6:11. See ibid., 5.

131. Ibid., 8.

132. Ibid., 116, 24, 27, 33.

133. The rally is described in "Sister Mcpherson Guest of Associated Churches," *Bridal Call-Crusader Foursquare*, November 7, 1934. It also forms the opening scene for

Matthew Avery Sutton, *Aimee Semple McPherson and the Resurrection of Christian America* (Cambridge, MA: Harvard University Press, 2009).

134. A sketch of the fifth scene may be found on the cover of the November 7, 1934, issue of *Bridal Call- Crusader Foursquare.*

135. She was hardly the only one to do so. Many Europeans adopted an apocalyptic framing of the Great War as well. See Philip Jenkins, *The Great and Holy War: How World War I Became a Religious Crusade* (New York: HarperOne, 2014).

136. "Modern Warfare—'Over the Top'" in Aimee Semple McPherson, *This Is That* (Los Angeles: Bridal Call Publishing House, 1919), 353.

137. Ibid., 345.

138. Specifically, the lens of "premillennial dispensationalism," a version of premillennial apocalypticism that had become increasingly popular among Anglophone Protestants since the mid-nineteenth century. This view differed from earlier versions of premillennial apocalypticism insofar as it divided history into various stages, or "dispensations." For McPherson's views, see her *The Second Coming of Christ* (Los Angeles: n.p., 1921). On the decline of postmillennialism, see James H. Moorhead, "The Erosion of Postmillennialism in American Religious Thought, 1865–1925," *Church History: Studies in Christianity and Culture* 53, no. 1 (1984); idem, *World Without End: Mainstream American Protestant Visions of the Last Things, 1880–1925* (Bloomington: Indiana University Press, 1999). On the rise of premillennialism, see Richard G. Kyle, *Apocalyptic Fever: End-Time Prophecies in Modern America* (Eugene, OR: Wipf and Stock Publishers, 2012); Clyde Norman Kraus, *Dispensationalism in America: Its Rise and Development* (Louisville, KY: John Knox Press, 1958).

139. However, I have not found any indication that she believed in a pretribulation Rapture, as most premillennial dispensationalists now do.

140. PDFs of the *Bridal Call* can be easily searched and accessed online at pentecostalarchives.com.

141. Grant Wacker, *Heaven Below: Early Pentecostals and American Culture* (Cambridge, MA: Harvard University Press, 2009).

142. Leo P. Ribuffo, *The Old Christian Right: The Protestant Far Right from the Great Depression to the Cold War* (Philadelphia: Temple University Press, 1983).

143. Thomas R. Pegram, *One Hundred Percent American: The Rebirth and Decline of the Ku Klux Klan in the 1920s* (Lanham, MD: Rowman & Littlefield, 2011).

144. Lisa McGirr, *Suburban Warriors: The Origins of the New American Right* (Princeton, NJ: Princeton University Press, 2002); David Mark Chalmers, *Hooded Americanism: The History of the Ku Klux Klan* (Durham, NC: Duke University Press, 1981).

145. The word "equality" does not appear a single time in the wartime sermons collected in McKim, *For God and Country.*

146. On this, see especially Walter A. McDougall, *Promised Land, Crusader State: The American Encounter with the World since 1776* (Boston: Houghton Mifflin Harcourt, 1997).

147. The seminal treatment remains James Davison Hunter, *Culture Wars: The Struggle to Define America* (New York: Basic Books, 1991). For a fuller treatment of the fundamentalist/modernist controversy, see George M. Marsden, *Fundamentalism and American Culture*, 2nd ed. (Oxford and New York: Oxford University Press, 2006).

CHAPTER 6. THE POST–WORLD WAR II PERIOD:
JEW, PROTESTANT, CATHOLIC

1. Hannah Arendt, *The Human Condition* (Chicago: University of Chicago Press, 2013).
2. Idem, *Between Past and Future: Eight Exercises in Political Thought* (New York: Penguin, 1968), 3–4.
3. Idem, *On Revolution* (New York: Penguin, 1965), 24.
4. Ibid., 118.
5. Ibid., 110.
6. Ibid., 227.
7. Ibid., 124.
8. Ibid., 142.
9. Most famously, Tom Hayden, "The Port Huron Statement," in *The New Radicals: A Report with Documents* (New York: Random House, 1962), 138.
10. Ibid., 204.
11. Hannah Arendt, *Crises of the Republic: Lying in Politics; Civil Disobedience; on Violence; Thoughts on Politics and Revolution* (Boston: Houghton Mifflin Harcourt, 1972), 212.
12. Carl Schmitt, *Political Theology: Four Chapters on the Concept of Sovereignty* (Chicago: University of Chicago Press, 2005).
13. Arendt, *Human Condition*, 238.
14. Luke 17:3.
15. Arendt, *Human Condition*, 237.
16. Ibid., 244.
17. Ibid.
18. Charles T. Mathewes, *Evil and the Augustinian Tradition* (Cambridge and New York: Cambridge University Press, 2001); Eric Gregory, *Politics and the Order of Love: An Augustinian Ethic of Democratic Citizenship* (Chicago: University of Chicago Press, 2008).
19. Max Weber, P. R. Baehr, and Gordon C. Wells, *The Protestant Ethic and the "Spirit" of Capitalism and Other Writings*, Penguin Twentieth-Century Classics (New York: Penguin Books, 2002).
20. Gregory, *Politics and the Order of Love*, 201.
21. George Kateb, "Freedom and Worldliness in the Thought of Hannah Arendt," *Political Theory* 5, no. 2 (1977): 164.
22. Eric J. Sundquist, *King's Dream* (New Haven, CT: Yale University Press, 2009). Nor is King's legacy confined to the United States. On the contrary, few Americans are more widely known and admired throughout the world. His speeches and writings are familiar to South Africans, Poles, Chinese, and Egyptians, among others. Inspired by Gandhi, King's tactic of nonviolent resistance was successfully deployed in Johannesburg and Gdansk, though unsuccessfully in Beijing and Cairo.
23. Shelby Steele, *The Content of Our Character* (New York: St. Martin's Press, 1990).
24. In doing so, they ignore King's demands that the federal government undertake a massive program of economic redistribution to redress the ongoing effects of slavery and Jim Crow on the black community.

25. For example, see Vincent Harding, *Martin Luther King, the Inconvenient Hero* (Mary-knoll, NY: Orbis Books, 2008). On the social views of the radical King, see Thomas F. Jackson, *From Civil Rights to Human Rights: Martin Luther King, Jr., and the Struggle for Economic Justice* (Philadelphia: University of Pennsylvania Press, 2011).

26. On this point, see especially David L. Chappell, *A Stone of Hope: Prophetic Religion and the Death of Jim Crow* (Chapel Hill: University of North Carolina Press, 2004). Of course, some conservative evangelicals also question King's faith on the grounds that he was not an "orthodox" Christian. Whether King was in fact "orthodox" in this sense is another matter.

27. Sam Harris, *The End of Faith: Religion, Terror, and the Future of Reason* (New York: W. W. Norton & Co., 2004); Christopher Hitchens, *God Is Not Great: How Religion Poisons Everything* (New York: 12/Warner Books, 2007).

28. Martin Luther King, Ralph Luker, and Penny A. Russell, *The Papers of Martin Luther King, Jr.: Advocate of the Social Gospel*, vol. 6, *September 1948–March 1963* (Berkeley: University of California Press, 2007), 534.

29. On King's relationship to Carmichael and Malcolm X, see James H. Cone, *Martin and Malcolm and America: A Dream or a Nightmare* (Maryknoll, NY: Orbis Books, 1992); Peniel E. Joseph, *Waiting'til the Midnight Hour: A Narrative History of Black Power in America* (New York: Macmillan, 2007).

30. Clayborne Carson and Kris Shepard, *A Call to Conscience: The Landmark Speeches of Dr. Martin Luther King, Jr.* (New York: Hachette Digital, 2001), 219.

31. Sundquist, *King's Dream.*

32. Wendy Wall, *Inventing the"American Way": The Politics of Consensus from the New Deal to the Civil Rights Movement* (New York: Oxford University Press, 2008); Lizabeth Cohen, *A Consumers' Republic: The Politics of Mass Consumption in Postwar America* (New York: Random House, 2004).

33. Kenneth L. Smith and Ira G. Zepp, *Search for the Beloved Community: The Thinking of Martin Luther King, Jr.* (Valley Forge, PA: Judson Press, 1998), 91.

34. Clayborne Carson and Peter Holloran, *A Knock at Midnight: Inspiration from the Great Sermons of Reverend Martin Luther King, Jr.* (New York: Hachette Digital, 2001), 92.

35. Martin Luther King Jr., *The Trumpet of Conscience* (Boston: Beacon Press, 2010), 70.

36. Idem, *A Gift of Love* (Boston: Beacon, 2012), 152.

37. Idem, *Where Do We Go from Here: Chaos or Community?* (Boston: Beacon Press, 2010), 96.

38. Adam Fairclough, *To Redeem the Soul of America: The Southern Christian Leadership Conference and Martin Luther King, Jr.* (Athens: University of Georgia Press, 2001).

39. King, *Where Do We Go from Here*, 60.

40. Ibid., 58.

41. Smith and Zepp, *Search for the Beloved Community*, 71.

42. Quoted in ibid., 83.

43. King, *Where Do We Go from Here*, 38.

44. Idem, *Strength to Love* (Minneapolis, MN: Fortress Press, 1977), 48–49.

45. Martin Luther King and James Melvin Washington, *A Testament of Hope: The Essential Writings of Martin Luther King* (San Francisco: Harper, 1986), 19.

46. Ibid., 20.

47. King, *Where Do We Go from Here*, 106.

48. Richard Lischer, *The Preacher King: Martin Luther King, Jr. and the Word That Moved America* (New York: Oxford University Press, 1997), 201.
49. Carson and Shepard, *A Call to Conscience*, 182.
50. Ibid., 22.
51. Carson and Holloran, *A Knock at Midnight*, 88.
52. Gary Younge, *The Speech: The Story Behind Dr. Martin Luther King Jr.'s Dream* (Chicago: Haymarket Books, 2013), 120.
53. Carson and Holloran, *A Knock at Midnight*, 10.
54. Carson and Shepard, *A Call to Conscience*, 39.
55. Ibid., 38–39.
56. Ibid., 32–33.
57. On this point, it is worth noting, King's position was actually somewhat closer to Augustine's and Aquinas's view of evil as "the absence of the good," or the omission of good acts, rather than to Augustine's (and Calvin's and Kant's) understanding of evil as the result of a fundamental "corruption of the will" that resulted in the commission of evil acts. (As we will see later, King did not put much stock in the notion of "will".)
58. Personalist philosophy comes in many varieties: American and French, theistic and nontheistic, idealist and realist. King's version was American, theistic, and idealist. For a brief overview, see Thomas D. Williams and Jan Olof Bengtsson, "Personalism," in Zalta, *Stanford Encyclopedia of Philosophy*.
59. Borden Parker Bowne, *Personalism* (Boston: Houghton, Mifflin, 1908); Edgar Sheffield Brightman, *Is God a Person?* (Boston: Association Publishers, 1932).
60. Carson and Shepard, *A Call to Conscience*, 20.
61. Carson and Holloran, *A Knock at Midnight*, 82.
62. Ibid., 81.
63. King and Washington, *A Testament of Hope*, 122.
64. Ibid.
65. Biographies include Donald E. Pelotte, *John Courtney Murray: Theologian in Conflict* (New York: Paulist Press, 1976). The best overview of Murray's thought is Robert W. McElroy, *The Search for an American Public Theology: The Contribution of John Courtney Murray* (New York: Paulist Press, 1989).
66. The new Christian view was based on a radical distinction between the order of the sacred and the order of the secular: "Two there are, august Emperor, by which this world is ruled on title of original and sovereign right—the consecrated authority of the priesthood and the royal power. In this celebrated sentence of Gelasius I, written to the Byzantine Emperor Anastasius I in 494 A.D., the emphasis laid on the word 'two' bespoke the revolutionary character of the Christian dispensation." John Courtney Murray, *We Hold These Truths: Catholic Reflections on the American Proposition*, Sheed & Ward Classic (Lanham, MD: Rowman & Littlefield, 2005), 187.
67. Ibid., 188.
68. Ibid., 155.
69. The fullest discussion of *ressourcement* and tradition may be found in the third volume of Paul Ricoeur, *Time and Narrative*, 3 vols. (Chicago: University of Chicago Press, 1984).
70. Murray, *We Hold These Truths*, 274.
71. Ibid., 275.
72. Ibid., 280–282.

73. McElroy, *Search for an American Public Theology*.
74. Murray, *We Hold These Truths*, 153.
75. Ibid., 90.
76. Idem, "The Return to Tribalism," *Catholic Mind* 60, no. 6 (1962): 26.
77. Idem, *We Hold These Truths*, 25.
78. Idem, *Bridging the Sacred and the Secular* (Washington, DC: Georgetown University Press, 1996), 147.
79. Idem, *We Hold These Truths*, xv.
80. Will Herberg, *Protestant, Catholic, Jew: An Essay in American Religious Sociology* (Chicago: University of Chicago Press, 1983).
81. Ruby Jo Reeves Kennedy, "Premarital Residential Propinquity and Ethnic Endogamy," *American Journal of Sociology* 48, no. 5 (1943); idem, "Single or Triple Melting-Pot?: Intermarriage in New Haven, 1870–1950," *American Journal of Sociology* 58, no. 1 (1952).
82. Herberg, *Protestant, Catholic, Jew*, 258.
83. Ibid., 257.
84. This episode and its aftereffects are discussed at great length in Kevin M. Schultz, *Tri-Faith America: How Catholics and Jews Held Postwar America to Its Protestant Promise* (New York: Oxford University Press, 2011).
85. Herberg, *Protestant, Catholic, Jew*, 260.
86. Ibid., 263.
87. Ibid., 260.
88. Ibid., 264.
89. Ibid., 263.
90. Karel Dobbelaere, "Towards an Integrated Perspective of the Processes Related to the Descriptive Concept of Secularization," *Sociology of Religion* 60, no. 3 (1999).

CHAPTER 7. FROM REAGAN TO OBAMA: TRADITION CORRUPTED AND (ALMOST) RECOVERED

1. See Rick Perlstein's trilogy: *Before the Storm: Barry Goldwater and the Unmaking of the American Consensus* (New York: Nation Books, 2009); *Nixonland: The Rise of a President and the Fracturing of America* (New York: Simon and Schuster, 2010); *The Invisible Bridge: The Fall of Nixon and the Rise of Reagan* (New York: Simon and Schuster, 2014).
2. Richard Nixon, *Richard Nixon: Speeches, Writings, Documents* (Princeton, NJ: Princeton University Press, 2010), 155.
3. Ibid., 157.
4. John P. Diggins, *Ronald Reagan: Fate, Freedom, and the Making of History* (W. W. Norton & Company, 2007). I am largely persuaded by Diggins's claim that Reagan was an "Emersonian."
5. Ibid., 30.
6. Ibid., 48.
7. Stephen Prothero, *The American Bible—Whose America Is This?: How Our Words Unite, Divide, and Define a Nation* (New York: HarperOne, 2012).
8. Michael Sean Winters, *God's Right Hand: How Jerry Falwell Made God a Republican and Baptized the American Right* (New York: HarperOne, 2012), 158.

9. In his book-length jeremiad *Listen, America!*, for instance, Falwell cites Jeremiah only twice, and then only in relationship to contemporary Israel. Jerry Falwell and Jose G. Simon, *Listen, America!* (Garden City, NY: Doubleday, 1980).

10. Secular humanism? In his 1923 book *Christianity and Liberalism*, the conservative Calvinist theologian Gresham Machen had argued that liberalism was actually a form of religion—a non-Christian one. This argument would be reprised a half century later by Francis Schaeffer, another conservative Calvinist, whose *Christian Manifesto* presented the "Humanist Manifesto" of 1933—a document unknown to most contemporary humanists—as a foundational creed, similar in significance to the Westminster Confession or the Communist Manifesto. John Gresham Machen, *Christianity and Liberalism* (Grand Rapids, MI: Wm. B. Eerdmans Publishing, 2009); Francis August Schaeffer, *A Christian Manifesto* (Wheaton, IL: Crossway Books, 1982).

11. W. Cleon Skousen, *The 5,000 Year Leap: A Miracle That Changed the World* (Franklin, TN: C&J Investments, 2011).

12. George H. W. Bush, *Speaking of Freedom: The Collected Speeches* (New York: Simon and Schuster, 2009), 13.

13. Ibid., 237, 41.

14. Ibid., 18.

15. Ibid., 13, 33, 218, 32.

16. Ibid., 171–174.

17. George W. Bush, "Third Presidential State of the Union Address," in *American Rhetoric: Online Speech Bank*, http://www.americanrhetoric.com/speeches/stateoftheunion2004.htm.

18. Idem, "Speech to National Religious Broadcasters 2008 Convention," Gaylord Opryland Resort and Convention Center, Nashville, Tennessee, March 11, 2008. By contrast, the terrorists were serving Satan's purposes: "These murderers were not instruments of a heavenly power; they were instruments of evil."

19. Idem, "State of the Union Address," U.S. Congress, Washington, DC, January 29, 2002.

20. Idem, "Second Inaugural Address," Washington, DC, January 20, 2005.

21. James T. Kloppenberg, *Reading Obama: Dreams, Hope, and the American Political Tradition* (Princeton, NJ: Princeton University Press, 2012).

22. This often happens with youthful expatriates. A missionary's son collects baseball cards in China. His sister obsessively twirls a baton. In Obama's case, the focus was the American intellectual tradition.

23. Barack Obama, "Address to Sojourners/Call to Renewal," Building a Covenant for a New America Conference, Washington, DC, June 26, 2006.

24. Idem, *The Audacity of Hope: Thoughts on Reclaiming the American Dream* (New York: Crown Publishers, 2007), 214.

25. Idem, "Address to Sojourners."

26. Cathleen Falsani, "Obama's Religious Beliefs: An Interview with Barack Obama," in *Want to Know*, http://wanttoknow.info/008/obama_religious_beliefs_views.

27. Barack Obama, "Remarks by the President on Comprehensive Immigration Reform," White House, Washington, DC, July 1, 2010.

28. Idem, "Remarks by the President at the National Prayer Breakfast," Washington, DC, February 3, 2011.

29. David Brooks, "Obama, Gospel and Verse," *New York Times*, April 26, 2007.

30. Barack Obama, "Civil Forum," CNN, August 16, 2008.

31. Idem, "Remarks by the President at the United States Military Academy," West Point, NY, May 22, 2010.

32. Ephesians 4:31.

33. Barack Obama, "Address to the Chicago Council on Foreign Relations," Chicago, October 2, 2007.

34. Barack Obama, "Remarks," Compassion Forum, Messiah College, Mechanicsburg, PA, April 13, 2008.

35. Newt Gingrich, *A Nation Like No Other: Why American Exceptionalism Matters* (Washington, DC: Regnery, 2011); Mitt Romney, *No Apology: The Case for American Greatness* (New York: Macmillan, 2010).

36. Barack Obama, "Remarks by the President at the Acceptance of the Nobel Peace Prize," Oslo City Hall, Oslo, Norway, December 10, 2009.

37. Idem, "Remarks by the President at the Martin Luther King, Jr. Memorial Dedication," Washington, DC, November 16, 2011.

38. Idem, "Civil Forum," CNN, August 17, 2008.

39. Idem, "President's Remarks to the National Prayer Breakfast," Washington, DC, February 4, 2010.

40. Idem, "President's Remarks at the UN," United Nations General Assembly, New York, September 23, 2010.

41. Idem, "Remarks by the President at the National Prayer Breakfast," Washington, DC, February 3, 2011.

42. Idem, "Remarks by the President at a Memorial Service," Missouri Southern University, Joplin, MO, May 29, 2011.

43. Idem, *Audacity of Hope*, 206.

44. Ibid., 55.

45. Ibid., 92.

46. Ibid., 56.

47. Contemporary American liberals tend to be more concerned with questions of personal freedom, and especially with sexual freedom. They want a strong state that can protect these liberties. Their conservative counterparts are generally more obsessed with issues of economic freedom, and especially with government regulation. They want a weak state that is unable to "interfere" with their economic activities.

48. Obama, *Audacity of Hope*, 53–54.

CHAPTER 8. THE CIVIL RELIGION:
CRITICS AND ALLIES

1. Smith, *Bible Made Impossible*, 4–5.

2. Amar, *America's Unwritten Constitution*.

3. John Rawls, *A Theory of Justice* (Cambridge, MA: Belknap Press of Harvard University Press, 1971), 224.

4. Ibid., 525.

5. Idem, *Political Liberalism*, expanded ed., Columbia Classics in Philosophy (New York: Columbia University Press, 2005), 441.

6. Ibid., 453.

7. Martha Nussbaum, "Patriotism and Cosmopolitanism," in Martha Craven Nussbaum and Joshua Cohen, *For Love of Country: Debating the Limits of Patriotism* (Boston: Beacon Press, 1996). Similar views can be found in George Kateb, *Patriotism and Other Mistakes* (New Haven, CT: Yale University Press, 2006); Steven Johnston, *The Truth about Patriotism* (Durham, NC: Duke University Press, 2007).

8. Nussbaum and Cohen, *For Love of Country*, 15.

9. Christopher Lasch, *The Revolt of the Elites and the Betrayal of Democracy* (New York: W. W. Norton & Company, 1996). For a similar argument, see also Christopher Hayes, *Twilight of the Elites: America after Meritocracy* (New York: Random House, 2013).

10. William Easterly and Ian Vásquez, *The Tyranny of Experts: Economists, Dictators, and the Forgotten Rights of the Poor* (New York: Basic Books, 2014).

11. The target of the critique is Maurizio Viroli's theory of "republican patriotism." See Maurizio Viroli, *For Love of Country: An Essay on Patriotism and Nationalism* (Oxford: Oxford University Press, 1997). Kateb, *Patriotism and Other Mistakes*.

12. Kateb, *Patriotism and Other Mistakes*, 7–8.

13. Paul Ricoeur, "Life in Quest of Narrative," in *On Paul Ricoeur: Narrative and Interpretation*, ed. David Wood (New York: Routledge, 1991); idem, "Can Fictional Narratives Be True?," in *The Phenomenology of Man and of the Human Condition*, ed. Anna-Teresa Tymieniecka (Dordrecht, The Netherlands: Springer, 1983). See also Jerome Bruner, "Life as Narrative," *Social Research* 54, no. 1 (1987).

14. See Charles Taylor, *Philosophical Papers*, vol. 1, *Human Agency and Language* (Cambridge and New York: Cambridge University Press, 1985), esp. chaps. 2 and 3. More generally, see idem, *Sources of the Self: The Making of the Modern Identity* (Cambridge, MA: Harvard University Press, 1989).

15. A highly sophisticated and well-elaborated version of this perspective may be found in "dialogical self theory." See, for instance, Hubert J. M. Hermans, "The Dialogical Self: Toward a Theory of Personal and Cultural Positioning," *Culture & Psychology* 7, no. 3 (2001).

16. Ernst Troeltsch, Olive Wyon, and H. Richard Niebuhr, *The Social Teaching of the Christian Churches*, Phoenix ed. (Chicago: University of Chicago Press, 1981); Weber, Baehr, and Wells, *Protestant Ethic and the "Spirit" of Capitalism*.

17. Troeltsch, Wyon, and Niebuhr, *Social Teaching of the Christian Churches*, 1:331.

18. For a critical overview, see especially R. R. Reno, "Stanley Hauerwas," in *The Blackwell Companion to Political Theology*, ed. Peter Scott and William T. Cavanaugh (Oxford: Blackwell, 2004).

19. Stanley Hauerwas, *Against the Nations: War and Survival in a Liberal Society* (Minneapolis, MN: Winston Press, 1985), 126.

20. Ibid., 127.

21. Ibid., 124.

22. Idem, *After Christendom?: How the Church Is to Behave If Freedom, Justice, and a Christian Nation Are Bad Ideas* (Nashville, TN: Abingdon Press, 1991), 70.

23. Ibid., 71.

24. Stanley Hauerwas and William H. Willimon, *Resident Aliens: Life in the Christian Colony* (Nashville, TN: Abingdon Press, 1989).

25. Hauerwas, *Against the Nations*, 130.

26. Ibid., 6.

27. Jeffrey Stout, "The Spirit of Democracy and the Rhetoric of Excess," *Journal of Religious Ethics* 35, no. 1 (2007); Richard John Neuhaus, *The Naked Public Square: Religion and Democracy in America* (Grand Rapids, MI: W. B. Eerdmans Pub. Co., 1984). See also Michael J. Quirk, "Beyond Sectarianism?," *Theology Today* 44, no. 1 (1987).

28. To his credit, Hauerwas would later acknowledge the influence of prophetic religion and civic republicanism on American democracy, if only skeptically and in passing.

29. James M. Gustafson, "The Sectarian Temptation: Reflections on Theology, the Church and the University," *Proceedings of the Catholic Theological Society of America* 40 (2013). See Hauerwas's response in Stanley Hauerwas, "Why the 'Sectarian Temptation'Is a Misrepresentation: A Response to James Gustafson," in *Hauerwas Reader*, ed. John Berkman and Michael Cartwright (Durham, NC: Duke University Press, 2001).

30. Jocelyn Maclure and Charles Taylor, *Secularism and Freedom of Conscience* (Cambridge, MA: Harvard University Press, 2011).

31. Walzer, *Exodus and Revolution*; H. Lehmann, "Pietism and Nationalism: The Relationship Between Protestant Revivalism and National Renewal in Nineteenth-Century Germany," *Church History* 51, no. 1 (1982).

32. Jurgen Habermas, "Notes on Post-Secular Society," *New Perspectives Quarterly* 25, no. 4 (2008).

33. William E. Connolly, *Pluralism* (Durham, NC: Duke University Press, 2005); Antonio Negri, *The Labor of Job: The Biblical Text as a Parable of Human Labor* (Durham, NC: Duke University Press, 2009); Alain Badiou, *Saint Paul: The Foundation of Universalism* (Stanford, CA: Stanford University Press, 1997); Giorgio Agamben, *The Highest Poverty: Monastic Rules and Form-of-Life* (Stanford, CA: Stanford University Press, 2013).

34. Hent De Vries and Lawrence Eugene Sullivan, *Political Theologies: Public Religions in a Post-Secular World* (New York: Fordham University Press, 2006); Hent De Vries, *Philosophy and the Turn to Religion* (Baltimore: Johns Hopkins University Press, 1999).

35. For a history of the concept and an overview of Habermas's use of it, see Jan Werner Müller, *Constitutional Patriotism* (Princeton, NJ: Princeton University Press, 2009).

36. Dolf Sternberger, *Schriften*, vol. 10 (Frankfurt: Inselverlag, 1990).

37. James Knowlton and Truett Cates, *Historikerstreit. Die Dokumentation der Kontroverse um die Einzigartigkeit der Nationalsozialistischen Judenvernichtung* (Munich: Piper, 1987).

38. Jürgen Habermas and Max Pensky, *The Postnational Constellation: Political Essays* (Cambridge, MA: MIT Press, 2001).

39. Jürgen Habermas, "Citizenship and National Identity: Some Reflections on the Future of Europe," *Praxis International* 12, no. 1 (1992).

40. Idem, *Between Facts and Norms*, trans. William Rehg (Cambridge, MA: MIT Press, 1996).

41. Jurgen Habermas, "The Hermeneutic Claim to Universality," in *The Hermeneutic Tradition: From Ast to Ricoeur*, ed. Gayle L. Ormiston and Aland D. Schrift (Albany, NY: SUNY Press, 1990). Critical reviews of the debates can be found in Ingrid H. Scheibler, *Gadamer: Between Heidegger and Habermas* (Lanham, MD: Rowman & Littlefield Publishers, 2000); Warnke, *Gadamer*, 1.

42. Paul Ricoeur, "Ethics and Culture: Habermas and Gadamer in Dialogue," *Philosophy Today* 17, no. 2 (1973).

43. For example, on German social policy, see Kees Van Kersbergen, *Social Capitalism: A Study of Christian Democracy and the Welfare State* (London and New York: Routledge, 2003).

44. Michael J. Sandel, "The Procedural Republic and the Unencumbered Self," *Political Theory* 12, no. 1 (1984).

45. For an effort to introduce personalist theory into social thought, see Christian Smith, *What Is a Person?: Rethinking Humanity, Social Life, and the Moral Good from the Person Up* (Chicago: University of Chicago Press, 2010).

46. Saul A. Kripke, *Wittgenstein on Rules and Private Language: An Elementary Exposition* (Cambridge, MA: Harvard University Press, 1982).

47. George Herbert Mead, *Mind, Self, and Society: From the Standpoint of a Social Behaviorist*, vol. 1 (Chicago: University of Chicago Press, 2009).

48. Smith, *What Is a Person?*.

49. See, for instance, recent work in "positive psychology" such as Martin E. P. Seligman, *Flourish: A Visionary New Understanding of Happiness and Well-Being* (New York: Simon and Schuster, 2012).

50. The seminal formulation of this argument is Richard A. Easterlin, "Does Economic Growth Improve the Human Lot? Some Empirical Evidence," *Nations and Households in Economic Growth* 89 (1974).

51. See, for instance, James Laidlaw, *The Subject of Virtue: An Anthropology of Ethics and Freedom* (Cambridge and New York: Cambridge University Press, 2013).

52. See, for instance, Martha Nussbaum, "Aristotelian Social Democracy," in *Necessary Goods: Our Responsibility to Meet Others' Needs* (Lanham, MD: Rowman & Littlefield, 1998).

53. As argued by "new institutionalist" political economists. For the seminal statement, see Douglass C. North, "Economic Performance Through Time," *American Economic Review* 84, no. 3 (1994).

54. Stuart White, *The Civic Minimum: On the Rights and Obligations of Economic Citizenship* (New York: Oxford University Press, 2003).

55. Will Kymlicka, *Multicultural Citizenship: A Liberal Theory of Minority Rights*, Oxford Political Theory (Oxford and New York: Clarendon Press, 1995); idem, *Politics in the Vernacular: Nationalism, Multiculturalism, and Citizenship* (Oxford: Oxford University Press, 2001).

56. David Miller, "In Defence of Nationality," *Journal of Applied Philosophy* 10, no. 1 (1993): 6–7. See more generally his *Citizenship and National Identity* (Cambridge: Polity Press, 2000).

57. Martha C. Nussbaum, "Human Functioning and Social Justice in Defense of Aristotelian Essentialism," *Political Theory* 20, no. 2 (1992); idem, "Non-Relative Virtues: An Aristotelian Approach," *Midwest Studies in Philosophy* 13, no. 1 (1988); idem, "Aristotelian Social Democracy."

CONCLUSION.
THE RIGHTEOUS REPUBLIC

1. For recent efforts to revive these concepts, see Jeffrey A. Winters and Benjamin I. Page, "Oligarchy in the United States?," *Perspectives on Politics* 7, no. 4 (2009); Jeffrey A. Winters, *Oligarchy* (Cambridge and New York: Cambridge University Press, 2011);

Zephyr Teachout, "The Anti-Corruption Principle," *Cornell Law Review* 94, no. 341 (2009); idem, *Corruption in America: From Benjamin Franklin's Snuff Box to Citizens United* (Cambridge, MA: Harvard University Press, 2014).

2. Thomas Piketty and Emmanuel Saez, *Income Inequality in the United States, 1913–1998* (Cambridge, MA: National Bureau of Economic Research, 2001); Jacob S. Hacker and Paul Pierson, "Winner-Take-All Politics: Public Policy, Political Organization, and the Precipitous Rise of Top Incomes in the United States," *Politics & Society* 38, no. 2 (2010).

3. Martin Gilens, *Affluence and Influence: Economic Inequality and Political Power in America* (Princeton, NJ: Princeton University Press, 2012); Jacob S. Hacker and Paul Pierson, *Winner-Take-All Politics: How Washington Made the Rich Richer—and Turned Its Back on the Middle Class* (New York: Simon and Schuster, 2011).

4. McCormick, *Machiavellian Democracy.*

5. Ibid., 181.

6. Ibid., 184.

7. This has been a theme in the recent writings of Andrew Bacevich and Chalmers Johnson. See, for instance, Andrew J. Bacevich, *Washington Rules: America's Path to Permanent War* (New York: Metropolitan Books, 2010).

8. Jean L. Cohen, *Civil Society and Political Theory* (Cambridge, MA: MIT Press, 1994); Robert D. Putnam, *Bowling Alone: The Collapse and Revival of American Community* (New York: Simon and Schuster, 2000); Jeffrey C. Alexander, *The Civil Sphere* (New York: Oxford University Press, 2006).

BIBLIOGRAPHY

Aalders, Gerhard Jean Daniël. *Die Theorie der gemischten Verfassung Im Altertum*. Amsterdam: Adolf M. Hakkert, 1968.

Aamodt, Terrie Dopp. *Righteous Armies, Holy Cause: Apocalyptic Imagery and the Civil War*. Macon, GA: Mercer University Press, 2002.

Adams, John. *The Portable John Adams*. New York: Penguin, 2004.

Addams, Jane. *Democracy and Social Ethics*. John Harvard Library. Cambridge, MA: Belknap Press of Harvard University Press, 1964.

———. *Twenty Years at Hull-House, with Autobiographical Notes*. New York: Macmillan Co., 1910.

Agamben, Giorgio. *The Highest Poverty: Monastic Rules and Form-of-Life*. Stanford, CA: Stanford University Press, 2013.

———. *The Time That Remains: A Comment on the Letter to the Romans*, trans. P. Dailey. Stanford, CA: Stanford University Press, 2000.

Akenson, Donald H. *God's Peoples: Covenant and Land in South Africa, Israel, and Ulster*. Montreal: McGill-Queen's University Press, 1991.

Alexander, Jeffrey C. *The Civil Sphere*. New York: Oxford University Press, 2006.

Allen, Brooke. *Moral Minority: Our Skeptical Founding Fathers*. Chicago: Ivan R. Dee, 2006.

Allitt, Patrick. *The Conservatives: Ideas and Personalities Throughout American History*. New Haven, CT: Yale University Press, 2009.

Amar, Akhil Reed. *America's Unwritten Constitution: The Precedents and Principles We Live By*. New York: Basic Books, 2012.

Anderson, Frederick M. "Dewey's Experiment with Greek Philosophy." *International Philosophical Quarterly* 7, no. 1 (1967).

Anscombe, Gertrude E. M. "Modern Moral Philosophy." *Philosophy* 33, no. 124 (1958).

Anton, John P. "John Dewey and Ancient Philosophies." *Philosophy and Phenomenological Research* 25, no. 4 (1965).

Appleby, Joyce Oldham. *Liberalism and Republicanism in the Historical Imagination*. Cambridge, MA: Harvard University Press, 1992.

Aquinas, Thomas, Aristotle, Robert William Mulligan, James V. McGlynn, Robert William Schmidt, Lottie H. Kendzierski, J. P. Reid, et al. *The Collected Works of St. Thomas Aquinas*. Charlottesville, VA: InteLex Corporation, 1993.

———. *Political Writings*. Trans. R. W. Dyson. Cambridge: Cambridge University Press, 2002.

Arendt, Hannah. *Between Past and Future: Eight Exercises in Political Thought*. New York: Penguin, 1968.

———. *Crises of the Republic: Lying in Politics; Civil Disobedience; on Violence; Thoughts on Politics and Revolution*. Boston: Houghton Mifflin Harcourt, 1972.

———. *The Human Condition*. Chicago: University of Chicago Press, 2013.

———. *On Revolution*. New York: Penguin, 1965.

Aristotle. *The Politics*. New York: Penguin, 1982.

Assmann, Aleida. *Erinnerungsräume: Formen und Wandlungen des kulturellen Gedächtnisses*. Munich: CH Beck, 2006.

Assmann, Jan, and Tonio Hölscher. *Kultur und Gedächtnis*, rev. ed. Suhrkamp Taschenbuch Wissenschaft. Frankfurt am Main: Suhrkamp, 1988.

Augst, Thomas, and Kenneth E. Carpenter. *Institutions of Reading: The Social Life of Libraries in the United States*. Studies in Print Culture and the History of the Book. Amherst: University of Massachusetts Press, 2007.

Axtell, James. *The Invasion Within: The Contest of Cultures in Colonial North America*. Oxford: Oxford University Press.

Bacevich, Andrew J. *Washington Rules: America's Path to Permanent War*. New York: Metropolitan Books, 2010.

Backus, Irena Dorota. *Reformation Readings of the Apocalypse: Geneva, Zurich, and Wittenberg*. New York: Oxford University Press, 2000.

Badiou, Alain. *Saint Paul: The Foundation of Universalism*. Stanford, CA: Stanford University Press, 1997.

Bailey, Richard A. *Race and Redemption in Puritan New England*. New York: Oxford University Press, 2011.

Bailyn, Bernard. "Religion and Revolution: Three Biographical Studies." *Perspectives in American History* 4 (1970).

Baker, James W. *Thanksgiving: The Biography of an American Holiday*. Durham, NH: University Press of New England, 2009.

Balkin, Jack M. *Constitutional Redemption*. Cambridge, MA: Harvard University Press, 2011.

———. *Living Originalism*. Harvard University Press, 2011.

Banning, Lance. "Jeffersonian Ideology Revisited: Liberal and Classical Ideas in the New American Republic." *William and Mary Quarterly* 43, no. 1 (1986).

———. *The Jeffersonian Persuasion: Evolution of a Party Ideology*. Ithaca, NY: Cornell University Press, 1980. Bannister, Robert. *Social Darwinism: Science and Myth in Anglo-American Social Thought*. Philadelphia: Temple University Press, 2010.

Baritz, Loren. *City on a Hill: A History of Ideas and Myths in America*. New York: Wiley, 1964.

Barkun, Michael. *Crucible of the Millennium: The Burned-over District of New York in the 1840s*. Syracuse, NY: Syracuse University Press, 1986.

Baron, Hans. *The Crisis of the Early Italian Renaissance; Civic Humanism and Republican Liberty in an Age of Classicism and Tyranny*, rev. 1 vol. ed. Princeton, NJ: Princeton University Press, 1967.

Barry, John M. *Roger Williams and the Creation of the American Soul: Church, State, and the Birth of Liberty*. New York: Penguin, 2012.

Bartlett, Irving H. *John C. Calhoun: A Biography*. New York: W. W. Norton & Co., 1993.

Barton, David. *America's Godly Heritage*. N.p.: WallBuilders, 1992.

———. "A Few Declarations of Founding Fathers and Early Statesment on Jesus, Christianity and the Bible." *WallBuilders*, May 2008. http://www.wallbuilders.com/LIBissues Articles.asp?id=8755.

Beaune, Colette, and Fredric L. Cheyette. *The Birth of an Ideology: Myths and Symbols of Nation in Late-Medieval France*. Berkeley: University of California Press, 1991.

Becker, Gary S, and Kevin M Murphy. "A Theory of Rational Addiction." *Journal of Political Economy* 96, no. 4 (1988).

Bellah, Robert Neelly. *The Broken Covenant: American Civil Religion in Time of Trial*. New York: Seabury Press, 1975.

———. *The Broken Covenant: American Civil Religion in Time of Trial*, 2nd ed. Chicago: University of Chicago Press, 1992.

———. "Civil Religion in America." *Daedalus* 96 (1967).

———. *Religion in Human Evolution: From the Paleolithic to the Axial Age*. Cambridge, MA: Harvard University Press, 2011.

Bellah, Robert Neelly, and Steven M. Tipton. *The Robert Bellah Reader*. Durham, NC: Duke University Press, 2006.

Bensel, Richard Franklin. *Yankee Leviathan: The Origins of Central State Authority in America, 1859–1877*. Cambridge and New York: Cambridge University Press, 1990.

Bercovitch, Sacvan. *The American Jeremiad*. Madison: University of Wisconsin Press, 1978.

———. *Typology and Early American Literature*. Amherst: University of Massachusetts Press, 1972.

Berger, Peter. "Two Modest Victories for Common Sense." *American Interest*, December 11, 2013.

Besier, Gerhard, Hermann Lübbe, and Hannah-Arendt-Institut für Totalitarismusforschung. *Politische Religion Und Religionspolitik: Zwischen Totalitarismus Und Bürgerfreiheit*. Schriften Des Hannah-Arendt-Instituts Für Totalitarismusforschung, Bd. 28. Göttingen: Vandenhoeck & Ruprecht, 2005.

Blakely, William Addison. *American State Papers Bearing on Sunday Legislation*. New York: National Religious Liberty Association, 1891.

Blight, David W. *Race and Reunion: The Civil War in American Memory*. Cambridge, MA: Belknap Press of Harvard University Press, 2001.

Bloch, Ruth H. *Visionary Republic: Millennial Themes in American Thought, 1756–1800*. Cambridge and New York: Cambridge University Press, 1988.

Blum, Edward J. *Reforging the White Republic: Race, Religion, and American Nationalism, 1865–1898*. Conflicting Worlds. Baton Rouge: Louisiana State University Press, 2005.

———. " 'There Won't Be Any Rich People in Heaven': The Black Christ, White Hypocrisy, and the Gospel According to W.E.B. Du Bois." *Journal of African American History* 90, no. 4 (2005).

———. *W.E.B. Du Bois: American Prophet*. Politics and Culture in Modern America. Philadelphia: University of Pennsylvania Press, 2007.

Blythe, James M. *Ideal Government and the Mixed Constitution in the Middle Ages*. Princeton, NJ: Princeton University Press, 2014.

Bourdieu, Pierre. "Social Space and Symbolic Power." *Sociological Theory* 7, no. 1 (1989).

Bowen, John Richard. *Why the French Don't Like Headscarves: Islam, the State, and Public Space*. Princeton, NJ: Princeton University Press, 2007.

Bowne, Borden Parker. *Personalism*. Boston: Houghton, Mifflin, 1908.

Boyer, Paul S. *When Time Shall Be No More: Prophecy Belief in Modern American Culture*. Studies in Cultural History. Cambridge, MA: Harvard University Press, 1992.

Brecht, Martin, Klaus Deppermann, Ulrich Gäbler, and Hartmut Lehmann. *Geschichte des Pietismus*, vol. 1. Göttingen: Vandenhoeck & Ruprecht, 1993.

Breen, Louise A. *Transgressing the Bounds: Subversive Enterprises among the Puritan Elite in Massachusetts, 1630–1692*. New York: Oxford University Press, 2001.

Breen, Timothy Hall. *The Character of the Good Ruler: A Study of Puritan Political Ideas in New England, 1630–1730*. Yale Historical Publications Miscellany 92. New Haven, CT: Yale University Press, 1970.

———. *Puritans and Adventurers: Change and Persistence in Early America*. New York: Oxford University Press, 1980.

Bremer, Francis J. *John Winthrop: America's Forgotten Founding Father*. New York: Oxford University Press, 2005.

Brightman, Edgar Sheffield. *Is God a Person?* Boston: Association Publishers, 1932.

Brooks, David. "Obama, Gospel and Verse." *New York Times*, April 26, 2007.

Brown, Victoria. *The Education of Jane Addams*. Politics and Culture in Modern America. Philadelphia: University of Pennsylvania Press, 2004.

Brueggemann, Walter. *Prophetic Imagination*, rev. ed. Minneapolis, MN: Fortress Press, 2001.

Bruner, Jerome. "Life as Narrative." *Social Research* 54, no. 1 (1987).

Burke, Peter. *Popular Culture in Early Modern Europe*. Burlington, VT: Ashgate Publishing, Ltd., 2009.

Bush, George H. W. *Speaking of Freedom: The Collected Speeches*. New York: Simon and Schuster, 2009.

Butler, Jon. "Enthusiasm Described and Decried: The Great Awakening as Interpretative Fiction." *Journal of American History* 69, no. 2 (1982).

Byrd, James P. *Sacred Scripture, Sacred War: The Bible and the American Revolution*. New York: Oxford University Press, 2013.

Caldwell, Patricia. *The Puritan Conversion Narrative: The Beginnings of American Expression*. Cambridge and New York: Cambridge University Press, 1983.

Calhoun, John C., and H. Lee Cheek. *John C. Calhoun: Selected Writings and Speeches*. Conservative Leadership Series. Washington, DC: Regnery, 2003.

Calhoun, John C., Robert Lee Meriwether, William Edwin Hemphill, and Clyde Norman Wilson. *The Papers of John C. Calhoun*. Columbia: University of South Carolina Press, 1959.

Carson, Clayborne, and Peter Holloran. *A Knock at Midnight: Inspiration from the Great Sermons of Reverend Martin Luther King, Jr*. New York: Hachette Digital, 2001.

Carson, Clayborne, and Kris Shepard. *A Call to Conscience: The Landmark Speeches of Dr. Martin Luther King, Jr*. New York: Hachette Digital, 2001.

Casanova, José. *Public Religions in the Modern World*. Chicago: University of Chicago Press, 1994.

Cavanaugh, William T. *Torture and Eucharist: Theology, Politics, and the Body of Christ*. Oxford: Blackwell, 1998.

Cave, Alfred A. *The Pequot War*. Amherst: University of Massachusetts Press, 1996.

Chadwick, Owen. *From Bossuet to Newman: The Idea of Doctrinal Development*. Cambridge: Cambridge University Press, 1957.

Chalmers, David Mark. *Hooded Americanism: The History of the Ku Klux Klan*. Durham, NC: Duke University Press, 1981.

Chambliss, J. J. "Common Ground in Aristotle." *Educational Theory* 43, no. 3 (1993).

———. *Educational Theory as Theory of Conduct: From Aristotle to Dewey*. Albany: State University of New York Press, 1987.

———. *The Influence of Plato and Aristotle on John Dewey's Philosophy*. Mellen Studies in Education 10. Lewiston, NY: E. Mellen Press, 1990.

Chappell, David L. *A Stone of Hope: Prophetic Religion and the Death of Jim Crow.* Chapel Hill: University of North Carolina Press, 2004.

Churchill, Winston. *A History of the English-Speaking Peoples.* 4 vols. London: Cassell, 1956.

Cicero, Marcus Tullius. *Cicero: On the Commonwealth and on the Laws*, ed. E. G. Zetzel. Cambridge and New York: Cambridge University Press, 1999.

Cohen, Charles Lloyd. *God's Caress: The Psychology of Puritan Religious Experience.* New York: Oxford University Press, 1986.

Cohen, Jean L. *Civil Society and Political Theory.* Cambridge, MA: MIT Press, 1994.

Cohen, Lizabeth. *A Consumers' Republic: The Politics of Mass Consumption in Postwar America.* New York: Random House, 2004.

Cohn, Norman. *The Pursuit of the Millennium.* Fairlawn, NJ: Essential Books, 1957.

Colley, Linda. *Britons: Forging the Nation, 1707–1837.* New Haven, CT: Yale University Press, 1992.

Collins, John Joseph. *The Apocalyptic Imagination: An Introduction to Jewish Apocalyptic Literature.* Grand Rapids, MI: Wm. B. Eerdmans Publishing, 1998.

Cone, James H. *A Black Theology of Liberation.* C. Eric Lincoln Series in Black Religion. Philadelphia: Lippincott, 1970.

———. *The Cross and the Lynching Tree.* Maryknoll, NY: Orbis Books, 2011.

———. *Martin and Malcolm and America: A Dream or a Nightmare.* Maryknoll, NY: Orbis Books, 1992.

———. *Risks of Faith: The Emergence of a Black Theology of Liberation, 1968–1998.* Boston: Beacon Press, 1999.

Congar, Yves. *The Meaning of Tradition.* San Francisco: Ignatius Press, 2004.

Connolly, William E. *Pluralism.* Durham, NC: Duke University Press, 2005.

Constant, Benjamin. *Constant: Political Writings*, ed. and trans. Biancamaria Fontana. Cambridge and New York: Cambridge University Press, 1988.

Cooper, William J. *Liberty and Slavery: Southern Politics to 1860.* New York: Knopf, 1983.

Cotton, John. *A Discourse about Civil Government in a New Plantation Whose Design Is Religion.* Cambridge, MA: Samuel Green and Marmaduke Johnson, 1663.

———. *Gods Promise to His Plantations: As It Was Delivered in a Sermon.* London: W. Jones, 1630.

———. *The Way of the Churches of Christ in New-England, or, the Way of Churches Walking in Brotherly Equality, or Co-Ordination, Without Subjection of One Church to Another. Measured and Examined by the Golden Reed of the Sanctuary, Containing a Full Declaration of the Church-Way in All Particulars.* London: Matthew Simmons, 1645.

Coyne, Jerry. "H. L. Mencken: The First New Atheist." In *Why Evolution Is True* (blog), May 19, 2012.

Cramer, Clarence Henley. *Royal Bob: The Life of Robert G. Ingersoll.* Indianapolis: Bobbs-Merrill, 1952.

Crapanzano, Vincent. *Serving the Word: Literalism in America from the Pulpit to the Bench.* New York: New Press, 2000.

Crisp, Roger, and Michael A. Slote. *Virtue Ethics.* Oxford Readings in Philosophy. Oxford and New York: Oxford University Press, 1997.

Cristi, Marcela. *From Civil to Political Religion: The Intersection of Culture, Religion and Politics.* Waterloo, ON: Wilfrid Laurier University Press, 2001.

Cross, Whitney R. *The Burned-over District: The Social and Intellectual History of Enthusiastic Religion in Western New York, 1800–1850.* Ithaca, NY: Cornell University Press, 1950.

Crouch, David J. F. *Piety, Fraternity, and Power: Religious Gilds in Late Medieval Yorkshire, 1389–1547.* Woodbridge, Suffolk, UK, and Rochester, NY: York Medieval Press, 2000.

Cunaeus, Petrus, and Clement Barksdale. *Petrus Cunæus of the Common-Wealth of the Hebrews.* London: T.W., 1653.

Curti, Merle. "The Great Mr. Locke: America's Philospher, 1783–1861." *Huntington Library Bulletin* 11 (April 1937).

Curtis, Bruce. *William Graham Sumner.* Twayne's United States Authors Series. Boston: Twayne, 1981.

Dagger, Richard. *Civic Virtues: Rights, Citizenship and Republican Liberalism.* New York and Oxford: Oxford University Press, 1997.

Davis, Thomas M. "The Exegetical Traditions of Puritan Typology." *Early American Literature* 5, no. 1 (1970).

Dawson, Hugh J. " 'Christian Charitie' as Colonial Discourse: Rereading Winthrop's Sermon in Its English Context." *Early American Literature* 35, no. 2 (1998).

——. "John Winthrop's Rite of Passage: The Origins of the 'Christian Charitie' Discourse." *Early American Literature* 26, no. 3 (1991).

D'Elia, Donald J. "Benjamin Rush: Philosopher of the American Revolution." *Transactions of the American Philosophical Society* 64, no. 5 (1974).

Desan, Suzanne. *Reclaiming the Sacred: Lay Religion and Popular Politics in Revolutionary France.* Ithaca, NY: Cornell University Press Ithaca, 1990.

De Vries, Hent. *Philosophy and the Turn to Religion.* Baltimore: Johns Hopkins University Press, 1999.

De Vries, Hent, and Lawrence Eugene Sullivan. *Political Theologies: Public Religions in a Post-Secular World.* New York: Fordham University Press, 2006.

Dewey, John. *The Early Works, 1882–1898.* Carbondale: Southern Illinois University Press, 1967.

——. *The Middle Works, 1899–1924.* 15 vols. Carbondale: Southern Illinois University Press, 1976.

Dewey, John, and Jo Ann Boydston. *The Later Works, 1925–1953.* 17 vols. Carbondale and London: Southern Illinois University Press, 1981.

Dickinson, John K. "William Graham Sumner, 1840–1910: Eine Biographische Und Theoretische Untersuchung Zur Frühen Amerikanischen Soziologie." Inaugural diss., Phillips-Universität, 1963.

Dickow, Helga. *Das Regenbogenvolk: Die Entstehung Einer Neuen Civil Religion in Südafrika,* rev. ed. Gesellschaft Und Bildung 12. Baden-Baden: Nomos Verlagsgesellschaft, 1996.

Diggins, John Patrick. "Republicanism and Progressivism." *American Quarterly* 37, no. 4 (1985).

——. *Ronald Reagan: Fate, Freedom, and the Making of History.* New York: W. W. Norton & Company, 2007.

Douglass, Frederick, and Philip Sheldon Foner. *The Life and Writings of Frederick Douglass.* 4 vols. New York: International Publishers, 1950.

Douglass, Frederick, Philip Sheldon Foner, and Yuval Taylor. *Frederick Douglass: Selected Speeches and Writings*. Chicago: Lawrence Hill Books, 1999.

Dreisbach, Daniel L. "Sowing Useful Truths and Principles: The Danbury Baptists, Thomas Jefferson, and the Wall of Seperation." *Journal of Church and State* 39 (1997).

———. *Thomas Jefferson and the Wall of Separation Between Church and State*. New York: New York University Press, 2002.

Du Bois, W.E.B. *Black Reconstruction: An Essay Toward a History of the Part Which Black Folk Played in the Attempt to Reconstruct Democracy in America, 1860–1880*. New York: Harcourt, Brace and Co., 1935.

———. *Darkwater: Voices from Within the Veil*. New York: Harcourt, Brace and Howe, 1920.

———. *The Gift of Black Folk: The Negroes in the Making of America*. Boston: Stratford Co., 1924.

———. *The Negro Church: Report of a Social Study Made under the Direction of Atlanta University; Together with the Proceedings of the Eighth Conference for the Study of Negro Problems, Held at Atlanta University, May 26th, 1903*. Atlanta University Publications. Atlanta: Atlanta University Press, 1903.

———. *The Philadelphia Negro: A Social Study*. Boston: Ginn & Co., 1899.

———. *The Souls of Black Folk: Essays and Sketches*. Chicago: A. C. McClurg & Co., 1903.

———. *The Suppression of the African Slave-Trade to the United States of America, 1638–1870*. Harvard Historical Studies 1. New York and London: Longmans, Green and Co., 1896.

Du Bois, W.E.B., and Herbert Aptheker. *The Correspondence of W.E.B. Du Bois*. Amherst: University of Massachusetts Press, 1973.

Du Bois, W.E.B., and David L. Lewis. *W.E.B. Du Bois: A Reader*. New York: Henry Holt and Company, 1995.

Du Bois, W.E.B., and Phil Zuckerman. *Du Bois on Religion*. Walnut Creek, CA: AltaMira Press, 2000.

Dunn, John. *The Political Thought of John Locke*. London: Cambridge University Press, 1969.

Dwight, Timothy. *The Duty of Americans at the Present Crisis: Illustrated in a Discourse, Preached on the Fourth of July, 1798*. New Haven, CT: Thomas and Samuel Green, 1798.

———. *The True Means of Establishing Public Happiness: A Sermon, Delivered on the 7th of July, 1795, Before the Connecticut Society of Cincinnati*. New Haven, CT: T. & S. Green, 1795.

Dworetz, Steven M. " 'See Locke on Government': The Two Treatises and the American Revolution." *Studies in Eighteenth-Century Culture* 21, no. 1 (1992).

———. *The Unvarnished Doctrine: Locke, Liberalism, and the American Revolution*. Durham, NC: Duke University Press, 1989.

Easterlin, Richard A. "Does Economic Growth Improve the Human Lot?: Some Empirical Evidence." *Nations and Households in Economic Growth* 89 (1974).

Easterly, William, and Ian Vásquez. *The Tyranny of Experts: Economists, Dictators, and the Forgotten Rights of the Poor*. New York: Basic Books, 2014.

Edwards, Jonathan. "Thoughts Concerning the Present Revival of Religion in New England." In *The Works of Jonathan Edwards*, ed. Edward Hickman. London: Ball, Arnold and Co., 1840 [1742].

Eisenstein, Elizabeth L. *The Printing Press as an Agent of Change*, vol. 1. Cambridge: Cambrdige University Press, 1980.

Elshtain, Jean Bethke. *Jane Addams and the Dream of American Democracy: A Life*. New York: Basic Books, 2002.

———. *The Jane Addams Reader*. New York: Basic Books, 2002.

Endy, Melvin B. "Just War, Holy War, and Millennialism in Revolutionary America." *William and Mary Quarterly* 42, no. 1 (1985).

Evans, Christopher Hodge, and William R. Herzog. *The Faith of Fifty Million: Baseball, Religion, and American Culture*. Louisville, KY: Westminster John Knox Press, 2002.

Fairclough, Adam. *To Redeem the Soul of America: The Southern Christian Leadership Conference and Martin Luther King, Jr*. Atlanta: University of Georgia Press, 2001.

FaithFacts. "The Bible and Government. Biblical Principles: Basis for America's Laws." http://www.faithfacts.org/christ-and-the-culture/the-bible-and-government.

Falsani, Cathleen. "Obama's Religious Beliefs: An Interview with Barack Obama." *Want to Know*, n.d. http://wanttoknow.info/008/obama_religious_beliefs_views.

Falwell, Jerry, and Jose G. Simon. *Listen, America!* Garden City, NY: Doubleday, 1980.

Farber, Daniel A. *Lincoln's Constitution*. Chicago: University of Chicago Press, 2003.

Farrow, Douglas. *Recognizing Religion in a Secular Society: Essays in Pluralism, Religion, and Public Policy*. Montreal and Ithaca, NY: McGill-Queen's University Press, 2004.

Faust, Drew Gilpin. *The Creation of Confederate Nationalism: Ideology and Identity in the Civil War South*. Walter Lynwood Fleming Lectures in Southern History. Baton Rouge: Louisiana State University Press, 1988.

———. *The Ideology of Slavery: Proslavery Thought in the Antebellum South, 1830–1860*. Library of Southern Civilization. Baton Rouge and London: Louisiana State University Press, 1981.

Feldman, Noah. *Divided by God: America's Church-State Problem—and What We Should Do About It*. New York: Farrar, Straus and Giroux, 2005.

Finley, Samuel. *The Curse of Meroz*. Philadelphia: Chattin, 1757.

Fitzmaurice, Andrew. *Humanism and America: An Intellectual History of English Colonisation, 1500–1625*, vol. 67. Cambridge and New York: Cambridge University Press, 2003.

Foner, Eric. *The Fiery Trial: Abraham Lincoln and American Slavery*. New York: W. W. Norton, 2010.

———. *Free Soil, Free Labor, Free Men: The Ideology of the Republican Party Before the Civil War*. Oxford and New York: Oxford University Press, 1971.

———. *A Short History of Reconstruction, 1863–1877*. New York: Harper & Row, 1990.

Ford, Caroline C. *Creating the Nation in Provincial France: Religion and Political Identity in Brittany*. Princeton, NJ: Princeton University Press, 1993.

Ford, Lacy K. "Recovering the Republic: Calhoun, South Carolina, and the Concurrent Majority." *South Carolina Historical Magazine* 89, no. 3 (1988).

———. "Republican Ideology in a Slave Society: The Political Economy of John C. Calhoun." *Journal of Southern History* 54, no. 3 (1988).

Foster, Gaines M. *Ghosts of the Confederacy: Defeat, the Lost Cause, and the Emergence of the New South, 1865 to 1913*. New York: Oxford University Press, 1987.

———. *Moral Reconstruction: Christian Lobbyists and the Federal Legislation of Morality, 1865–1920*. Chapel Hill: University of North Carolina Press, 2002.

Foster, Stephen. *The Long Argument: English Puritanism and the Shaping of New England Culture, 1570–1700*. Chapel Hill: University of North Carolina Press, 1996.

Fox, Richard Wightman. *Reinhold Niebuhr: A Biography*. New York: Pantheon Books, 1985.

Fox-Genovese, Elizabeth, and Eugene D. Genovese. "The Divine Sanction of Social Order: Religious Foundations of the Southern Slaveholders' World View." *Journal of the American Academy of Religion* 55, no. 2 (1987).

———. *The Mind of the Master Class: History and Faith in the Southern Slaveholders' Worldview*. Cambridge and New York: Cambridge University Press, 2005.

Franzen, Jonathan. *Freedom*. New York: Farrar, Straus & Giroux, 2010.

Friedland, Roger. "The Institutional Logic of Religious Nationalism: Sex, Violence and the Ends of History." *Politics, Religion and Ideology* 12, no. 1 (March 2011).

Fullinwider, S. P. *The Mind and Mood of Black America; 20th Century Thought*. Dorsey Series in American History. Homewood, IL: Dorsey Press, 1969.

Gadamer, Hans Georg. *Truth and Method*, 2nd rev. ed. New York: Crossroad, 1989.

Gallagher, Gary W. *Jubal A. Early, the Lost Cause, and Civil War History: A Persistent Legacy*. Frank L. Klement Lectures 4. Milwaukee, WI: Marquette University Press, 1995.

Garnsey, Peter. *Ideas of Slavery from Aristotle to Augustine*. W. B. Stanford Memorial Lectures. Cambridge: Cambridge University Press, 1996.

Garsten, Bryan. *Saving Persuasion: A Defense of Rhetoric and Judgment*. Cambridge, MA: Harvard University Press, 2009.

Gaukroger, Stephen. *The Emergence of a Scientific Culture: Science and the Shaping of Modernity, 1210–1685*. Oxford: Oxford University Press, 2006.

Gehrig, Gail. *American Civil Religion: An Assessment*. Storrs, CT: Society for the Scientific Study of Religion, 1981.

Genovese, Eugene D., and Elizabeth Fox-Genovese. "The Religious Ideals of Southern Slave Society." *Georgia Historical Quarterly* 70, no. 1 (1986).

Gilders, William K. *Blood Ritual in the Hebrew Bible: Meaning and Power*. Baltimore: Johns Hopkins University Press, 2004.

Gildrie, Richard P. *The Profane, the Civil, and the Godly: The Reformation of Manners in Orthodox New England, 1679–1749*. University Park: Penn State University Press.

Gilens, Martin. *Affluence and Influence: Economic Inequality and Political Power in America*. Princeton, NJ: Princeton University Press, 2012.

Gilsdorf, Joy. *The Puritan Apocalypse: New England Eschatology in the Seventeenth Century*. New York: Garland, 1989.

Gingrich, Newt. *A Nation Like No Other: Why American Exceptionalism Matters*. Washington, DC: Regnery, 2011.

Go, Julian. *American Empire and the Politics of Meaning: Elite Political Cultures in the Philippines and Puerto Rico During U.S. Colonialism*. Politics, History, and Culture. Durham, NC: Duke University Press, 2008.

Goldie, Mark. "The Civil Religion of James Harrington." *Languages of Political Theory in Early Modern Europe* 198 (1987).

Gorman, Frank H. "Sacrifices and Offerings." In *The New Interpreter's Dictionary of the Bible*, ed. Katharine Doob Sakenfeld, Sameuel E. Balentine, and Brian K. Blounk. Nashville, TN: Abingdon, 2009.

Gorski, P. "Calvinism and Revolution: The Walzer Thesis Re-Considered." In *Meaning and Modernity: Religion, Polity and Self*, ed. Richard Madsen, Ann Swidler, and Steven Tipton. Berkeley and Los Angeles: University of California Press, 2001.

———. "Premodern Nationalism: An Oxymoron? The Evidence from England." In *Sage Handbook of Nationalism*, ed. Gerard Delanty and Krishan Kumar. New York: Russell Sage, 2006.

Gourevitch, Alex. "Labor and Republican Liberty." *Constellations* 18, no. 3 (2011).

Grabill, Stephen John. *Rediscovering the Natural Law in Reformed Theological Ethics.* Grand Rapids, MI: Wm. B. Eerdmans, 2006.

Grayson, John Christopher. "The Civic Militia in the County of Holland, 1560–81: Politics and Public Order in the Dutch Revolt." *BMGN-Low Countries Historical Review* 95, no. 1 (1980).

Green, Steven Keith. "The Rhetoric and Reality of the 'Christian Nation' Maxim in American Law, 1810–1920." PhD diss., University of North Carolina, 1997.

———. *The Second Disestablishment: Church and State in Nineteenth-Century America.* Oxford and New York: Oxford University Press, 2010.

Gregory, Eric. *Politics and the Order of Love: An Augustinian Ethic of Democratic Citizenship.* Chicago: University of Chicago Press, 2008.

Gribbin, William. "Republican Religion and the American Churches in the Early National Period." *Historian* 35, no. 1 (1972).

Grosby, Steven Elliott. *Biblical Ideas of Nationality: Ancient and Modern.* Winona Lake, IN: Eisenbrauns, 2002.

Gustafson, James M. "The Sectarian Temptation: Reflections on Theology, the Church and the University." *Proceedings of the Catholic Theological Society of America* 40 (2013).

———. "Notes on Post-Secular Society." *New Perspectives Quarterly* 25, no. 4 (2008).

Habermas, Jürgen. *Between Facts and Norms.* Trans. William Rehg. Cambridge, MA: MIT Press, 1996.

———. "Citizenship and National Identity: Some Reflections on the Future of Europe." *Praxis International* 12, no. 1 (1992).

———. "The Hermeneutic Claim to Universality." In *The Hermeneutic Tradition: From Ast to Ricoeur,* ed. Gayle L. Ormiston and Aland D. Schrift. Albany: SUNY Press, 1990.

Habermas, Jürgen, and Max Pensky. *The Postnational Constellation: Political Essays.* Cambridge, MA: MIT Press, 2001.

Hacker, Jacob S., and Paul Pierson. *Winner-Take-All Politics: How Washington Made the Rich Richer—and Turned Its Back on the Middle Class.* New York: Simon and Schuster, 2011.

———. "Winner-Take-All Politics: Public Policy, Political Organization, and the Precipitous Rise of Top Incomes in the United States." *Politics and Society* 38, no. 2 (2010).

Hackett, David G. *Religion and American Culture: A Reader,* 2nd ed. New York: Routledge, 2003.

Hadfield, Andrew. *Shakespeare and Republicanism.* Cambridge and New York: Cambridge University Press, 2008.

Hahm, David E. "The Mixed Constitution in Greek Thought." *Companion to Greek and Roman Political Thought* 32 (2009).

Halbwachs, Maurice. *On Collective Memory.* Chicago: University of Chicago Press, 1992.

Hall, David D. *Puritans in the New World: A Critical Anthology.* Princeton, NJ: Princeton University Press, 2004.

———. *A Reforming People: Puritanism and the Transformation of Public Life in New England.* Chapel Hill: University of North Carolina Press, 2012.

———. *Worlds of Wonder, Days of Judgment: Popular Religious Belief in Early New England.* Cambridge, MA: Harvard University Press, 1990.

Hall, Timothy. *Separating Church and State: Roger Williams and Religious Liberty.* Urbana and London: University of Illinois Press, 1998.

Haller, William. *The Elect Nation: The Meaning and Relevance of Foxe's* Book of Martyrs. New York: Harper & Row, 1963.

Hambrick-Stowe, Charles E. "Practical Divinity and Spirituality." In *The Cambridge Companion to Puritanism*, ed. John Coffey and Paul C. H. Lim. New York: Cambridge University Press, 2008.

——. *The Practice of Piety: Puritan Devotional Exercises in Seventeenth Century New England*. Chapel Hill: University of North Carolina Press, 1982.

Hamburger, Philip. *Separation of Church and State*. Cambridge, MA: Harvard University Press, 2002.

Hamilton, Alexander. *Writings*. New York: Library of America, 2001.

Hammond, James Henry. *Selections from the Letters and Speeches of the Hon. James H. Hammond of South Carolina*. New York: J. F. Trow & Co., 1866.

Handlin, Oscar. *The Uprooted*, 2nd ed. Boston: Little, 1973.

Hanf, Theodor. *Dealing with Difference: Religion, Ethnicity, and Politics: Comparing Cases and Concepts*. Baden-Baden: Nomos, 1999.

Hann, C. M., and Max-Planck-Institut für ethnologische Forschung Religion und Zivilgesellschaft. *The Postsocialist Religious Question: Faith and Power in Central Asia and East-Central Europe*. Berlin and Piscataway, NJ: Transaction, 2006.

Hansen, Jonathan M. *The Lost Promise of Patriotism: Debating American Identity, 1890–1920*. Chicago: University of Chicago Press, 2003.

Harding, Vincent. *Martin Luther King, the Inconvenient Hero*. Maryknoll, NY: Orbis Books, 2008.

Harris, Sam. *The End of Faith: Religion, Terror, and the Future of Reason*. New York. W. W. Norton & Co., 2004.

Harry Houdini Collection. *The Truth Seeker Collection of Forms, Hymns, and Recitations: Original and Selected*. New York: D. M. Bennett, 1877.

Hartz, Louis. *The Liberal Tradition in America: An Interpretation of American Political Thought since the Revolution*. New York: Harcourt, 1955.

Haskins, George Lee. *Law and Authority in Early Massachusetts: A Study in Tradition and Design*. Hamden, CT: Archon Books, 1968.

Hastings, Adrian. *The Construction of Nationhood: Ethnicity, Religion, and Nationalism*. Cambridge and New York: Cambridge University Press, 1997.

Hatch, Nathan O. "The Origins of Civil Millennialism in America: New England Clergymen, War with France, and the Revolution." *William and Mary Quarterly* 31, no. 3 (1974).

——. *The Sacred Cause of Liberty: Republican Thought and the Millennium in Revolutionary New England*. New Haven, CT: Yale University Press, 1977.

Hauerwas, Stanley. *After Christendom?: How the Church Is to Behave If Freedom, Justice, and a Christian Nation Are Bad Ideas*. Nashville, TN: Abingdon Press, 1991.

——. *Against the Nations: War and Survival in a Liberal Society*. Minneapolis, MN: Winston Press, 1985.

——. "Why the 'Sectarian Temptation' Is a Misrepresentation: A Response to James Gustafson." In *The Hauerwas Reader*, ed. John Berkman and Michael Cartwright. Durham, NC: Duke University Press, 2001.

Hauerwas, Stanley, and William H. Willimon. *Resident Aliens: Life in the Christian Colony*. Nashville, TN: Abingdon Press, 1989.

Hayden, Tom. "The Port Huron Statement." In *The New Radicals: A Report with Documents*. New York: Random House, 1962.

Hayes, Christopher. *Twilight of the Elites: America after Meritocracy*. New York: Random House, 2013.

Heimert, Alan. *Religion and the American Mind*. Cambridge, MA: Harvard University Press, 1933.

Helgerson, Richard. *Forms of Nationhood: The Elizabethan Writing of England*. Chicago: University of Chicago Press, 1992.

Herberg, Will. *Protestant Catholic Jew: An Essay in American Religious Sociology*. Chicago: University of Chicago Press, 1983.

Hermans, Hubert J. M. "The Dialogical Self: Toward a Theory of Personal and Cultural Positioning." *Culture and Psychology* 7, no. 3 (2001).

Hietala, Thomas R. *Manifest Design: Anxious Aggrandizement in Late Jacksonian America*. Ithaca, NY: Cornell University Press, 1985.

Hildebrandt, Mathias. *Politische Kultur Und Zivilreligion*. Epistemata: Reihe Philosophie 202. Würzburg: Königshausen & Neumann, 1996.

Hill, Christopher. *God's Englishman: Oliver Cromwell and the English Revolution*. New York: Dial Press, 1970.

Hillers, Delbert R. *Covenant: The History of a Biblical Idea*. Baltimore: Johns Hopkins University Press, 1969.

Hitchens, Christopher. *God Is Not Great: How Religion Poisons Everything*. New York: 12/ Warner Books, 2007.

Hobbes, Thomas. *Leviathan*. Harmondsworth: Penguin, 1968.

Hobbes, Thomas, John Bramhall, and Vere Chappell. *Hobbes and Bramhall on Liberty and Necessity*. Cambridge and New York: Cambridge University Press, 1999.

Hobsbawm, Eric, and Terence Ranger, eds. *The Invention of Tradition*. Cambridge: Cambridge University Press, 1992.

Hofstadter, Richard. *The American Political Tradition and the Men Who Made It*. New York: A. A. Knopf, 1948.

——. *The American Political Tradition and the Men Who Made It*, Vintage Books ed. New York: Vintage Books, 1989.

——. "William Graham Sumner, Social Darwinist." *New England Quarterly* 14, no. 3 (1941).

Holifield, E. Brooks. *Theology in America: Christian Thought from the Age of the Puritans to the Civil War*. New Haven, CT: Yale University Press, 2003.

Holstun, James. "John Eliot's Empirical Millenarianism." *Representations* no. 4 (1983).

Honohan, Iseult. *Civic Republicanism*. Routledge, 2003.

Horsman, Reginald. *Race and Manifest Destiny: The Origins of American Racial Anglo-Saxonism*. Cambridge, MA: Harvard University Press, 1981.

Howard-Pitney, David, and David Howard-Pitney. *The African American Jeremiad: Appeals for Justice in America*, rev. and expanded ed. Philadelphia: Temple University Press, 2005.

Hunter, James Davison. *Culture Wars: The Struggle to Define America*. New York: Basic Books, 1991.

Hutchison, William R. *Religious Pluralism in America: The Contentious History of a Founding Ideal*. New Haven, CT: Yale University Press, 2003.

Hutchison, William R., and Hartmut Lehmann. *Many Are Chosen: Divine Election and Western Nationalism*. Harvard Theological Studies 38. Minneapolis, MN: Fortress Press, 1994.

Huxley, Thomas Henry. *Collected Essays*. New York: Macmillan, 1893.

Ingersoll, Robert Green. *The Gods, and Other Lectures*. Peoria, IL: C. P. Farrell, 1889.
——. *The Works of Robert G. Ingersoll*. 12 vols. Dresden, NY: Dresden Publishing Company, 1912.
Irons, Charles F. *The Origins of Proslavery Christianity: White and Black Evangelicals in Colonial and Antebellum Virginia*. Chapel Hill: University of North Carolina Press, 2008.
Jackson, Thomas F. *From Civil Rights to Human Rights: Martin Luther King, Jr., and the Struggle for Economic Justice*. Philadelphia: University of Pennsylvania Press, 2011.
Jacobson, Matthew Frye. *Whiteness of a Different Color: European Immigrants and the Alchemy of Race*. Cambridge, MA, and London: Harvard University Press, 1998.
Jacoby, Susan. *Freethinkers: A History of American Secularism*. New York: Metropolitan Books, 2004.
——. *The Great Agnostic: Robert Ingersoll and American Freethought*. New Haven, CT: Yale University Press, 2013.
Jefferson, Thomas, Joyce Oldham Appleby, and Terence Ball. *Thomas Jefferson, Political Writings*. Cambridge Texts in the History of Political Thought. Cambridge and New York: Cambridge University Press, 1999.
Jenkins, Philip. *The Great and Holy War: How World War I Became a Religious Crusade*. New York: HarperOne, 2014.
Johnston, Steven. *The Truth about Patriotism*. Durham, NC: Duke University Press, 2007.
Joseph, Peniel E. *Waiting 'til the Midnight Hour: A Narrative History of Black Power in America*. New York: Macmillan, 2007.
Juc, Jeffrey K. "Puritan Millenarianism in Old and New England." In *The Cambridge Companion to Puritanism*, ed. John Coffey and Paul C. H. Lim. New York: Cambridge University Press, 2008.
Juergensmeyer, Mark. *The New Cold War?: Religious Nationalism Confronts the Secular State*. Comparative Studies in Religion and Society 5. Berkley: University of California Press, 1993.
Kahn, Jonathon Samuel. *Divine Discontent: The Religious Imagination of W.E.B. Du Bois*. Oxford and New York: Oxford University Press, 2009.
Kant, Immanuel. *Political Writings*. Trans. H. B. Nisbet. Cambridge: Cambridge University Press, 1991.
Kateb, George. "Freedom and Worldliness in the Thought of Hannah Arendt." *Political Theory* 5, no. 2 (1977).
——. *Patriotism and Other Mistakes*. New Haven, CT: Yale University Press, 2006.
Katznelson, Ira, and Andreas Kalyvas. *Liberal Beginnings: Making a Republic for the Moderns*. Cambridge and New York: Cambridge University Press, 2008.
Kennedy, Ruby Jo Reeves. "Premarital Residential Propinquity and Ethnic Endogamy." *American Journal of Sociology* 48, no. 5 (1943).
——. "Single or Triple Melting-Pot? Intermarriage in New Haven, 1870–1950." *American Journal of Sociology* 58, no. 1 (1952).
Kerber, Linda. "The Republican Mother: Women and the Enlightenment—an American Perspective." *American Quarterly* 28, no. 2 (1976).
——. *Women of the Republic: Intellect and Ideology in Revolutionary America*. Williamsburg, VA: Institute of Early American History and Culture, 1980.
Kidd, Colin. *British Identities Before Nationalism: Ethnicity and Nationhood in the Atlantic World, 1600–1800*. Cambridge and New York: Cambridge University Press, 1999.

Kidd, Thomas S. *God of Liberty: A Religious History of the American Revolution*. New York: Basic Books, 2012.

———. *The Great Awakening: The Roots of Evangelical Christianity in Colonial America*. New Haven, CT: Yale University Press, 2007.

———. *The Protestant Interest: New England after Puritanism*. New Haven, CT: Yale University Press, 2004.

King, Martin Luther, Jr. *A Gift of Love*. Boston: Beacon, 2012.

———. *Strength to Love*. Minneapolis, MN: Fortress Press, 1977.

———. *The Trumpet of Conscience*. Boston: Beacon Press, 2010.

———. *Where Do We Go from Here: Chaos or Community?* Boston: Beacon Press, 2010.

King, Martin Luther, Ralph Luker, and Penny A. Russell. *The Papers of Martin Luther King, Jr: Advocate of the Social Gospel*, vol. 6, *September 1948–March 1963*. Berkeley: University of California Press, 2007.

King, Martin Luther, and James Melvin Washington. *A Testament of Hope: The Essential Writings of Martin Luther King*. San Francisco: Harper, 1986.

Kingdon, Robert M. "The Political Resistance of the Calvinists in France and the Low Countries." *Church History: Studies in Christianity and Culture* 27, no. 3 (1958).

Kirk, Russell. *The Conservative Mind, from Burke to Santayana*, 2nd rev. ed. Chicago: H. Regnery, 1953.

Klein, Herbert S. *A Population History of the United States*. Cambridge, UK, and New York: Cambridge University Press, 2004.

Kloppenberg, James T. *Reading Obama: Dreams, Hope, and the American Political Tradition*. Princeton, NJ: Princeton University Press, 2012.

———. *The Virtues of Liberalism*. New York and Oxford: Oxford University Press, 1998.

Knight, Louise W. *Citizen: Jane Addams and the Struggle for Democracy*. Chicago: University of Chicago Press, 2005.

———. *Jane Addams: Spirit in Action*. New York: W. W. Norton, 2010.

Knowlton, James, and Truett Cates. *Historikerstreit: Die Dokumentation der Kontroverse um die Einzigartigkeit der Nationalsozialistischen Judenvernichtung*. Munich: Piper, 1987.

Kramnick, Isaac, and R. Laurence Moore. *The Godless Constitution: A Moral Defense of the Secular State*, new chapter ed. New York and London: Norton, 2005.

Kraus, Clyde Norman. *Dispensationalism in America: Its Rise and Development*. Louisville, KY: John Knox Press, 1958.

Kraybill, J. Nelson. *Apocalypse and Allegiance: Worship, Politics, and Devotion in the Book of Revelation*. Grand Rapids, MI: Brazos Press, 2010.

Kripke, Saul A. *Wittgenstein on Rules and Private Language: An Elementary Exposition*. Cambridge, MA: Harvard University Press, 1982.

Kuhn, Thomas S. *The Structure of Scientific Revolutions*. Chicago: University of Chicago Press, 1962.

Kupperman, Karen Ordahl. *The Jamestown Project*. Cambridge, MA: Harvard University Press, 2009.

Kyle, Richard G. *Apocalyptic Fever: End-Time Prophecies in Modern America*. Eugene, OR: Wipf and Stock, 2012.

Kymlicka, Will. *Multicultural Citizenship: A Liberal Theory of Minority Rights*. Oxford Political Theory. Oxford and New York: Clarendon Press, 1995.

———. *Politics in the Vernacular: Nationalism, Multiculturalism, and Citizenship*. Oxford: Oxford University Press, 2001.

Laidlaw, James. *The Subject of Virtue: An Anthropology of Ethics and Freedom*. Cambridge and New York: Cambridge University Press, 2013.

Lambert, Frank. *Inventing the" Great Awakening."* Princeton, NJ: Princeton University Press, 2001.

Langdon, Samuel. *Government Corrupted by Vice, and Recovered by Righteousness*. Watertown, MA: Benjamin Edes, 1775.

———. *Joy and Gratitude to God for the Long Life of a Good King*. Portsmouth, NH: Daniel Fowle, 1760.

———. *The Republic of the Israelites: An Example to the American States*. Exeter, NH: John Lamson and Henry Ranlet, 1788.

Lasch, Christopher. *The Revolt of the Elites and the Betrayal of Democracy*. New York: W. W. Norton & Company, 1996.

Lawson, Melinda. *Patriot Fires: Forging a New American Nationalism in the Civil War North*. American Political Thought. Lawrence: University Press of Kansas, 2002.

Lear, Jonathan. *Aristotle: The Desire to Understand*. Cambridge and New York: Cambridge University Press, 1988.

Lears, J. "The Sophomore." *New Republic* 228, no. 3 (2003).

Lehmann, H. "Pietism and Nationalism: The Relationship Between Protestant Revivalism and National Renewal in Nineteenth-Century Germany." *Church History* 51, no. 1 (1982).

Lepore, Jill. *The Name of War: King Philip's War and the Origins of American Identity*. New York: Vintage Books, 1999.

Lewis, David L. *W.E.B. Dubois—Biography of a Race, 1868–1919*. New York: H. Holt, 1993.

Lincoln, Abraham. *Selected Speeches and Writings*. New York: Vintage, 1992.

Lincoln, Abraham, and Roy P. Basler. *Collected Works*. Contributions in American Studies. New Brunswick, NJ: Rutgers University Press, 1953.

Lischer, Richard. *The Preacher King: Martin Luther King, Jr. and the Word That Moved America*. New York: Oxford University Press, 1997.

Lissak, Rivka Shpak. *Pluralism and Progressives: Hull House and the New Immigrants, 1890–1919*. Chicago: University of Chicago Press, 1989.

Locke, John. *An Essay Concerning Human Understanding*. London: Penguin, 1997.

———. *Two Treatises of Government*. New York: Cambridge University Press, 1988.

———. *Works of John Locke*, 12th ed. 9 vols. London: C. and J. Rivington, 1824.

Lockridge, Kenneth A. *A New England Town: The First Hundred Years: Dedham, Massachusetts, 1636–1736*. New York: Norton, 1970.

Lovejoy, David S. "Satanizing the American Indian." *New England Quarterly* 67, no. 4 (1994).

Lutz, Donald S. "The Relative Influence of European Writers on Late Eighteenth-Century American Political Thought." *American Political Science Review* 78, no. 1 (1984).

Macedo, Stephen. *Liberal Virtues: Citizenship, Virtue, and Community in Liberal Constitutionalism*. Oxford: Clarendon Press, 1990.

Machen, John Gresham. *Christianity and Liberalism*. Grand Rapids, MI: Wm. B. Eerdmans, 2009.

Machiavelli, Niccolò, Harvey Claflin Mansfield, and Nathan Tarcov. *Discourses on Livy*. Chicago: University of Chicago Press, 1996.

MacIntyre, Alasdair. *After Virtue*. Notre Dame, IN: University of Notre Dame Press, 1984.

———. "Epistemological Crises, Dramatic Narrative and the Philosophy of Science." *Monist* 60, no. 4 (1977).

———. *Three Rival Versions of Moral Enquiry: Encyclopedia, Genealogy, and Tradition.* Notre Dame, IN: University of Notre Dame Press, 1990.

Maclear, James F. "New England and the Fifth Monarchy: The Quest for the Millennium in Early American Puritanism." *William and Mary Quarterly* 32, no. 2 (1975).

Maclure, Jocelyn, and Charles Taylor. *Secularism and Freedom of Conscience.* Cambridge, MA: Harvard University Press, 2011.

Macpherson, C. B. *The Political Theory of Possessive Individualism.* Oxford: Clarendon Press, 1962.

Madison, James. *Writings.* Library of America 109. New York: Library of America, 1999.

Maier, Pauline. "The Road Not Taken: Nullification, John C. Calhoun, and the Revolutionary Tradition in South Carolina." *South Carolina Historical Magazine* 82, no. 1 (1981).

Mandeville, Bernard, and E. J. Hundert. *The Fable of the Bees, and Other Writings.* Indianapolis: Hackett, 1997.

Marsden, George M. *Fundamentalism and American Culture,* 2nd ed. Oxford and New York: Oxford University Press, 2006.

Marty, Martin E. *Civil Religion, Church and State.* Modern American Protestantism and Its World 3. Munich and New York: K. G. Saur, 1992.

Marvin, Carolyn, and David W. Ingle. "Blood Sacrifice and the Nation: Revisiting Civil Religion." *Journal of the American Academy of Religion* 64, no. 4 (1996).

Mather, Cotton. *Magnalia Christi Americana.* London: Thoas Parkhurst, 1702.

Mather, Richard, Peters Hugh, John Davenport, and Richard Mather. *Church-Government and Church-Covenant Discussed: In an Answer of the Elders of the Severall Churches in New-England to Two and Thirty Questions, Sent over to Them by Divers Ministers in England, to Declare Their Judgements Therein: Together with an Apologie of the Said Elders in New-England for Church-Covenant, Sent over in Answer to Master Bernard in the Yeare 1639: As Also in an Answer to Nine Positions About Church-Government.* London: R. O. and G. D., 1643.

Mathewes, Charles T. *Evil and the Augustinian Tradition.* Cambridge and New York: Cambridge University Press, 2001.

May, Stephen, Tariq Modood, and Judith Squires. *Ethnicity, Nationalism, and Minority Rights.* Cambridge, UK, and New York: Cambridge University Press, 2004.

Mayhew, Jonathan. *A Defence of the Observations on the Charter and Conduct of the Society for the Propagation of the Gospel in Foreign Parts: Against an Anonymous Pamphlet Falsly Intitled, a Candid Examination of Dr. Mayhew's Observations, &C. And Also Against the Letter to a Friend Annexed Thereto, Said to Contain a Short Vindication of Said Society. By One of Its Members.* Boston: R. and S. Draper, Edes and Gill, and T. & J. Fleet, 1763.

———. *A Discourse Concerning Unlimited Submission and Non-Resistance to the Higher Powers with Some Reflections on the Resistance Made to King Charles I. And on the Anniversary of His Death: In Which the Mysterious Doctrine of That Prince's Saintship and Martyrdom Is Unriddled: The Substance of Which Was Delivered in a Sermon Preached in the West Meeting-House in Boston the Lord's-Day after the 30th of January, 1749/50.* Boston: D. Fowle and D. Gookin, 1750.

———. *A Discourse Occasioned by the Death of George II.* Boston: Edes & Gill, 1761.

———. *The Expected Dissolution of All Things, a Motive to Universal Holiness: Two Sermons Preached in Boston, N. E. on the Lord's Day, Nov. 23, 1755; Occasioned by the Earthquakes Which Happened on the Tuesday Morning, and Saturday Evening Preceeding.* Boston: Edes & Gill and R. Draper, 1755.

———. *God's Hand and Providence to Be Religiously Acknowledged in Public Calamities. A Sermon Occasioned by the Great Fire in Boston, New-England, Thursday March 20 1760 and Preached on the Lord's-Day Following.* Boston: Richard Draper, Edes and Gill, and Thomas and John Fleet, 1760.

———. *A Letter of Reproof to Mr. John Cleaveland of Ipswich, Occasioned by a Defamatory Libel Published under His Name, Intitled, an Essay to Defend Some of the Most Important Principles in the Protestant Reformed System of Christianity, &C.—Against the Injurious Aspersions Cast on the Same.* Boston: R. and S. Draper, Edes and Gill, and T. & J. Fleet, 1764.

———. *Popish Idolatry: A Discourse Delivered in the Chapel of Harvard-College in Cambridge, New-England, May 8, 1765, at the Lecture Founded by the Honorable Paul Dudley, Esquire.* Boston: R. & S. Draper, 1765.

———. *A Sermon Preach'd in the Audience of His Excellency William Shirley, Esq; Captain-General, Governor and Commander in Chief, the Honourable His Majesty's Council, and the Honourable House of Representatives, of the Province of the Massachusetts-Bay, in New-England, May 29, 1754, Being the Anniversary for the Election of His Majesty's Council for the Province.* Boston and London: G. Woodfall, 1754.

———. *Seven Sermons Upon the Follow Subjects; Viz. the Difference Betwixt Truth and Falshood, Right and Wrong. The Natural Abilities of Men for Discerning These Differences. The Right and Duty of Private Judgement. Objections Considered. The Love of God. The Love of Our Neighbor. The First and Great Commandment, &c.* Boston: Rogers and Fowlse, 1749.

———. *The Snare Broken. A Thanksgiving-Discourse, Preached at the Desire of the West Church in Boston, N. E. Friday May 23, 1766,* 2nd ed. Boston: R. & S. Draper, Edes & Gill, and T. & J. Fleet, 1766.

———. *Striving to Enter in at the Strait Gate Explain'd and Inculcated; and the Connexion of Salvation Therewith, Proved from the Holy Scriptures in Two Sermons on Luke XIII: 24.* Boston: Richard Draper, Edes & Gill, and Thomas & John Fleet, 1761.

Mayhew, Jonathan, Benjamin Edes, and John Gill. *A Discourse on Rev. Xv. 3d, 4th. Occasioned by the Earthquakes in November 1755: Delivered in the West-Meeting-House, Boston, Thursday December 18.* Boston: Edes & Gill and R. Draper, 1755.

McCloskey, Robert Green. *American Conservatism in the Age of Enterprise: 1865–1910: A Study of William Graham Sumner, Stephen J. Field and Andrew Carnegie.* Cambridge, MA: Harvard University Press, 1951.

McCormick, John P. *Machiavellian Democracy.* Cambridge and New York: Cambridge University Press, 2011.

McCurry, Stephanie. "The Two Faces of Republicanism: Gender and Proslavery Politics in Antebellum South Carolina." *Journal of American History* 78, no. 4 (1992).

McDougall, Walter A. *Promised Land, Crusader State: The American Encounter with the World since 1776.* Boston: Houghton Mifflin Harcourt, 1997.

McElroy, Robert W. *The Search for an American Public Theology: The Contribution of John Courtney Murray.* New York: Paulist Press, 1989.

McGinn, Bernard. *Visions of the End: Apocalyptic Traditions in the Middle Ages*. New York: Columbia University Press, 1998.

McGirr, Lisa. *Suburban Warriors: The Origins of the New American Right*. Princeton, NJ: Princeton University Press, 2002.

McKenna, George. *The Puritan Origins of American Patriotism*. New Haven, CT: Yale University Press, 2008.

McKim, Randolph H. *For God and Country or the Christian Pulpit in War*. New York: E. P. Dutton & Company, 1918.

———. *The Motives and Aims of the Soldiers of the South in the Civil War*. N.p: United Confederate Veterans, 1904.

———. *The Numerical Strength of the Confederate Army: An Examination of the Argument of the Hon. Charles Francis Adams and Others*. New York: Neale Publishing Company, 1912.

———. *Problem of the Pentateuch: An Examination of the Higher Criticism*. New York: Longmans, Green, 1906.

———. *A Soldier's Recollections: Leaves from the Diary of a Young Confederate, with an Oration on the Motives and Aims of the Soldiers of the South*. New York: Longmans, Green, and Company, 1910.

McPherson, Aimee Semple. *The Second Coming of Christ*. Los Angeles: n.p., 1921.

———. *This Is That*. Los Angeles: Bridal Call Publishing House, 1919.

McPherson, James M. *The Struggle for Equality; Abolitionists and the Negro in the Civil War and Reconstruction*. Princeton, NJ: Princeton University Press, 1964.

Mead, George Herbert. *Mind, Self, and Society: From the Standpoint of a Social Behaviorist*, vol. 1. Chicago: University of Chicago Press, 2009.

Mencken, H. L. "Bryan." *Baltimore Evening Sun*, July 27, 1925.

———. "Hitlerismus." *American Mercury* (December 1933).

———. "The Mailed Fist and Its Prophet." *Atlantic Monthly* 114 (1914).

———. *Minority Report*. Baltimore: Johns Hopkins University Press, 2006.

———. *Notes on Democracy*. New York: Random House, 2013.

Middlekauff, Robert. *The Mathers: Three Generations of Puritan Intellectuals, 1596–1728*. Berkeley: University of California Press, 1999.

Miller, David. *Citizenship and National Identity*. Cambridge: Polity Press, 2000.

———. "In Defence of Nationality." *Journal of Applied Philosophy* 10, no. 1 (1993).

Miller, Perry. "The Half-Way Covenant." *New England Quarterly* 6, no. 4 (1933).

———. *The New England Mind: From Colony to Province*. Cambridge, MA: Belknap Press of Harvard University Press, 1983.

———. *The New England Mind: The Seventeenth Century*. New York: Macmillan, 1939.

———. *Roger Williams: His Contribution to the American Tradition*. Indianapolis: Bobbs-Merrill, 1953.

Miller, Randall M., Harry S. Stout, and Charles Reagan Wilson, eds. *Religion and the American Civil War*. New York: Oxford University Press, 1993.

Milton, John. *John Milton: Prose: Major Writings on Liberty, Politics, Religion, and Education*. Oxford: Wiley-Blackwell, 2013.

Montesquieu, Charles. *The Spirit of the Laws*. Trans. Basia Miller, Anne Cohler, and Harold Stone. Cambridge, UK: Cambridge University Press, 1989.

Moorhead, James H. "The Erosion of Postmillennialism in American Religious Thought, 1865–1925." *Church History: Studies in Christianity and Culture* 53, no. 1 (1984).

———. *World Without End: Mainstream American Protestant Visions of the Last Things, 1880–1925*. Bloomington: Indiana University Press, 1999.

Morgan, Edmund Sears. *The Puritan Dilemma: The Story of John Winthrop*. Library of American Biography. Boston: Little, 1958.

———. *Roger Williams: The Church and the State*. New York: Harcourt, 1967.

———. *Visible Saints: The History of a Puritan Idea*. Ithaca, NY: Cornell University Press, 1965.

Moulakis, Athanasios. "Civic Humanism." In *The Stanford Encyclopedia of Philosophy*, ed. Edward N. Zalta. Stanford, CA: Stanford University, 2002.

Müller, Jan-Werner. *Constitutional Patriotism*. Princeton, NJ: Princeton University Press, 2009.

Murdoch, Iris. *The Sovereignty of Good*. London: Routledge, 2013.

Murphey, Murray G. "The Psychodynamics of Puritan Conversion." *American Quarterly* 31, no. 2 (1979).

Murphy, Andrew R. *Prodigal Nation: Moral Decline and Divine Punishment from New England to 9/11*. Oxford and New York: Oxford University Press, 2009.

Murray, Bruce T. *Religious Liberty in America: The First Amendment in Historical and Contemporary Perspective*. Amherst: University of Massachusetts Press and Foundation for American Communications, 2008.

Murray, John Courtney. *Bridging the Sacred and the Secular*. Washington, DC: Georgetown University Press, 1996.

———. "The Return to Tribalism." *Catholic Mind* 60, no. 6 (1962).

———. *We Hold These Truths: Catholic Reflections on the American Proposition*. Sheed & Ward Classic. Lanham, MD: Rowman & Littlefield, 2005.

Negri, Antonio. *The Labor of Job: The Biblical Text as a Parable of Human Labor*. Durham, NC: Duke University Press, 2009.

Nelson, Eric. *The Greek Tradition in Republican Thought*. Ideas in Context 69. Cambridge, UK, and New York: Cambridge University Press, 2004.

———. *The Hebrew Republic*. Cambridge, MA: Harvard University Press, 2010.

———. "Patriot Royalism: The Stuart Monarchy in American Political Thought, 1769–75." *William and Mary Quarterly* 68, no. 4 (2011).

———. *The Royalist Revolution: Monarchy and the American Founding*. Cambridge, MA: Harvard University Press, 2014.

Neuhaus, Richard John. *The Naked Public Square: Religion and Democracy in America*. Grand Rapids, MI: W. B. Eerdmans, 1984.

Neuman, Kalman. "Political Hebraism and the Early Modern 'Respublica Hebraeorum': On Defining the Field." *Hebraic Political Studies* 1, no. 1 (2005).

Newman, John Henry. *An Essay on the Development of Christian Doctrine*. London: Toovey, 1846.

Niebuhr, Reinhold. *Children of Light and the Children of Darkness: A Vindication of Democracy and a Critique of Its Traditional Defence*. New York: Charles Scribner's Sons, 1944.

———. *An Interpretation of Christian Ethics*. New York: Harper & Brothers, 1935.

———. *The Irony of American History*. New York: Scribner, 1952.

———. *Moral Man and Immoral Society: A Study in Ethics and Politics*. New York and London: C. Scribner's, 1932.

———. *The Nature and Destiny of Man: A Christian Interpretation*. Gifford Lectures. New York: Charles Scribner's Sons, 1948.

Niebuhr, Reinhold, and Robert McAfee Brown. *The Essential Reinhold Niebuhr: Selected Essays and Addresses*. New Haven, CT: Yale University Press, 1986.

Niebuhr, Reinhold, and D. B. Robertson. *Love and Justice: Selections from the Shorter Writings of Reinhold Niebuhr*. Gloucester, MA: P. Smith, 1976.

Nixon, Richard. *Richard Nixon: Speeches, Writings, Documents*. Princeton, NJ: Princeton University Press, 2010.

Noll, Mark A. *America's God: From Jonathan Edwards to Abraham Lincoln*. Oxford and New York: Oxford University Press, 2002.

Noll, Mark A., and William A. Blair. *The Civil War as a Theological Crisis*. Steven and Janice Brose Lectures in the Civil War Era. Chapel Hill: University of North Carolina Press, 2006.

North, Douglass C. "Economic Performance Through Time." *American Economic Review* 84, no. 3 (1994).

Novak, David. *The Jewish Social Contract: An Essay in Political Theology*. Princeton, NJ: Princeton University Press, 2009.

Nowell, Samuel. *Abraham in Arms; or the First Religious General with His Army Engaging in a War for Which He Had Wisely Prepared, and by Which, Not Only an Eminent Victory Was Obtained, but a Blessing Gained Also. Delivered in an Artillery-Election-Sermon, June, 3. 1678*. Boston: John Foster, 1678.

Nussbaum, Martha. "Aristotelian Social Democracy." In *Necessary Goods: Our Responsibility to Meet Others' Needs*, ed. Gillian Brock (Boulder, CO, and London: Rowman & Littlefield, 1998).

———. "Human Functioning and Social Justice in Defense of Aristotelian Essentialism." *Political Theory* 20, no. 2 (1992).

———. "Non-Relative Virtues: An Aristotelian Approach." *Midwest Studies in Philosophy* 13, no. 1 (1988).

Nussbaum, Martha Craven, and Joshua Cohen. *For Love of Country: Debating the Limits of Patriotism*. Boston: Beacon Press, 1996.

O'Brien, Michael. "The American Experience of Secularisation." In *Religion and the Political Imagination*, ed. Ira Katznelson and Gareth Stedman Jones. New York: Cambridge University Press, 2010.

Obama, Barack. *The Audacity of Hope: Thoughts on Reclaiming the American Dream*. New York: Crown Books, 2007.

Olick, Jeffrey K, and Joyce Robbins. "Social Memory Studies: From 'Collective Memory' to the Historical Sociology of Mnemonic Practices." *Annual Review of Sociology* 24, no. 1 (1998).

Pagan, Nicholas. "Configuring the Moral Self: Aristotle and Dewey." *Foundations of Science* 13, no. 3/4 (2008).

Paganini, Gianni, and Edoardo Tortarolo. *Pluralismo E Religione Civile: Una Prospettiva Storica E Filosofica: Atti Del Convegno Di Vercelli (Università Del Piemonte Orientale), 24–25 Giugno 2001*. Milan: B. Mondadori, 2004.

Paine, Thomas. *Collected Writings*. New York: Library of America, 1995.

Parrington, Vernon L. *Main Currents in American Thought (New York, 1930)*. New York: Harcourt Brace, 1954.

Parry, Richard. "Ancient Ethical Theory." In *The Stanford Encyclopedia of Philosophy*, ed. Edward N. Zalta. Stanford, CA: Stanford University Press, 2014.

Pegram, Thomas R. *One Hundred Percent American: The Rebirth and Decline of the Ku Klux Klan in the 1920s*. Lanham, MD: Rowman & Littlefield, 2011.

Pelikan, Jaroslav. *The Vindication of Tradition*. New Haven, CT: Yale University Press, 1986.

Pelotte, Donald E. *John Courtney Murray: Theologian in Conflict*. New York: Paulist Press, 1976.

Peltonen, Markku. *Classical Humanism and Republicanism in English Political Thought, 1570–1640*, vol. 36. Cambridge and New York: Cambridge University Press, 2004.

Perl-Rosenthal, Nathan R. "The 'Divine Right of Republics': Hebraic Republicanism and the Debate over Kingless Government in Revolutionary America." *William and Mary Quarterly* 66, no. 3 (2009).

Perlstein, Rick. *Before the Storm: Barry Goldwater and the Unmaking of the American Consensus*. New York: Nation Books, 2009.

———. *Nixonland: The Rise of a President and the Fracturing of America*. New York: Simon and Schuster, 2010.

Pettit, Philip. *Just Freedom: A Moral Compass for a Complex World*. New York: W. W. Norton, 2014.

———. *Republicanism: A Theory of Freedom and Government*. Oxford Political Theory. New York: Oxford University Press, 1997.

Piercey, Robert. "Ricoeur's Account of Tradition and the Gadamer–Habermas Debate." *Human Studies* 27, no. 3 (2004).

Piketty, Thomas, and Emmanuel Saez. "Income Inequality in the United States, 1913–1998 (Series Updated to 2000 Available)." Cambridge, MA: National Bureau of Economic Research, 2001.

Pleck, Elizabeth. "The Making of the Domestic Occasion: The History of Thanksgiving in the United States." *Journal of Social History* 32, no. 4 (1999).

Polybius. *The Rise of the Roman Empire*. Trans. Ian Scott Kilvert. London: Penguin, 1981.

Pope, Robert G. *The Half-Way Covenant: Church Membership in Puritan New England*. Princeton, NJ: Princeton University Press, 1969.

Prothero, Stephen. *The American Bible—Whose America Is This?: How Our Words Unite, Divide, and Define a Nation*. New York: HarperCollins, 2012.

———. *American Jesus: How the Son of God Became a National Icon*. New York: Farrar, Straus and Giroux, 2003.

Putnam, Robert D. *Bowling Alone: The Collapse and Revival of American Community*. New York: Simon and Schuster, 2000.

Quirk, Michael J. "Beyond Sectarianism?" *Theology Today* 44, no. 1 (1987).

Raab, Felix. *The English Face of Machiavelli*, reprint ed. New York: Routledge, 2013.

Rable, George C. *The Confederate Republic: A Revolution Against Politics*. Civil War America. Chapel Hill: University of North Carolina Press, 1994.

———. *God's Almost Chosen Peoples: A Religious History of the American Civil War*. Littlefield History of the Civil War Era. Chapel Hill: University of North Carolina Press, 2010.

Rahe, Paul. *Republics Ancient and Modern*. 3 vols. Chapel Hill: University of North Carolina Press, 1994.

———. *Aristotle*. New York: Columbia University Press, 1960.

———. "Dewey's Interpretation of the Philosophy of History." In *The Philosophy of John Dewey*, ed. Paul Arthur Schilpp and Lewis Edwin Hahn. LaSalle, IL: Open Court, 1939.

"Randolph Harris Mckim (1842–1920)." In *Encyclopedia of Virginia Biography*, ed. Lyon Gardiner Tylor. New York: Lewis Historical Pub. Co., 1915.

Rawls, John. *Political Liberalism*, expanded ed. Columbia Classics in Philosophy. New York: Columbia University Press, 2005.

——. *A Theory of Justice*. Cambridge, MA: Belknap Press of Harvard University Press, 1971.

Reno, R. R. "Stanley Hauerwas." In *The Blackwell Companion to Political Theology*, ed. Peter Scott and William T. Cavanaugh. Oxford: Blackwell, 2004.

Ribuffo, Leo P. *The Old Christian Right: The Protestant Far Right from the Great Depression to the Cold War*. Philadelphia: Temple University Press, 1983.

Richard, Carl J. *The Founders and the Classics: Greece, Rome, and the American Enlightenment*. Cambridge, MA: Harvard University Press, 1994.

Ricoeur, Paul. *The Phenomenology of Man and of the Human Condition*. Dordrecht, The Netherlands: Springer, 1983.

——. "Ethics and Culture: Habermas and Gadamer in Dialogue." *Philosophy Today* 17, no. 2 (1973).

——. "Life in Quest of Narrative." In *On Paul Ricoeur: Narrative and Interpretation*, ed. David Wood. New York: Routledge, 1991.

——. *Time and Narrative*. 3 vols. Chicago: University of Chicago Press, 1984.

Rockefeller, Steven C. *John Dewey, Religious Faith and Democratic Humanism*. New York: Columbia University Press, 1991.

Rodgers, Daniel T. "Republicanism: The Career of a Concept." *Journal of American History* 79, no. 1 (1992).

Roediger, David R. *The Wages of Whiteness: Race and the Making of the American Working Class*. Haymarket Series. London and New York: Verso, 1991.

Rogers, Melvin L. *The Undiscovered Dewey: Religion, Morality, and the Ethos of Democracy*. New York: Columbia University Press, 2012.

Romney, Mitt. *No Apology: The Case for American Greatness*. New York: Macmillan, 2010.

Rorty, Richard. *Contingency, Irony, and Solidarity*. Cambridge and New York: Cambridge University Press, 1989.

Rouner, Leroy S. *Civil Religion and Political Theology*. Boston University Studies in Philosophy and Religion 8. Notre Dame, IN: University of Notre Dame Press, 1986.

Rousseau, Jean-Jacques, and Victor Gourevitch. *The Social Contract and Other Later Political Writings*. Cambridge Texts in the History of Political Thought. Cambridge and New York: Cambridge University Press, 1997.

Royle, Edward. *Radicals, Secularists, and Republicans: Popular Freethought in Britain, 1866–1915*. Manchester: Manchester University Press, 1980.

Rush, Benjamin. *An Inquiry into the Influence of Physical Causes Upon the Moral Faculty. Delivered before a Meeting of the American Philosophical Society, Etc.* Philadelphia: Haswell, Barrington, and Haswell, 1839.

——. *A Plan for the Establishment of Public Schools and the Diffusion of Knowledge in Pennsylvania: To Which Are Added Thoughts Upon the Mode of Education, Proper in a Republic. Addressed to the Legislature and Citizens of the State*. Philadelphia: Thomas Dobson, 1786.

Rush, Benjamin, and L. H. Butterfield. *Letters*. Memoirs of the American Philosophical Society 30, Pts. 1–2. Princeton, NJ: Princeton University Press, 1951.

Rush, Benjamin, Frederick Rudolph, ACLS Humanities E-Book Organization, and American Council of Learned Societies. *Essays on Education in the Early Republic*. Cambridge, MA: Belknap Press of Harvard University Press, 1965.

Rushdoony, Rousas John. *The Nature of the American System*. Nutley, NJ: Craig Press, 1965.

Salisbury, Neal. "Red Puritans: The 'Praying Indians' of Massachusetts Bay and John Eliot." *William and Mary Quarterly* 31, no. 3 (1974).

Sandel, Michael J. *Democracy's Discontent: America in Search of a Public Philosophy*. Cambridge, MA: Belknap Press of Harvard University Press, 1996.

———. "The Procedural Republic and the Unencumbered Self." *Political Theory* 12, no. 1 (1984).

Saxton, Alexander. *The Rise and Fall of the White Republic: Class Politics and Mass Culture in Nineteenth Century America*. Haymarket Series. London and New York: Verso, 1990.

Scaff, Lawrence A. *Max Weber in America*. Princeton, NJ: Princeton University Press, 2011.

Schaeffer, Francis August. *A Christian Manifesto*. Wheaton, IL: Crossway Books, 1982.

Scheibler, Ingrid H. *Gadamer: Between Heidegger and Habermas*. Lanham, MD: Rowman & Littlefield, 2000.

Schlesinger, Arthur M., Jr. "Not Left, Not Right, but a Vital Center." *New York Times*, April 4, 1948.

———. *The Vital Center, the Politics of Freedom*. Boston: Houghton Mifflin Co., 1949.

Schmitt, Carl. *Political Theology: Four Chapters on the Concept of Sovereignty*. Chicago: University of Chicago Press, 2005.

Schultz, Kevin M. *Tri-Faith America: How Catholics and Jews Held Postwar America to Its Protestant Promise*. New York: Oxford University Press, 2011.

Scobey, David M. "Revising the Errand: New England's Ways and the Puritan Sense of the Past." *William and Mary Quarterly* 41, no. 1 (1984).

Sehat, David. *The Myth of American Religious Freedom*. New York: Oxford University Press, 2010.

Seidman, Aaron B. "Church and State in the Early Years of the Massachusetts Bay Colony." *New England Quarterly* 18, no. 2 (June 1945).

Selby, Gary S. *Martin Luther King and the Rhetoric of Freedom: The Exodus Narrative in America's Struggle for Civil Rights*. Studies in Rhetoric and Religion. Waco, TX: Baylor University Press, 2008.

Seligman, Martin E. P. *Flourish: A Visionary New Understanding of Happiness and Well-Being*. New York: Simon and Schuster, 2012.

Sellers, M.N.S. *American Republicanism: Roman Ideology in the United States Constitution*. Studies in Modern History. Houndmills, Basingstoke, Hampshire: Macmillan, 1994.

Sells, Michael. *The Bridge Betrayed: Religion and Genocide in Bosnia*. Berkeley and Los Angeles: University of California Press, 1998.

Shalev, Eran. *American Zion*. New Haven, CT: Yale University Press, 2013.

———. *Rome Reborn on Western Shores: Historical Imagination and the Creation of the American Republic*. Charlottesville: University of Virginia Press, 2009.

Shalhope, Robert E. "Republicanism and Early American Historiography." *William and Mary Quarterly* 39, no. 2 (1982).

———. "Toward a Republican Synthesis: The Emergence of an Understanding of Republicanism in American Historiography." *William and Mary Quarterly* 29, no. 1 (1972).

Sheldon, Charles Monroe. *In His Steps: "What Would Jesus Do?"* Chicago: Advance Pub. Co., 1897.

Sheldon, Garrett Ward. *The Political Philosophy of Thomas Jefferson*. Baltimore: Johns Hopkins University Press, 1991.

Shepard, Thomas, and Michael McGiffert. *God's Plot: The Paradoxes of Puritan Piety; Being the Autobiography and Journal of Thomas Shepard*. Amherst: University of Massachusetts Press, 1972.

Shklar, Judith N. "Ideology Hunting: The Case of James Harrington." *American Political Science Review* 53, no. 3 (1959).

Shurtleff, Nathaniel Bradstreet, and Massachusetts General Court. *Records of the Governor and Company of the Massachusetts Bay in New England*. New York: AMS Press, 1968.

"Sister Mcpherson Guest of Associated Churches." *Bridal Call-Crusader Foursquare*, November 7, 1934, 13, 22.

Skinner, Quentin. *Hobbes and Republican Liberty*. Cambridge: Cambridge University Press, 2008.

——. *Liberty Before Liberalism*. Cambridge and New York: Cambridge University Press, 1998.

Skocpol, Theda. *Protecting Soldiers and Mothers: The Political Origins of Social Policy in the United States*. Cambridge, MA: Belknap Press of Harvard University Press, 1992.

Skousen, W. Cleon. *The Five Thousand Year Leap*. Franklin, TN: W. Cleon Skousen, 2009.

Skowronek, Stephen. *Building a New American State: The Expansion of National Administrative Capacities, 1877–1920*. Cambridge and New York: Cambridge University Press, 1982.

Sleeper, James. "Our Puritan Heritage." *Democracy* 37 (Summer 2015).

Smith, Christian. *The Bible Made Impossible: Why Biblicism Is Not a Truly Evangelical Reading of Scripture*. Grand Rapids, MI: Baker Books, 2012.

——. *The Secular Revolution: Power, Interests, and Conflict in the Secularization of American Public Life*. Berkeley: University of California Press, 2003.

——. *What Is a Person?: Rethinking Humanity, Social Life, and the Moral Good from the Person Up*. Chicago: University of Chicago Press, 2010.

Smith, Kenneth L., and Ira G. Zepp. *Search for the Beloved Community: The Thinking of Martin Luther King, Jr*. King of Prussia, PA: Judson Press, 1998.

Smith, Philip. *Why War?: The Cultural Logic of Iraq, the Gulf War, and Suez*. Chicago: University of Chicago Press, 2005.

Smith, Rogers M. *Civic Ideals: Conflicting Visions of Citizenship in U.S. History*. New Haven, CT, and London: Yale University Press, 1997.

Smith, Steven D. *The Rise and Decline of American Religious Freedom*. Cambridge, MA: Harvard University Press, 2014.

Snyder, K. Alan. "Foundations of Liberty: The Christian Republicanism of Timothy Dwight and Jedidiah Morse." *New England Quarterly* 56, no. 3 (1983).

Snyder, R. Claire. *Citizen-Soldiers and Manly Warriors: Military Service and Gender in the Civic Republican Tradition*. Lanham, MD: Rowman & Littlefield, 1999.

Somers, Margaret R. "Rights, Relationality, and Membership: Rethinking the Making and Meaning of Citizenship." *Law and Social Inquiry* 19, no. 1 (Winter 1994).

Starr, Harris E. *William Graham Sumner*. New York: H. Holt and Company, 1925.

Steele, Shelby. *The Content of Our Character*. New York: St. Martin's Press, 1990.

Stein, Stephen J. "Transatlantic Extensions: Apocalyptic in Early New England." In *The Apocalypse in English Renaissance Thought and Literature*, ed. C. A. Patrides and Joseph Wittreich. Ithaca, NY: Cornell University Press, 1984.

Sternberger, Dolf. *Schriften*. Frankfurt: Inselverlag, 1990.

Stewart, Matthew. *Nature's God: The Heretical Origins of the American Republic*. New York: W. W. Norton, 2014.

Stout, Harry S. *The New England Soul: Preaching and Religious Culture in Colonial New England*. New York: Oxford University Press, 1986.

———. "Rhetoric and Reality in the Early Republic: The Case of the Federalist Clergy." In *Religion and American Politics: From the Colonial Period to the 1980s*, ed. Mark Noll. New York: Oxford Universtiy Press, 1990.

———. *Upon the Altar of the Nation: A Moral History of the American Civil War*. New York: Viking, 2006.

Stout, Jeffrey. *Democracy and Tradition*. Princeton, NJ: Princeton University Press, 2009.

———. *The Flight from Authority: Religion, Morality, and the Quest for Autonomy*. Notre Dame, IN: University of Notre Dame Press, 1981.

———. "The Spirit of Democracy and the Rhetoric of Excess." *Journal of Religious Ethics* 35, no. 1 (2007).

Strauss, Leo. *Liberalism Ancient and Modern*. Chicago: University of Chicago Press, 1995.

Stringfellow, Thornton. *A Brief Examination of Scripture Testimony on the Institution of Slavery in an Essay, First Published in the Religious Herald, and Republished by Request, with Remarks on a Review of the Essay*. Richmond, VA: Religious Herald, 1841.

Strom, Jonathan, Hartmut Lehmann, and James Van Horn Melton. *Pietism in Germany and North America 1680–1820*. Farnham, England, and Burlington, VT: Ashgate Publishing, 2009.

Sturgis, Amy H. "Prophesies and Politics: Millenarians, Rabbis, and the Jewish Indian Theory." *Seventeenth Century* 14, no. 1 (1999).

Sumner, William Graham. *Essays*. New Haven, CT: Yale University Press, 1913.

———. *The Forgotten Man, and Other Essays*, ed. Albert Galloway Keller. New Haven, CT: Yale University Press.

———. *War, and Other Essays*. New Haven, CT: Yale University Press, 1919.

———. *What Social Classes Owe to Each Other*. New York: Harper & Brothers, 1883.

Sumner, William Graham, and Robert C. Bannister. *On Liberty, Society, and Politics: The Essential Essays of William Graham Sumner*. Indianapolis, IN: Liberty Fund, 1992.

"'Sumnerology'—the Social Philosophy of Prof. W. G. Sumner." *New York Times*, April 17, 1910.

Sundquist, Eric J. *King's Dream*. New Haven, CT: Yale University Press, 2009.

Sunstein, Cass R. "Beyond the Republican Revival." *Yale Law Journal* 97, no. 8 (1988).

———. "The Enduring Legacy of Republicanism." *A New Constitutionalism: Designing Political Institutions for a Good Society* 38 (1993).

Sutton, Matthew Avery. *Aimee Semple McPherson and the Resurrection of Christian America*. Cambridge, MA: Harvard University Press, 2009.

Tackett, Timothy. *Religion, Revolution, and Regional Culture in Eighteenth-Century France: The Ecclesiastical Oath of 1791*. Princeton, NJ: Princeton University Press.

Taylor, Charles. *Philosophical Papers*, vol. 1, *Human Agency and Language*. Cambridge and New York: Cambridge University Press, 1985.

———. *Sources of the Self: The Making of the Modern Identity*. Cambridge, MA: Harvard University Press, 1989.

Teachout, Terry. *The Skeptic: A Life of H. L. Mencken*. New York: HarperCollins, 2003.

Teachout, Zephyr. "The Anti-Corruption Principle." *Cornell Law Review* 94, no. 341 (2009).

———. *Corruption in America: From Benjamin Franklin's Snuff Box to Citizens United.* Cambridge, MA: Harvard University Press, 2014.

Terpstra, Nicholas. *Lay Confraternities and Civic Religion in Renaissance Bologna.* Cambridge Studies in Italian History and Culture. Cambridge and New York: Cambridge University Press, 1995.

Thomas, Keith. *Religion and the Decline of Magic: Studies in Popular Beliefs in Sixteenth and Seventeenth-Century England.* London: Penguin UK, 1991.

Tise, Larry E. *Proslavery: A History of the Defense of Slavery in America, 1701–1840.* Athens: University of Georgia Press, 1987.

Tocqueville, Alexis de. *Democracy in America.* New York: HarperPerennial, 1988.

Trask, Kerry A. "In the Pursuit of Shadows: A Study of Collective Hope and Despair in Provincial Massachussetts During the Era of the Seven Years War, 1748–1764." PhD diss., University of Minnesota, 1971.

Troeltsch, Ernst, Olive Wyon, and H. Richard Niebuhr. *The Social Teaching of the Christian Churches*, Phoenix ed. Chicago: University of Chicago Press, 1981.

Turner, James. *Without God, Without Creed: The Origins of Unbelief in America.* Baltimore: Johns Hopkins University Press, 1985.

United Confederate Veterans. "Minutes UCV." New Orleans: United Confederate Veterans, 1909.

Vajda, Zoltán. "John C. Calhoun's Republicanism Revisited." *Rhetoric and Public Affairs* 4, no. 3 (Fall 2001).

Van Kersbergen, Kees. *Social Capitalism: A Study of Christian Democracy and the Welfare State.* London: Routledge, 2003.

Van Kley, Dale K. *The Religious Origins of the French Revolution: From Calvin to the Civil Constitution, 1560–1791.* New Haven, CT: Yale University Press, 1996.

Viroli, Maurizio. *For Love of Country: An Essay on Patriotism and Nationalism.* Oxford: Oxford University Press, 1997.

Wacker, Grant. *Heaven Below: Early Pentecostals and American Culture.* Cambridge, MA: Harvard University Press, 2009.

Waldman, Steven. *Founding Faith: Providence, Politics, and the Birth of Religious Freedom in America.* New York: Random House Digital, 2008.

Waldron, Jeremy. *God, Locke, and Equality: Christian Foundations in Locke's Political Thought.* Cambridge and New York: Cambridge University Press, 2002.

Walker, Williston. *The Creeds and Platforms of Congregationalism.* Boston: Pilgrim Press, 1960.

Wall, Wendy. *Inventing the "American Way": The Politics of Consensus from the New Deal to the Civil Rights Movement.* New York: Oxford University Press, 2008.

Walzer, Michael. *Exodus and Revolution.* New York: Basic Books, 1985.

———. *In God's Shadow: Politics in the Hebrew Bible.* New Haven, CT: Yale University Press, 2012.

Warnke, Georgia. *Gadamer: Hermeneutics, Tradition, and Reason*, vol. 1. Stanford, CA: Stanford University Press, 1987.

Washington, Booker T., and W.E.B. Du Bois. *The Negro in the South, His Economic Progress in Relation to His Moral and Religious Development, Being the William Levi Bull Lectures for the Year 1907.* Philadelphia: G. W. Jacobs & Company, 1907.

Watts, James W. *Ritual and Rhetoric in Leviticus: From Sacrifice to Scripture.* New York: Cambridge University Press, 2007.

Weber, Eugen. *Apocalypses: Prophecies, Cults, and Millennial Beliefs Through the Ages.* Cambridge, MA: Harvard University Press, 2000.

Weber, Max, P. R. Baehr, and Gordon C. Wells. *The Protestant Ethic and the "Spirit" of Capitalism and Other Writings.* Penguin Twentieth-Century Classics. New York: Penguin Books, 2002.

Weber, Max, and Edward Shils. *The Methodology of the Social Sciences.* New York: Free Press, 1949.

Weir, David A. *Early New England: A Covenanted Society.* Emory University Studies in Law and Religion. Grand Rapids, MI: W. B. Eerdmans, 2004.

Westbrook, Robert B. *John Dewey and American Democracy.* Ithaca, NY: Cornell University Press, 1991.

White, Stuart. *The Civic Minimum: On the Rights and Obligations of Economic Citizenship.* New York: Oxford University Press, 2003.

Williams, Colin W., Sydney E. Ahlstrom, and Charles William Powers. *The Changing Nature of America's Civil Religion.* New York: Aspen Institute for Humanistic Studies, 1973.

Williams, Solomon. *The Duty of Christian Soldiers.* New London: T & J Green, 1755.

Williams, Thomas D., and Jan Olof Bengtsson. "Personalism." In *The Stanford Encyclopedia of Philosophy*, ed. Edward N. Zalta. Stanford, CA: Metaphysics Research Lab Center for the Study of Language and Information, 2014.

Wilson, Catherine. *Epicureanism at the Origins of Modernity.* New York: Oxford University Press, 2008.

Wilson, Charles Reagan. *Baptized in Blood: The Religion of the Lost Cause, 1865–1920.* Athens: University of Georgia Press, 1983.

———. "The Religion of the Lost Cause: Ritual and Organization of the Southern Civil Religion, 1865–1920." *Journal of Southern History 46*, no. 2 (1980).

Wilson, John Frederick. *Religion and the American Nation: Historiography and History.* George H. Shriver Lecture Series in Religion in American History 1. Athens: University of Georgia Press, 2003.

Wilson, Woodrow. *The New Freedom: A Call for the Emancipation of the Generous Energies of a People.* Garden City, NY: Doubleday, Page & Company, 1913.

Winship, Michael P. *Godly Republicanism: Puritans, Pilgrims, and a City on a Hill.* Cambridge, MA: Harvard University Press, 2012.

———. "Godly Republicanism and the Origins of the Massachusetts Polity." *William and Mary Quarterly 63*, no. 3 (2006).

Winterer, Caroline. *The Culture of Classicism: Ancient Greece and Rome in American Intellectual Life, 1780–1910.* Baltimore: Johns Hopkins University Press, 2004.

Winters, Jeffrey A. *Oligarchy.* Cambridge and New York: Cambridge University Press, 2011.

Winters, Jeffrey A, and Benjamin I. Page. "Oligarchy in the United States?" *Perspectives on Politics 7*, no. 4 (2009).

Winters, Michael Sean. *God's Right Hand: How Jerry Falwell Made God a Republican and Baptized the American Right.* New York: HarperCollins, 2012.

Winthrop, John. *Winthrop Papers, 1498–1649.* 5 vols. Boston: Massachusetts Historical Society, 1929.

Wolterstorff, Nicholas. *Justice: Rights and Wrongs.* Princeton, NJ: Princeton University Press, 2010.

Wood, Amy Louise. *Lynching and Spectacle: Witnessing Racial Violence in America, 1890–1940*. Chapel Hill: University of North Carolina Press, 2011.

Wood, Ralph C., and John E. Collins. *Civil Religion and Transcendent Experience: Studies in Theology and History, Psychology and Mysticism*. Macon, GA: Mercer University Press, 1988.

Younge, Gary. *The Speech: The Story Behind Dr. Martin Luther King Jr.'s Dream*. Chicago: Haymarket Books, 2013.

Zakai, Avihu. *Exile and Kingdom: Reformation, Separation, and the Millennial Quest in the Formation of Massachusetts and Its Relationship with England, 1628–1660*. Baltimore: Johns Hopkins University Press, 1982.

———. "Puritan Millennialism and Theocracy in Early Massachusetts." *History of European Ideas* 8, no. 3 (1987).

———. "Reformation, History, and Eschatology in English Protestantism." *History and Theory* 26, no. 3 (1987).

Zubrzycki, Geneviève. *The Crosses of Auschwitz: Nationalism and Religion in Post-Communist Poland*. Chicago: University of Chicago Press, 2006.

Zuckert, Michael P. *Natural Rights and the New Republicanism*. Princeton, NJ: Princeton University Press, 1994.

INDEX